NATURE AND STRUCTURE OF RURAL HABITATIONS

NATURE AND STRUCTURE OF RURAL HABITATIONS

S.K. CHANDHOKE

FOREWORD
AMOS RAPOPORT

INTRODUCTION
B.K. ROY BURMAN

CONCEPT PUBLISHING COMPANY, NEW DELHI - 110 059
and
SCHOOL OF PLANNING AND ARCHITECTURE, NEW DELHI - 110 002

ISBN 81-7022-253-2

First Published 1990

Published by
Ashok Kumar Mittal
Concept Publishing Company
A/15-16, Commercial Block, Mohan Garden
NEW DELHI - 110 059 (India)

Lasertypeset by
Microtech Advance Printing Systems (Pvt.) Ltd.
H-13, Bali Nagar,
NEW DELHI - 110 015

Printed in India by
Taj Press
DELHI - 110 006

to
my father

FOREWORD

THE SOCIAL and behavioral sciences have studied people but have typically ignored the built environment. Architecture and planning have concentrated on buildings and settlements, but have ignored human behavior, culture and social relations; they have ignored the users or occupants of built environments – their activity systems, life-styles, values and culture; the meanings they attach to environments and the choices they make. Moreover, architecture and planning have been concerned only with that minute portion of the built environment designed by professionals, neglecting what is variously called folk, vernacular or popular design. Yet that constitutes the bulk of the built environment and is also the context within which professionally designed elements exist, and relationships among elements are often at least as important as the elements themselves. Furthermore, buildings, even vernacular buildings, have tended to be considered in isolation rather than as part of the larger environment – that system of settings within which people live and which constitutes the cultural landscape.

The need to consider social, cultural, behavioral and physical aspects together has become more accepted over the past 20 years, as some of us started and developed environment-behavior studies (EBS), first in the United States, then western Europe and now world-wide. Although I have emphasized the need to work at the scale of the cultural landscape, most work is still on buildings or other isolated bits. Similarly, cross-cultural research in a wide variety of cultures is still rare, although that is starting to change. Although recently major growth in interest and emphasis has been in culture-built environment relations, cross-cultural approaches to general EBS questions are still rare.

Such work, however, is difficult partly because data is lacking.

What I recently called "natural history" has been neglected, so that there are few really thorough EBS-oriented case-studies in a variety of cultures (particularly in non-Western settings) which consider the whole cultural landscape: the buildings. spaces, settlements and beyond; the relationships among different elements and scales and with behavior, meaning and culture, generally. Also lacking is such work by researchers from within the cultures concerned who, if they are concerned with users, can more easily understand, communicate and explain these users – the **real** insiders.

Many more such studies are needed, as well as comparable historical studies, before generalizations can be made and theory development begun. This will require the most extensive and varied body of evidences: all of the environment (the cultural landscape), all environments in all cultures and over the whole time span (almost two million years even excluding animal environments). Yet such generalizations and theory are essential if one is to learn from the knowledge contained in all these environments – and such learning is essential.

Four attitudes are possible to this full range of built environments. They can be ignored, rejected, copied – or one can try and learn from them. By far the most common have been the first two: 'primitive', vernacular, popular and spontaneous environments were (and are) seen as of no value or interest and not worth studying because they have nothing to teach us; that position seems untenable. I will not deal with copying here; I have shown elsewhere that it does not work. Learning by means of concepts and theory from EBS is thus the only possible approach. The recent explosive growth of interest in culture-environment relations and traditional environments (mentioned above) suggests that this may be starting.

The rich cultural and environmental traditions of the countries of Asia, Africa and the other continents have thus been ignored, in many cases even after independence – in fact, often even more in the early decades of independence. Yet these traditions are a major source of environmental knowledge and experience, not only for people in the places concerned but for EBS generally. If adequate studies of these riches were available people like me could use them to generalize and develop theory. This, in turn, would allow lessons to be learned relevant not only locally, regionally or nationally, but for EBS as a whole, because these environments have many general lessons. **The learning would then be mutual.**

There is a real danger that many of these environments will rapidly disappear or will be changed so radically that much knowledge and many lessons will be lost. Also lost will be the opportunity to study the processes of change themselves.

The present book is an example of the kind of case-study to which I have just referred and which is all too rare. I have known Dr. Chandhoke's published work on Indian villages for some time and have cited it in my own work. I have used his specific data, among others, in my broad more general theorizing. I was, therefore, both honored and pleased to have been asked to write a foreword to this book which collects, elaborates and integrates his previous work.

But pleased as I was to read the manuscript and write a foreword, an obvious question immediately arose: why should one have forewords? This raises an even more fundamental question: **What is a foreword and what is it supposed to do?**

On the one hand it is not helpful to make a general argument of interest to the writer but unrelated to the book. On the other hand it seems useless to summarize the book – after all it is there before the reader. Nor is it the place to evaluate the book – that is the role of the book reviewer. What then is one to do? After all, the author clearly knows much more about the specific subject and can say more about it than anyone else – certainly more than I can. The author can also put that topic into a specific framework. The purpose of a foreword then seems to be to **provide a larger framework within which the book can be seen.**

This answer shapes this foreword. What I have already written, and what follows, is intended to make it easier and more likely that a single work will transcend its apparent subject matter and will be seen as part of the larger, collective enterprise of scholarship and research. It should help develop the interplay (or tension) between the particular and the general, the idiographic and the nomothetic, the descriptive and the conceptual/theoretical and so on.

Although this book has a background (or "theory") section, based partly on my work and that of others, this plays a secondary role. It is primarily a case-study – a detailed, in depth, unusually detailed study of a place, its people, their life in that place, their beliefs and so on. My foreword can most usefully complement that by concerning itself with broader issues, with placing the case-study in a context, providing a framework within which the book can be seen. One can think of three levels: broad theory and concept development, a "local" framework and, within that, case-study. My foreword is then meant to provide the third level, the global framework within which can fit both the "local" framework and case-study of Chhatera.

The "local" framework of Part I can help the study of a single village in one region of India to be related to India as a whole, although the broader framework will still be needed, particularly in distinguishing between generalities and specifics. After all India itself is highly varied, with numerous different cultural landscapes created by many groups. Whatever their commonalities, these differ in their cultures as expressed in world views, values, beliefs, life-styles and activity systems. They also vary in some of their social characteristics, e.g. roles, family and kinship, deriving from these cultural differences and degree of modernization. Thus, in order to be able to generalize even to India (let alone more broadly) many critical EBS questions arise immediately: what are valid or relevant groups? (For example, can findings on caste become relevant to apparently very different social groupings?). This then raises the question of how one identifies commonalities and differences, how one distinguishes between important differences and trivial or superficial ones. How can one identify commonalities among apparent diversity? When is diversity real? How does one study constancy and change?

Not only does this allow many such important questions to be generated easily. It also makes clear that considering such questions is essential before one can generalize beyond region, e.g. to villages in India. It is also essential to make the detailed and highly specific data about one village in India useful to those whose primary interest may not be with villages in India but with how to plan or design truly Indian environments or concerned with villages in developing countries, with change and development; or with culture change and constancy vs. change; or even larger issues of models or theory about environment-behavior interaction. In this way such a study can become of interest to those who have no interest in villages as such or villages in India, and even less in Chhatera. In this way examples from numerous places can become mutually relevant. All can then contribute to the field of EBS.

It follows that these levels of relevance are not mutually exclusive, although my own interest and, I believe, ultimately the essential step is through the collective and cumulative enterprise of research and scholarship to move through ever broader generalization to the development of explanatory theory in EBS.

These different levels of interest are partly related to disciplines, some of which emphasize the descriptive and particular, others the conceptual and general. But they also relate to researchers' interests in considering the many variables involved in understanding environment-behavior relations (EBR). Two general approaches can be taken, which, of course, merely mark the two ends of a continuum. One can take a macro-approach and look at broad conceptual and theoretical issues and patterns across many varied examples. This favours breadth, scope and generality rather than depth, specificity and detail. Alternatively, one can emphasize the latter and adopt a micro-approach, dealing with the interplay of the many forces in a single place which one gets to know intimately in great detail and in depth.

My work is an extreme example of the former approach, this book exemplifies the latter.

Of course, most research shares aspects of both approaches – some conceptual framework is needed for any case-study and specific instances are essential for broad theorizing; the two approaches are generally complementary, not conflicting. Theory and concept formation without empirical data is just waffling and vacuous, and must be based on solid and adequate foundations. Case studies that do not contribute to theory are of little use. Thus, both are needed. One needs descriptions and analyses of cases on the basis of which one may theorize. On the other hand general questions or hypotheses require specific evidence although, as already emphasized, this should be as extensive and varied as possible.

The studies comprising such evidence need to combine the physical, cultural and social aspects, need to examine buildings as just one part of the often extensive system of settings of which they are part and need to discuss how activities take place within these. Of course, within the larger framework with which I am dealing latent aspects of activities need to be considered, not only manifest or instrumental aspects. Thus how activities are carried out, how are assembled into systems and their meaning need to be considered as well as the activities themselves at their manifest level. Activities vary more and more as one goes from the manifest to the latent aspects, hence the extraordinary variety of environments when considered cross-culturally and through time, in spite of the apparently much smaller range of activities. This is also the reason why we need the broadest and most varied body of evidence, i.e., many case studies.

If one can adequately answer an apparently simple question: who does what, where, when, including or excluding whom, and why, one can go a long way towards beginning to understand EBR. To go further, on the basis of many studies, requires answers to what I have called the three basic questions of EBS:

1. What characteristics of people as members of a species, of various groups and as individuals influence (or, in design, should influence) and how built environments are shaped?
2. What effects do which characteristics of built environments have on which groups in terms of behavior, mood, satisfaction, well-being and so on, and under what sets of circumstances?
3. A corollary question: given such a mutual interaction between people and environments there must be mechanisms linking them. What are these mechanisms?

Any research question in EBS can be understood in terms of these; they also provide one way of fitting material from this book into broader frameworks – the book provides data relevant to each of these questions. Once again, note that a diverse body of evidences is needed in order to answer these questions adequately; for any specific case much detailed knowledge is required.

Since my earliest work I have argued against single cause explanations; multiple causes are inevitable. At the same time I have suggested the primacy of cultural and social variables and the secondary or modifying influence of site, climate, materials, technology, defence and economics. I believe that in the last 20 years this position has been confirmed repeatedly, although the relative influence of the various factors may differ from case to case. I believe that this study also supports the primacy of factors such as culture, religious practices and beliefs, values, rule systems, prejudice and the like in determining morphology orientation, organization and so on.

Other views, of course, can be found. Be that as it may, and whatever hierarchy one accepts (and the answer ultimately depends on more and more thorough use studies of which this book is an example) one thing now seems generally accepted – that in order to understand built environments multiple variables must be considered and monocausal explanations are untenable.

In a foreword I cannot further develop the many points raised. But I hope that enough has been said to suggest the kind of framework that should be used while reading the book, so that it can contribute to the larger enterprise of understanding EBR. To make this clearer I will, in conclusion, discuss a few examples of how information provided by this case study, when placed into the larger framework, will reveal patterns and show principles that operate across different scales and across many situations; how data might contribute to theory. I hope readers will be able to think of many more. This is because this study provides enough data to do so; because it does look at the larger system of settings from the house interior to well beyond the village. Thus, not only do we see the relation of part of house to house, street, neighbourhood, village, fields, boundary of village estate, system of villages, town, city etc. We also find that members of a single household actually use three house locations (**Ghar, Baithak** and **Gher**). This is a very important finding in itself, but it is most significant for broader theory and methodology – even that system we call "house" or "dwelling" varies and **needs to be discovered rather than assumed.**

This example of a culturally highly specific system of settings, and how it works, can then help clarify highly general issues such as valid definition of housing that can be used in cross-cultural research, or the nature of systems of settings, among many others. In turn, this specific example is greatly clarified through the use of such concepts. Readers should also be able to think of their own examples because this book considers activity systems, life-style, beliefs and social variables as aspects of culture (even if not always explicitly) and because it draws on a range of disciplines. Too many case studies only consider small parts of the system and, thus, only bits of information. But let me give a few more examples related to my own work.

Many of the variables which I proposed in **House Form and Culture** as the primary influences on the form of dwellings and villages are considered in this most detailed study. Its use to people like me is that an Indian example can be used to complement others and fit into larger theory. Also, in my work over the past 20 years I have referred to Indian examples. This study can then allow me (and others) to see whether we have used examples correctly or whether we have tended to overgeneralize and so on. It can also, because of its comprehensiveness and detail, suggest additional research questions and hypotheses to be tested – if seen in the broader framework.

One topic, which I have explored in **Human Aspects of Urban Form** and other publications, concerns the existence (and persistence) of areas homogeneous on the basis of perceived similarity and using attributes such as ethnicity, race, language, life-style, occupation, caste and many others. Villages, other settlements and cultural landscapes clearly show the existence of a social geography – people rarely seem to be distributed randomly in space. This study discusses in great detail a single example which both reinforces general theory and becomes much more significant when seen not as a unique curiosity or anomaly but as a specific expression of a very general pattern. In that sense what at first glance seems specific to a single village becomes a characteristic of India, including very large cities. It is also seen to be a very general phenomenon (although, possibly, not universal; to determine that many more case studies will be needed in many cultures). The specifics apply to how homogeneous areas are organized, what form of homogeneity applies, the scale or size of such areas, their morphology, how and through which cues their homogeneity is communicated and so on. How a single village work becomes a useful instance of a more general theory and supports it? Also while caste may appear to be relevant only in India, and increasingly less so there, the principles revealed through theory, which influence environments, apply very broadly – if not universally. This is an example of how by asking the question – who does what, where, when, including or excluding whom and why – apparently highly specific answers can lead to very general conclusions.

In many places in this book suggestive ideas are found which are not developed, or even made explicit. One I would interpret in terms of **meaning** which, while not discussed explicitly, seems to play a very important role in the analysis. This makes it possible to use findings of this book in studies of meaning, even though it does not seem to deal with that topic. The findings also well support my argument (in **The Meaning of the Built Environment** and elsewhere) that meaning is possibly the most important function of the built environment rather than something added to function, and that the built environment is not merely a container of culture but is used actively within culture as an important part of it. Thus, these kinds of issues, raised by the broader framework, even though they are implicit and not developed, raise questions, suggest comparisons with other places in India and environments more generally. This not only allows the generalization and conceptual development that I have been emphasizing. Reading the book in this way, made possible by the broader framework, also increases its fertility, i.e., the book can suggest research questions, applications and so on.

Because of the 100-year time-span covered – a rare and most important aspect of the study – change and constancy can be studied. The detailed baseline in the 1970s provides further opportunities (for future study). The changing relations between the village and the city, and effects of urbanization and of innovations in transportation and other technology can be identified. For example, changes in transportation change the relationships between systems of activities and systems of settings, and hence change what I have called units of settlement. One small example in this book is the shift in the conceptual place of receiving and greeting guests to the railway station as a function of new transportation technology. This is not only a striking example in itself, but can be related to comparable re-orientations in other places, for example, the shift that occurred due to the changes from communication along rivers to one along roads (e.g. among the Fang in Africa). It can also be related to the literature on changes in subjective distance and size of settlements due to new transport technology. At the larger scale, changes among unit of settlements relate what happens in villages to what occurs in towns and even very large cities and metropolis. Such findings can also be related to other places. For example, the study concludes that density is being reduced, that residences are moving from the **Abadi** to the periphery, and that there is a tendency towards scatteration of the village. This can be related both to changes in life-style and expectations (and increased resources) and to comparable changes elsewhere (as just one example to analogous changes among many Pueblos in the south-western United States). If found among other studies, one might even hypothesize that this reveals a regular pattern; further case studies could test this hypothesis. A related finding in this study is that there is increasing variability of house forms, that non-traditional forms are becoming more common. In that process **choice** plays an increasing role (and sometimes results in conflict). This, again, is fully in accord with findings from very many other places. In this sense it also fits into some fairly high-level theoretical work that I have done on housing generally and into models of change in developing countries. As a result, once again, this study of a single village becomes of **general** interest and utility; it also makes those conceptual models potentially relevant to India. **A large variety of work becomes mutually relevant.** Similar arguments can be made about changes in standards and expectations, in relations to animals or among people and so on; all can be subsumed under a single model: changes in culture lead to changes in life-style and those, in turn, change environment in (often) predictable ways.

The discussion of rules and how they are handled provides another good example. Not only are the descriptions and analysis most useful in themselves, for example, in clarifying orientation and showing that it applies not only to fixed-feature elements like the house, but semi-fixed feature elements (furnishings) and even non-fixed – people. The discussion of rules about separating various categories of people (by caste, gender, age and so on), or people and animals, fits into very general models that I have developed, for example, on the importance of such rules in how settings work. Again, the specific material helps these models and at the same time achieves greater generality through them. For example, the role of the school (**Sakul**) in meetings and interaction seems clearly related to what I call a "neutral place". As such it fits into a model of such places that I have developed from Anglo-American data, eventhough the **specifics** are very different. This increases the generality of both model and data. Similarly, the **chaupal** becomes another neutral place, but only within caste lines – a good example of the hierarchical organization of system of settings in settlements; this, again, is of great generality. In fact, much of this book can very usefully be analyzed in terms of my model of system of activities in system of settings. Who does what, where, when including or excluding whom, and why, is codified through rules and highly routinized (as behavior always is – this is a major function of culture). The localization of activities is very striking and fits the model very well; it also suggests comparisons with other places regarding the nature of such systems and their organization, the codification of behavior and the extent of its localization, processes of change in all of these with changing life-styles and so on.

I thus welcome this case-study from India with its interesting and useful data, rich description and suggestive partial analysis. I hope that many more will be forthcoming as the field of EBS matures and develops in India – and I hope this happens quickly. There is much to be done and time is short. The knowledge embodied in traditional environments needs to be discovered and preserved before these environments disappear or change beyond recognition; this process of change itself also needs to be studied. At the same time the lessons need to be learned quickly. These may help preserve environments which should not be destroyed, because of higher quality than what replaces them; they may contribute to the development of truly Indian built environments, and they may help prevent and avoid mistakes in development, planning and design, not only in India but more generally. Such lessons are of the most general importance for the development of explanatory theory in environment-behavior studies.

Distinguished Professor AMOS RAPOPORT
The School of Architecture & Urban Planning
The University of Wisconsin
MILWAUKEE

INTRODUCTION

ATHARVA VEDA contains a profound realisation of man: soil is the mother and water is the father. The physical quality of life is primarily determined by soil and water. But man is not a mere creature of nature. Man also makes himself in the image of his inspired vision. It has been very apt for Chandhoke to look into the philosophical and religious background while examining the nature and structure of rural habitat in India. The moot question is whether in case of the societies in other parts of the world – the advanced industrialised countries, for instance – philosophical and religious considerations are relevant for habitat planning or whether these are important only for 'traditional' societies, the 'modern' societies being guided by only 'rational' technological considerations. The question is not a matter of academic interest only: in the International Year for the Shelterless, it has great practical implications. When millions of persons are homeless or have only ramshackled structures over their heads, it is natural to think in terms of solution on a mass-scale: and, in the context of the same, many would like to perceive philosophy and religion or in broader term local cultures, as luxuries in habitat planning. There are several assumptions which define the contours of such a perception. Among them, three will be particularly mentioned here.

(A) Emergence of a world technological culture, making the historical cultural differences matters of secondary importance.

(B) Relationship of dependence between the techno-bureaucrat and the rest of the society resulting from incapacity of the general mass of the population to creatively move in the direction of solving their problems.

(C) Operational rationality is identical with societal rationality.

According to the first assumption, technology interacting strongly with nature, but cutting across society and men in their political, psychological, anthropological and other dimensions, provides a mechanistic model of planning. This model requires that the goals are given from outside, the programmes are related to specified outcome and are controlled by external policy. It is essentially an elitist model and the second assumption fits into it almost with gliding smoothness.

But in this model the concept of rationality deserves special attention. In an extremely narrow sense rationality is related to the convenience of the operative apparatus of the techno-bureaucratic set up, and not to the fulfilment of the societal goal of need satisfaction of the concerned segments of the population. Rationality can also be conceptualised in a different sense of economic rationality, which some would like to brush aside as belonging to the realm of philosophy rather than of anthropology (Clammer, John 1985: *Anthropology and Political Economy*, p.30: The Macmillan Press Ltd, London). But this is not true. As pointed out by Chatterjee (Chatterjee Partha 1986: *Nationalist thought and the colonial world* p.11; Zed Book Depot, U.N. University, Tokyo), there is a deep rooted cultural arrogance in treating the question of rationality in this manner. In fact, the concept of rationality has come to be organised around such matters as productive efficiency, accumulation of wealth, 'progress' of some 'interest' in the society, without too closely examining whose interest it is.

As against the mechanistic model is the human action model. In this, man-nature interaction and planning processes are self-adaptive and self-regulatory to a large extent. The essential feature of this model is general introduction of normative thinking and valuation planning, thus making it non-deterministic and continuously creative.

In India, the mechanistic model has been tried again and again, but the administrative and technological elites do not appear to have learnt much from the history of the failures. In the 1950s, housing colonies were built in different parts of the country for the benefit of the tribals and untouchable castes. More frequently than not, these colonies remained unoccupied or were abandoned after being occupied. Studies conducted at that time showed that the values, the social, psychological and economic needs and constraints and in some cases even the ecological considerations were generally overlooked. In a Rabha village in West Bengal, the beneficiaries continued to stay in their old huts, and kept their poultry and cattle in the 'improved' houses, as these did not provide for privacy. In Orissa in the housing colonies, families with too heterogeneous social background were brought together, making it difficult for the emergence of effective leadership from within for looking after the matters of common interest. In Bihar, in a colony the location of the residential area was found to be far away from the source – places of economic activities. In Madhya Pradesh, the housing colony did not make provision for the common socio-cultural activities of the population. In a hilly tract in Eastern Himalaya, the plan for replacing the stilt houses had to be abandoned as the substitutes were found to be ecologically unsuitable, besides requiring too many adjustments to be made in the hygienic habits and other behavioral aspect of the concerned population. As a result of these experiences, the programme of setting up housing colonies as a welfare measure was given up during the third and fourth Five-Year Plans in many areas of the country. Housing programmes were of course there, in which the selection of the site was the concern of the beneficiaries themselves. By and large, establishment of housing colonies in rural area was confined to the rehabilitation of the oustees of major industrial and hydro-electric projects. But since the mid 1970s the programme of establishing housing colonies has been resumed with some vigour and the same mistakes, as in the 1950s and the early 1960s, have been found to be repeated.

It is not only in India, that such mechanistic planning takes place. In South Korea, as a defence-need, in many cases the old villages where removed from the hillsides to the plains, well connected by roads. The hills in the old villages served as protective screens against the chilly wind blowing from the North Pole; in the new villages this protective screen was not there. The mortality rate went up: many of the aged persons moved over to the towns, and the villages showed features of anomie (Roy Burman, B.K. 1982: Discussion arranged by Futurology Commission of Seol. Cultural Research Future. Arizona University). In Tashkent, after the great earthquake in the late 1960s, a massive programme of constructing modern houses was taken up for the rehabilitation of the affected population. But many preferred to repair their traditional type of houses with backyard, as these provided scope for many of their social activities and hobbies to be pursued.

All these are mentioned here to bring out the relevance of normative thinking in the matter of habitat planning. By treating rural habitation as a dimension of continuity and change in culture and at the same time by highlighting some of the relevant issues of political-economy, Chandhoke has made a useful attempt to stimulate normative thinking in this field. He has also considered aspects of constructional technology, as prevalent among the villagers. This is a matter of great importance and merits intensive study all over the country as a part of the programme of fulfilling the challenging task of co-operating with the shelterless millions to have not only their 'shelters' but their 'homes'. A study in the tribal and non-tribal villages in Manipur and Nagaland shows that large number of adaptive innovations are made by the people in their housing technology, compatible with their resource base and demographic and economic constraints. The study also shows that it is only with intimate knowledge about the ethno-technology prevailing among the people that it is possible to co-operate with them in improving the quality of the habitat. Chandhoke's study relates to a different area: but with a very similar canvass of cognitive mapping. The intellectual quest he has made has an ethical thrust; and this is what the Third World countries require of their scholars, for a long time to come.

Visiting Senior Fellow B.K. ROY BURMAN
Centre for the Study of Developing Societies
NEW DELHI
Chairman
Advisory Committee on Social Dimensions of Environment
Government of India

CONTENTS

Part III
ELEMENT OF PATTERNS OF HABITATION

Part IV
CONCLUSION: SETS AND PATTERNS

LIST OF PLATES

LIST OF TABLES

LIST OF FIGURES

NOTE OF PRESENTATION

HUMAN HABITATION is an area of great interest and concern. It has been the subject of study under several aspects—socio-economic, cultural and historical, etc. The complex process of its growth and development is, however, comprehended more vividly in the context of a more simple, less complex, society.

Mr. Chandhoke's work is a valuable contribution to the study of the rural habitat. His most significant contribution is that he goes beyond the views of a sociologist, that he is, and dwells in details related to architectural and physical planning. The book is very topical particularly because of the great revival of interest amongst professionals and academicians in trying to resolve the problems of shelter in a more humane and basic adaptive forms and materials. The search for the vernacular and understanding of its social and environmental context are reflected not only in academic curricula and research but also in the new directions of professional work of architects particularly in developing countries. Mr. Chandhoke brings to bear on his work his vast knowledge and experience of field-work, teaching and working with architects as well as his contributions in several papers presented nationally and internationally. This is evident in his analysis of the physical aspects of the rural habitat, which he weaves, with his insight as a sociologist, into case studies of village life.

Director
School of Planning and Architecture
NEW DELHI

BRUNO DIAS SOUZA

ACKNOWLEDGEMENTS

BEHIND THE successful accomplishment of any venture there is always the 'invisible' support of a number of persons. All the more so when one undertaking the venture is not of a masterly type.

The learned advice of Professor J.P.S. Uberoi of the Department of Sociology, University of Delhi, at different stages of this study illuminated the dark alleys of the subject. I am really at my wit's end to find an appropriate way to express my heart-felt gratitude to him.

The study of classic Sanskritic literature on the subject could be possible only because of the learned guidance and blessings of the saint-scholar, the late Professor Mohan Singh Uberoi Deewana. My respectful homage to him.

My sincere thanks are also due to Professor A.M. Shah of the University of Delhi for providing encouragement for this work.

I owe my gratitude to the residents of Chhatera and surrounding villages for providing me an excellent opportunity to study their life styles, culture and habitat by staying with them. Among them the village Headman, Choudhary Partap Singh, and his brothers, the late Master Rattan Singh, Choudhary Ran Singh, Dr. Maha Singh's mother, Pt. Sant Ram Sharma and his family, the late Pt. Ganga Dutt, the late Pt. Giri Lal Sharma and Pt. Tika Ram and his wife deserve a special mention.

Thanks are due to our present Director, Professor V.P. Raou for providing guidance and encouragement at different stages of this work. I am also grateful to my friend and colleague, Mr. M. Chandra Mouli, who always made himself readily available for useful discussions.

The late Professor Bijit Ghosh was kind enough to allow me to use some of the illustrative material prepared by his students during their study of the village. Mr. B.G. Verghese, former Editor-in-Chief, The

Hindustan Times, also allowed me to use the photographs of Chhatera from his rich photo archives. My thanks to both of them. The drawings included in this book have been prepared by Mr. P.C. Sharma, formerly a student and now a colleague. He genuinely deserves an affectionate pat. I am thankful to Mr. S.L. Sharma, also of the School, for his photographic assistance. Jacket design is by Prof. Mohammad Shaheer and coloured photographs are by Mr. Z.H. Khan. Mr. R.L. Kalra put his heart and soul in typing the manuscript. Mr. B.N. Saraf and his team of the Publication Unit of the School have seen this publication through.

I have no words to express my deep sense of gratitude to Professor Amos Rapoport for his thoughtful foreword in which he has brought to bear his vast knowledge and rich experience - both as an architect as well as anthropologist and a leader in the field of Environment Behavior Studies - to throw light on the intricate field of anthropology of space and human habitations which has added to the value of my work by placing it in its proper perspective.

Professor B.K. Roy Burman has put this work in its proper perspective and infused added meaning to it by writing an introduction. He had given useful and learned suggestions for the improvement of the manuscript earlier also. I am extremely indebted to him.

I am grateful to the authorities of the School, especially the then Director, Professor Bruno Dias Souza, for sponsoring the publication of this work. My thanks are also due to him for his note of presentation to this book.

I know I must have missed many names in this list. They all deserve my thanks anonymously.

School of Planning and Architecture S.K. CHANDHOKE
NEW DELHI.

PREFACE

HUMAN HABITATION is a very legitimate area for systematic study by a number of disciplines. Since cave-dwelling stage - when shelter enjoyed pre-eminence even over clothing - man has been making continuous efforts for the increased satisfaction of the three fundamental needs. While revolutionary advances, mainly as a result of tremendous achievements in the fields of science and technology, have been brought about in the realms of food and clothing, precious little has been done in the domain of human habitations. A majority of the mankind still continues to reel under the burden of finding a suitable and reasonably decent place to live in.

Whatever little breakthrough has been achieved in the field of human habitation, it pertains mainly to building materials and construction techniques. The pattern, i.e., the design, form and texture of human habitation, has attracted very little attention of the intelligentsia, policy-maker, technocrat and the scholar alike. An important parameter, that of the social and cultural dimensions, has somehow remained neglected in whatever little has been done on this front.

House building, for example, is undertaken not as a result of the dictates of the physical factors, it is a cultural necessity. In the decisions about the choice of various elements - material as well as non-material - their sizes, shapes, combinations and arrangements, social and cultural factors play an over-ridingly important role. More important is the decision with regard to the alternate uses of these elements and the actors there.

Most of the existing theories in this field are quite inadequate in themselves as they suffer from a predominant physical bias and, therefore, cannot help us in understanding human habitation in a realistic perspective, the way a sociological approach promises to do.

Various disciplines studying human habitation have approached the problem from certain specific angles but almost all have focussed on one dimension or the other of only its three dimensional tangible aspects.

This author firmly believes what Spate has observed, in respect of habitation at the level of the house "Not only the site and layout of the village, but the geography of the house often reflects age-old religious and magical traditions" (Spate, O.H.K. 1961: 255), is equally true at all other levels of habitation also.

Sociologists and anthropologists have also been making some attempts in this direction. Such attempts have, however, been of a fragmentary nature touching only a few aspects of human habitation, thus leaving a void, consequently generating a palpable need for a systematic and serious work on a comprehensive scale. The present work is a modest attempt in this direction.

A comparative review of the existing literature and a survey to identify the various potential secondary sources of data and information form an important part of this study.

Information on the subject in the classical Sanskritic literature was imperative as field-work for this study was to be undertaken in India. Lack of knowledge of Sanskrit language on the part of the author was a handicap in studying the original sources directly, but a more serious impediment was lack of identification of the sources themselves.

Next step was the selection of a suitable community for field-work. Jats being a typical ethno-linguistic group in Northern India with a distinct culture and history of their own constitute an important segment of the population in the villages of Haryana and Delhi. Moreover, this author's knowledge of the regional language and familiarity with the local culture was an additional advantage. His long professional association with village Chhatera offered a potential area for field-work.

To collect information through observation as well as interviews with the villagers, the author stayed in village Chhatera during a summer vacation and again for about an equal period during winter the same year.

Visits to a number of villages in the region also provided opportunities for discussions with cross-sections of the people. Study of very old (non-governmental) records of Chhatera and surrounding villages in the possession of some inhabitants of Sasana and Kharkhauda provided insight into the problem.

Discussions with the respective *Purohits* of the Jats and Brahmans, the Head Master of Mandora High School and the Bhat of the Jats and others provided useful information. Interaction with the village level government functionaries, the Block Development Officer, the Tehsildar, District Magistrate, Revenue Officer and others as well as scrutiny of some of the old government records in the District Archives at Rohtak yielded useful results.

The reader may wonder about the implications of the detailed case study in the context of the theoretical formulations and cross-cultural and historical appraisal in the first two chapters.

The aim of this case study is to find out the factors responsible for the behavior patterns of the unit and its relationships with the social factors and forces involved in its surrounding milieu. To sum up, this method helps in understanding the complex of forces that are operative within a social unit as an integrated totality. A lone case study, admittedly, cannot explain all the situations. However, the purpose of this method is to highlight the common elements. The utility and appropriateness of this approach for the present work becomes self-explanatory when viewed in the light of its objectives.

The conclusions of the present study would be directly applicable to villages of Delhi, Haryana, Punjab, Rajasthan and Uttar Pradesh as well. It is not this author's intention to claim that the method for the study of the socio-cultural dimensions of any human habitation has been fully developed and refined here, nonetheless it is a pioneering work.

The book is divided into four parts. Part I contains introduction to the subject, description of different approaches adopted by various disciplines for the study of human habitation and review of the concerned works in sociology and anthropology as well as in Sanskritic literature.

An account of village Chhatera; its location, history, social structure, physical aspects and economic life, the various levels of living in the village and cultural aspects related to habitation form Part II.

Part III comprises a description of the elements of patterns of habitation at the macro – as well as micro-level. "Conclusion : Sets and Patterns" and Summary constitute Part IV. An attempt has also been made in this Part to identify the various pairs of complimentary relationships (which form a part of the System of Classification) as relevant to the habitation under study and classify them, according to their respective roles, into Primary and Secondary.

At the end of the main text there is an exhaustive bibliography of references cited in the text and also a glossary of the native terms used.

The system of transliteration followed is that of Platt. In the main body of the text the native terms have been put in Italics. In the case of native terms (ending with the letter s) when used in plural sense the accepted practice has, however, not been followed. The diacritical marks have been given in the glossary only.

The last portion of the book is formed of ten appendices based partly on data from the author's own field-work and partly on that collected from secondary sources. A number of photographs and drawings have been included in the book.

The author shall consider his labour to have been amply rewarded if the book proves to be useful to those for whom it is intended and succeeds in motivating some others to take up works in this fascinating field, hardly explored so far.

School of Planning and Architecture S.K. CHANDHOKE
NEW DELHI,

ONE

APPROACHES

1.1 INTRODUCTION

1.1.1 *Definition and objectives*

THE PURPOSE of the present study is to know the factors that go into the shaping of a human habitation and those that help sustain the pattern so formed, and also, if possible, the respective roles of these factors: to have an understanding of the character of rural habitations and their internal structure. The entire process or mechanism of the origin, growth, change and decay of rural habitations, as it has evolved over ages, is the most fundamental issue.

This understanding is an essential prerequisite for the successful formulation and implementation of any programme of rural development, especially those concerning the physical environment.

To settle means 'to colonize', 'the act of settling', 'to decide', 'to compromise', to compose or regulate. The term settlement, therefore, signifies the residential areas or colonies planned and developed according to some particular design, generally, along newly-dug canals or areas made newly-cultivable, or near some industrial places, etc.,[1] unlike those *abadis* which originate and develop in a slow and natural way and grow like a natural organism. It is because of this reason that we often talk about the 'village morphology', meaning the structure of the organism of the village.

The terms 'settlement' and 'habitation' are often used interchangeably which is not correct. The dictionary meaning of the term 'habitation' is a place of abode and its physical environment, and this happens to be also one of the meanings of the term 'habituation' itself. 'Habitation pattern' of a community, therefore, is an indication of the practice or custom of any community with regard to the pattern of its place of abode. The connotation of the term, in the rural context, is not restricted only to the *abadi* including the environs but also includes the individual dwelling at the micro-level. The concept of habitation pattern is, therefore, the physical aspect of a locality, the community inhabiting it and the associated social and cultural norms, tendencies and behaviour. The term 'rural', I believe, is too well-known to need any explanation here.

Social factors play a very prominent role in shaping any habitation and it is only a sociological approach that can help us have a proper understanding of the complex subject of human habitations. One important limitation of all the existing theories of human habitations is that they have a predominant physical bias and, therefore, cannot help us in understanding the human habitations the way a sociological approach can. In this sense, the existing theories are quite inadequate by themselves. Hence, as its caption "Social Patterns of Rural Habitations" shows, the subject matter of the present work is to evolve a sociological approach to the understanding of human habitations in rural areas and highlight its significance. The physical extent, the number of inhabitants and the structure and functioning of this physical unit of economic, social and administrative and political life of the people are aspects of rural settlements which naturally attract our serious attention and are unfortunately either not mentioned or, if mentioned, very perfunctorily so, in old literature and inscriptions (Ghurye, 1960: xxi).

The way people build their houses, group them and the way arteries of internal and external communications are formed would lend itself to ecological and anthropological analysis (Karve, 1957: 100). The study of settlements is also the study of human reactions to the environmental factors, because the settlement is the product of adjustment between the social forces and the physical conditions of the habitat (Mukerji, 1957: 102). Definite grouping of rural populations is a conscious human response to a number of factors (Aurrouseau, 1920: 237). Any specific environment, to some degree, forces a material way of living upon the people subjected to it (Firth, 1956: 41). A study of the rural populations in the Sone Valley (India) has revealed that definite grouping is a conscious human response to physiography and a number of other factors (Bhattacharya and Verma, 1956-57: 303). "Two common orientations of villages are observed on flat terrain where village water supply is dependent on artificial tanks or bunds. In villages originally founded by Muslims, the tanks and bunds are invariably oriented east-west, that is, the longer arms are stretched that way and villages arranged around them. In the villages founded by Hindus, the tanks or bunds invariably stretch north-south with the settlement around them. Thus, the prevalent forms represent various stages of social and economic orgnisation and resource mobilization" (Mitra, 1966:11). Sarma (1953) has very clearly brought out as to how the habitation pattern of any community is related to its economic activity and the stages of economy and its development. Further, the ecological process of the supply and distribution of resources governs both the size and character of the human community (Mukerjee, 1928:343). Kinship ties are one of the important factors that influence the settlement pattern (Bose and Malhotra, 1963: 241).

"In many cases it is not the geographical conditions but the social heritage that become the determinants of the elements of geographical reality" (Mukerji, 1957: 303). "Settlement types seem to have more to do with tradition than either geography or agriculture" (Bose and Sinha, 1961: 3). Although the pattern of any habitation is very much conditioned by social life of those inhabiting it, once a pattern has been formed, the social life in the village is influenced by its physical character and human endowment (Bracey, 1959; Nicholas, 1963).

1.1.2 *Factors that shape and sustain a pattern*

Each pattern is formed and sustained by different factors or groups of factors (Karve, 1957; Mobgunje; Janki 1953; Mukerji, 1957; Bhattacharya and Verma, 1956-57) like:

(a) Cultural and Community factors
(b) Economic factors
(c) Historical factors
(d) Physical factors

Social factors, like the history of the area, customs and traditions of the communities inhabiting it, and their social organization have a direct or indirect influence on the habitations in the area. Folk beliefs, caste, kinship, family, marriage, rules of inheritance of property and of succession, etc., play an important role in the evolution of particular patterns of village habitations. "... The successional changes in the socio-economic trends and historical events also influence the human habitations" (Kaushic, 1959: 2). In countries with social freedom each natural region tends to develop a characteristic pattern of habitation (Aurrousseau, 1920: 224).

Economic factors like the occupations of those inhabiting a habitation, their state of economic development, the type of farming they are engaged in, etc., also have their own role to play in patterning the habitation.

The physical conditions include factors like topography, soil, water supply and other conditions which are by and large beyond the control of human beings whether acting individually or in social groups (Janki, 1953: 45; Mukerji, 1957: 102; Semple, 1947). Although, under certain exceptional circumstances, even a single factor may cause a habitation to acquire a particular pattern, it is seldom possible to give any one reason for the formation of a particular pattern (Janki, 1953; Mukerji, 1957). An attempt may be made to find out as to what pattern roughly a rural habitation is likely to take under a particular set of circumstances. And this by itself, if achieved, would be no mean a contribution. In fact, it is always a group of them responsible for it. Similarly, it is also always difficult to disentangle and isolate the various factors responsible for the shaping of a habitation, and to identify the exact role played by each one of them in this process. Though individually each factor may be having the potentialities of influencing the habitation pattern in a particular manner, its impact under different sets of circumstances is different. The number of permutations and combinations, especially with differential weightages and behaviour patterns of the various factors in different settings, is very large. As such, it is difficult to pinpoint the specific role of any individual factor in this respect.

Each village has a pattern and mode of life which is to some extent unique. Villages next door to each other differ considerably (Dube, 1954: 526; Ray, 1960: 12; Srinivas, 1954: 606). No two villages are alike (Ali, Amir, 1937: 335). Different villages under almost similar physical conditions, economic circumstances and law and order conditions have assumed different patterns and the factors causing dissimilarities are mainly sociological. Within a radius of eight kms. from the Govind Ballabh Pant University of Agriculture and Technology (Nainital, U.P.) four different types of villages—Bhotia, Rai Sikh, Bengali and local — exist. It is a newly developed region where people from different parts of the country have been settled/rehabilitated. These new settlers have, as if it were, brought along with them the entire villages and houses from their native places. Similar situations have been observed in Medak and Nizamabad districts of Andhra Pradesh. These are the villages put up by the migrants from the delta districts of the State. "...The inhabitants make it appear as though an entire coastal delta village had been uprooted and planted in the midst of the wet land of the project..." (Mitra, 1966: 335). Another manifestation of the tribal and caste control of the rural habitation is that of the Bhoksa villages on the border of Bijnore and Garhwal districts of Uttar Pradesh (Bhattacharya, A.N., 1956: 99). These villages are distinct than those of the other groups living in the same area. Everywhere the Bhoksa village plan and the house form are the same. The distinction of the Bhoksa village is, therefore, due to the tribal factor, its traditions and mode of adaptation to the environmental conditions and not so much due to the direct environmental control. Another case as instance to show that the pattern of housing varies within the same region according to social factors is that of villages inhabited mainly by the Meos, Brahmans, Jats, Ahirs, Gujjars, Girasias and Bhils within the Alwar district of Rajasthan (Mitra, 1966: 184a). The same is true of the style of villages inhabited by the various communities in the Bharatpur district of Rajasthan and some other parts of the State (Mitra, 1966: 185a, from Rajasthan and Ajmer Merwara 1911: 29). The Japanese while spreading from south to north took with them the house identified with their culture, although this house was extremely uncomfortable (at least during certain parts of the year) in their new habitat (Rapoport, 1969: 22). Similarly, the Santhals generally carry the linear type of village layout pattern wherever they go (Bose and Sinha, 1961: 5). The habitations of non-Malayalee Hindus in Kerala (where the predominant pattern is that of dispersal), most of whom are of Tamil origin, are nucleated. "The Tamilians seem to have introduced into Kerala the traditional nucleated village of their home origin. Examples of those are usually found in border areas south of Alagappapuram, Maharajapuram, Ramanddupuram and Pattancherry" (Janki, 1953: 53). Hence the necessity of studying the sociological aspects of the subject - a fact which is now being increasingly acknowledged even by scholars in other disciplines (Rapoport, 1969: 48).

1.1.3 *Broad patterns of rural habitations in India*

There are two[2] extreme patterns of habitation, namely, (a) nucleated or clustered, where houses are clustered together to form a compact habitation area clearly dema cated from the surrounding agricultural fields and (b) the dispersed or scattered type, where houses are built apart either in small clusters of two or three or separately, each in its own farm. Between the tightly nucleated and the widely dispersed villages there are a number of variant forms (Mitra, 1966; Malhotra and Bharara, 1963; Hudson, 1970; Vanne Troph, 1965). The two types have their relative advantages and disadvantages over each other (Jones, 1964: 118-119; Slucum, 1962: 118-119).

The basic mechanism of nucleation and dispersal has been discussed by Janki thus:

> Man is a gregarious animal whose fundamental tendency is to remain grouped, sometimes in a family, often in a clan. Theoretically one might put forward a case that the small nucleated settlement is the primary form, and that all dispersal is subsequent. Among the simpler societies the cohesion of social groups is often reflected in communal dwellings.
>
> This primary urge toward nucleation is emphasised by the need for protection of man from beast. This applies to temporary as well as permanent settlement...
>
> But it is rarely that close nucleation is the product of only one factor. One cannot dissociate pressure on land from need for protection - the Iranian villages are walled - and as the need for either diminishes, nuclearity may still persist, for, it is a form which also reflects social cohesion and may be found in association with specific kinds of land tenure (1953: 42).

In India there are no clear-cut areas having the various types of habitations. Although every region has a predominant pattern, perhaps very few regions can claim to be not having any other pattern. For example, dispersed villages are not confined to the West Coast of India - they occur elsewhere also, for instance, in the Bhil country to the East and North of Gujarat and Coorg and western Mysore. Even in Kerala there is a striking contrast between the settlements of the west side of the sahyadri and those of the east. "A true Malayalee never seems to have lived in villages of the East Coast, that is houses built in streets" (Janki, 1953: 41, Innes and Evans, 1907: 139). Nor do they show any inclination to live in colonies (Janki, 1953: 42). On the Coimbatore-Palghat highway in the centre of the highway gap, settlements on the eastern half of the highway passing through Kanjikode are of the Tamil

Nadu type while those on the western half are of the Kerala type" (Mitra, 1966: 2). "In the agricultural village Lousiana, farmsteads are concentrated along a road, riverfront, or lakefront with the farming lands in long strips behind them. Smith, who has studied this form of settlement extensively, attributes its presence in the United States principally to French culture. In Southern Lousiana, which Bertrand calls French Lousiana, the Line Village is the principal type of settlement" (Slocum, 1922: 122).

Even in those areas where complete dispersal is the geneal rule of rural habitations, exceptions to it are found. This may be the result of historical, cultural, economic or physical factors.

About the distribution of the various forms of villages in the country, Bose and Sinha have observed thus:

> The boundaries of the culture areas or sub-areas do not tally with Grierson's boundaries of either linguistic families like Indo-Aryan or Dravidian or of branches within either of these families. Material items of culture seem to have independent extensions of their own; and these may roughly tend to be in accord with one another. On their basis, India becomes divided very roughly into two distinguishable and overlapping regions meeting at a broad zone which runs from Maharashtra to Bihar in some cases and to Orissa or Bengal in others...
>
> Regionalization in respect of social organization is less than that in material traits...
>
> Thus, for instance, village plans in India have a certain rough distribution between North and South. The North is the area of the shapeless clusters, often broken up in dispersed units, while Southern villages are, on the whole, distinguishable by the presence of open streets as an integral part of the layout (1961: introduction).

Again, according to the same authors:

> From the point of view of the physical form taken by a village, the following different orders can be distinguished in India (each type having a fairly wide range of variations):
>
> 1. Shapeless cluster or agglomerate with streets not forming an integral part of the design. These may be of the (i) massive or (ii) dispersed type, in whch the village is reckoned to consist of an

> assemblage of discrete clusters of comparatively small size...
> 2. Linear cluster or assemblage with a regular open space or straight street provided between parallel rows of houses.
> 3. Square or rectangular cluster or agglomerate with straight streets running parallel or at right angles to one another.
> 4. Villages formed of isolated homesteads, a number of which are treated together as a *mauza* for convenience of collection of rent or taxes.
>
> The four patterns do enjoy regional exclusiveness to a certain extent but they interpenetrate in many areas other than border zones, the greatest tract of interpenetration being Madhya Pradesh, on which the main regions seem to converge, they run into each other in a complicated tangle (1961: 1-2).

It would be useful to have a Distribution Map of the entire country depicting the locations of villages with various types of layout patterns. This map would become quite meaningful when studied in conjunction with, or in relation to, the other distribution maps depicting various factors like the social organization and physiographic conditions.

The pattern of habitation is also related to the stage and type of agriculture (Janki, 1953: 61). "...Wherever the food-producing revolution effectively replaced earlier hunting and gathering patterns, village life became established" (Sills, 1968: 318). It is often said that the agglomerated habitations are associated with extensive farming (due to security in large farms) and the dispersed habitations are associated with intensive farming (due to close devotion to their fields and careful methods of farming) (Bhattacharya, A.N., 1956: 95). But this is not always so, sometimes even evidence to the contrary is available. In fact, co-operation (in agriculture and other fields) among the villagers leads to compactness (Ahmad, Enayat, 1952: 231-32; Forde 1963: 55; Janki 1953: 61). "The compact village may be held to imply the existence, at least at the origin, of some form of communal cultivation" [Ahmad, Enayat, 1952: 231 from Demangeon, A. Agricultural systems and schemes of distribution of population in Western Europe, The Geographical Teacher XII (1925-1926): 199-205; Kaushic, 1959: 7]. Irregularity of relief leads to diffusion of resources and general sameness of scene fosters a sense of community (Ahmad, Enayat, 1952: 230).

> ... Originally, at any rate, throughout entire regions, villages must

> have been established in a country covered with forest or jungle; and the labour of clearing this, as well as of maintaining an unceasing struggle against the re-growth of semi-tropical vegetation, required co-operation and union would also be necessary for defence against the depredations of deer, pigs and other animals which are dangerous not only to the cultivation but to human life. And any group of cultivators would have to be prepared to present a common front against neighbours with whom they were probably at feud... (Baden-Powell, 1913: 67-68).

There is an implicit reference to this aspect in the writings of Shah also:

> All the members of the hamlet used to work in lah. That is whenever a man required help for any work involving the co-operation of many, such as harvesting, house-building, tile-making, or cutting wood in the jungle, he invited people to lah. Sometimes he would invite only a few kinsmen and friends, but sometimes he may need the help of all the members of a hamlet. He has to provide the guests with a meal in return for their help (1955: 113).

Some observations of Chandoke (1972: 128-44) among the Tana Bhagats of Chotanagpur also support this.

Clan solidarity, social and economic bonds (including the division of labour) and religion and folk beliefs have led to agglomeration (Ahmad, Enayat, 1952: 232; Mitra, 1966: 22).

Writing about the village layout pattern of the Mormons, Slocum observes thus:

> ... that the main reason for their departure from the prevalent form of settlement is to be found in their religious ideology, which held among other things that a second coming of the saviour was imminent and the city of Zion was to be re-built as his headquarters during his reign on earth. This design was used as the basic plan for all Mormon settlements... (1962: 120 from Nelson Lowry).

The caste factor itself is often responsible for scattered hamlets (Bhattacharya and Verma, 1956-57: 302). Some scholars (Ahmad, Enayat, 1952: 233; Kaushic, 1959: 17) have emphasized also the role played by the religious and other folk beliefs in determining the habitation pattern of any village.

"...The social gatherings in the centre of the village, usually under some shady tree or near the temple; the mutual rejoicings on festivals; the gathering of neighbours after the day's work near the well in summer and around the fire in winter when tales are told and talks of fields and crops exchanged; all these have contributed their influence in the direction of compact settlements" (Ahmad, Enayat, 1952: 233). Sasikumar (1963: 231) has shown as to how the habitation patterns in the coastal areas of Kerala are interwoven in the matrix of the rich coconut groves of the coast-line. "The orderliness evident in the arrangement of the dwelling houses along definite streets at different sites in Sind and Baluchistan has also been found to exist in the settlements of Egypt, Europe and South Russia. Such orderliness of spatial arrangement seems to be the expression of a definite form of socio-economic organization, based mainly upon mutual co-operation" (Ghose, 1953: 32 from Gordon, Childe V. *What happened in history*. 1948, p. 569). Ray (1960: 23) has shown as to how the stage of mixed economy of the Veddas of Ceylon, the Chenchus of Hyderabad and the Birhors of Chotanagpur is reflected in the patterns of their respective villages. Nicholas (1963) has shown by a comparison of two Bengal villages - one an active delta village and the other in a moribund delta - in which technology, economy and culture are generally similar, but environments were different, as to how differences between social structure and environment are connected with each other. In the Ganges Valley there is intimate relationship between the types of habitations and the nature of rainfall and water supply. But, once formed, a pattern does not change so easily, even with a change in the water supply position. For example, "... about 1865, the average water table depth in Bulandshahar district was some 80 feet below the surface. Now it is probably not deeper than 30 feet. The rise of water table in the Doab is comparatively a recent phenomenon and does not appear to have modified the original compactness of settlements" (Ahmad, Enayat, 1952: 230-31).

One of the important factors responsible for the seasonal movement of the populations is the source of livelihood (Bose and Jodha, 1967: 247). The roles that the economic pursuits followed by the members of a community play in shaping their habitations can be seen from the following observations of Mitra:

In the high Himalayan ranges, where people dwell with their flocks

> which also help them in transporting merchandise between India and Tibet (formerly), villages tend to be clustered and sometimes there is a summer and winter encampment, each of which remains unoccupied for some months in the year. But when the same people settle down nearer the northern plains of India and begin to cultivate potato for the market, their isolated houses are set in the midst of fields which need constant attention or watching (1966: 2).

Same is true of the Bhotias (Ghose, 1953: 16), Gujjars (Pandit, 1959) and some other communities (Newell, 1952). In Dehra Dun district there are also crop-raising villages like Sirkanda and field houses or cattle-sheds called *chans* (Gerald, 1963: 34). There are several instances of temporary dwellings noted along the low banks of the Sone which are often damaged by the annual overflow of the stream in rainy season. Such settlements spring up, as if by magic, on rich Pehariraman on which rice and kodon are grown just after the flood season is over (Bhattacharya and Verma, 1956-57: 303-304). In the arid regions of Rajasthan the cattle breeders lead semi-nomadic life during acute scarcity condtions (Malhotra, Bharara, Joshi, 1966: 228). A similar case is that of the Gujjars of Kashmir (Pandit, 1959: 64-71). Same is the position in this regard in the high valleys of Uttar Khand and Kumaon also (Bose, S.C., 1960).

The Kharias are divided into two groups, one called Hill Kharias whose habitations consist of about a dozen of homesteads. The other group, which is agriculturist and settled one, is called Dudh Kharias. Their habitation pattern is agglomerated, amorphous and nucleated (Ray, 1960: 11).

An example of how the physical factors in a region and the stage of economy of the communities inhabiting it simultaneously play their role in shaping human habitations can be seen from the following description by Ray:

> The Chenchus of Hyderabad can be divided into two groups. One group lives in the jungle and hilly areas of the higher ranges of the Amrabad plateau. They are still in the primitive hunting and food-gathering stage. Usually the settlements of this group of Chenchus consist of seven or eight houses, and generally only the kin groups inhabit these small settlements which consist mostly of temporary grasshuts and leaf-shelters. The other group, called Village Chenchus, is more permanently settled. ... Chenchu villages on the

> plateau are more traditional in type. There are two distinct settlement patterns; in one pattern, the houses are usually arranged in the form of a crescent, generally open to the east, and surrounded by trees. The other type is found on the stretches of the naked rock, and the arrangement of the houses in this type of settlement is adapted to the surface of the rock formation ... (1960: 14).

Similarly, Sarma (1952) has described that in two different settings - physical as well as economical - the patterns of the habitations of the two groups of the same tribe are different. The Kanikhars, who live in the interior reserved forest ranges of the southern and central sections of the Travancore State, select most inaccessible areas in the hills so that they will not be bothered with visits from the non-tribal people. The population within these settlements is small and shifting one. In contrast to this, the habitations of the Kanikhars near Palode, etc., are in areas easily accessible from the plains and are bigger in size. The people here are engaged in more stable agriculture.

"A village may be defined as a small permanent collection of people with their homes and other material and cultural tools." "The Toda name for a village 'mad' or 'mand', according to Rivers, denotes rather a place - a place connected in any way with the active life of the people". The origin of the village may, however, be traced to the active life of a group of people which needs and makes possible permanent collective dwelling in more or less fixed space..." (Rivers, 1906). As the physical conditions may effect the economy so the economy also effects the habitation pattern (Forde, 1963: 465). In spite of all this the settlement types seem to have more to do with tradition than either geography or agriculture (Mitra, 1966: 7).

Sociologists have observed that where the services of the village craftsmen are not necessary this causes a tendency towards dispersal. About certain parts of Gujarat, Shah (1956: 65) has observed that "the industrial, administrative and trading centres are everywhere nucleated settlements. The dispersed settlements are populated predominantly by tribal and semi-tribal rural folk". In one of his other studies, Shah (1955: 67) has observed that the trading, priestly and the various artisan and servicing castes are found mostly in towns and nucleated villages. Chamhua, Kolgar, Kudra, Magraha are the depressed caste hamlets in Madhya Pradesh. These castes are seasonally hired for field operations, otherwise, for the rest of the time, they are found engaged in cottage industries. Besides caste differences, other social customs have helped in the fragmentation of settlements. Agricultural labourers used to be bought and sold and powerful feudal lords used to have a good number of landless labourers to be employed in their fields. Sometimes these landlords settled amidst their holding for supervision and they also made their tenants and labourers gather round them because of the latter's dependence on the former for economic reasons as well as perforce of law. Lastly, the village sites used to be shifted in the Baghelkhand region and all houses used to be built on a new site within the same *mauza* in every ten or twelve years. This system also fostered hamletted dwellings to a large extent (Bhattacharya and Verma, 1956-57: 301-02). Some scholars (Bhattacharya and Verma, 1956-57: 300; Carstairs, 1952: 231; Kaushic, 1959: 7; Mitra, 1966: 40) have also observed that habitations on higher altitudes are generally scattered while those in the plains are nucleated. Even the mere fact that two sub-groups of the same ethnic group who are living in two different administrative areas make a difference in the pattern of their villages. Shah (1955: 68) has observed that "...even though the Palias have always been living in dispersed settlements, there is some difference between those living in the former British territory and the others in the former State of Deugadhbaria". Not only that, he has further observed that the prestige enjoyed by the two sub-groups is also different. "The Barias of nucleated villages are regarded as higher than those of dispersed villages. The former take their wives from, but never give their daughters to, the latter. Such hypergamous relations are not, however, wide spread."

The law and order situation also plays a role in this sphere. Wherever there has been security of life and property, the villages have a tendency to disperse, and in the 'Law and Order Problem Areas' the villages have a tendency towards nucleation. Defence against various enemies also plays an important role in shaping human habitations. In the Wardha area of Maharashtra, "...in the days when a visit from the Pindharis or some other lawless band from across the village was no extraordinary occurrence, the agriculturists were obliged to flock together for purposes of mutual protection and defence, and sacrifcing convenience to safety to take up their quarters at some central spot at, perhaps, a considerable distance from their fields" (Mitra, 1966: 137). In periods of peace, there is a tendency towards dispersal (Ahlmann, 1928: 108; Baden-Powell, 1913: 67; Bhattacharya and Verma, 1956-57: 300, Carstaris, 1952: 231; Ghose, 1953: 19-20; Jones, 1964: 119; Spate, 1957: 177).

Writing about very closed type of tightly nucleated introvert housing clusters inhabited by closely related kin groups, Karve observes that :

> This particular plan with houses all round and a central courtyard is found among many people in India... The main idea of this plan was followed by merchant caravans travelling long distances in bullock-carts. We are told in a Jataka story how the Buddha, who in that particular birth was a merchant, wisely guided the caravan and how he protected it every night by arranging all the carts in a circle with men, merchants and the bullocks in the middle of the protecting wall made by the carts (1957: 90).

Natural and political disturbances also transform the prevalent pattern of rural habitations in any area. In northern India, early Aryan villages were transformed by successive natural and political disturbances. In Southern India, villages had a more peaceful history and Hindu civilization was preserved better and, therefore, the ideal village type of the Aryan race, settled according to the Mansara Silpasastra, has been retained in South India, while in Northern India they were transformed by successive natural and political disturbances.

The presence or otherwise of village amenities also influence the form of rural habitation (Bhattacharya and Verma, 1956-57: 297-98).

1.1.4 *Internal structure of the Indian village*

Within the habitations, whether dispersed or nucleated, there are again many factors that govern their particular formation (Janki, 1953: 43; Mukerji, 1957). There is very little in the Indian village that looks like a "plan", but within the seemingly chaotic agglomeration, there is, as a rule, a strong internal differentiation, that of the separate quarters for various castes (Ali, H.A., 1970: 49; Bose, N.K., 1958: 149; Jones, 1964: 121-22; Gough, 1960: 93-94; Masters, 1957: 52; Spate, 1957: 172).

About caste concentrations in rural habitations, Karve observes thus :

> This tendency to have separate sub-areas for habitation within a larger unit called a village can be explained in various ways and on different grounds, like caste-hierarchy, ideas of impurity and pollu-

> tion, the need for certain occupations to have room for carrying out the different processes needed for their craft. The first reason applies to the house complexes generally, the second applies to the distance found between the untouchable quarters and the rest, the third applies to the castes like potters, brickmakers, weavers and dyers, shepherds, wool carders and blanket makers, etc. To me it appears that there is an inherent tendency in the Indian culture to form separate groups and remain separate. The arguments listed above all strengthen this tendency and the phenomenon called "caste", apart from its historical structure, is the direct outcome of this tendency. The primary group is the large family, sometimes unilateral. This group extends into the caste. The family as well as the caste are based on territory...(1957: 102).

The reason for segregation of caste sectors are the ban on contact between castes and the solidarity of a sub-caste (Srinivas, 1965: 27).

There are villages inhabited mainly by particular castes, but the mono-caste villages are very few in number and generally small in size, that too these are mainly in the hilly areas. Karve (1957: 87) has reported having come across in Gujarat a "one-house" village, and several "one-family" villages. She has also reported some villages in Maharashtra called "eklahare", meaning "only one house" or "all alone". She has reported having come across even a village which seemed to be made up of only one long hut called "karaguda" belonging to the Savara tribe. There are also some single-caste villages. Where these villages are of artisans they sell their goods in nearby towns, or more frequently in the weekly markets, which is eloquent testimony to the Indian village's lack of self sufficiency (Srinivas and Shah, 1960: 1376). At the same time, there is hardly any village having households of all the castes existing in the region. This again points to the lack of self-sufficiency of the Indian villages. Some scholars have reported even single-lineage villages (Nath, Y.V.S., 1954: 1356) and single-*gotra* villages (Jones, 1964). There are cases, though rare, of groups of four villages inhabited by the same (i.e., only one) lineage (Nath, Y.V.S., 1954: 1356). Majority of villages have some (numerically) dominant caste/s.

Within the caste sectors there are again physical divisions on the basis of sub-caste, *gotra* and lineage, and further beyond on the basis of kinship. Even at the level of a kinship group, the physical configuration generally reflect the social/biological closeness. Groupings of human beings based on space or locality and those centred on interests of all kinds are more recent than groupings based on kinship (Ghurye, 1960: XI; Sastri, 1967: 37). Hardly any village ever has as many sectors as the number of castes inhabiting it. Some of the sectors, therefore, have to accommodate two or more castes. The location of various caste quarters in a village more or less reflects the position occupied by each one of them in the Caste Pyramid, and the social status enjoyed by each of the castes in the village. Social distances are reflected in the physical distances in the *abadi* qualified, of course, by approachability.

Sarma has observed that :

> Although within the village members of each of the castes live together in separate neighbourhoods, and these areas are called by the names of the castes living in them. However, there is no uniform rule about it, and members of the same caste may be found to be living together at great distances if it is so convenient, and lower caste people may be found to settle near about high caste houses, especially if they are the tenants of the latter (1953: 901).

The following observations of Chauhan about a Rajasthan village are quite useful in this connection :

> The residences in the neighbourhood of the fortress can be classified into two types : houses facing the fortress, and houses adjacent to the fortress but having no entrance or exit to it on either side.
>
> The Rajput family units live in the houses that face the fortress, whereas families of other castes are found on the other side of the walls of the fortress. Thus nearness in the physical sense is qualified by approachability. Among the Rajputs the two go together.
>
> In case of the Rajput and the Teli, the Gadri and the Jat, the houses are so located as to appear with backs turned towards one another. The Rajputs thus show the pattern of habitation in which the caste happens to be living in one concentration, within which the houses have the entrance gate nearest to one another. This case supports the view of caste concentration in a village community.
>
> It is more helpful to look both at the concentrations of a caste

> group and the non-concentrated residences of its members to come to an understanding of the social structure of the village (1967: 284-85).

In any human habitation each configuration is more or less a true reflection of the social configuration (a part of the social structure itself) of the community inhabiting it.

It can be said that in a village, man's nearest neighbours generally tend to be the agnates or the affinal kin. The larger circle of neighbours consists of caste fellows. Then come the untouchables (Karve and Damle, 1963: 17). About a tribal village of Bihar, however, Sachidananda (1953) has observed that kinship relations are unrelated to territorial and residential groupings. It is not always essential that the castes closest to each other in the social hierarchy will be closest in the physical location also. But at least the highest and the lowest castes never live together or near each other.

"...It is understandable when the status of the patron is viewed as economically secure by the serving castes, it acts as a significant attraction for them to move nearer their patrons; and that a patronage is not confined merely to the old feudal groups..." (Chauhan, 1964: 178). How the economic considerations soften the effect of social factors can be further seen from the following observations of Chauhan in his studies of a Rajasthan village :

> Groups which interact with each other more frequently are residing nearer than those interacting less frequently.
>
> On the negative side, evidence, equally strong, that persons not residing near one another can have more frequent interaction can be advanced.
>
> However, the factor of physical nearness can be used to study the interaction of the nature of master-servant, patron-client relationship of a higher caste chief with his serves of clean castes (1964: 178-79).

Writing about a South Indian village, Miller (1954: 413) has observed that "in all these social relations - whether judicial, economic or ritual - structural distance was expressed in terms of spatial segregation. The member of a higher caste was ritually polluted if a lower caste person approached within a specified distance - the greater the gap of rank, the greater the spatial segregation."

In certain villages, place also acquires a prestige and economic value. Height of the base (or the roof) has been an important factor in distinguishing the residence of rulers and feudal chiefs in Rajasthan. Even two storeyed houses could be built by only a selected few. The need for a fuller enquiry in the hierarchy of places of residence has been realized by sociologists (Chauhan, 1964: 179). "In many parts of India the lowest castes were not allowed to have tiled roofs for their houses. Nor were they allowed to build two storeyed houses" (Srinivas, 1965: 29).

The difficulty one often experiences in understanding the physical configurations of a village (with the help of normal principles of human habitations), where human-cattle segregation is practised in a manner that there are separate residences for human beings and cattle, can be partly overcome by the following explanation of Chauhan :

> In a village where residences for men and animals are separate, an increase in the next generation of human families is at times followed by an extension of the residential area to the one demarcated for cattle and storing fodder. The divergence in individual cases can also be explained by this shifting, since the rules that explain the residential pattern were different than those for explaining cattleyards (1964: 180).

"...The manner in which houses have been extended to cattleyards indicate further the nature of intrinsic change occurring in the village.." (Chauhan, 1967: viii).

The discussion can be summed up thus :

> The study of a few small village communities provides several explanations of residential concentrations. Where caste is found inadequate for explaining the distribution in space, it is fruitful to inquire into various kin groups of each caste, and a number of exceptions become amenable to suitable explanation around a politically, economically and ritually dominant individual or group (Srinivas, 1955).
>
> Dependent castes of clean groups can be located, but such an explanation does not apply to lower groups. When even kin groups are not sufficient to explain the divergencies, it may be a case of separation from the larger family, conversion of a cattleyard into a residential area or late arrival of individuals either as heirs or on in-

> vitations of business. Deviations from the general rule of caste-concentration may thus be explained in terms of kin concentrations; and whenever this modification is not sufficient, the point can be understood by the (a) internal mobility in cattleyard being converted into residential quarters, separation of lineage groups or of family tensions leading to physical separation; (b) mobility or by the arrival of different groups from outside which have arrived at later stages (Chauhan, 1964: 181).

"...Further, the stage of a village population in being at the receiving end of the population transfers or at the exporting end has to be borne in mind..." (Chauhan, 1964: 179).

The higher castes always have a tendency to occupy more advantageous locations (Bose and Malhotra, 1963: 246). "The Brahmin houses are built on rather more favourable sites than those of the other castes (Sivertsen, 1963: 51). But even this physical separation of the caste sectors is different in the various regions. In the villages where orthodoxy and conservatism cannot tolerate the untouchables living near the caste Hindus, it has led to the creation of separate habitations (Ahmad, Nafis, 1956; Bhattacharya and Verma, 1956-57; Bose and Sen, 1963). In areas where the untouchables are not subjected to such a harsh treatment they are allowed to live in village premises but in a separate corner (Ambedkar, 1948; Bailey, 1960; Bhattacharya and Verma, 1956-57: 301-02; Collin, 1952; Kaushic, 1959: 7; Mukerji, 1957). In some of the areas the Harijans live on the periphery of the *abadi* (Ali, H.A., 1970: 50), for example, among the Meos of Gurgaon. Often these people are "outsiders" not only physically, but also socially as well as psychologically (Collin, 1952).

Similar cases have been observed in some of the other countries also. Mayer (1961: 28) has reported that even among the Indians settled in Fiji there is a tendency for people with same socio-religious background to form separate clusters of homesteads. In primitive times, a Welsh village was a collection of homesteads. The homesteads were separated into two groups, the homesteads of the Free-tenants and the homesteads of the Un-free tenants (Ambedkar, 1948: 87). There is also a parallel (though not completely parallel) example, that of the Liberated and Unliberated villages of Japan. Here the total village is inhabited by either members of one group or of the other.

Besides these hamlets of the depressed castes, every large village in some of the regions has attached hamlets of specialized castes, who, because of greater convenience as well as scarcity of living space in the main village, left it and established separate hamlets not far from the main village. Such attached hamlets consist either of a single caste or of more than one castes. Certain castes prefer to live in certain areas useful from the point of view of their vocation (Ahirs, Gadarias, etc., who depend on animals). Fishing castes prefer to live near water sources. Even after the fall of the water transport, when they have changed their occupation and taken to agriculture, there has been very little change in the distribution and shape of such caste villages (Karve, 1957: 83). Mayer (1960: 1953-57) has drawn a very good pen-picture of how caste segregation is practised in Central Indian villages at different levels like village parts, sectors, wells as also different parts of the house.

Miller has observed about the South Indian villages thus:

> Within any one village the order of caste ranking was always known and accepted, and disputes over precedence never arose. Perhaps the only exceptions were the parallel sub-castes of Nayar barbers and washermen. Nowadays there are disputes over rank between those Nayar sub-castes who served Nambudiris and those who served royal lineages, each claiming to be higher than the other. In the traditional system the two different kinds of Nayars lived in different villages, and if they met at all it was in situations where their relative rank was irrelevant (1954: 417).

Not only that, the ritual status also dictates rules about entering houses of the touchables. These rules vary for different rooms and spaces, with the most barred to visitors being, of course, the kitchen (Mayer, 1960: 56). "...All over the village there is a certain amount of intermingling. But in the Harijan wards there is clear separation, both from other castes and between the Hairjan castes themselves. ...The sweepers are to one side of the village and the tanners to the other..." (Mayer, 1960: 56).

The pictures, respectively, of a Central Indian village drawn by Mayer (1960) and of a Rajasthan village by Bose and Sen (1963) are quite representative of a large number of Indian villages. "Everyone, including Harijans, can walk freely through all parts of the village. But people should go to the tanner and sweeper wards only on business..." (Mayer, 1960: 57).

Most public places are barred to the Harijans. The most strictly

> closed is the main village temple. This is maintained by a Brahmin who does not allow Harijans even within the temple wall, let alone the platform on which stands the actual shrine...Besides this, there is one other large platform which extends around the shrines of the Shakti Goddess and is maintained by the Gosain. Harijans are not ordinarily allowed here, but when the Smallpox Goddess was worshipped by the entire village even the sweeper was allowed to go to her shrine on the platform (1960: 57).

Bose and Sen have reported a similar situation about a Rajasthan village thus :

> The village has its sacred places, temples and shrines. Structurally the temples have a larger built-up space and look more sophisticated and imposing, while the shrines vary from a simple stone slab on the ground or on a built platform to a small structure built of stone. The villagers, however, distinguish between the two in the sense that a temple has a priest or *Sewa-Karne-Wala* while the shrines lie in the open and do not have the daily attention of any priest. Shrines are believed to be more responsive in granting relief from certain specific ailments like snake-bite, etc. None of the shrines has been built recently. They have been in existence for several generations and are associated with different saints. These temples and shrines hub with activity on appropriate occasions. The villagers have considerable faith in the shrines and stories are told about how people have been cured when brought to the shrine. After marriage it is customary for the newly-wedded couple to go round all the shrines and temples and make religious observances. It is interesting to note that whereas restrictions have existed regarding the entrance of the lower castes to temples, they have been in enjoyment of free access to the shrines (1963: 16-17).

The territorial segmentation of castes has two functions. First, it promotes localized interdependent relations for all castes. Secondly, it supports the hierarchical order of castes by permitting greater mobility and a greater range of inter-caste relations for those at the top of the scale than those at the bottom (Miller, 1954: 410). "...I suggest, however, that territorial divisions fundamentally similar to those I have described for Malabar were an essential concomitant of what is called the traditional castes system, and further that the caste system survives most strongly where the territorial cleavages are least impaired. As soon as the territorial alignment loosens its force, castes develop broader internal bonds of solidarity at the expense of their local complimentary interdependence" (Miller, 1954: 419).

In South India the problem of caste sectors aggrevated with the arrival of Christians and Muslims and there are instances of Hindus vacating the entire villages for the fear of pollution (Janki, 1957: 61). Moreover, history is reflected in the siting of village houses. Old streets are relatively populated by one caste, new streets are for practical reasons heterogeneous (Bailey, 1960: 124). The way the arrival of some service caste people from outside a village affects the habitation pattern of that village is clearly reflected in the following remarks of Chauhan :

> Arrival of such persons from other villages requires the building of fresh houses, and such new allotments disturb the old setting of the initial or earlier stages. Discrepencies in kin concentrations can thus serve as a starting point for analyzing the time at which the 'deviant' had come to the village. Dube indicates the probability that in the beginning different castes marked out different blocks for themselves on the proposed site for the settlement. People coming later to the village either found a place to construct their houses in their caste blocks or had to choose a plot elsewhere (1964: 180: from Dube, 1956: 25).

Ahlmann (1928: 108) has given an idea of the historical sequence of settlements. Settlement study is meaningless unless it takes into consideration the changes which time has imposed. The student looks at a stage in the settlement pattern, and the core of his study is the process by which such a stage develops (Jones, 1964: 124).

An appropriate illustration of the role played by the law of inheritance of property prevalent among a people in shaping their habitations is the Tharawad system (Janki, 1953: 44). More or less similar to the Tharawad is example of the Bhera (in Jaunsar Bawar) - the common house of the families having a common ancestry (Mitra, 1966: 188). Another example in this connection is that of the Korwas where the new house is constructed very close to the old one, or the old house itself is partitioned (Bhandari, 1936: 81). Other similar examples are those of the Bhils (Nath, Y.V.S., 1954: 1355), the Gaddis (Newell, 1952: 209), the Gonds and the Bhumias (Stephen, 1960: 25).

Although house has always enjoyed an important position in the life of man, different communities sometimes view its importance from different angles. Among the Gaddis of Chamba, a house is considered to be important "...because a man has his eye on marrying some particular girl and the best way of convincing her parents that the marriage would be a success is to produce visible evidence of a good property...The Gaddi house is always in the thoughts of these agriculturists and herdsmen wherever they be. As the most valuable single piece of property which they possess and the most difficult task which they accomplish, a good house is the end-all of every Gaddi's ambition" (Newell, 1957: 24-25).

Availability of potable water is an important factor wielding considerable influence on the pattern of any human habitation (Kaushic, 1959: 7). Seed of clustering was the well within the village *abadi* (Mukerji, 1957: 111; Bose and Sen, 1963: 18). Caste segregation is exercised on the water source also; on tanks and wells, and even on rivers. At places where both touchable as well as untouchable castes are allowed to take water from the same well, separate spots are marked for both touchables and untouchables for bathing, filling water, washing clothes, etc. (Malhotra and Bharara, 1963: 23). "There has been, up to recent years, a rigid caste control... over the drinking water reservoirs in Jaunsar-Bawar... The Koltas were not allowed to touch the drinking-water reservoir, lest it should get polluted. There fixed timings, when Kolta women gather, with their pitchers, around the water-site and wait the arrival of a higher caste woman, who pours water into their pitchers" (Kaushic, 1959: 7). The role of water source in shaping human habitations becomes all the more important in areas where it is very scarce and especially where more than one village cooperate with each other in arranging water (Karve and Damle, 1963: 5; Kaushic, 1959: 7; Malhotra, Bharara and Joshi, 1966: 24; Mayer, 1960: 53). Sometimes, even on a river there are separate places for touchables and untouchables for washing clothes, for bathing and for filling water. The place for untouchables being lower down the stream, so that the water flows from the touchable *Panotha* (the colloquial term for the water spot) to the untouchable *Panotha* (Karve and Damle, 1963: 5).

An example of how economic compulsions soften the callousness of social restrictions has been reported by Sivertsen (1963: 53) about a South Indian village. In dry seasons the Brahmins allow their servants and tenants to draw water from the wells in the houses of the former.

Muslims are marginal between touchables and untouchables. In villages, they also behave like touchables (Karve and Damle, 1963: 5). In the Punjab villages, the Sikhs also behave like touchables, although, strictly speaking, there is no caste system in Sikhism.

A very good example of how social, economic and physical factors play a role in shaping up human habitations can be had from the description of the Nicobar islands by Chaudhury (1955). Pati is a big beehive typed house located overlooking the sea. This village house serves as the beacon for village canoes plying far away from the coast. This is used mainly as a place of social assembly and entertainment on the occasion of races with other villages. Post-funeral feasts of important households are arranged here. The place is also used to keep big sized canoes and bows and arrows, etc. Similarly, there are houses for confinement of expectant mothers - *Pati Yongi* - as well as houses where women stay for some time after having delivered their children. There are other places like pre-burial houses, etc., also.

To sum up in the words of Mitra :

> Apart from the age-old mores and hierarchies regulating the Indian village community the broad determining features of the rural settlements seem to be four. First, the terrain and water point; secondly, the need of cultivation; thirdly, the needs of security and defence; and, fourthly, the inter-relationships and hierarchy of castes and the strength of the Jajmani system. It is one or other or combination of several or all that gives a village its distinctive settlement pattern. This also explains how in the same natural zone one may come across one or several or all the types (1966: 7).

The fundamental ecological processes and the exploitation of the natural milieu by the population of the region determine the spatial distribution and the density of habitations; and not only the stage of technology but also the standard of sanitation, social tradition regarding caste and social classes, religious beliefs, use of magic as an aid in the performance of habitation and outside cultural contact exert their influence on the style and pattern of habitations" (Kaushic, 1959: 22).

To quote Doxiadis in this connection :

> We can perhaps draw one conclusion about the variations in the different forms of human settlements. They are mainly, due to the economic purpose of the settlement, a big divergence which may

> lead to big differences in the size, dimension, shape and structure of settlements. Differences in systems of political organization, administration and defence also have an impact but not as strong as that of economic purpose. Differences of Nature have an impact only in the micro-scale of the settlements and on its architectural details. Man, as an element of human settlements, does not lead to different solutions. All major differences, with the exception of those due to the economic purpose of the settlement, are mainly in the micro-scale. In the middle and macro-scale all settlements have similar characteristics that depend mainly on the variable of functions, which, of course, comprises the incomes of the inhabitants and general economic conditions (1968: 109).

Similar comprehensive summings up have also been given by Jones (1964: 133), and also by Bhattacharya and Verma (1956-57 : 301) where they have quoted Mukerjee, R.K., *Man and his habitation* (1940: 65 & 68).

1.2 DISCIPLINES CONCERNED WITH THE STUDY OF THE SUBJECT

1.2.1 *Various disciplines and the scope of their studies*

The field of human habitations is so extensive, the problem so complicated and the knowledge so limited, that there is an imperative need for contribution from all quarters. Important among the disciplines studying the habitations are : (A) Geography, (B) Sociology & Anthropology, (C) Economics, (D) Regional Science, (E) Ekistics.

> "The two basic elements of human settlements, the content and the container, can be further sub-divided into five elements like:
>
> Nature, providing the foundation upon which the settlement is created and the frame within which it can function.
>
> Man.
>
> Society.
>
> Shells, or the structures within which man lives and carries out his different functions.
>
> Networks, or the natural and man-made systems which facilitate the functioning of the settlement, as, for example, roads, water

supply, electricity, etc." (Doxiadis, 1968: 21).

To quote the same scholar further :

> One of the greatest mistakes made in the study of human settlements is considering them as containing of the container only (Nature, Shells and Networks) and thus depriving of the fourth dimension, time, and of their life which is expressed in functions. In this respect, we are making the same mistake as the medical science, which for centuries had concerned itself with the human body, and studied its structure mainly through anatomy, but overlooked its functioning, which could be studied through physiology, until the time when modern medicine established the co-ordinated study of functions and structures.
>
> In actual life we are interested in functions, in living, working, running, walking; but these are not easily expressed physically; therefore, we tend to think of a settlement in terms of its Shells, even though what really matters is the men who live in it or use it in another way (Doxiadis, 1968: 24).

Social scientists are concerned with Man and Society; Engineers deal with certain Networks such as roads; Geographers are more interested in Nature; while the Architects and Physical Planners deal mostly with Shells. Yet the habitations consist of all these elements and the Ekisticians claim that they study all these simultaneously to find their relationships (Doxiadis, 1968: 35).

Describing the lead given by geography in this field, Doxiadis further states :

> The oldest science dealing with the human settlements, geography, has been dealing with the topic through its branch of Human Geography. The habitation (which throughout the geographical literature has been referred to as 'settlement') is central of all human geography, as it modifies the natural environment by introducing a cultural element. Any settlement, the geographers feel, to be adequately appreciated, must be correlated with other facts of geography, e.g., relief, climate, geology and the social and economic conditions (1968: 35).

Regional Science has made several efforts to define mathematical laws relating the Ekisties functions to each other.

> Ekisties is the science of human settlements. Ekistics demonstrates the existence of an overall science of human settlements conditioned by man and influenced by economics, social, political, administrative and technical sciences, and the disciplines relating to art (Ekistics; Back Page).

The Ekisticians claim that theirs is a science whose task is to examine all human settlements from every possible point of view in order to develop skills for the solution of the problems involved. Ekistics and Regional Science both are descriptive and prescriptive. Geography has generally been limited to description of human settlements and not prescriptive action. Although during the last one or two decades some efforts have been made to turn it into a prescriptive science as well. Regional Science has been concerned much more with production and transportation on a macro-scale; and Ekistics has been mainly concerned with residence and more actively so in the middle 57, 61 and micro-scale ... (Doxiadis, 1968: 57, 61). Human ecology centres in the study of relations between man and environment. Broadly conceived, human ecology comprehends the study of every aspect of man-environment relations. Within the broad field, however, each of the several traditional disciplines has emphasized its own problems.

During recent years an increasing number of sociologists has come to identify human ecology with studies of communities and regions (James, 1950: 3-4). "The current crisis in human settlements and the obvious inability of the disciplines traditionally concerned to handle it in a satisfactory way has caused other disciplines to enter the field. Some of them - economics, sociology, anthropology, psychology, medicine - are already greatly concerned with specific aspects of settlements. There is also a dawning interest in biology, ecology, mathematics and other disciplines. It is too early to say how much each of these disciplines can contribute to the problem. Indeed success or failure depends not only on the content, objectives and methods of a discipline, but also on the people who try to develop them and the conditions which excite them ..." (Doxiadis, 1968: 57).

However, the greatest movement, a turning of interest to the field of human settlements, has been in the social sciences, especially in those directly related to man and his health. The increasing interest of health experts in human settlements is a result of the evolution in medicine and psychiatry, which has gradually led to an increased interest in Man not only from the point of view of medicine and psychiatry, but also from the biological, psychological and social aspects (Doxiadis, 1968: 62-63).

Some of the economists (Gangulee, 1935) have written about the village life as it is related to the different systems of land tenure. The economists have generally discussed habitations purely from the point of view of the locations of the various elements. They also discuss the somewhat mathematical way of calculating the advantages of the location of the *abadi* at distances from (a) the five most basic elements which none can dispense; grazing land, arable land, water, fuel, building materials and (b) links with the outside world - lines of communication and their inhabited centres. The economists have also discussed the problems of dispersal, etc. (Chisholm, 1970).

Books, written by administrators, do not contain even a proper description of village lay-outs and house types. Even a scholar like Tod (1957) who has discussed in detail the life-style, history, etc., of the inhabitants of a particular region and has even written on topics like, *"Foundations of States and cities by the different tribes"*, *"The fortification of Udaipur"*, etc., has not mentioned any thing about village patterns and house designs.

Another approach to the study of the subject, and a recent one, is that of the Proxemics. Edward Hall coined the term 'proxemics' and devised a system of notation for recording proxemic behaviour. Proxemics is the study of how man structures micro-space, how he relates physically to other persons with whom he is interacting and what is communicated by these physical relationships. "...the study of how man unconsciously structures micro-space - the distance between man in the conduct of daily transactions, the organisation of space in his house and buildings, and ultimately the layout of his town..." (Waston and Graves, 1966: 971).

1.2.2 *Studies by geographers and sociologists and anthropologists*

Geographers have studied the types of human settlements by size, according to the occupations of their inhabitants, and tried to identify the respective shapes these villages generally assume (Hudson, 1970: 48-50,61; Money, 1967; Sharma, 1972: 91,93). Geographers have also studied the regional distributions of rural settlements (Hudson, 1970: 61; Money, 1967) in relation to: (a) Administrative Units, (b) Physiographic Regions, etc. They have also studied the Settlement Hierarchy (Ahmad, Enayat, 1952: 233; Janki, 1953; 1957: Sharma,

1972). Geographers have done the 'Intervening Distance Analysis', the 'Cluster Analysis' and the 'Dot Distribution' (Sharma, 1972: 107, 108, 132). Another aspect of human settlements of perenial interest to the geographers is the Geometric Pattern of Roads and Properties and the arrangement of buildings in relation to them (Kohn, 1954: 154).

One of the important aspects on which a lot of work has been done by the geographers is the characteristics of the two types of settlement; nucleated and dispersed (Ahlmann, 1928; Ahmad, Enayat, 1952: 242-243; Augelli, 1952; Platt, 1959; Dicktinson, 1949; Sharma, 1972: 110; Trewertha, 1946), and also the factors leading to nuclearity and dispersal (Ahlmann, 1928: 230-238; Ahmad, Nafis, 1956: 388; Blache, 1956; Bhattacharya and Verma, 1956-57: 100; Hudson, 1970: 63,65-69; Janki, 1953: 42; 1957; Mukerji, 1957: 102; Scofield, 1938; Yonekura, 1961). Facilities in the settlements have also been used by the geographers as a criterion for their classification (Kohn, 1954: 136). They have also studied the origins of villages (Sharma, 1972: 93; Cozens, 1938).

Interest of geographers in the settlement features *per se* is a comparatively recent one. One of the oldest interests of geographers in this field is the study of occupation sequences (Ackerman, 1941; Whittlesey, 1929, etc.). A leading geographer (Ahlmann, 1928: 95) has submitted a scheme for the study of human settlements which, according to him, rests on the conception of the whole process of settlement "...as a great unified complex; a living thing, constantly changing, advancing, retrogressing. However great may be the differences, the settlements show between the different series, however various may be the forms it assumes, it nevertheless seems to me certain that, on the whole, man takes possession of the country for settlement in a similar manner within regions where the dominating conditions of physical geography are similar and men have there attained a similar degree of civilization". Ahlmann (1928: 108) has also evolved a concept of 'Settlement Series', "...within each climatologically determined settlement region are found areas of such varying topographic character that settlement presents marked differences of form, grouping, location and development. In the course of its evolution it exhibits stages which bear a definite relation to each other...".

Now a new "Functions of cultural geography series" is coming up in the geographical literature. "The authors of the series report and evaluate current thought centred on the question : How do widely different systems of ideas and practice influence what people do to recreate and utilize their habitats? How do human efforts change environments, and with what effect?" (Philip, 1969).

Sociologists have studied the reasons for nuclearity and dispersal (Bose, Malhotra and Bharara, 1963: 124; Bose and Sen, 1963: 12-13), the causes for settling in the core and in the hamlets, relative advantages of settling in the core and hamlets (Bose and Malhotra, 1963: 240-241); (Bose and Sen, 1963: 22), who are the people living in the core and in the hamlets, respectively? (Bose and Malhotra, 1965: 174; Bose, Malhotra and Bharara, 1963: 124; Karve, 1957: 83), caste distribution and occupational distribution of those living in the core and in the hamlets (Bose, Malhotra and Bharara, 1963: 129; Bose and Sen, 1963: 21; Karve, 1957: 83), age and sex composition of the population, size and composition of households in the core and the hamlets, respectively (Bose, Malhotra and Bharara, 1963: 126; Karve, 1957: 83); age of males and females at the time of marriage, for those living in the core and the hamlets, respectively, nuclearity or jointness of families living in the core and the hamlets (Bose, Malhotra and Bharara, 1963: 122), average size of land holdings and number of fragments per household in the core and the hamlets (Bose, Malhotra and Bharara, 1963: 129; Bose and Sen, 1963: 22) and even factors like the number of livestock per household and sale value of the livestock produce per year (Bose, Malhotra and Bharara, 1963: 130); intensity of cropping and the cropping pattern (Malhotra, Bharara and Joshi, 1966: 25); and also the shift from traditional occupations among the households living in the core and hamlets, respectively (Bose, Malhotra and Bharara, 1963: 126).

There is a long list of points connected with the habitation patterns studied by geographers, sociologists and anthropologists. But the geographers' interest has been confined mainly to the physical forms and the physical factors related to it. They have primarily described the way a village or a part of it looks like (Blache, 1956). During recent years, of course, even the geographers have been realizing the importance of sociological factors in explaining these phenomena (Bhattacharya and Verma, 1956-57: 100; Hudson, 1970: 27; Sharma, 1972: 42,104; Spate, 1957: 177; Yonekura, 1961). Sociologists and anthropologists, on the other hand, have been trying to explore and explain the deeper reasons underlying these patterns and the ways of life associated with them.

Even when studying common points, the approaches adopted by the geographers and sociologists have been different. For instance, while dealing with division of *abadi* into caste sectors, the geographers have simply described this phenomenon (Bhattacharya and Verma, 1956-57: 100; Janki, 1957; Mukerji, 1957: 22-23; Yonekura, 1961), while sociologists have provided explanation for this, as to (a) why this phenomenon takes place? (b) what are its functions or advantages? (Bose and Malhotra, 1963: 246; , 1965: 173), (c) how this reflects the social distances, etc. Within the caste sectors what provided the explanation for the different kinds of groupings under different sets of circumstances, e.g., sub-caste, clan, lineage, kinship etc. ? (Chauhan, 1964: 181), (e) explanation for those cases not given by the normal rule in this regard, (f) why is it that some caste groups reside near each other, while some other members of the same caste are residing in some other sectors? (Chauhan, 1964: 178; Ali, H.A., 1970: 49), (g) effects of caste segregation on the growth of the village as a coherent social group, etc., etc., (Mitra, 1966: 234). Some sociologists (Nath, V., 1962) have studied as to how an *abadi* expands and why the new *abadis* are not always close to the old ones.

The distinction between the settlement or revenue/ administrative village, on the one hand, and the social village, on the other, has been emphasized by some scholars (Srinivas and Shah, 1960; Davis, 1951). Though not always using these terms, sociologists and anthropologists have often emphasized that the village is an entity *per se* (Dube, 1954: 526; Miller, 1954: 413; Nath, V., 1962: Nath, Y.V.S., 1954: 1360).

Writing about that part of the Punjab where the villages are generally walled, Smith (1952) states that "...even in villages which are not walled, I have been told several times by the Sikhs that the punishments meted out by village *panchayats* occurred at the "gate" of the village. Both physically and conceptually, therefore, the village is a unit". Some others (like Singh, R.D., 1956), however, have remarked that taking into consideration all aspects of village life one begins to wonder whether an Indian village can at all be characterized as a functioning social unit distinguishable from others. In this respect Srinivas feels thus:

> It is normally not visible, but some incident suddenly and strikingly reveals its existence. When the village is threatened with an epidemic or floods or fire, or when the government passes an order which the villagers regard as unjust, or on certain religious occasions, or in a fight with a neighbouring village, the unity of the village reveals itself in an unmistakable manner (1954: 607).

Similarly, geographers have described the phenomenon of hamlets, sometimes also giving a few geographical reasons for it (Bhattacharya and Verma, 1956-57: 98). Sociologists have explained at length as to why this phenomenon takes place and several details about the life and living in the core and the hamlets. There is a long list of aspects of life (discussed earlier in this chapter) in the core and the hamlets studied by the sociologists and anthropologists. Similarly, there are many other common aspects of habitations studied by the geographers and sociologists. But in all these studies also the approaches of the two disciplines are different.

To sum up, all that the geographers have done in this field is reflected in the very term they use, i.e., "Settlement", while work done by the sociologists and anthropologists is reflected in the term they prefer, i.e., "Habitation".

1.3 STUDY OF HUMAN HABITATIONS AT THE MICRO-LEVEL

In the concerned disciplines either the topic of dwellings is neglected or treated as secondary (even when relevant).

Cultural Geography, which has seen the dwelling as important, has either used it as a diagnostic tool or concentrated on morphological classification (Rapoport, 1969: viii), i.e., listing of the House Types and description of features. Little has been done to link these forms to life patterns, beliefs and desires although life is difficult to understand outside the context of its setting, culture and the way of life it shelters (Rapoport, 1969: 17). Such descriptions in the sociological literature are mainly descriptive rather than analytical. The built-up environment of man is mainly the result of Vernacular (or Folk or Popular) Architecture and has been largely ignored in Architectural History and Theory (Rapoport, 1969: 1).

In archaeology the interest shifted a while ago from temples, palaces and tombs to the whole city as an expression of culture and a way of life, although the house, the most typically vernacular type, is still frequently ignored. Similar shifts have taken place in general history, in the history of art and also perhaps in that of music to some extent. In architecture, however, such an interest is only now starting and it has not yet gone very far nor beyond the purely visual. It is, therefore, a topic which has been rather neglected (Rapoport, 1969: 1). Even such books like those by Bever (1959, 1965), Morris and Mogey

(1965), which apparently appear to be having a lot of information on the topic, give a very superficial treatment to the subject of human habitations.

Dwellings by Finlay and Scott (1940) and Gates (1933), a report on certain Mexican House Types by Cozzens (1938) are the examples. In a few cases the American geographers have also studied the houses in relation to the climatic conditions in which they are built and the artificial climates produced in them for the human comfort. Notable among these studies are those by Lee (1951).

The studies of dwellings by geographers are less even than the studies of habitations (at the macro-level) by them.

Recenlty, a geographer (Sharma, 1972: 157) has himself said: "In any study of settlements, study of the house type is necessary as well as fascinating. Somehow it has not received its due attention in geographical studies."

Similarly, Spate (1961: 255) has observed that "a geographical study of Indian house types would be a work vast in scope and rich in instruction...Not only the site and layout of the village, but the geography of the house often reflects age-old religious and magical traditions..."

The house has many aspects: the form or the shape, i.e., as the house appears outwardly; the layout, which is the plan of fixing up of the building/s in relation to the plot and the approach roads; section or plan is what we get when we cut a building horizontally or vertically; the plan, i.e., as we see a building from its top or from above. The geographers have confined themselves to the study of the form and elevation, and sometimes even the layout. But they have not studied the plans of the houses. Even when they claim that they are studying the plan, they are simply classifying the houses into Single, Compact and Multiple Dwellings. It is really difficult to understand as to how one can call it the plan, when he is not even touching the Site Plan (i.e., the outline of a building as seen from the top) or the sections.

Geographers have confined themselves mainly to the study of forms, materials and of house groupings. Their approach is also more of a quantitative nature, i.e., where things can be classified into categories and put into tables and charts.

But some of the recent works of geographers show that they have started realizing the limitation of the classical geographical approach to the subject of habitations, and that they are also now becoming vocal about their realization of the significance of studying the sociological dimensions of the problem. "In geographical studies the house is primarily an element of landscape, expressing the physical conditions of a region in collaboration with the economic and cultural stages of the inhabitants. House types are treated as a functional response to the physical and human characteristics of the region (Sharma, 1972: 38).

To quote the same author further:

> The influence of climatic conditions, the local resources, the medium of building materials and the cultural traditions of the inhabitants explain the external appearance of house type. But the plan of the house and the layout of the farm buildings can only be explained in terms of social and eonomic factors. In fact, the layout and arrangement are detailed by a strict social order and by form of the economic activities of the community as a whole (1972: 42).

NOTES

1. a. Ernest Weekly, and Anne Scott., 1954
   b. William Geddie. 1964
   c. Macdonald, A.M. 1972
2. Dube (1961) has structurally divided the village communities into three groups: the "Single Settlement" Village, in which the community shares a common and compact site, the "Nucleated" Village which has a central settlement as the nucleus around which there are a number of smaller satellite settlements, and the "Dispersed" Village community, in which the community consists of a series of dispersed homesteads having well-defined ties with one another.

TWO

HUMAN HABITATIONS IN SANSKRITIC LITERATURE AND IN SOCIOLOGY AND ANTHROPOLOGY

2.1 SANSKRITIC LITERATURE

2.1.1 *Philosophical and religious background of Indian architecture*

INDIAN CULTURE is historic rather than historical. Architecture being the hallmark of civilization must be very old in India.

In India, we cannot draw a line of demarcation between science and philosophy. The truth is, a science without a philosophy or religious background is not a complete science according to the Hindu view of life. The cosmological, metaphysical, astronomical, mathematical and other aspects are very closely linked with and cannot be separated from science. Even the science of architecture has a lofty philosophical theory, as Vastu Bramvada or Vastu Purusvada as its background (Shukla, 1961: 34, 340).

Architecture in India is intimately associated with religion. The ritualistic origin and evolution of the Indian architecture may be taken as an established canon. The standards for house construction were rigid, codified and given the sanctity of religious character so that they may never be violated (Shukla, 1961: 321, 353). According to the scriptures there are different *lokas*, which have their own particular positions in the celestial horizon in terms of the points of the campass, etc., and they have their symbolic meanings. There are also seven islands (continents) which are guided by seven seas. *Meru* is the king of sixteen mountains. India is one of the countries that lie towards the south of these mountains. The abode of God Brahma is in these mountains. The *lokpals*, such as God Indra, etc., also reside therein (Shastri, 1967: 434, 435, 476, 478 etc.). "Intimate relationship between astronomy, astrology, and architecture has been established" (Shukla, 1961: 337). The entire way of life which is also directly reflected, among other things, in the human habitations also - at the micro- as well as macro-levels - is related to these things.

There is a very strong emphasis on symbolism in Hindu architecture (Havell, 1927).

Buildings are mainly of four types; (a) for Gods, (b) for kings, (c) public buildings and (d) individual houses for the common man. In the texts belonging to a certain period of Indian history these buildings have been named as *salas*. Temple was the chief feature of Indian architecture during ancient as well as the medieval periods of history. Some scholars have even observed that Indian architecture is exclusively religious, i.e., it is suitable only for the religious buildings because in old times the main buidlings were for the Gods, and those for human beings were very insignificant in scale and construction material, etc. But from the time of King Bhoja of Dhara - who ruled the country from 1018 to 1060 A.D. - popular architecture came in (Shukla, 1961: 25, 303, 323).

2.1.2 *Meaning of architecture in Sanskritic literature*

Vastu means architecture in the broadest sense implying the earth, buildings, conveyance, and bedstead. The term denotes also villages, towns, forts, commercial cities, etc. (Archarya, 1934).

To quote a reputed authority on the subject:

> Extent of architectural term–comprehended in the *Vastu-Sastras* architecture–is taken in its broadest sense and implies what is built or constructed. Thus, in the first place, it denotes all sorts of buildings–religious, residential and military, and their auxiliary members and component buildings. Secondly, it implies town-planning; laying out gardens; constructing market places; making roads, bridges, gates; digging wells, tanks, trenches, drains, sewers, moats; buidling enclosure walls, embankments, dams, railways, ghats, flights of steps for hills, ladders, etc. Thirdly, it denotes articles of house furniture, such as bedsteads, couches, tables, chairs, thrones, fans, wardrobes, clocks, baskets, conveyances, cages, nests, mills, etc.
>
> Architecture also implies sculpture and deals with the making of phalli, idols of deities, statues of sages, images of animals and birds. It includes the making of garments and ornaments, etc.

Architecture is also concerned with such preliminary matters as the selection of site, testing of soil, planning, designing, finding out cardinal points by means of a gnomon dialling; and astronomical calculations (Acharya, 1934: 105-106).

A good architect, it was, therefore, prescribed, should not only be good in his own art but should also possess a detailed knowledge of the *shastras* (scriptures) as well as of the customary law of the region in which he was working. It was also essential for him to have intuitive power. Because of this, the qualification or the syllabus (if one may call it so), prescribed for the architects, also includes a large number of other subjects, besides pure architecture itself (Acharya, 1934: 68-96; Shukla, 1961: 37,45).

2.1.3 *Sources of information on Indian architecture*

Information on architecture is available in *Rig Veda*. It has clues of the architectural tradtion. The latter *Vedas* present a picture of more religious architecture than the civil one, a glimpse of which one finds in the *Rig Veda* itself.

Sutras are also treasure house of knowledge in this respect.
Epic period literature - Ramayana, Mahabharata, etc.
Buddhist literature - *Jatakas* and the *canons.*
Pali canons.

Then comes the category of literature like the Kautilya's *Arthashastra*, etc.

Puranas - *Matsya, Skanda, Garuda, Agni.*
Agmas. These are many more than the *Puranas.*
Tantras also contain a lot of information on architecture. But much work has not been done on the *Tantras.*
Brhatsmhita - written by a leading astronomer of the Gupta period.
Miscellaneous works like the *Silpa* texts, *Vastu Shastras* and *Silpa Shastras*, etc.

2.1.4 *Prescriptive nature of the Sanskritic literature about architecture*

Eminent scholars have remarked that the ancient Indian social and economic pattern evolved integrally from the basic aboriginal (tribal and rural) pattern of life, and as a corollary the architectural forms and types, that we find on early Indian bas-reliefs, also evolved from the rural and urban house types and forms, not only in their general outline, but in many architectural details as well (Ray, 1960: 3).

In some of the Sanskritic literature village is taken to be a town in miniature and it is said that a group of villages give rise to a town (an example of this is Patliputra). And, hence, unlike the present-day rural-urban dichotomy from the stand-point of planning and house design, there is no difference between a village and town (Agarvala, 1953: 63). Of course, the town had a ditch and a wall and was lived in by the king and his appertenances, while the village did not have the above and was lived in mostly by people engaged in agriculture. In fact, "...The first problem of rural India is to analyze the definition of an Indian village" (Bhattacharya, Vivek Ranjan, 1971: 1).

To quote the same scholar again :

> There were no two opinions on the concept of a *grama* in ancient, medieval, or modern India so long as it denoted 'an aggregate' of several families sharing the habitation.
>
> The finer distinction between a hamlet and a village as noted in the West is more or less recent as compared to the distinction between the *grama* and a *palli* in ancient India.
>
> ... the conception of *grama* and *palli* means exactly what their Western counterparts - village and hamlet - signify, 1971: 2).

"The earliest Indian literature, e.g., *Rig Veda* refers to village - *grama* - as an aggregate of several families sharing the same habitation" (Bhattacharya, Vivek Ranjan, 1971: 2, from Dube, 1956). It cannot, however, be said that the village always had a natural origin and growth. Because the *Artha Sastra* as well as the *Jatakas* throw enough light as to how these were to be established by the king, and how these are to be planned, etc. (Shamasastry, 1967: 45).

Raja Bhoj, in *Samrangana*, even makes a distinction between villages and towns for the purpose of National Planning (physical planning) at three levels, taking village to be the unit of planning (Shukla, 1961). Raja Bhoj was so careful that he even stated that the development of towns should be confined to particular regions of a kingdom, and that these should not be allowed to come up everywhere indiscriminately, lest they disturb the peaceful rural way of life in the villages. There used to be some Grant Villages also. Certain categories of people were allotted tax-free land grants.

> Those who perform sacrifices *(rivik)*, spiritual guides, priests and those learned in the *Vedas* shall be granted *Brahmandeya* lands yielding sufficient produce and exempted from taxes and fines (*anandakarani*).
>
> Superintendents, accountants, *Gopas*, *Sthanikas*, veterianary surgeon (*anikastha*), physician, horsetrainers and messengers shall also be endowed with lands which they shall have no right to alienate by sale or mortgage (Shamasastry, 1967: 45-46).

The villages were marked by their natural boundaries such as forest, thickets, rivulets, hills, jungle and rocks (Agarvala, 1953: 141). In case of any boundary dispute between neighbouring villages they had a prescribed and accepted way of settling the same (Shastri, 1967: 926-927).

Every village had a guardian deity.

> ...A city or a village, etc., protected by a deity, becomes thriving and prosperous; and imparts victory, enjoyment of earthly goods and finally salvation to its inhabitants (Shastri, 1967: 431).
>
> The Indian village differed very little from that of the present day, but while most villages in the North are now open and undeveloped, in earlier times they were usually walled or stockaded, as they are still in many parts of the Deccan. The village was a cluster of huts, small or large, often grouped round a well or a pond, near which was a small open space with a few trees. In earlier times villages often had clubrooms, which served as rest houses for travellers and as centres of social life; later the place of these halls was taken by the village temples. The villagers formed a self-conscious community, and often had an energetic communal life... (Basham, 1967: 190).

Apte described the love a person always had for his habitation (village as well as house) thus:

> When a person leaves his village on a journey, he mutters 'Free from danger may we be. May the village entrust me to the care of the forest and looks at his house and says 'Do ye both, Mitra and

> Varuna, protect this house for me. When he enters the village at the end of his journey he should mutter "May the forest entrust me to the care of the village: and should not enter it without carrying something with him such as fuel, flowers, etc.
>
> The words with which he addresses the house while approaching it and looking at it before actually entering it are touching and show us how the house had become the rallying point and centre of material prosperity in the eyes of the house-holder...Similarly the love and respect that house inspired in the mind of the house-holder are seen from the instructions that he should avoid all quarrelling on the day on which he has arrived and should utter auspicious words and then accept water for washing the feet (Apte, 1954 : 144-145).

A definition of the 'Home' is implicit in the *Mantras* that one chants on such occasions.

2.1.5 *Prescriptions about habitations at the micro- as-well as macro-level*

For the pattern to be followed in the village there is a very strict code with a sanctified religious character the violation of which was beyond contemplation (Shamasastry, 1967:54). There is a lot of emphasis on the customary law (Acharya, 1934:45; Shukla, 1961:45). The stages and process of village planning and house construction have been very elaborately laid down (Acharya, 1934:63). The ancient buildings in any habitation must be preserved (Acharya, 1934:91).

There are detailed prescriptions about the selection of site (Havell, 1915:35). There is an emphasis on the point that the site must be an undisputed property, i.e., there must not by any ownership dispute. The land should be non-disputed property and non-salinous (Oldenberg and Max Muller, 1964). "The A.G.S. gives the most detailed instructions : the ground upon which he intends to build should be undisputed property first of all; then it should be non-salinous; with herbs or trees growing...". "The land should be compact, one-coloured, not swampy, not dry, not surrounded by sandy tracts and free from the danger of inundation" (Apte, 1954:138,139). There are three main divisions of soil and sixteen varieties of different kinds of lands. "...the text describes the different soils - fit for all castes and fit only for the Brahmans, Kshatriyas or Vaishyas, and Sudras" (Shukla, 1961:105,106).

Even the colour, smell and taste of the earth for construction of houses upon has been prescribed caste-wise (Shastri, 1967:889). Similar details about the caste-wise prescription of soils in the Sanskritic literature have also been given by Apte (1954:139). It has even been prescribed that the land with particular types of vegetation on it is good for the various castes. Sites clouded (with smoke) from the dye-factories, surrounded by workshops of blacksmiths, and those at the junction of four paths, three paths, two paths, or city path (trade route) all are to be avoided. Residential buildings, it is further prescribed, should be built in quarters free from conveyances. If not, all prosperity would be ruined (Acharya, 1934:12,14,90). There are also detailed prescriptions about the preparation of sites (Shastri, 1967:890).

Majority of the villages is likely to have contained a heterogeneous population, but there were others inhabited exclusively or mainly by the members of a single caste or followers of or single occupation (Jha, 1955). According to Shukla (1961:106), in ancient India the towns and villages were planned caste-wise. Acharya (1934:63-96) and Shamasastry (1967) have also written about the prescriptions for the establishment of different types of villages for different castes, (i.e., mono-caste villages). "The Manasara recognizes 40 different classes of villages..." (Acharya, 1927). There are certain types of villages which can be used by various castes. But the name given to a village of this type depends upon the caste inhabiting it (Acharya, 1934).

About the *Vedic* villages, Ray observes thus:

> The *Vedic* village or *grama* was indeed an aggregate of several *kulas* or families; each *Kula*, lived in the detached houses or *grihas* within a boundary or enclosure and was presided over by the father or the eldest brother of the family, called *Kulapa* or *Kulpati*. Since individual system of ownership and inheritance of private property was recognized the house was demarcated by a boundary... (1960:24).

There are prescriptions about the percentage of the total land of any village to be used for habitation and for agricultural purposes, respectively, (Acharya, 1927). There is also mention of the special habitations of the Herdsmen *(Ghosha)* and Hamlets *(Khetas)* in Panini (Agarvala, 1953:63). There is presumption for a special type of village - a very small one - suitable for the retired people, villages suitable for kings and for hermits (Acharya 1934:63, 65, 69) have also been prescribed.

Very detailed planning instructions for these villages have been given. Even their lengths and breadths have been prescribed. The planning of a village has followed that of the Cosmic Cross and the Magic Square (Havell, 1915:26). It has also been given as to where the various types of villages should be located - on the river bank, etc. (Acharya, 1934:87). Some of the castes were required to live outside the main habitation area of the village. Even Manu says "But the dwellings of the *Chandalas* and the *Shvapakas* shall be outside the village, they must be made *Apatras* and their wealth (shall be) dogs and donkeyṣ" (Ambedkar, 1948:25, from Manu). It was further prescribed that the *Malechhas* and other low caste people should have their dwellings in quarters situated at the angular quarters of a city (Shastri, 1967:430).

Some of the villages are settled on the Centre-Periphery basis/Plan. The places for the location of houses, etc., of the people following different occupations (and occupation, of course, goes with caste) are prescribed "round wise" for such villages (Acharya, 1934:72-78).

One finds a detailed knowledge of the science of Landscape Architecture (Jha, 1955; Shastri, 1967:891-892; Shukla, 1961:317). Keeping in view the level of technology and the needs of the people during those days, the wealth of knowledge of Traffic and Transportation Planning has been extremely vast (Acharya, 1934; Jha, 1955; Shamasastry, 1967:53). The wealth of knowledge about use of wood as a building material is tremendous. Various trees suitable for different purposes have been mentioned. There is also a very detailed list of names of trees that should be avoided (Shukla, 1961:115).

To quote Shukla again on this point:

> Practically all the important ancient treatises of architecture have treated this topic of brining timber from the forest for the use of house construction. This they call 'Collection of Wood'.
>
> Most of the wooden architecture in those days was related to pillars, beams and lintels. Door frames and roofing, too, were done by wood. Wood was used for load-bearing components like pillars, etc. It is perhaps due to this that there is such an emphasis on wood (1961:329,330).

Several procedures "ritualistic and non-ritualistic are prescribed and the import of all this is to select the best wood to secure the best results. This only indicates how meticulous our forefathers were in matters mundane" (Shukla, 1961:331).

There is also mention about arrangement of drainage in the human habitations (Acharya, 1934). For this, there is prescription for selecting the site with a slope in a particular direction (Acharya, 1934:12; Apte, 1954:138-139; Oldenberg and Max Muller, 1964:211). These texts are all the more particular about the slope of the site for the location of assembly hall (drawing-room). It should be built on a spot where the water flow off easily in all directions. Indian architecture was so developed, that there was provision of even rain-gauging devices, built in the buildings (Shamasastry, 1967:46).

Scholars of those days were well aware that a house cannot be planned without regard for its surroundings and for the region, etc. (Shukla, 1961:35). While planning a village the architect was supposed to keep in mind the future extension of the *abadi* also (Acharya, 1934:90). Provision of drinking water has always been an important consideration for the location and pattern of human habitations the world over. Indian architects have also been very particular about it. "There was one well for every ten houses" (Shamasastry, 1967:56).

Within the village *abadis*, the places where the different castes should be located is clearly stated (Acharya, 1934:63-96; Shamasastry, 1967:53-54; Shastri, 1967:430; Upadhyaya, 1947:171). There is a very detailed and minute planning about it. Places are decided with reference to the points of the compass (Acharya, 1934:68-96; Shamsastry, 1967:56; Shastri, 1967:82). In fact, in an ancient village a (permanent) temple of a god was not invariably built (as is the practice now-a-days). Even the gods whose statues or idols should be placed on the watch-towers on the ramparts of the *abadi* have been specifically named (Acharya, 1934:82, 90).

Prescriptions have also been very clearly given about the placing of the various types of gates in a village (Acharya, 1934:79; Shamasastry, 1967:54; Jha, 1955). As a matter of courtesy a host used to come to the Village Gate to see his guest off (Jha, 1955).

There are also instructions about the location of the shops of various kinds (Acharya, 1934:87; Shamasastry, 1967; Shastri, 1967:430). Similarly places have also been prescribed for the location of Guest Houses, Drinking Houses/bars (Acharya, 1934:70, 75), Hospitals (Shamasastry, 1967:54), burial grounds, stables, etc., grounds for the inspection of parades (Acharya, 1934:85). Caste segregation was practised even on the cremation and burial grounds.

"Either to the north or the east, burial or cremation grounds shall be situated; but that of the people of highest caste shall be to the south (of the city)" (Shamasastry, 1967:54).

Even the locations for the various government offices and other government departments and organs have been prescribed (Shamasastry, 1967:53-54). Locations of residential quarters for those at different rungs of the bureaucracy (clerks, chiefs, army general, etc.) have also been prescribed (Acharya, 1934:68-96). The physicians and forces should be spread all over a habitation (Shastri, 1967:430). Interestingly enough the prescriptions are that the houses for both the *Vaishyas* (trading class) and the *Shudras* (menial class) should be located in rows in the south side of the village (Acharya, 1934:70). "...Heretics and *Chandalas* shall live beyond the burial grounds..." (Shamasastry, 1967:56).

Houses were owned individually, these were single household units (according to the *Griha Sutras*), while the pastures, etc., were owned jointly by the community (Acharya, 1953:142). An individual house sheltering one family formed the unit of village life (Agarvala, 1953:141; Nilkanthasastri, 1963:37). House planning was never left to the caprice of the individual in India. It was the responsibility of the State or the ruler to see that a certain minimum standard was adhered to by every house-holder in matters of building his house. These standards were very rigid, codified and given the sanctity of religious character, so that they may never be violated (Shukla, 1961:321,353). The way the members of a community should co-operate in the matter of house building and village development has also been prescribed (Shamasastry, 1967:47). There was also emphasis on co-operative work for improving life and living in the villages (Jha, 1955).

Within a village, not only were the various sectors fixed for the different castes, even detailed instructions about the size and shape of the plot, orientation of the house (Acharya, 1934:62-64, 68-96; Apte, 1954:, 141), number of storeys (Acharya, 1934:92; Shukla, 1961:39), number of storeys suitable for various castes (Acharya, 1934:92), materials to be used for construction (Shukla, 1961:109), heights of buildings (Acharya, 1934:92; Shukla, 1961:118), shape of the columns, i.e., square, rectangular, etc., and even such mundane things like the wood of the pegs and the material of ropes to be used for laying out the central lines of the buildings and for the plums, dimensions of the nails and wood for the nails have been prescribed caste-wise (Shukla, 1961:109). In fact everything in the house; form, plan, materials, and construction techniques are related to the caste of the house builder. Caste has a very central position in this respect. It is the '*axis*' around which the entire human habitation revolves.

One possible explanation (for such minute prescriptions on the caste basis) that strikes my mind is that, because the caste sectors are fixed, so in order to give suitable visual effects (in tune with the general spirit and philosophy of the caste system) to the total human habitations, i.e., human habitations (at the macro-level) when completed, all the other rules have also been prescribed accordingly. But this explanation needs to be examined more thoroughly, and such a thorough examination by itself may perhaps lead to certain further more meaningful and revealing explanations.

In some of the texts, of course, it is also mentioned that the length, breadth and the height of houses varied according to the status of their owners. There are also detailed instructions about the furniture to be provided in the various types of buidlings (Shukla, 1961:38-39, 322 and 324).

The appearance of a buidling, it is prescribed, should clearly indicate its purpose (Shukla, 1961:321). The greatest emphasis in Indian architecture is perhaps on the proportions (Acharya, 1934; Shukla, 1961:118). The proportion of the length and breadth of the house plots is also prescribed (Acharya, 1934:12). For the buildings situated on the main roads, even the length of the side of the building abutting the road is prescribed. In fact, this emphasis on the proportions has been taken to such an extreme that some of the scholars from the West have remarked that this emphasis on the exactitude of proportions, especially in the field of iconography, was over-done (Shukla, 1961:68, 322).

There are also prescriptions about numbers. Some numbers are auspicious, some inauspicious, while some others are, naturally, neutral (Shastri, 1967:432). Symbolism, especially as contained in the Sanskritic texts, also enjoys an important place in Indian architecture (Havell, 1927). The auspicious and inauspicious months, dates and times for starting house construction and for the *Griha Pravesh* - House Warming - ceremony and for various other stages, between these two, are also given (Shukla, 1961:120; Shastri, 1967:487). The way circumambulation is to be performed at the time of entering a new village has also been spelled out. The way the architect - repeatedly referred to as the 'Wise Man' - is to be honoured by the house owner has also been very elaborately described (Acharya, 1934:90, 92).

In the house plan there is an emphasis on the proper grouping of the various parts of the house (Apte, 1954:141-142; Shukla, 1961:23) and also of the units of measurement. Instructions about the location of the drawing-room, store-room and of other spaces have been given (Apte, 1954:139; Shamasastry, 1967; Shastri, 1967:431; Shukla, 1961:313-323). "That a nursery, a bed-room and a privy were parts of the house appears from the description of the places where the daily *Bali* oblations were offered. A drawing-room, provision-room, and resting-place or retiring-room were parts of the house. A span and an arrow were the units of measurement" (Apte, 1954:141-142). A diagram consisting of 64 rectilineal chambers should be delineated on the plot on which the house is to be constructed. Different gods are to be worshipped in the various chambers. They are considered to be the presiding gods of their respective chambers (Shastri, 1967:890).

There is a homestead god. There are occult nerves which run through the various (81) parts of his body. There are eight gods who are the presiding deities of a household. They are to be worshipped in the eight angular points (Shastri, 1967:425,890). In some of the texts the house site has been compared with the human body divided into 81 parts. Different parts are considered to be the places or abode of the various gods, and these are connected with different functions. The house plan, therefore, is to follow that arrangement strictly (Apte, 1954:153; Shamasastry, 1967; Shastri, 1967:423,425,431,889-890,921-926). "The general idea underlying the construction of a house is that it is fashioned after the body of a human being lying on the site, with his head towards the north-east and his feet to the south-west, reclining on his left arm and facing the east" (Rao, 1923-24).

Many of these prescriptions might have lost their hold in various parts of the country by now, but at least the Brahman houses in South India are still built according to these prescriptions in the *Shastras*. Even doors, etc., in these houses are placed along a particular axis (Sivertsen, 1963:51). Writing about Cochin State (India), Forde (1963:281) says: "The residence of a wealthy Brahman or a Nayar should be planned and built according to a number of rules which have a religious sanction. The house should occupy the north-eastern or, less propitiously, the south-western quarter; the burial ground and cow-sheds should be in the south-east and the bathing tank and shrines in the north-west".

2.1.6 *Classical Indian architecture and modern architecture*

Comparing Indian architecture with modern architecture, Volwahsen has observed thus:

> Once one has grasped the geometric principles underlying Indian architecture, one is bound to draw comparisons with corresponding epochs of the European architecture. Parallels with modern architecture are also manifest; modern architecture is sometimes reproached for being poorer than that of earlier eras, since most buildings today are constructed on the basis of a grid plan. Yet by contrast Indian architecture does not seem to have suffered any kind of limitation upon its wealth of forms by using such grids, even figures so rigid and unyielding as squares. It is possible that this profusion was only able to develop because it was based upon a grid.
>
> In Indian architecture the use of square as the basic unit and the triangle as the principle governing the layout was chiefly a matter of religious significance. Each square in the centre of each building was the seat of Brahma. The Indian architect was solely concerned with the religious significance of the grid he used. Thus, a Hindu temple can be interpreted as a model of the Cosmos serving purposes of religious worship.
>
> When we employ a grid in a modern functional building, we do so mainly from economic considerations (or so at least it seems from a superficial point of view). We try to use identical architectural elements which can be mass-produced. We are also prepared to modify the grids upon which our buildings are based whenever this seems expedient or economically worthwhile.
>
> The Indian architect could not modify his basic geometrical figures, because these were of religious origin. Therefore, he kept to the ancient forms and repeated them, in completely different materials, as the centuries passed. It follows that Indian architects were familiar with the notion of building in such a way as to do justice to the qualities of the materials instead the canonization of forms which was uppermost in their work. Such concepts as thrust, support and arch were taken from European architecture. Indeed, even the term facade carries a different connotation (1969:3,4,5).

Iconography enjoyed an important position in the architecture of that period (Shastri, 1967). There was also emphasis on the aesthetics. A building should be good in its look also. A beautiful building was considered to be auspicious also (Shukla, 1961:118-119).

There are details of pillars, building materials, especially wood, construction techniques and defects in construction, along with the in-auspicious results associated with each of these defects, obstructions (called *Vedhas*) to the building with the different types of respective calamities each of these *Vedhas* are believed to attract (Shukla, 1961:36-37,109,105,115,312,328,330,337-350), etc., have also been given in great details. Almost all the manuals deal with this topic.

There are detailed prescriptions about the various types of doors and windows (along with their sizes, etc.) to be used for different purposes (Acharya, 1934:92; Shukla, 1961: 332; Upadhyaya, 1947:250-251). There are detailed instruction about the placing of the main door (Apte, 1954:141; Shukla, 1961:326-335). According to Acharya the door in a house should follow the (following) special rule :

> The length of the house on the side of the street being divided into the nine parts, there should be left, both in the interior and exterior (of the wall), five parts on the right-side and out of the (remaining) four parts there should be left three parts on the left side, and on the remaining (one) part the (entrance) door (of a house) should be constructed, otherwise the (entrance) door may be opened (anywhere) on the left side of the middle line (drawn through the house).
>
> The entrance-door of the houses in a village should be (generally) constructed by the south side (of a house)... (1934:91-92).

Never place a door in the middle of the house. No two doors should be exactly opposite each other (Shukla, 1961:326).

About the orientation of doors, Apte has made the following observations :

> ...he who is desirous of fame or strength should build his house with its main door to the east. The door should be to the north if one is desirous of children or cattle; and to the south if one desires all these things but it should not be to the west. The back-door should not be to the west. The back-door should not face the door

> of another house, and should be so constructed that the householder should not be seen by unholly persons while performing religious acts or while dining in his house and passers-by should not be able to see the valuables in the house. The frequent reference to the 'Threshold' indicates strong door-frames with a strong sill (1954:141).

There is also some work on typonomy (Agarvala, 1953:63). Typonomy helps in understanding origins of habitations and the impact of culture on them. Sanskritic literature also exhibits consciousness/awareness of the role of the law of inheritance of property in the house design (Shukla, 1961:921-926). Segregation of sexes as reflected in the arrangement and use of spaces in the house is also there (Apte, 1954; Chakladar, 1954; Shamasastry, 1967:54). There are two principal parts of the house (Shukla, 1961:322).

These Sanskritic texts contain mainly prescriptions. These texts are primarily construction manuals. These manuals were meant for the planners and architects, for the executors of building projects and for the individual house builders of those days. The intention was that the different works of various planners and architects could be of a reasonable standard - aesthetically, functionally, structurally as well as economy-wise, and that there could also be some symmetry, some uniformity in the various buildings in such a way that the human habitations at the macro, local, regional and national levels could also be functional, aesthetical and in conformity with and depictions of the cultural traditions of those communities.

These texts only prescribe what should be done. There is hardly any work on architecture to show that what was prescribed was practised also. In fact, there is a wide gulf between the canons of village planning and the universal practice in India regarding the most fundamental canon of town planning, namely, fortification.[1]

According to Volwahsen :

> *Vastu-Vidya*, the science of architecture, was already a branch of occult knowledge of *Vedic* times. It was handed down orally from father to son. Not until the middle ages did it become necessary to put this knowledge in writing. For during the flourishing period of temple-building the instructions relating to the rules of proportion became so numerous and the ritual so complex that it was no longer possible to avoid compiling manuals and reference works in which

these instructions were laid down. The manuscripts relating to *Vastu-Vidya*, in most cases incised on palm-leaves which were then dried, are still today venerated in the Hindu temples by the performance of a sacrificial rite.

Only in rare cases have historians of architecture had the opportunity to analyze the form and structure of surviving buildings in the light of these original palm-leaf manuscripts. Even the 19th century British authors of the '*Archaeological Survey of India*' were obliged to confine themselves. to recording and restoring abandoned temples (1969:43).

The knowledge of architecture in the Sanskritic literature (or during that period) has stemmed from ritualistic belief in religion. It is, therefore, dogmatic. The architects of those days did not have scientific training and arrived at conclusions/results/solutions mainly by intuition (which, we with scientific training, fail to understand and appreciate). Then how is it that in spite of all these limitations they produced some very perfect works? Each work was a perfect one and unique in itself.

The situation can better be understood in the light of the conditions in which architecture developed in India. For a long period in history the main buildings were for the gods and later on for the kings, houses for the lesser mortals were not of much significance and, therefore, not of much concern to the professionals. So the trade of planning and construction was highly patronized and restricted to only a few hands/families. Architects of those days had long experiences and by the 'trial and error' method they arrived at perfections. They were highly devoted to their work which they took as a religion and way of life and not merely as a job. Their training was such that they had a real 'feel' of things - a quality which the present-day architects in general and those in India in particular badly lack. Knowledge was not documented but was handed down from generation to generation as a part of their social heritage.

A study of way the fission of science from religion took place and of the circumstances under which it so happened would perhaps be a great contribution to the subject.

2.2 SELECTED WORKS OF SOCIOLOGISTS AND ANTHROPOLOGISTS

In the recent past, some interesting contributions in the field of human habitations have also been made by various sociologists and anthropologists.

2.2.1 *Comparatively older works*

The first such work is by Lewis Henry Morgan who published his book entitled "*Houses and house life of the American aboriginals*", in 1881.[2] Morgan says that family in those stages - the upper stages of savagery and the lower stages of barbarism - was too weak an organization to face alone the struggle of life and sought shelter for itself in larger households composed of several families. Moreover they were occupied as joint tenement houses. The house for a single family was an exception rather than the rule.

Morgan begins with a detailed account of the genes, phratry, tribe and the confederacy of tribes - a knowledge which, he feels, is indispensable for an understanding of the house life of the aborigines. He has also described certain usages and customs of the American aborigines that explain their plan of life. These are:

(a) The law of inheritance
(b) The law of hospitality
(c) Communism in living
(d) The ownership of land in common
(e) The practice of having one meal a day - a dinner
(f) Separation at meals - men eating first by themselves, and the women and children afterwards.

Morgan has also given an idea of the forms and plans of the houses of some of these tribes. These houses were so much adapted to the surrounding conditions that the tent used by some of these tribes under the name of "Sibly Tent" was later on used, with some modification of plan, in the U.S. army for services in the plains. With the arrival of the Europeans in the area the change gradually set in. After coming into contact with the Whites, they started adopting the new way of life. It came in stages; first breaking up the old plan of living together in the old Long Houses, and with the substitution of single houses for each family which ended communism and living in the large households, and substituted the subsistence of a single family through individual efforts.

Morgan's idea, in a nutshell, is "that in the upper stages of savagery and also in the lower stages of barbarism the Indian household was formed of a number of families of gentile kin that they practised communism in living in the household and this principle found expression in their house architecture and pre-determined its character" (Bohannan, 1965).

To quote Bohannan further:

> Although this book can no longer be accepted today, no book of similar scope has replaced it.
>
> Indeed the theoretical point of Morgan's book is only today beginning to be taken up by the specialist subject of proxemics which is in Edward Hall's words for the study of the relationships between the social structure and space, particularly the buildings and their placement.
>
> Morgan's problem in this book is a basic one : what does domestic architecture show anthropologists — either ethnologists or archaeologists - about social organization and how does social organization combine with a system of production technology and an ecological adjustment to influence domestic and public architecture.
>
> Morgan's method of procedure can only be called functional evolutionary. In fact Morgan failed, as we all do, whenever his model for explanation illfitted his data. His mode was not flexible (1965: ix,x,xii,xiii).

Singh, S.J. in his article "Habitations of the Maities" (1933) has given a very good account of the dwellings of this tribe. These houses are rectangular in shape and are constructed on the ground level (as one of the regular type of houses described in the *Rig Veda*), while the general practice in the region is to build houses on stilts. The importance of these Manipuri habitations is that they have still the fully preserved customs and canons about the rites connected with its various parts.

Singh distinguishes the various spaces in the house, their measurements and the folk-beliefs attached to each. Different spaces are rigidly assigned to different members of the joint family, and various spaces and elements in the house have different names, some having a magico-religious significance. The whole house is divided into two halves, one reserved for women and the other for men. The paper gives a detailed description of the *central hall*.

The Maitie dwelling houses are all of the same type. Maities have very strict rules as regards building their houses. They take great care in buidling operations. These houses are built on the basis of an analogy with human body. The "compound" is divided into nine parts in such a way that the length is divided into three equal parts so also the breadth. If the plot is not right-angled, the house is built on the side which is wider. Each part has a name and is fixed for a certain purpose/use. These places are sometimes changed in consultation with the astrologer according to the horoscope of the builder (owner). The house is supposed to be inhabited by some gods and goddesses and respective places are rigidly attributed to them.

The paper also has a mention of the orientation of houses and the building materials used. The Maities are not strict about the material used except for the *'first pole'*. The paper is more like a manual of rules for constructing and using the house, and a list of certain don'ts. There is no mention of any other aspect of the life of the Maities. It is possible, the author says, that the Maitie received the ancient Indian culture very early. The paper very much resembles the Sanskritic literature on the subject.

Iyer, L.K. Anantakrishna in his presidential address titled "An Ethnographic Study of the Coorgs" delivered to the Anthropology Section of the Indian Science Congress Association in 1937, while discussing the history of the Coorgs, their social organization, etc., has briefly described their houses also.

The Coorgs live in a semi-isolated portion of the Western Ghats. They are basically agriculturists, hunters and grow cardamom jungles and live in extended joint very big-sized patriarchal families.

> Their racial history like that of the Todas is a puzzle to the anthropologists...Hinduism has had no influence on them. Their traditional customs and manners are gradually changing in favour of Western culture.
>
> The Coorg houses, like those of Nayars of Malabar, are generally situated close to their paddy fields on a sheltering slope of 'Bane' land surrounded by clamps of mountain trees... The position and the type of building very much resemble those of the Nayars of Malabar and Cochin. The approaches of the old Coorg house strongly mark the design of fortification and tradition points back to a time of general feuds, when chief fought with chief, and clan with clan. Deep Kadangas or trenches with high embankments

still testify to the memorials of the warlike state of affairs in former times. These war ditches intersect the mountainous district in every direction. They have resisted both the furious attacks of the contending armies and the forces of the annual monsoon. A deeply cut passage (*woni*) paved with rough stones and overgrown with shady trees, its sloping side walls decked with variety of ferns, leads one in angular lines to door-way passing under an outhouse. Houses are situated in the middle of their plantations far removed from the public road. A paved courtyard is surrounded on all sides by stables, store-rooms and servant's quarters, in front of which is the quadrangular building which is provided with one storey, and is raised about three feet from the ground. All the buildings are roofed with bamboos and thatched with rice straw which is annually repaired and renewed. Many of the houses... conform themselves to the original plan and design and are tiled. There is generally an open square hall in the centre known as mudumane or butte, the four sides of which are provided with rooms for the inmates to occupy. On the front side of the building there is an open verandah which is the reception hall. It is raised and covered with a wooden plank aimara two or three feet broad, so as to form convenient seats for the male members and visitors. From it rise three or four wooden pillars, square, round and tapering and sometimes carved. The floor is well beaten with mud and cleaned with cowdung. The ceiling is of wood, arranged in small compartments. In some, the verandah is separated from the inner hall by a wall with a sort of window or latice made of wood. This aperture like the principal door-posts is elaborately and handsomely carved in flowers and figures, leaving open space between, just large enough to peep through without being seen. It is a contrivance designed chiefly for the benefit of the Coorg women who are curious to see visitors as their Musalman sisters behind the *purda* or screen. On the right side of the verandah there is the main door leading to the inner hall which is lit by the sky light formed by the junction of the four slopes of the inner roof into an open space (*nittam*) which is a masonry reservoir in which rain water is collected and drained off by an underground passage. The inner roof is supported on four pillars, resting on thick broad slabs of jack wood open the walls of the reservoir, and forming convenient seats for the inmates of the house, the inner rooms of which are without windows and open by small doors into the central hall only. On the sides diagonally opposite to the door of the verandah and like the inner right corner, there are two doors leading to the exterior of the house. The first room of the inner hall is occupied by the master of the house and his wife. The next room is the kitchen (*adu-mane* or *umbala-mane*) dining room whence the smoke issues and fills the whole house coating and preserving the wood-work. The small rooms of the remaining two wings are tenanted by the married couple, the widows and unmarried women, one room near the left corner is set apart as sacred to the family deity (*mane-devata*) and also known as *Kanni-Kombare*. From the ceiling are suspended matchlocks, the wooden bells for cattle, the trappings for pack bullocks and other domestic utensils. The space under the roof and above the ceiling, the wooden floor covered with a thick layer of earth to keep the rooms below dry and fire-proof, serve for storing bags of rice, baskets, pots and culinary provisions. There is a deep well built with stone in the compound to supply water for cooking purposes and another hut is built by the side of the paddy fields for bathing in hot water.

On the morning of the wedding day at about nine O'clock the invited guests assemble in festive array at the houses of the bride and bridegroom; and while the women go inside the house, and give a helping hand to the mistress, the men are accommodated in the spacious verandah or in temporary sheds in the courtyard, and served with *pan supari* to assist 'the flow of village gossip' which is now and then interrupted by the noisy band of musicians.

The furniture in a Coorg house bear ample testimony to the simple habits of the inmates...On days of religious ceremonies they sit on mats. A wooden shelf is fixed to the wall in each room to keep their brass vessels, plates and lamps. Rattan or wooden boxes contain their clothes and jewels. There is always a spittoon in one of the corners of the room. Where there is a baby a rattan cradle is suspended from the ceiling within reach of the mother's bed. The air of the room with closed doors and no window is at night very stuffy, and extremely unwholesome in cases of sickness (Iyer, 1937:319-321,330,332).

2.2.2 *After the Second World War : 1945 - 1960*

Opler, Morris and Singh, Rudra Datt, in their article "The Division of Labour in an Indian Village" (1948) have thrown light on life in a village in Uttar Pradesh (India) by clearly bringing out the ways in which the various castes interlock and form a whole - an aspect of village life an idea of which is really indispensable for a proper understanding of any rural habitation anywhere in India where the entire life revolves round the caste axis. Opler and Singh have also traced the history of that village and given detailed information about the various castes living in it.

The paper contains two drawings; one showing the habitation area in the village, and the other a caste-wise distribution of houses in its central part. But the authors have not explained the drawings much. I think it is so because their main aim was not to analyze the habitation pattern in the village. Regarding the dwellings, they have mentioned the building materials, house forms, the preferred orientations of houses and the number of rooms. There is no mention of the house plan, not to speak of the parts of the house and their uses reflecting the way of life of their inhabitants.

Srinivas, M.N. in his well-known work on the Coorgs (1952) has also made a mention of their habitations. The Coorgs live in extended joint families called *OKA*. The Coorg house is a substantial stone structure built usually on an elevated site with a narrow high-wall and a winding lane leading to it. The house is a fort-like construction with windows only on the first floor. This design is a result of the old disturbed times in the region when raids by hostile *OKAS* were quite common.

Srinivas has given a description of different parts of the ancestral estate. He also mentions in some detail the Coorg house, the various spaces and elements in the house, and their uses with the taboos, wherever applicable. The author has also given an idea of the attitudes of the Coorgs towards various parts of their ancestral estate and about the cardinal directions. The classification of places and spaces into sacred and profane has also been mentioned.

Honigman, J. (1954) has described the Men's Houses in Pakistan, on the background of the existence of similar institutions among the Indians of western Alaska, south-western Pueblo Tribes and in Turkey. Honigman's study describes the situation in this respect in each of the three main regions of Pakistan - Sind, Punjab and North-West Frontier Provinces - where the men's house is known as *Otak*, *Batok* and *Hudzra*, respectively.

This study describes the plan, construction and the use of these houses. It also analyzes, to a limited extent though, the utility of having such separate structures for men only. But this description is not very exhaustive and the main limitation of this work is that one cannot properly understand this institution of the Pakistanis in the absence of sufficient knowledge about the total life styles of the people in each of the three regions of that country.

Karve, Iravati (1957) has given a description of "human habitation areas", the internal and external communication systems and their regional distribution over Maharashtra, Andhra Pradesh and certain coastal areas of India, which she claims to be the first attempt at such a description. Karve has also undertaken a limited exercise in typonomy. She has described at quite some length the phenomenon of hamlets, discussing as to how the hamlets come up and how these grow into villages, etc. This information is quite useful.

Karve has given a very illustrative description of some of the house groupages called *khadki*. All the inhabitants of such a groupage claim descent from a common ancestor. As such, it is one agnatic *khadki* or *vado*, and naturally, therefore, all the inhabitants of a *khadki* marry only outside it, i.e., they practice *khadki* exogamy. But these observations relate to the urban areas. The entire village may be made up of such *khadkis* standing wall to wall with narrow passages joining them. This whole complex makes a village.

Karve's entire work, including what she has observed in Baroda, i.e., the house groupages, is at the macro-level. The main emphasis in this study is on the communication systems. Moreover, Karve is concerned here only with the physical form of the village, what she calls its Gestalt without any effort to relate this form, i.e., Gestalt to the way of life lived in these habitations.

Singh, R.L., in his article "Typical Rural Dwellings in the Umland of Banaras" (1957), while describing the houses of the people in the Banaras villages has confined himself mainly to a description of the house in an engineer-like fashion.[3] The main emphasis is on the form of the house, its dimensions and the materials used, etc.. There is also a mention of the orientation of these houses.

Singh, of course, has enumerated some parts of the house like; *deorhi*, *aangan*, courtyard, verandah, etc. It is a definite contribution that he has given brief accounts of the different uses to which these spaces in the house are put. But the list of spaces is not a comprehensive one, and the uses of various spaces have not been given in detail. Moreover, Singh does not explain the manner in which the various spaces are arranged in the house plan.

Masters, A. (1957) has described the Mudaliar houses in a South Indian village. He has described the various important spaces in a Mudaliar house and the common uses of these spaces.

Needham, Rodney in his article "A Structural Analysis of the Purum Society" (1958) has shown that the entire life of the Purum is based on a *Right vs Left* classification, and he has tried to show that this classification is clearly reflected even in the design of the Purum house, and also in the use of the various spaces in it. The Purum is an old Kuki tribe of Manipur, on the Tibeto-Burmese border. They are from the Mangoloid stock and are divided into six patrilineal clans. They have a system of matrilineal connubium.

The Purum house is divided length-wise into two parts. The right half is considered to be superior than the left half. The master of the house with his unmarried sons and daughters sleeps in the right half, while his future sons-in-law, and other casual guests as well as his married daughters whenever visiting their parents' home sleep in the left half. This *Right vs Left* classification is also observed in every element of the house and even in its construction method. The very names for the right and left parts of the house, respectively, mean *Private* and *Public*, *Superior* and *Inferior*, *Family* and *Outsiders* leading one to an equation :

Right : Left :: Private : Public
Right : Left :: Superior : Inferior
Right : Left :: Family : Outsiders

2.2.3 *After the Second World War : 1960 - 1975*

Chauhan, Brij Raj has also done some good work on the subject of rural habitations. His three works in this connection are : two articles "An Indian Village : Some Questions" (1960) and "Residential Concentrations and Caste Groupings in the Rural Setting" (1964), and a book "*A Rajasthan Village*" (1967). Though very useful, these works deal with the habitations at the macro-level only, i.e., at the level of the village layout, especially the concentration of the houses of people belonging to different castes in particular sectors. Chauhan has not touched the habitation problem at the micro-level, i.e., he has not studied the house as such.

Stephen, Fuchs (1960) has described the preferred and avoided orientations of the Bhumia houses giving reasons for the same, and the folk beliefs of the Gonds and so many formalities (elaborate procedure and rituals) observed by them for starting house construction. The Bhumias living with the Gonds, and in the same ecological and geographical conditions, are not particular about these folk beliefs and formalities. Stephen has also given some idea about the various spaces, the use of these spaces and the construction material, etc., of the Gond and Bhumia houses and their groupings, i.e., House Groupages. The paper contains similar information about the Kuki and Lushai houses also.

Trivedi, H.R. (1961) has also given a brief description of the traditional Mer house. The book has a layout drawing and a brief mention of the uses to which some of the spaces are put. The main emphasis is on the segregation of sexes as reflected in the use of space. Trivedi has also mentioned some of the important household goods of the Mers. The Mers consider a new house to be unfit for living till it is equipped more or less in traditional ways.

Bose, N.K. and Sinha, S. in their publication: "*Peasant Life in India, Unity in Diversity*" (1961), have also touched the habitations under the headings, 'Settlement pattern', 'House types' and 'Sanitation'. But as the survey covered thirty and odd material traits of culture in the selected villages all over the country, it has not been able to throw sufficient light on habitations. I also studied at Calcutta the basic data collected by the survey for this particular study. At the macro-level, there are mentions only of the types of settlement of particular villages, i.e., description of the village layout. Neither the layout has been adequately explained, nor there is any mention of any factor that has led the settlement to take the particular shape it has.

At the level of the individual dwelling, the data is very inadequate. There are only rough sketches of some houses, sometimes describing (in local terms) the various spaces in it. Beyond this there are no details. Moreover, the greatest weakness of this data is that the information on various aspects is about different groups of people, i.e., the information on house type is about one group, that on another trait about another group, and so on, making it impossible to relate these to one another and draw meanings out of them. Perhaps nothing better could be expected from a survey of this nature with such a wide coverage.

Recently, an important work on rural habitations has been done by Cunningham, Clarke. E. "*Order in the Atoni House*" (1964). The Atoni are a tribe in Indonesia. Numbering about a quarter million, the Atoni practice patrilineal descent, shifting cultivation, keep cattle, pigs, etc. Their villages are inaccessible. They have an exchange economy. Most of the Atoni live by their traditions in a village environment. Atoni have nuclear families. There are no communal houses or communal granaries. There is the minimum of economic co-operation among the households.

"The Atoni do not build houses to express abstract notions. They build homes. However, they do so in a way thought and managed by the elders, according to rules regarded as a vital part of their heritage, and houses follow patterns not individual whims" -- again a characteristic feature of vernacular architecture. "There is a fixed way of making and using the parts, sections and appurtenances. Same is applicable in the case of the village. When a question is asked to an Atoni about this, the answer is: "This is the order or arrangement". This concept of 'Order' in building expresses ideas symbolically and the house depicts them vividly for every individual from birth to death. Furthermore, Order concerns not just discrete ideas of symbols, but a system, and the system expresess both the principles of classification *per se*, the definition of unity and difference. There is also a description of the values these people attach to the various cardinal directions and to the various colours and numbers. Cunningham has also brought out the fact that the design of the house reflects their conceptions of the Cosmos.

House is, for Atoni, a ritual centre for prayer, sacrifice, and feasts. Rituals of life-cycle are conducted here. Even the agricultural rituals begin in the house. There is a division of the house into two parts; inner and outer. The various uses of the two parts and the persons who can use each are given. There is also a detailed description of the various spaces, elements and construction techniques of the house. As one reads through this paper, one forms an impression as if the Atoni house has some characteristics of the Hindu Architecture. May be, there was some Hindu influence during early periods, or these people also belong to the same racial stock.

Bose, A.B and Malhotra, S.P. in their article "Residential Segregation and Housing in a Desert Village" (1965) mention the storeys of houses, building materials used and the *kacha-pacca* distinction. They have described the shapes, dimensions and orientations of houses as well as the priority that housing enjoys in the life of these desert (Rajasthan) people. The houses are designed to achieve the segregation of sexes and those who can afford to do so build separate rooms for guests. Due to the fear of theft, cattle are tied in a separate portion of the house. The paper contains a brief list of the various parts of the house which have been described mainly in material terms without giving any information about their respective uses and the ways these parts fit into the total plan of the house.

The paper "Rural House Types" by Unni, K.R. (1956) is a study from the point of view of house groupages in respect of two villages; one in Rajasthan and the other in Delhi. Unni gives some idea about the structures to be used mainly by males and females, respectively, reflecting the segregation of sexes. The paper does not give any information about the individual house. The observations made by Unni, even at the macro-level, suffer from certain basic limitations.

Chandhoke, S.K. and Singh K.B. have conducted a number of studies on human habitations in rural areas. Some of these are: The Study of Planning Pattern of Existing Houses in Villages - Bharatpur Region - (Rupbas and Bayanna Tehsils in particular) (1968), The Study of Existing Planning Pattern of House in Villages - Saharanpur Region - (Roorkee Tehsil in particular) (1969), The Study of Existing Planning Pattern of Houses in Villages - Delhi Region - (Mehrauli Block in particular) and Village Housing Conditions in the Bharatpur Region, Eastern Rajasthan, India (1974). The first three studies deal with the rural habitations at both the micro - as well as macro-level in the Bharatpur, Saharanpur and Delhi regions, respectively. The fourth one is a detailed study of houses and house groupages against the background of the physical conditions of the region, and the social and economic aspects of life of the communities inhabiting it.

Chandhoke has been working in this field for over the last two decades. He submitted a dissertation titled Types of Rural Habitation Patterns in the University of Delhi in 1976.

Beginning with an introduction, review of the literature on the subject and information about the Haryana region, the dissertation is focussed on Chhatera, a Jat village, in Sonepat District adjoining the Union Territory of Delhi. There is a brief description - physical, economic as well as socio-cultural - of this and surrounding villages followed by a detailed analysis of the various elements of habitation. In addition to giving a physical description of the various elements of habitation, the dissertation discusses the various alternative uses to which these elements/spaces are put (on different occasions), the actors there and the significance of these elements/spaces in the background of the culture and life styles of the people in the village/region. Chandhoke further identifies a number of pairs of complimentary relations. These relations are the Sub-System of Classification constituting the total System of Classification which, in its turn, is itself embedded in the culture of the community. The respective roles of these relations, in the habitations under study, have been analyzed and, on this basis, have been classified into Primary and Secondary categories. The second half of the present book has, to an extent, drawn from that dissertation.

Taking up various aspects of this theme and discussing them in the light of some of the published works, Chandhoke has published a number of papers some of which deserve a mention here. All of these papers are based mainly on the author's field-work in the States of Haryana, Rajasthan and Uttar Pradesh and the Union Territory of Delhi and his long professional experiences in the Punjab as well as Bihar villages. Therefore, the range of applicability of the observations made in these papers is quite wide, though the main focus of many of these is village Chhatera and villages in the region around. These works also include a number of illustrations - photographs and typical detailed drawings - especially produced for the purpose which provide a considerable help in understanding the text in a realistic perspective.

These papers can be grouped into four broad categories. In papers in the first (i.e., A.) category, though Chandhoke has portrayed certain aspects of life of the local communities, the main subject matter of all these has been woven around some physical element/structure. In the second (i.e., B.) category, the author has discussed mainly the sociological aspects as related to the habitation in this region. In his papers falling in category C, the author has attempted to understand and explain the fact that the habitation pattern of any human group is an indication of the practice or custom of that group with relation to its abode, it is nothing but a physical manifestation of the cultural configurations of the group and how, therefore, an anthropological approach alone can help us to understand the complicated mechanism of the origin growth, stability and decay of human habitations while all other approaches fail us - at least partially - in this venture. In the last (i.e., D.) category, Chandhoke has also contributed a number of papers describing and discussing various aspects of the housing problem in rural India in general and those concerning the depressed sections of its population in particular.

Category A

"The Habitation Patterns of a Jat Village of Haryana, India" (1978) is based on the premise that one way to understand certain aspects of the habitat of any community, which itself is basically a resultant of the complicated and long-drawn process of continuous interaction between its cultural and physical environment, is to look at the component parts of the habitation and observe the various uses of these parts. The paper portrays, though on a modest scale, a method that can be fruitfully followed for a realistic understanding of the habitation pattern of any human group, especially those having some similarities with the one under reference.

"*Chaupal* - The Men's Community Place in a Jat Village of Haryana" (1977) and "*Chaupal* : The Traditional Village Centre - Haryana, India" (1978) are about one of the most important institutions - a physical structure into which the social aspects of the life of the local people are inextricably interwoven - of the communities inhabiting a good part of North India. Buildings occupied or used exclusively by man have an extensive distribution around the world. *Chaupal* is a very rough parallel of a Club House in a Western Society. But as segregation among the sexes is exercised in an extreme and peculiar form among the communities in this region, it is an all man's place and his exclusive domain. A good part of life at the level of the individual, small groups as well as total community of the males is spent at, and revolves around, the *chaupal*. The two articles trace the history of this institution from primitive times, describe the entire process as to how a *chaupal* is built, who builds it, who are its various users and how it is maintained - financially as well as otherwise - and also give an idea of the winds of change (in this respect) flowing among the local communities.

Similarly, "*Kuwan* : Water Source And the Traditional Social Centre For Women" (1987) is a comprehensive presentation of the water well - the main source of at least potable water not only in this region but over a sizable part of the entire globe - highlighting its role, which has virtually become an institution, in the life of especially the women folk, whose life would really become unliveable in the absence of the well.

Category B

"Haryana Village : A Study Of Ethno-Linguistic Groups" (1978) describes the ethnic composition of the local population, their social, economic and religious lives, the Proprietary Body of the Villages and the Village Council as also the pattern of interaction among the various groups. The most significant aspect of this work is about the roles and rights of these various groups and the often-talked-about vertical as well as horizontal unity of the Indian villages, in general, and of those in this region, in particular, as related to and reflected in the habitation pattern at the level of a village and also smaller units (*i.e.*, village layout patterns, housing clusters, land uses, etc., as related to the various actors).

"The Multi-Village Panchayat : A Nesting Series of The Jat Villages of Haryana, India" (1983) is a protrayal of the built-in mechanism to exercise social control and maintain social discipline among the members of the village communities in Haryana. How the local communities - at the level of the individual villages as well as higher formation — functions as "in-groups" with "we-feeling" have a way of determining leadership and code of conduct to regulate life within these habitations and also their relations with the people in surrounding areas has been analyzed and compared with some parallel cases elsewhere. The subject can be best understood in a very realistic perspective when studied in conjunction with Appendixes II, III and VII of this book.

Category C

In this category fall Chandhoke's papers, like, "Human Habitations : An Anthropological Approach" (1978) and "Human Habitations in India : An Anthropological Approach" (1980).

In another paper in this category, "The Human Environment : Role of Socio-Cultural Factors in Man's Adaptation To Physical Environment - With Special Reference To Habitat" (1983), beginning with an introduction to the subject and role of socio-cultural factors in it, the author describes in detail the role of these factors in man's built environment especially at the levels of individual houses and house groupages. It has been clearly brought out as to how aggregation, segregation and segmentation on various fronts (including cattle-human) in the human habitations in India, especially in its countryside, is a function of the culture of the communities inhabiting them and how the cultural factors have influenced other aspects and elements of habitations. Even the provision and maintenance of community facilities is conditioned by cultural considerations. The work is full of examples from different actual life situations based mainly on author's own field work and field experiences.

Some of the other works of Chandhoke falling in this category are:

The Study of Planning Pattern of Existing Houses in Villages - Saharanpur Region - (Roorkee Tehsil in particular) (1969)

Village Housing Conditions in The Bharatpur Region, Eastern Rajasthan, India (1974)

Environmental Impact Assessment : Some Socio-Cultural Dimensions (1985)

Housing and Planning : Cultural Factors and Innovations (1986)

Socio-Cultural Dimensions of Human Settlements (1987)

Category D

"Housing Conditions in Rural India" (1977), "Caste Segregation in Villages" (1976) and "Towards A Better Rural Habitat" (1976) are some of the other papers in this category in whch the author has explained both the quantitative as well as qualitative aspects of the problem viewed from different, especially anthropological, angles and suggested a number of remedies.

Some of the other works of Chandhoke falling in this category are:

Housing and the Weaker Sections (1983)

Human Settlements in India in 2000 and Beyond With Special Reference to Delhi - A Case Study (1985)

The Under-priviledged Sections and Their Habitations (1986)

Housing and Built Environment in Rural North India (1986)

Role of Informal (Co-operative) Associations in Providing Urban/Civic Amenities - Three Case Studies in Delhi (1987)

A recently published paper "Animals Are Good To Think And Good To Prohibit", by Tambiah, S.J. (1969), is based on work in a Thai village. Tambiah has given the drawings of a house, depicted and described the various spaces in a house, mentioned the various uses to which these are put, and through that he has attempted to show as to how these reflect the way and philosophy of life of those who live in these houses. But Tambiah has not taken this point too far. The main stress in Tambiah's study is on the attitude of the Thai people towards certain animals, like, cat, dog and horse, the values these animals symbolise for a Thai and how this philosophy is reflected in the latitude given to each of these animals in the various spaces in the house. In other words, the main discussion is about the relation between the attitudes of the Thai towards different animals, on the one hand, and the parts of the house to which each one of them is, respectively, allowed access, on the other. Anyway, it is a good work.

Another recent work on the subject is by Hilda, Kuper, "The Language of Sites in the Politics of Space", (1971). Kuper argues that there is a condensation of values in special sites, and the transactions that constitute the totality of social life may be spatially mapped with sites expressing relatively durable social structure. But this paper deals with the sites alone and not with the sites constructed upon or, if one may like to call it so, with the built-up structures.

A recent work in this field, "Spatial Concepts of the Ainu of the North-West Coast of Southern Sakhalin" (1972) is by Ekimo, Ohnuki-Tierney. Ekimo has presented the basic cognitive structure underlying the concept of space among the Ainu of the north-west coast of Southern Sakhalin now settled in Hokaido. To use Ekimo's own words, "The spatial structure is examined by analyzing cultural meanings attached to the spatial categories and directions. The basic spatial structure may be best understood as a dyadic structure comprising a series of contrast sets in binary opposition, with the Super-Ainu quality as the minimal distance feature."

Ekimo's discussion of the Ainu spatial concepts begins with a brief presentation of the framework of the Ainu Universe. Next, he discusses the universe and division of the horizontal plane of the universe in order to examine the cultural meanings of the divisions. He further attempts to examine the horizontal plane by analyzing the spatial arrangements of the Ainu house, which the Ainu consider to be miniature universe. The paper then gives an analysis of the directional terms of the horizontal plane in order to further understand the cultural meanings assigned to these directions and the spatial categories which correspond to each direction. Ekimo further examines the vertical plane and its directional terms in order to arrive at the categories and meanings of the vertical plane. Lastly, the possible locations of various enclaves of the universe are examined. These enclaves include the world of the dead Ainu, the world of the demons and world of the dead members of various beings of the universe - these worlds are belived to be invisible to ordinary living Ainu.

Ekimo's work is mainly an attempt at identifying the system of classification, with special refrence to spatial aspects, in the life of the

Ainu. To quote Ekimo himself, "I have attempted to convey the basic structure of Ainu spatial concepts - how the Ainu classify the universe..."

Some work on rural habitations has been done by the Census organization also. Since the 1961 decennial Census the scope of this aspect in the Census framework has been considerably expanded. Information on village layout patterns and on house types is available in the all-India as well as in the State volumes (Part IV, A and B), the District Census Handbooks, as well as in a large number of Village Survey Monographs. Besides these, a special volume, "Report on House Types and Village Settlement Patterns in India", was published as a part of the 1961 Census Programme.

Limitation of space here does not permit me to enter into a detailed discussion of what information about habitations is available in the Census volumes. However, one thing is clear that the data is not always adequate to enable one to relate any habitation pattern - at either the micro- or macro-level with the way of life of those who inhabit it. Perhaps, it is so because the Census data are not collected with this specific end in view.

Scanty information about human habitations is also available in some of the Gazetteers - especially in the District Gazetteers published under the New Series after the Independence of India.

Settlement Reports of the Revenue Department generally do not touch this topic. But some of these, like the one by Ibbetson (1883), do contain some excellent information on human habitations.

Studies of rural habitations conducted by the administrators deal mainly with the types of villages related to the different systems of revenue administration, i.e., joint and severalty villages, and the nature of relationships that exist among the differnt groups of people in the two type of villages.

The basic approach of the administrators is through the Land Holdings and the Land Ownership System, although a few of them have also given very good accounts of the layouts of villages and some impressions about the life being lived in them (Baden-Powell 1913).

2.3 HOUSE AS A PART OF CULTURE

The house itself is not merely a shell for protection but it is also an effective means to communicate ideas from generation to generation : it reflects the life and culture of its inhabitants. There is an 'order' in the house. Physical aspects or spaces have social meanings. The universe is sometimes considered to be analogous to the human body, so is the miniature universe; the village or the house. Different parts of the miniature universe are in that case believed to be symbolic representations of the human body.

To quote (*Encyclopaedia Britannica*)

> All land animals except the hoofed mammals regularly make use ot shelters if only for the period of rearing their young. Their shelters are fixed by instinct; in contrast, human dwellings are diverse products of invention and cultural tradition. Housing provides shelter from the elements, protection from human enemies and predatory animals, security for infants and a place for social intercourse (1969 : Vol. 7, p.810).

According to Ghose, since the dawn of human society the dwelling house has served three fundamental human needs:-

(i) the need for protection from weather and enemy (generally beasts)
(ii) the need for storage of food and property, personal and communal, and
(iii) the need for free family life and sexual privacy.

As these needs can be grouped as (a) the need for self-preservation and (b) the need for reproduction, they may be broadly called 'biological needs'. A house which does not fulfil these basic biological needs is not worthy of being called a 'dwelling house'.

The house is a tool invented by man to help him in his adaptation to his environment. But the needs of man are not determined by physiological drives alone, they are determined under conditions of culture also in a more or less round-about process. "Culture" is not simply an "instrumental reality" and "apparatus" for the satisfaction of fundamental needs. It is a total dynamic reality in which physiological, economic, political, religious, educational and aesthetic needs and responses are all combined and integrated. The house does not serve "biological needs" alone, but satisfies other "cultural needs" also. The house, in this sense, is both a "material tool" and a "cultural symbol". It is founded upon the primary

> biological and economic needs, and is structured and roofed with the secondary or derived socio-cultural needs - religious, educational and aesthetic. In this sense, the dwelling house is not only a 'tool of culture', but also super-structure (1953:4-5).

Adaptations also involve availability of materials and their utility. In spite of abundance, limitations may exist. Mud, though often used as building material, is impractical where rainfall is heavy. Adaptations are not made anew by each individual; rather the selection of materials and the form of house are dictated primarily by the traditional building practice (*Encyclopaedia Britannica*, 1969: Vol. 7; p. 810).

Rapoport has very clearly brought out this point, i.e., how house is a part of culture thus:

> While it would be impossible to deny the great importance of shelter as an aspect of the house and as a human need, the basic necessity of shelter itself has been questioned. It has been suggested that house building is not a natural act and is not universal, since South-East Asia, South America and Australia contain a number of tribes without houses.
>
> Conversely, elaborate dwellings are found in areas where, in terms of climate alone, the need for shelter is minimal, as in part of the South Seas... The principle that religious prescriptions and taboos introduce discomfort and complications, and become more important than climatic imperatives is more important than any specific example which could be given.
>
> There are cases in which the way of life may lead to almost anti-climatic solutions, with the dwelling form related to the economic activity rather than climate. For example, the Hidatsa of the Missouri Valley were agriculturists from April to November, growing corn, greens and beans. During that period they lived in circular wooden houses, 30 to 40 feet in diameter, with five-foot-high walls made of tree trunks and four central columns 14 feet high supporting rafters carrying branches, earth and grass roofing. These houses were in large villages and lasted several generations. From December to March they hunted buffalo and used tepees like those of the plains Indians. The two dwelling types were thus adopted to the two ways of life and the dual economic base, although climatically the reverse, would be expected (as is found in Siberia) . . .(1969:19-21).

Hall has expressed his views on the subject thus:

> The Japanese rural house is distinctly an implement of agriculture and as such varies with agricultural systems. It is also a product chiefly of its local environment and so varies in construction and form with the heterogeneity of environments found in Japan. Nevertheless, the rural house conforms to the homogeneity of the Japanese culture complex. The basic Japanese house seems to be rectangular structure of three rooms. There are many variations of and additions to the basic form, as can be noted from the different ground plans presented. Japanese tradition, like Chinese, encourages each family to live under one roof. Houses of two and three storeys, containing dozens of rooms, accommodate 50 or more people of all the living generations of one family. The same tradition has discouraged the building of apartment houses and tenements in urban centres despite crowded conditions (1931:122-123).

The Japanese while spreading from south to north took with them the house, identified with their culture, although this house was extremely uncomfortable (at least during certain parts of the year) in their new habitat (Rapoport, 1969:22).

Mankind's dwellings...stand as the concrete expressions of complex interaction among cultural skills and norms, climatic conditions and the potentialities of natural materials. (Rapoport has shown how the houses of the world's people thus reflect the physical conditions of their environments as well as cultural preferences and capabilities in a wide variety of solutions to the basic problem of house design (Wagner, 1969:vi).

To use the words of Wagner himself:

> Rapoport has very rightly described that: The house is an institution, not just a structure, created for a complex set of purposes, because building a house is a cutlural phenomenon, its form and organization are generally influenced by the cultural milieu to which it belongs...If provision of shelter is the passive function of the house, then its positive function is the creation of an environment best suited to the way of life of people.
>
> It is often what a culture makes impossible by prohibiting it either implicitly or explicitly, rather what it makes inevitable,

which is significant.

The physical setting provides the possibilities among which choices are made through the taboos, customs and traditional ways of culture. Even when the physical possibilities are numerous, the actual choices may be severely limited by the cultural matrix; this limitation may be the most typical aspect of the dwellings and settlements of a culture (1969:6).

Rapoport observes that inside the dwelling, symbolic attitudes account for the prevalence of symbolic space distribution in the house, courtyard or tent - there seems to be no purely physical basis. He further observes that :

> It is implicitly accepted that there is a link between behaviour and form in two senses: first, in the sense that an understanding of behaviour patterns, including desires, motivations and feelings, is essential to the understanding of built form, since built form is the physical embodiment of these patterns; and, second, in the sense that forms once built, affect behaviour and the way of life...The question, in fact, is concerned with how changes in culture, expressed in behaviour, relate to changes in the environment, as shown by physical form (1969:16).

A good (house) plan reflects a family's social organization. A poor plan usually reflects a building's organization, in terms of structure, or style. As structure and style have but secondary relevance to family life, they are inadequate criteria for design (Kennedy, 1953:105).

The following observations of Charles about houses in Indian villages are very appropriate in this connection :

> The village house, in all of its caste and regional variations, is, first of all, the full material expression of a way of life. It states in a compact and elemental form the summation of village culture. All of the social and religious energy, that is brought to play in the village, finds tangible expression in the form of the house. Each man's attitude towards life, his family, his place in the community, his religious convictions — the totality of his cultural experience - here makes its most direct and elemental statement. To know the village house, is to know the mind of the people who live in it - to see their way of life and understand its architectural implications. (1965:43).

Writing about houses in the Car Nicobar Islands, Mathur (1967:115) states: "A scheme for the welfare of Backward Classes under which good type of timber which is not locally available is procured from Port Blair and made available to the people on subsidised rates has given further impetus to the construction of improved type of houses. Most of these improved types of houses are more or less on the same pattern as the traditional houses".

About a village in Jaunpur, Uttar Pradesh (India) : Previously a closed village but recently opened up, Opler and Singh (1952:8) have observed that "the plan of the houses has not changed essentially, but cement, brick and iron are displacing the old mud walls. To be considered substantial, a *pacca* (brick) house now requires metal beams. Cement is replacing mortar in construction".

It is recognized that villagers have a tradition of building houses, which each region has evolved over a long period of time (Chandhoke, S.K. and Singh, K.B., 1974:67).

Housing conditions in the Saharanpur region of Uttar Pradesh (India), it has been observed, are also to a great extent dependent on and are explained by socio-economic considerations (Singh and Chandhoke, 1969:3).

In a large-scale house construction activity in a predominantly Mina (Scheduled Tribe) inhabited village in Rajasthan where a considerable change in the condition of individual houses has taken place is that *katcha* houses have given place to *pacca* houses and also there is a shift from smaller accommodations to larger ones. Architecturally, however, the construction activity has perpetuated the traditional Court-House Plan form in the village (Singh and Chandhoke, 1967:17-18).

Similarly, in village Bhawanpura, also in Rajasthan, where a set of demonstration houses embodying a number of new ideas and techniques were constructed and a lot of extension activities were carried out by the Regional Rural Housing Centre of the Ministry of Works and Housing, Government of India, then functioning in the School of Planning and Architecture, New Delhi, an Assessment Survey of the Project conducted by the Centre itself showed that out of the nine houses constructed in the village during a period of three to four years after the completion of the demonstration project, six followed the traditional Court-House design. "The three houses constructed on the pattern of the demonstration houses belong to villagers who, of late, have been enjoying the reputation of being *netas* (leaders) of the local community. They owe their allegiance to a political party some of the leaders of which were largely, although indirectly, associated with the choice of the location of this demonstration project in Bhawanpura (Singh and Chandhoke, 1967:3). Moreover, all these three houses belonged to the *gair-biswedaran* whose houses, not being very elaborate and substantial ones, are even otherwise not built on the Court-House plan.

An idea of the reason for selecting a rural house design for study is clear in the observations of Charles (quoted earlier) and the following views of Rapoport :

> Modern man has lost the mythological and cosmological orientation, which was so important to primitive man, or has substituted new mythologies in place of the old.
>
> It is the tract house rather than the architect-designed house that needs to be discussed in order to discover which of the values it represents might help explain its success.
>
> We may say that the monuments - buildings of the grand design tradition - are built to impress either the populace with the power of the patron, or the peer group of designers and cognoscenti with the cleverness of the designer and good taste of the patron. The folk tradition, on the other hand, is the direct and unself-conscious translation into physical form of a culture, its needs and values - as well as the desires, dreams and passions of a people. It is the worldview writ small, the "Ideal" environment of a people expressed in buildings and settlements, with no designer, artist, or architect with an axe to grind (although to what extent the designer is really a form giver is a moot point). The folk tradition is much more closely related to the culture of the majority and life as it is really lived than is the grand design tradition, which represents the culture of the elite. The folk tradition also represents the bulk of the built environment (1969:2).

There is some confusion about the extension of human settlements. In this connection a number of questions occur to one's mind. Some of the questions raised by Doxiadis (1968:25) are: Is a human settlement only the built up space created by man for his uses? Is it only the covered space? If so, a house is a settlement and its garden is not, or the house and the garden are a settlement but the part beyond the garden wall is not. And even assuming that all these and the streets as well belong to the settlement, can we also say that the park within the city is a part of it? If so, can we extend the boundaries of the settlement into the open countryside? Is a natural park part of a settlement?

No human habitation can be studied effectively at any one level - micro or macro. The two levels are very much interrelated and these must be studied in conjunction with each other. Rapoport (1969:69) has very rightly observed that the house cannot be seen in isolation from the settlement, but must be viewed as part of a total social and spatial system which relates the house, way of life, settlement and even landscape. Man lives in the whole settlement of which the house is only a part, and the way in which he uses the settlement affects house form. Geography, as well as architecture, has usually separated study of the house from that of the settlement, yet the need to look at the house as part of a larger system confirms that the house conveys little sense outside of its setting and context. Because the living pattern always extends beyond the house to some degree, the form of the house is affected by the extent to which one lives in it and the range of activities that takes place in it.

To quote Rapoport further in this connection:

> There is a perceptive comment by Karl Capek regarding England: "The poetry of the English home exists at the expense of the English street which is devoid of poetry" and that street has been described as "the empty street, the lonely street". This does not fully apply to the working class streets, i.e., the more vernacular setting, where the street is used, although far less than it is in Latin countries.
>
> It is clear that the form of the settlement affects the way of life and the house...
>
> The settlement pattern can also affect attitudes to innovations, as in the cases of the Navajo and Zuni. When veterans came back after World War II, the Navajo, who have a dispersed living pattern, were able to accept innovation because it affected only the single household and did not disrupt the community. Among the Zuni, whose settlement pattern is compact, any innovation would have affected the whole community and was resisted.
>
> Houses, settlements and landscapes are products of the same cultural system and worldview, and are, therefore, part of a single system. In traditional Japan, for example, the separation of domains results in each house being isolated and each household doing what

it wishes; as long as common values are shared, variations in house form within an order produce good results. Once the shared values disappear or are weakened, the same attitudes produce the visual chaos of the Japanese city today. No one takes responsibility for the public area because it is little used as part of the total living realm. The Japanese word for town is the same as that for street. Since the street was never meant to be used by the citizens, it and its houses are regarded very differently than they are in the West.

It is, therefore, important to see the house not only in relation to the basic dichotomy of settlement types as settings for life and their variants along the total space-use scale, but also as part of the specific system to which it belongs. It needs to be viewed in relation to the town, its monumental parts, non-domestic areas and social meeting places, and the way they and the urban spaces are used - we need only think of the different ways in which the dwelling is used in Paris and in Los Angeles for this need to become clear. In addition we must consider movement from the house, through the various transitions to the street, and then to the other parts of the settlement.

There are two ways in which the effect of the site on the building can be considered. The first would deal with the physical nature of the site - its slope, type of rock or soil, run-off, vegetative cover, micro-climate and so on; the second would consider the symbolic religious or cultural values of the site and their consequences. While the physical nature of the site does affect builing form, as in the case of steeply sloping site, it is the initial choice of site that introduces this variable. In this choice access to food or water, exposure to wind, defensive potential, the sparing of land for agriculture, and transformation all play a role. Defence may lead to the choice of a high point in the curve of a river, the shore of a lake, or a steep hill. For trade the presence of a ford may be a consideration, and for transportation in a jungle the bank of a river may be important. In the final analysis the choice of site depends largely on socio-cultural values, which help explain why the Meo in South-east Asia pick hills for their houses. While the need to preserve arable land plays a role in the siting of the Peruvian marca, the houses of New Caledonia, or the Pueblos, the latter are found on both the plains and mesa tops, their siting related to the six cardinal points and the sacred directions of North and East.

Siting and, to a degree, building form are mainly the result of

> social factors which may include family or clan structure and grouping; relation to animals and the spatial relations with them, as with the Masai; relation to grain, as in the Cameroons and the Pueblos; attitudes to nature; the needs of magic and sacred orientation; and the symbolism of landscape features. The choice of what is regarded as a good site brings with it physical effects and some consequent adjustments. The influence of physical effects on the siting of buildings and hence on their forms and relations can be strong...
>
> The fact that sites are chosen on the basis of myth, religion and way of life rather than on utilitarian or physical grounds has been pointed out by a number of writers... (1969:72-74).

The following observations of Sims (1928) about the American farm home are also, to a certain extent, true of the dispersed habitations in other parts of the world including India:

> To the farm family, home means not merely the house but the whole farm. It is a little world - homestead - encompassing the domestic sphere with the domains of other families fenced out. Said a farm woman: "You don't think of your home on a farm as just a space inside four walls. The feeling of home spreads out all around into the garden, the orchards, the hen-houses, the barn, the springhouse, because you are all the time helping to produce live things on those places and they, or their products, are all the time coming back into your kitchen from garden, orchard, barn or hen-house, as a part of the thing you handle or prepare for meals or market every day. It is one of those peculiarities of making a home on the farm.

The ideas of a people about their houses reflect their ideas of the universe and their world view. Their ideas about sacred and profane, their native system of classification in general and categorization of spaces in particular, and their concepts of space are more important than the use of space. The divisions and interrelations of space are more important than the elements of house construction. The internal system is more important than the external system, structure is more important than the environment, intrinsic structure is more meaningful than the extrinsic environment.

After a detailed study of the published literature on the subject and a reasonably good deal of theoretical work, I explored the value of some concrete data to handle the theoretical material, especially because the subject of rural habitation is of a relatively unexplored character. So, I undertook field-work in a Haryana village, near Delhi, in the summer of, 1972 and in the winter of, 1972-73, although I had otherwise already been working on the improvement of physical environment in this and surrounding villages since the late 1960s. Ever since then, I have been maintaining constant contacts with the village and its inhabitants by frequent visits and otherwise. In certain respects, the information about the village contained in this book has been updated till August, 1987, while in some others, where any change, it was feared, could distort the total picture and analysis, it has been intentionally kept unchanged.

For the subsequent discussions and analysis, etc., I have also extensively drawn upon my own three decades of field experiences in other regions of Haryana and in villages (including tribal habitations) in some other parts of the country, especially in the States of Bihar, Rajasthan and Uttar Pradesh and the Union Territory of Delhi.

NOTES

1. Lack of space here does not permit a detailed discussion of the topic which itself can be the subject matter of at least a number of articles, if not a couple of books.
2. Actually, the material contained in this book formed the fifth part of the original manuscript of "Ancient Society" under the title "Growth of the Idea of House Architecture."
3. Singh is basically a geographer.

THREE

THE VILLAGE, ITS LOCATION AND HISTORY

3.1 LOCATION OF THE VILLAGE

CHHATERA BAHADARPUR, named after its founder Chhatar Singh, is a medium-sized Jat village of Haryana, located at 77° 2' 30" east longitudes and 28° 54' 40" north latitudes. Situated about 40 km north of Delhi, the village falls in Sonepat Tehsil of the same district.[1] (Please refer to Fig. 3.1)

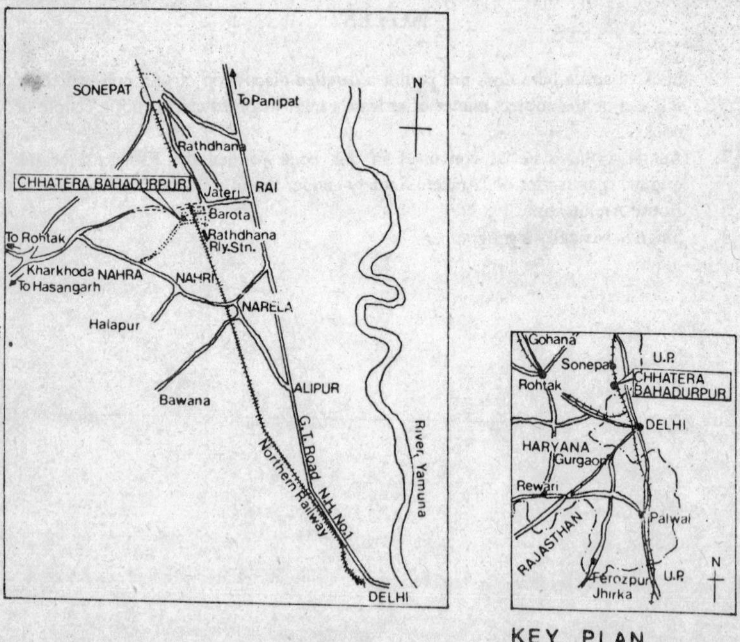

Figure 3.1: Location Plan of Chhatera

The village is located near two important drains (No. 6 and No. 8) which play an important role in the life and living in the village. During the rainy season, these drains flood some of the fields in the village and create pools of stagnant water which act as breeding grounds for mosquitoes. Drain No. 8 passes through the village *abadi* itself and divides its agricultural fields into two parts. Till about 1971 when there was no bridge over this drain, the village used to get partially cut-off from the rest of the State for about three-four months in a year. Every year a few human as well as cattle lives used to drown while crossing the drain. A temporary narrow cradle-like hanging bridge did exist on this drain. But it catered to the pedestrians only, and in that too the wooden planks on its base used to get submerged, at times even washed away, whenever the drain-water was in its fury. In 1972, a two-lane *pacca* bridge was constructed on this drain. Now heavy vehicles can also ply on this bridge. A *pacca* road was constructed by the Public Works Department of the Haryana government which connects Chhatera with Nahra, Bahadargarh and some other important places. This bridge and the connecting roads have opened up Chhatera to the rest of the country.

The nearest railway station, Rathdhana, (on the Delhi-Amritsar main line) is only one mile from the village *abadi*. A major part of the approach road to the railway station has now been metalled. By road, the village can be approached from Narela. Chhatera can also now be reached from Biswan Mil on the Grand Trunk Road (National Highway No. 1) through a seven km stretch of road. Moreover, there is a drain between Chhatera and Biswan Mil which does not have a bridge over it and cannot be easily crossed during the rainy season. There is as yet no bus service connecting Chhatera with the other parts of the State. The nearest bus stops are at Nahra for Rohtak, Rai for Sonepat and Delhi, and Lampur for Narela and Delhi.

The Block Development Office and the Police Station at Rai are seven km away. The nearest government dispensary in village Halalpur is also seven km from Chhatera. The village has a co-educational government middle school. The nearest high schools at Nahra and Mondora, and the nearest college at Sonepat are two, five and eleven km away, respectively.

3.1.1 *The Region*

The information regarding climate, topography and crops, mentioned here, is about Village Chhatera and the region around it. The climate of the region is dry with a very hot summer and a cold winter, and there are four seasons. The cold season starts by late November and extends till about the middle of March. This is followed by the hot season which continues till about the end of June. July to September is the South-West Monsoon season. October and November constitute a transitional period between the monsoon and winter.

January is the coldest month when the mean daily maximum temperature is about 21°C (69.8°F) and the mean daily minimum about 7°C (44.6°F). In the winter months, minimum temperature may sometimes go down to the freezing point and frost may occur. From about the middle of March, temperature begins to rise rapidly. May and June are the hotest months. From April, the hot westerly winds, locally known as *luh*, blow and the heat is extreme. In May and June, the maximum temperature may sometimes reach about 47°C (116.6°F). With the advance of the South-West Monsoon into the area towards the end of June, day temperature drops appreciably while night temperature continues to be as high as in the summer. Even during the brief South-West Monsoon, the weather is damp and the air being stagnant uncomfortable, in between the spells of rain. In October, the day temperature is as high as during the monsoon months but the nights are cooler.

The air is dry during the greater part of the year. During the monsoon months, the humidity is high. April and May are usually the driest months, humidity in the afternoon being less than 20 per cent. On an average, there are 16 rainy days (i.e., days with rainfall as 2.5 mm or more) in a year. The average annual rainfall is around 41 mm. Winds are generally light during the post-monsoon and winter months and are a little stronger during the summer and monsoon months. April to June is the period with the highest incidence of thunderstorms and duststorms.

Chhatera falls in the upland plain. The region slopes towards the south.

There are two well-defined crops, kharif and rabi. The main kharif crops are sugarcane, cotton, *jawar* (green small sprouts of barley), *bajra* (Indian corn, pearl millet), rice, maize and *gwara* (an annual plant whose seeds are used as pulse); the minor crops are chillies, pulses, vegetables, *til* (the sesamum plant and its seeds), *san* (a kind of flax, hemp), fruits, etc. The main rabi crops are: wheat, gram, barley, oil-seeds, *barseem* (a sort of green fodder), *methi* (fenugreek), tobacco, potato and vegetables.

3.2 VILLAGE HISTORY

Village Chhatera is about 120 years old. There are different versions about the history of the village. One version is that of the Jats of Chhatera themselves, the second is that of the Brahmans of Chhatera which is also supported by some of the Jat residents of the neighbouring village Malha Majra, the third is the record of the Bhat[2], while the fourth version is the one contained in the records of the Revenue Department. In this region, the "... local tradition tells of three or four old sites within the area of almost every estate, but many of these have disappeared under the plough" (Purser and Fanshawe, 1880:10).

3.2.1 *Version of the Jats of Chhatera*

According to the Jats of Chhatera, one Chhatar Singh - an ex-Serviceman - originally of village Kundlain (district Karnal) was allotted this land by the British Government as a reward for his meritorious services in the army, Chhatar Singh came here and settled down at the site where the *laihnda* (community/collective place for cattle) of the present village is located. But soon after that, an epidemic broke out here. So, Chhatar Singh shifted to the nearby village of Malha Majra. While in Majra, Chhatar Singh started the work of founding a village at the present site of Chhatera and shifted here after the *kot*, etc., had been completed. They further say that when Chhatar Singh shifted to the present site, he also brought a cook, Pandit Kewal Ram, with him. Chhatar Singh had four sons one of whom died issueless. The share of that son, in Chhatar Singh's property, was given to Kewal Ram. It is due to this reason, they say, that the ownership of the village is shared by the Jats and Brahmans in the proportion of three : one, i.e., 75 per cent and 25 per cent, respectively, or, to put it colloquially, twelve annas and four annas, respectively.[3]

3.2.2 *Version of the Brahmans of Chhatera supported by the Jats of Majra*

As per the version of the Brahmans of Chhatera - which is also supported by the Jats of Majra - goes, Chhatar Singh came here from Kundlain. At that time the present site of the Chhatera *abadi* and the area around it was a dense jungle having wild vegetation infested with ferocious animals. Chhatar first settled at the *thal*, a higher land near the present *abadi* of the village. Some time after that there occurred an epidemic and these people shifted to Malha Majra. At that time there were two *tholas* (sectors) of Jats in Majra, namely, *Birkhan-thola* and *Pauli-thola*. These Chhaterans settled in the *Pauli-thola*. In their talks, there is also reference to a fierce fight between these new-comers and a passing contingent of the Muslim army which was infuriated due to firing by a local *Teli* (oil man) at one of the Muslim soldiers offering prayers near the village *johar*. A large number of Jats died during this fight. Those who survived fled away from village Majra and settled down temporarily in nearby villages, whereever they could get shelter. After a few years they started returning to Majra - a typical characteristic of the Jats.[4] While living in Majra they cleared the present site, dug a *johar* and a *kuwan* and built a *kot*. They also constructed a wall along the *kot*, built a few *ghars* inside it and shifted there.

The Chhaterans felt insecure because, being new-comers, they had no friends or relatives around. During those disturbed periods in the history (of this region) it was very difficult for a small village to defend itself all alone. Villages in this region belong to Dahiya Jats. But all the Jats of Chhatera belong to Jun *gotra*. So, therefore, before shifting from Majra to the new site of Chhatera they married out five of their daughters to the Jats of the neighbouring villages. Now they were no longer strangers. The *sala-jija* relationship thus established, automatically developed into *mama-bhanja* relationship in the next generation. So, these new settlers shifted to the new site under the umbrella of support and protection of their new relations in the surrounding villages.

Excepting the Jats, all members of all other castes - Brahmans, Jogis, *Nais, Lohars, Khatis, Chamars* and *Bhangis* - who came to Chhatera at the time of its founding at the present site were originally the permanent residents of Majra. While some families of these castes moved to Chhatera, others stayed back in Majra. In fact, there were cases where even some members of the same family migrated to Chhatera while others remained in Majra. These service caste people were sent to Chhatera by the village community of Majra with a firm assurance that if the former faced any difficulty in the new village, they would be taken back into Majra and adequately helped to re-settle there.

For quite some time after migrating to the new village some of the Chhaterans had been tilling some of their lands in Majra. For a long time, the two villages had even a common *chaukidar*. The boundary line between Chhatera and Majra is a long diagonal one. This provides, to the residents of the two villages, the maximum opportunity to have intensive social interaction, meet each other in their *khets* every day and exchange news and notes. The two villages, thus, have very strong common bonds.

3.2.3 *Version of the bahi bhat*

It is difficult to use the *bahi bhat*, i.e., the records of the *bhat* of Chhatera for tracing the history of the village. Their *bhat* died long ago without leaving any male issue. His *bahis* were transferred to his son-in-law who also subsequently died without any male issue. The *bahis* were ultimately inherited by the sister's son of the new *bhat*. The present *bhat* has inherited the records of the original *bhat* of Chhatera, but he utterly lacks the skill and a lot of other information which the sons of *bhats* automatically inherit verbally (during the course of their up-bringing) from their fathers, grandfathers and other retatives. So the present *bhat* is not able to interpret the records properly to the extent that these may throw enough light on the founding and history of the village.

3.2.4 *Version in the revenue records*

Records of the revenue department (Settlement Report of Chhatera 1880) give yet a different picture of the history of the village. These records mention : It is heard that one Mohan, chief heir of the Jat community and of Jun *got*, was originally the resident of *mauza* Kundlain of Karnal district. After coming to Delhi he joined service on some post in the *darbar* of the king of that time. One Kewal, chief heir of the Brahman caste, resident of *mauza* Balamb, district Hissar, was also working there in the *darbar* on some post. Mohan and Kewal did some work which was very highly appreciated by the officers of the *darbar*. As a reward for this meritorious service rendered by Mohan and Kewal, the officers awarded to them the ownership of this village (which at that time was an un-inhabited jungle) for inhabiting it.

So, Mohan and Kewal obtained possession of this land. Since then ownership of the village has been of these two *gotras*. Possession of the adjoining *bhur* (waste land) was subsequently given to one Ram Rattan, vide order of the revenue department dated 5th July, 1864. There has not been any distribution of shares among them, i.e., and Jats and Brahmans, but the collectors of revenue have been mentioned. There are sectors named as *thola*-Jatan and *thola*-Brahmanan; and as per the tradition, one share is for *thola*-Brahmanan and three shares for *thola*-Jatan.

On getting possession of the land, Mohan and Kewal founded a new village and for some time they lived here. Mohan was also known as Chhehatar. Therefore, he named this village as Chhatera - a case of typonomy. But after a few years, due to their inability to pay revenue to the government these new settlers got uprooted from here, went to Malha Majra and settled there. They also started cultivating land in Malha Majra and, therefore, the *abadi* of Chhatera became uninhabited. At that time a person named Bahadar was appointed by the revenue department as the royal *ahlkar* and posted at Chhatera for managing the land revenue of this village. Bahadar re-named the village as Chhatera Bahadarpur - another case of typonomy.

It would have been 60[5] years ago, the Report (Settlement Report of Chhatera of 1880) states, that these people came back from Malha Majra and again settled down at the same place.

3.3 THE TYPE OF VILLAGE FROM THE POINT OF VIEW OF REVENUE SETTLEMENT (LAND TENURE SYSTEM)

Regarding the geneal variety of revenue settlement of the villages in India as a whole, Srinivas states thus :

> Earlier writers like Maine distinguished between twin type of villages in India - the Joint and the Severalty. The 'Joint type' may further be sub-divided into the *Pattidari* and *Zamindari* sub-types, in both of which the village lands constitute the joint property of an organized proprietary body. But while in the *Pattidari* system the joint families constituting the proprietary body own separate shares in the cultivable land and hold the waste and pasture lands in common, in the *Zamindari* system all land is held and managed in common and not divided. In the latter sub-type, the tenants, if any, are the tenants of the whole body of proprietors, their rents and other receipts are paid into a common fund from which common expenses are met; and the annual profits are divided among the co-sharers according to their respective shares. In a Joint village, there are two classes of men, one with proprietary rights, the other without them, power resting exclusively with the former.

(1951:1051).

Ibbetson has given the following classification of villages in Rohtak district :

(A) Villages held wholly in common by the body of owners - *Zamindari*

(B) Villages divided among the several branches of the community according to the ancestral shares - *Pattidari*

(C) Villages held in severalty by the individual households, the holding of each being quite independent of any fixed scale - *Bhayachara* (Ibbetson 1883).

According to this classification, Chhatera is a Joint type of village, falling in the *Pattidari* sub-type.

3.4 CONSTITUTION OF THE PROPRIETARY BODY

The households of the agriculturist group, who settle in a village at the time it is founded, constitute its proprietary body. The non-agriculturists, even those who come at the time the village is founded, are not included in the proprietary body. Those agriculturist households who migrate into the village, after it has already been founded and occupied, are also normally not given these rights. It is only under very exceptional circumstances that such agriculturists can acquire the proprietary rights. Even when an outsider purchases agricultural land in a village, unless he gets it specifically mentioned in the sale deed that the seller is transferring to the purchaser his rights (which are always in proportion to the amount of land sold) in the common lands of the village also, i.e., the proprietary rights, the purchaser does not acquire these rights automatically.

To quote Ibbetson in this connection :

> The proprietary body proper, which forms the nucleus, round which the subsidiary parts of the community are grouped, includes all those who have rights of ownership in the common land of the village. It is seldom wholly confined to one single family, strangers having almost always obtained admission in some or the other ways ... and very often the community will consist of two distinct tribes, or gentes of the same tribe, holding more or less equal share in the

village (1883:92).

Members of the proprietary body are called *biswedaran*, and others *be-biswedaran*[6] or *gair-biswedaran.*

Nath, Y.V.S. (1954:1356 & 1358) has also noted a similar distinction among the Bhils of Ratanmals. These groups are called *Bhaibetta* (literally, Children of Brothers, here 'kindred') of the village, and the *Karhan* (literally, tenant), respectively.

In the words of Ellis :

> The site of the *abadi* originally belongs to the proprietary body. And the *Gair Malik* settled in the village even if it has extended into a town, cannot sell either the site or the house...when the land is given for building the presumption is that the donee acquires occupancy rights and cannot be evicted at will (1917:305).

Similarly, Baden-Powell (1913:71-72) has also given a description of this phenomenon, while Gangulee (1935: xvii-xviii) has mentioned the main classifications of the Indian land system, viz., *ryotwari* and *zamindari*.

3.5 OWNERSHIP OF LAND WITHIN THE *ABADI*

All the membres of the proprietary body have a share in the rights in the village. Certain parts of the village, like the *abadi* land (leaving, of course, certain places like the *chaupal* etc.) are divided. But there are certain parts of the village, like the *charagah, chehanrin*, jungles etc. which can never be divided at all. These are always to be held in common. In every village there is always some confusion and consequently sometimes a dispute, on this issue, i.e., about the distribution of the divisible land.

According to the Customary Law of the region, a *biswedar* has share in the *abadi* land in the same proportion as his share in the land outside the *abadi* (i.e., in the *khets*). For example, in a village with 1,000 acres of agricultural land and ten acres of *abadi* land, if a person owns 100 acres (i.e., 10 per cent) of agricltural land in the village, then his share in the *abadi* land would be one acre (also 10 per cent). Generally it is because of this reason that density in the various sectors of *abadi* inhabited by the different sections of the village community is different. Density is the highest in the sectors occupied by the *be-*

biswedaran. But in actual practice, the entire *abadi* land in any village is seldom fully divided. From time to time, villagers ask the elders of the proprietary body for plots of land, and are allotted the same on the merits of each individual case. Hence, in every village some residential land (divisible land within the *abadi*) is always lying undivided. Those who have influence in the village, often cleverly manage to corner (grab) more land than their due share. In such a situation, the remedy open to the aggrieved villagers is that one or more members of the proprietary body may file a petition in a Civil Court praying for a proper and equitable re-distribution of the *abadi* land. After the preliminary hearing, if the case is admitted, the Court appoints a Commission (consisting of an experienced member of the bar) to study the matter in detail and submit its report. The Commission, taking the help of some technical person, conducts a physical survey of the *abadi* area and submits the results of this also along with its report, to the Court. After completing the necessary formalities, the Court pronounces its verdict.

This process of re-distribution of *abadi* land is called *bhai-batwara*, meaning the distribution among brothers. *Bhai-batwara* is also of two types. One type is called *qabza bahal* (literally, re-instating the occupation / possession) and the other is *qabza tor* (literally, breaking or evicting the occupation / possession). In both the cases, the land which any person is occupying above his normal / due share is taken away from him and restored to those who are in possession of less land than their due share. The main difference between the two methods - *qabza bahal* and *qabza tor* - being, that while in the case of *qabza bahal* if one has put up any structure, i.e., if the land has been constructed upon, its occupant is not evicted from that land, while in the case of *qabza tor*, if necessary, even demolitions are resorted to. In actual life, cases of *qabza tor* are very few in villages in this region. This is so because the process involved in it is very lenghty; time-consuming and cumbersome. Moreover, it creates lasting animosity among the concerned individuals, households and bigger groups. In the entire history of village Chhatera, there has been only one case of *qabza bahal*. The petition was filed in 1948, and the case was decided in 1951. It is really an interesting and informative experience to go through the details of the entire case.

NOTES

1. Till December 1972, Sonepat Tehsil formed a part of Rohtak district of Haryana. For details please see Appendix IX.
2. In many parts of India, there is a specialized caste called Bhat, somewhat akin to that of the bards. The male members of this caste group maintain detailed accounts of their *jajman* (patron) households, their histories, geneological trees and important events. The records maintained by these Bhats are considered to be so authentic that it is not uncommon to summon the same in Courts of Law to assist in deciding cases.
3. Before 1957 when India, switched over its currency to the metric system, a rupee was divided into 16 annas.
4. For details please refer to Appendix V.
5. It may be remembered that this report was published in 1920.
6. *Biswa* is a locally used measure of land. Hence, the term *biswedar* (plural, *biswedaran*), meaning the landlord/s.

FOUR

SOCIAL STRUCTURE

4.1 POPULATION AND CASTE COMPOSITION

CHHATERA IS inhabited by about 1,200 persons living in 158 households. The caste-wise break-up of these households is given in Table 4.1.

TABLE 4.1: Caste composition of Chhatera village

(Total population = 1,200

Sl. No.	Caste Group	No. of Households
1.	Upper	89
2.	Middle	33
3.	Lower	36
	Total	158

Source: Field data 1972.

The upper caste group includes Jats, Brahmans and Baniyas. The middle caste group consists of *Jogi, Lohar, Khati, Nai, Kumhar* and *Sunar* castes. The lower caste group comprises of *Chamars* and *Bhangis*. *Jogis* and *Sunars* are included in Backward Classes while *Chamars* and *Bhangis* are treated as Scheduled Castes in Haryana. The percentage that the Jats, Harijans and Brahmans, respectively, form of the total population of the village and the average size of household of these caste groups is given in Table 4.2.

TABLE 4.2: Population percentage and average size of household of Jats, Harijans and Brahmans in Chhatera village

Sl. No.	Name of the Caste Group	Population as percentage of Total Village Population	Average size of Household
1.	Jats	44.8	8.4
2.	Harijans	34.9	6.9
3.	Brahmans	20.3	7.0
	Total	100.0	7.6

Source: (a) Field data 1972
(b) Ghosh and Kulsreshta 1973

4.2 THE VILLAGE / LOCAL COMMUNITY - A PROFILE

The following observations of Sachchidananda are quite appropriate in this connection:

> Village communities all over India present certain common features. The structural bonds of a village are quite distinct from the bonds of kin, caste and class. This bond plays a significant role in the socialization of children and in social control. The different castes and communities living in the village are knit together in an economic, social and cultural configuration based on mutual obligations, common customs and a common past (1956:327).

Quite in line with these remarks of Sachchidananda, the Chhatera community too is an inter-woven check-pattern of various castes. In the Indian village, there is a very well and intricately worked out system of exchange of services. This system, called *jajmani* system (from the word *jajman*, meaning patron), clearly lays down the rights and obligations of the various caste groups in the village. The *jajmani* institution is one of the forces that sustain the vertical unity of the village communities. Not all the castes in a village are necessarily always linked by this net of relationships. The roles and rights of the various sections of every village community are documented in the *shart-wajib-ul-arz* (an appendix to the revenue settlement report of the village). This appendix is reviewed and revised at the time of every subsequent settlement of the village. But these rules are otherwise too well-known to every villager. The rights of the service castes, as contained in the above-said document, are the minimum and it has been observed that, in actual practice, the service castes get much more than what has been enshrined in the revenue record.[1]

Since economic production is the basic activity of a human aggregate, the mode of production (productive forces and social forces of production) play a determining role in shaping the social structure, the psychology and ideology of that human aggregate (Desai, 1961:28). Among those sections of the Chhatera community who are on the *jajmani* system, a cultivator is addressed as *jajman* by his *Purohit* and *Nai* only, while others, like, *Lohar*, *Khati* and *Bhangi* address him as their *kisan*. The cultivator addresses all of them by their respective caste names like, *Nai*, *Lohar* and *Khati*. In this respect, he makes no distinction between different castes.

JAT : There are 44 Jat households in Chhatera. All of them, barring two, who came here later, are the direct descendants of Chhatar Singh, the founder of the village, and belong to Jun *gotra* (non-localized patrilineal clan). Although immediately before coming to Chhatera, they had been living in the neighbouring village of Malha Majra, they originally came from village Kundlain (about 80 kms. in the north-west of Chhatera) in Karnal district of Haryana. The two non-Jun households in the village are those of the sons of one Ram Chand of Dagar *gotra*. Ram Chand had been adopted by his *nana* (mother's father) who had no son. Ram Chand's paternal village is Kilhor, about 15 kms. from Chhatera. So far as government records are concerned, Ram Chand had adopted Jun *gotra*, because without that, under the law existing at that time, it would not have been possible for him to inherit his *nana*'s property. Ram Chand's descendants practise exogamy in respect of both the *gotras*, i.e., their own (Dagar) as well as of Ram Chand's *nana*'s (Jun).

The Jats of Chhatera are agriculturists. So far as proprietary rights in the village are concerned, Jats are the masters of practically the entire village, holding 75 per cent share in the proprietary rights. Jats have been rightly referred to by Campbell as admirable cultivators. He has truly written that:

> They have great physical and moral energy, are admirable cultivators and, under a fair system, excellent revenue payers, are prodigiously tenacious of their rights in land and very orderly and well behaved when in possession of these rights, in fact in every

way they are beyond doubt the finest population in India (Purser and Fanshawe, 1880:54 from Campbell).

To quote Purser and Fanshawe further in this connection:

Mr. Gubbins has noted that the Jats of Rohtak are inferior to none of their tribe for patient industry and skill, and to those commendations I have nothing to add. The jats call themselves as a tribe "*zamindar*", and they are the true lords of the soil. They are intensely clannish and a man is a clansman before he is a tribesman, and calls himself a *Dahiya, Malik, Hudah* or *Jakkar*, when asked what race he is before he calls himself a Jat. The women assist the men in all tasks of agriculture, except ploughing and driving carts, and to their efforts the renown of the tribe as cultivators is largely due. The Jats are somewhat looked down upon because of the custom of retaining married girls in their father's house for a long number of years, and of *Karewa*, or widow re-marriage, which prevail among them, and in scorn of the latter, this alleged saying of Jat fathers to their daughters is quoted-

Aja Beti, lele phere – yih mar Jawe aur Bahutere

meaning, thereby, come daughter go round the sacred fire,[2] and if this man dies there are many others.

The Jat women help their men to the extent that it is proverbially said:

Bhali Jat Jatin ki Khurpi hat
Khet Nirave Apne Khavind ke Sath

meaning thereby, that the Jat woman has an hoe in her hand and goes to the field weeding with her husband (Purser and Fanshawe, 1880:54).

The Jats are traditionally vegetarians. They neither eat meat nor drink liquor. But now, due to their contact with the outside world, especially of those in the army, a few of them have, to use the expression of the Jats themselves, contacted this 'infection'. As regards smoking, not to speak of the Jats alone, there are not even half a dozen grown up males in the entire village who do not smoke *huka* - the life blood of the *Haryanvis*. Many of the Jat women also smoke, though privately (at least not in the presence of outside men).

The Jats by and large practise monogamy. But in cases, like, barenness and desertion, or in the event of the death of a brother, it is not uncommon for a man to go in for another wife. In such a case, the widow is married to one of the brothers of the deceased. Though senior levirate is not completely barred among them the Jats generally practise junior levirate (Ibbetson, 1883:135). The Jats practise sororate also. Majority of the Jats in the older generation are not educated. The daily routine in the life of the Jats does not leave them enough time for cultural development. To quote Mukherji, "... The daily routine in the lives of these peasants passionately devoted to the realm of agriculture does not leave them enough time for their cultural development whether material, intellectual or spiritual..." (1957:20-21).

Till the introduction of statutory *panchayats* (selected village councils to run general administration of the villages) in Haryana, in 1960, the Jats had always been completely dominating on all fronts of the village scene in an unquestionable and almost an unfettered manner. Even today the social, economic, political and practically all other spheres of village life are dominated by them. Except for a short spell of seven years (1965-1972), when a Brahman of Ladpur (a small adjoining village which also forms a part of the Chhatera *panchayat* in order to fulfil the statutory obligation of having at least 1,200 souls in a *panchayat*) was its *sarpanch* (chairman of the village *panchayat*), the Chhetera *panchayat* has always been headed by a Jat. Although with the implementation of the universal adult franchise, the balance of power has slightly changed now still the Jats generally get everything that they want done. About 40 persons among the Jats of Chhatera are working outside the village, most of them in Delhi. Quite a few Jats from Chhatera, as from other villages in the region, are serving in the armed forces.

BRAHMANS: There are 44 Brahman households in Chhatera. The caste-prescribed traditional occupation of Brahmans is teaching and preaching. Except the *purohit* (the priest who presides over the religious, social and life-cycle ceremonies) all the other Brahmans of Chhatera are the direct descendants of one Kewal Ram, who came here from village Malha Majra and settled here at the time Chhatera was founded. Only the *Purohit* came afterwards. Brahmans of Chhatera are of Alamba *gotra* (non-localized patrilineal clan). Their original *nikas* (place of origin, or, more, literally, the outlet) is from village Balam, near Sonepat. The Brahmans of Chhatera are all agriculturists. They hold 25 per cent share in the proprietary rights in the village. But their population is almost half that of the Jats. As the land within the *abadi* (inhabited area) is owned in the proportion of one's share in the proprietary rights in the agricultural land in the village, density in the Brahman sector of the *abadi* is almost 50 per cent as high as that in the Jat sector. Though owning only 25 per cent share in the proprietary rights in the village, the Brahmans occupy the highest position in the caste hierarchy.

All the Brahmans of Chhatera are strictly vegetarian, they neither eat meat nor drink liquor. But almost all of them smoke *huka* (hubble-bubble). The Brahmans are comparatively more religious-minded, orthodox, conservative and ritualistic than the Jats and other sections of the Chhatera community. They are mild in their manners, talk and behaviour. Brahmans do not practise widow re-marriage, though sororate is permissible among them. Although among older generations one does not find more literacy among the Brahmans than among the Jats, the former are more informed of and acquainted with the scriptures and other classical Hindu philosophy. As stated earlier, the population of Brahmans is almost 50 per cent as that of the Jats. But land with them being only one-fourth of the total land in the village, a large number of educated members of the former group have taken up salaried jobs in Delhi and other places. Though the Jats and Brahmans live side by side and peacefully there has never been any open conflict between the two groups — there is a perpetual feeling of rivalry among them and an urge to dominate over each other as well as over the affairs of the village.

PUROHIT: In Hinduism there is an institution of the *Purohit*. The *Purohit* has invariably to be a Brahman. The *Purohit* presides over all the religious and life-cycle ceremonies in the family of his *jajman* (patron). No such function can be performed without the *Purohit*. As all the Brahmans of Chhatera are agriculturists, none of them performs the functions of the *Purohit*. So, soon after founding the new village, the Jats of Chhatera invited a *Purohit* household from village Malha Majra to come and live in Chhatera and was immediately given a plot of land. The *Purohit* belongs to the same *gotra* as the other Brahman households of Chhatera. But he is not from the same lineage. The descendants of this *Purohit* act as the *Purohit*s only of the Jats and not of any other caste group of Chhatera.

The Jats have always had a great sense of regard for their *Purohit* who acts as a priest on all the religious festivals and life-cycle ceremonies, right from birth till before the death of all the members of his *jajman* households. The *Purohit* does not preside over the death as well as the post-death ceremonies till the thirteenth day after the death. These ceremonies are presided over by a member of another group called *acharaj* (also known as Maha Brahmans), living in the adjoining village of Ladpur. The wife of the *Purohit*, called *Mishrayn*, conducts ceremonies connected with women and children. She also officiates for the *Purohit* during the latter's absence.

The *Purohit* is paid in cash and kind on festivals and religious ceremonies and on innumerable other occasions in the life of the members of the *jajman* households. The *Purohit* has also been getting land in *dauhli*. Previously this land was scattered in small pieces. The respective *jajmans*, who had given a piece of land to the *Purohit* in *dauhli*, used to cultivate that land and give its produce to the *Purohit* at the time of each harvest. At the time of consolidation of holdings in the village, in 1956, the entire land of the *Purohit* was consolidated into one plot. So, now he cultivates these lands himself. The *Purohit* would never accept *katcha* food (cooked food which is not fried) from any one nor would others accept any food or presents (gifts) from the *Purohit*. The fomer practice is explained by the fear of ritual pollution and the latter by the fear of being involved in the sin of accepting something material from one to whom they must always give and not take from. It has always to be a one-way traffic, the only exception to this rule being *Prashad* (any consecrated eatable given by the *Purohit*). The *purohit* does not share *huka* with any one. For certain purposes, like, eating *khir* (pudding of rice cooked in milk) on occasions like *sankrant* (the first day of every month according to the Bikrami Calendar), the Brahmans of Chhatera act as *Purohit*s for each others. But for all the major ceremonies, the Brahmans too have a *Purohit*. He is one Bala Pandit living in village Mandora, seven km. away.

With the changing times, the attitude of the *jajmans* towards their *Purohit* has also changed and *Purohitgiri* (the profession of a *Purohit*) is no longer a very profitable one. So, the *Purohit* of the Jats of Chhatera has now taken to agriculture and *Purohitgiri* has become his secondary occupation. The local Post Office and the Public Call Telephone Office, attached to it, are in the charge of this *Purohit* - Pandit Tika Ram. One of his sons is serving in Delhi and another in a factory in village Ganaur (near Sonepat).

BANIYA: There are ten Baniya households in Chhatera. One

Baniya, Molar Chand, came to Chhatera about 90 years ago. Molar Chand belonged to Village Derjana - a *nawabi* (Muslim ruler's) village - near Beri, in district Rohtak. Molar was married in a Baniya family of village Mandori, about five kms. from Chhatera. Due to certain reasons Molar quarrelled with his parents and went to *pardes* (outside one's native place) where he earned some *nama* (wealth). After accumulating some wealth, Molar came to village Mandori. Due to the strained relations with his parents, Molar did not want to go back to his native village. Molar's father-in-law requested Molar to settle down with him. But as Molar was a self-respecting man, he declined the offer. Molar's in-laws had business dealings with a few Brahman families of Chhatera and there was no Baniya household in Chhatera at that time. So, through the contacts of his in-laws, Molar came to settle in Chhatera. As there was shortage of population at that time and people had *prem* (affection) for each other, Molar was offered, though temporarily, a house in the village. He was later allotted a plot of land in the Brahman Sector of the *abadi*. Molar was about 25 years old at that time. After settling down in Chhatera, Molar got two sons, Sri Chand and Ram Kishan. All the Baniyas of Chhatera are the direct descendants of Molar Chand and they belong to Bindal *gotra*. They are Vaish Aggarwal.

Traditionally, Baniyas are traders and money-lenders. In times of need they used to lend grains also to the needy villagers. Baniyas used to write the *bahis* (account books) of the *zamindars* (agriculturists), especially of the Jats. Previously the *zamindars* seldom took their produce to the *mandi* for disposal. Generally they used to sell their produce to the Baniya in the village. At times, some outside purchasers would also come to the village for purchasing grains. On reaching the village, these outside purchasers used to contact the local Baniya because the Baniyas also worked as food grain commission as well as weighing agents. It is commonly told by elderly people, belonging to all sections of the village, that Baniyas used to do manipulation in respect of rates, weights, as well as in the matter of making entries in the *bahis*. Even when a *zamindar* entered into an agreement with any trader directly, the former would immediately go to the Baniya, as the grains had to be weighed by the Baniya and entered in the *bahi*. At the time of harvest, the Baniyas would purchase grains from the *kisans* (farmers) at a nominal rate and sell the same back to them during the off season at exorbitant prices or charge very high rate of interest, if given on credit. Baniyas are known in Chhatera, and in the nearby villages, for their notoriety in exploiting the ignorant *zamindars*. It is said, if once anyone comes into the clutches of a Baniya, it would not be possible for him to get out of it, at least for a few generations. On the one hand, the Baniyas would fleece the poor ignorant villagers, on the other, in order to keep their position secured, they would keep the *lambardars* (those in charge of collection of land revenue in a sector of the village), *chawdhris* (headmen) and other such influential people in the village in good homour by making presents of *khil* (charred rice) and *patashe* (sugar drops) to them on occasions like *Diwali, Dussehra* and other festivals.

Agriculturists used to even mortgage their lands and take loan from the Baniyas at such high rates of interest that in 1932-33, during the time of Sir Chhotu Ram (a Jat of Haryana, and a minister in the coalition ministry in the then undivided Punjab under the British), the Baniyas were legally debarred from owning any agricultural land. In fact, nobody belonging to any non-agriculturist caste was allowed to purcahse agricultural land from any member of any agriculturist caste. It is only after Independence, especially since 1953, that the Baniyas have also entered into agriculture. During the days when the Baniyas were not allowed to purchase or mortgage land, they used to overcome the restriction by executing *amanti kawalas* (i.e., trust mortgage) - a novel method by which the land of an agriculturist taking loan from a Baniya would be mortgaged in the name of some other member of the agriculturist group in whom the Baniya had faith. In 1947, the Baniyas of Chhatera suffered a severe financial blow, because all the Muslim residents of the neighbouring village Akbarpur Barota, to whom the Baniyas of Chhatera had lent money, were either killed in the communal riots that followed the partition of the country, or left for Pakistan.

There is a flour mill and a small general merchandise shop in Chhatera run by the Baniyas. One of them is a village doctor while quite a few of them are in service at Delhi. Of all the sections of the local community, the Baniyas, perhaps, have the highest rate of literacy and the highest level of education. As a group, the Baniyas are quite different from other sections of the Chhatera community. In spite of their having lived in the village for almost a hundred years now, the Baniyas of Chhatera look, in all aspects of life, more like urban folk than like ruralites. Baniyas are strict vegetarians, rather teetotallers. They have their separate *huka* and do not inter-dine with any other caste in the village. Baniyas have their houses in the Brahman Sector of the village. If ever, due to the neighbourly persuasion, they eat in the house of any Brahman, they take only *pacca bhojan* (fried food) and even for that they pay *dakshina* to the latter. They have a *Kul dewta* (family deity) and also worship *Durga Bhawani* (Goddess of Power).

KHATI: *Khati* is the village carpenter. There are seven *Khati* households in Chhatera, all of them being the direct descendants of a *Khati* who came here from village Malha Majra at the time Chhatera was founded. *Khati* has to make and repair the *hal* (plough), *gadi* (bullock-cart) and *rahat* (wooden part of the Persian wheel). He also makes and repairs *barnas* (doors), *janglas* (windows), *khats* (bedsteads) as well as many other wooden elements in the house, items of furniture and agricultural implements, of his *kisan* (farmer). During a marriage in his *kisan's* household, the *Khati* helps in splitting up fuel wood into smaller pieces. The workshop of the *Khati*, called *khataur*, is generally attached to his *ghar* (residential house), but often he has to go to the *khets* (agricultural fields) of *kisans* to work there (Please see plate 4.1). For any new thing made by the *Khati*, he is immediately paid in cash or kind, both for the materials used as well as for the labour involved, but the minor repair works he does on *jajmani* basis.

Plate 4.1: Khati (Carpenter) working in the *khataur* attached to his *ghar* (Completely blind man doing all jobs of his trade)

Every year, each of *kisan* household gives to the *Khati* 50 kg. of grain (25 kg. of gram and 25 kg. of *bajra*) for each *hal* used by the *kisan*. A household having only one bullock would give only 25 kg. of grain to the Khati. The *Khati* also gets 200 kg. of *tura* (straw; dry fodder) - 60 kg. wheat straw, 60 kg *jawar* (green small sprouts of barley) straw, and 80 kg. *methi* (fenugreek) and/or *barseem* (a sort of green fodder) straw. The *Khati* is also allowed to take grass (for his own cattle only) from the *khets* (fields) of his *kisans*. During a marriage in his *kisan* household, the *Khati* is paid extra. At the time of sowing every season, the *Khati* visits his *kisan* in the latter's *khets* for carrying out repairs to the *hal* and to other agricultural implements needed there. The *hali* (man behind the plough) gives to the *Khati* between three to five kg. of grain being sown. A *kisan*, who grows sugarcane, gives a *bheli* (lump weighing about four kg.) of *gur* (molasses) to *Khati*. Those who grow sugarcane on bigger plots of land, give to the *Khati* 10 kg. of *gur* for every 40 quintals of sugarcane grown by them. Whenever the *Khati* comes to the *ghar* (residential house) of *kisan* to repair the *chaki* (grinding wheel) of the latter, he is given a *jholi* (lap)-full (i.e., about two to two-and-a-half kg.) of grain.

Though *Khati* is not considered to be an untouchable, the Jats and the Brahmans do not share food and smoke with him. They do not even accept water from the *Khati*.

LOHAR: *Lohar* is the village blacksmith, and a *Lohar* household or two are almost a must for every village. There are Lohars among Hindus as well as among *Mussalmans* (Muhammadans). All the *Lohars* of Chhatera are Hindus. Of the seven *Lohar* households in Chhatera, six are the direct descendants of two *Lohar* brothers, Kale and Gurdial, who came here from village Malha Majra at the time Chhatera was founded while the seventh household came to Chhatera (about 40 years ago) from the neighbouring village of Rathdhana. The *dadi* (father's mother) of Ram Sarup (the present head of this seventh *Lohar* household) was the sister of a *Lohar* of Chhatera. There were too many *Lohar* households in village Rathdhana at that time, so this household shifted to Chhatera.

Lohar has to make and repair the iron parts of the agricultural implements of *kisan* and iron chains for the latter's cattle. During a marraige in *kisan*'s household, the *Lohar* supplies an iron ring which is tied, by the *Purohit*, on the wrist of the person getting married. A major part of *Lohar's* work is done in his *aranrn* (workshop), generally attached to his *ghar* (residential house) (please see plate 4.2). A *kisan* pays to Lohar exactly in the same way as he pays to his *Khati*.

Plate 4.2: Village *Lohar* in his newly-established *Aranrn* getting reddy to start work

For the past some time, some of the *Lohars* have also started cultivating land on *batai* (share-cropping) while three *Lohar* boys of Chhatera have joined government serivice in Delhi. Jats and Brahmans do not share food and *huka* with the *Lohars*.

NAI: *Nai* is the village barber. The two *Nai* households in Chhatera are of two real brothers, the grandsons of one Tokha *Nai* who was brought here by the founders of Chhatera, from village Malha Majra, at the time Chhatera was founded. These two *Nai* households[3] serve only the *biswedaran* of the village. Due to certain reasons, like dispute over payment of dues, some of the Brahman households of Chhatera have also ceased to be the *jajmans* of these two *Nai* households and have become the *jajmans* of a *Nai* of a neighbouring village Akbarpur Barota. This *Nai* (of Akbarpur Barota) serves four Brahman households and also all the Baniya, *Jogi*, *Lohar*, *Khati*, *Sunar* and *Kumhar* households of Chhatera. But hs is not a *hissedar* (partner; shareholder) in the village. If and when the local *Nais* want, they can remove him. This *Nai* has some *jajman* households in his own village also.

Previously (some 40 years ago), one Sibal *Nai* of village Kheri (about three kms. away) came and settled down in Chhatera. According to one version, Tokha *Nai* of Chhatera, having financially fallen in bad times, "mortgaged"[4] some of his clients of Sibal. When Tokha's financial condition improved, he paid back his dues to Sibal and got these "mortagaged" clients released. Thereafter, Sibal and his family went back to their native village Kheri. According to another version, which, on detailed enquiries with a cross-section of the village community, seems to be more authentic, an old *lambardar* (person incharge of collection of land revenue from a sector of the village) suffered an attack of paralysis and Sibal was invited from Kheri to attend on the ailing *lambardar*. After the death of the old *lambardar*, Sibal was given a house-plot near the *chaupal* (men's community place), where the local families are also living. It is further reported, that Sibal had no issue and after his death, therefore, the family ended.

The *Nai* is a man's, rather an household's, most intimate *kamin* (a colloquial expression for the service caste people working on *jajmani* system). Of all the service caste people, the *Nai* is needed most and he is naturally paid the maximum. Duties of the *Nai* include; cropping the hair, shaving and clipping the nails of all the male members of his *jajman* household and of their male guests. When the tobacco crop is harvested, the *Nai* prepares tobacco of his *jajman* to be used in the *huka* for the entire year. In a marriage party or in a *panchayat* (assembly), whenever the *Nai* is present - and he is almost invariably present on all such occasions - he has to fill-in the *chilam* (top earthen portion of *huka* in which tobacco is kept). The *Nai* goes to inform and invite male guests on the occasion of any function in his *jajman* household. He makes *patals* (tree-leaf plates for serving meals, snacks, etc.), assists the *halwai* (sweet-meet maker) by cleaning his utensils and removes the *juth* (left-overs) after the guests have eaten. But the *Nai* does not take the *juth* himself, it is given to the *Bhangi*. In a girl's marriage, the *Nai* also prepares a *mor* (Crown-like headgear of coloured papers) to be worn by the *banri* (bride). During festivals and also on the occasion of functions in the families of their daughters, the Chhaterans send presents of sweets, grains, clothes and money to their daughters. These presents are carried by the Nai. When the *Nai* goes with the presents to the household of his *jajman's* daughter, he is well looked after there. He is respected, fed well and paid also.

The *Nai* is the go-between for all marriages in his *jajman* household. He is the traditional match-maker. On the occasion of a marriage, he has to apply *batna* (paste made of gram flour, turmeric and mustard oil) to the *banra* (bridegroom) and bathe him every day for five to seven days preceding the actual day of marriage. In a girl's marriage, the *Nai* of her father's household loads the *dahej* (dowry) on the conveyance of the *barat* party and he is paid Rs. five for this by the *banra*'s father. Similarly, the *Nai's* wife, called *Nainrn* cleans, oils and ties the hair and clips the nails of the women of her *jajman* household and of their female guests. She removes the *jui* (lice) from their heads. The *Nainrn* also arranges for removal of unwanted hair from secret parts of the body of lady members of her *jajman* household. The *Nainrn* visits her *jajman's ghar* (residential house) once in a week and does all this. Every time the *Nainrn* visits her *jajman*'s *ghar*, irrespective of the number of women she serves in the *ghar*, she is given one kg. of grain. Besides this, she is fed and given something in cash or kind. The *Nainrn* applies *batna* on the body of the *banri* (bride) and bathes her every day for five to seven days preceding the day of marriage. She also goes to inform and invite female guests for functions in her *jajman's* household. The *Nainrn* accompanies the *banri* in her *doli* (bridal coach) to her *sasural* (in-law's place). She is given clothes, cash and other presents by the in-laws of the bride. In the absence of the *Nai*, sometimes the *Nainrn* acts for him also.

On every harvest, the *Nai* is given 30 to 50 kg. of grains by 30 each of his *jajman's* households. At the time of every harvest, Ishwar *Nai* collects about 16 quintals of grain. When *gur* (molasses) is prepared, the *Nai* gets one *bheli* (lump weighing about four kg.) of *gur*. While preparing the tobacoo of his *jajman*, the *nai* takes away his own share of it. On the occasion of a marriage, when a man comes to Chhatera to give *bhat* (presents to one's sister on the occasion of the marriage of her son/daughter) he also pays in cash the *Nai* of his sister's household. On all the other functions also the *Nai* is paid well. Whenever there is any function in the household of the *Nai*, even then he receives presents from his *jajmans*. It is commonly said in villages that *jajman* to a *Nai* is like land to a *kisan*.

Although the *Nai* is very helpful and useful to his *jajman*, if the *Nai* is not paid adequately and is not shown the courtesy and regard that is his due, he creates troubles. At the same time, if he is paid well, the *Nai* can help his *jajman* in building the latter's reputation. To an extent, the reputation and goodwill of a person depends upon the attitude of his *Nai* towards him. In spite of having such a close relation with his

Nai, a *jajman* does not accept water touched by the *Nai*, because it is felt that the *Nai* has to do unclean jobs like cleaning the hair, etc. *Nais* are not on inter-dining or smoking terms with any other section of the village community.

KUMHAR: *Kumhar* is the village potter. There are three *Kumhar* households in Chhatera. The ancestor of the present *Kumhars* of Chhatera, one Mehar Chand, came here from village Dasghara near Delhi Cantt., about 30 years ago. During those days there were too many *Kumhar* households in village Dasghara. So Mehar Chand started moving from village to village in search of a place where he could possibly get suitable livelihood. The non-land-owners feel that they actually do not belong to any particular village. *be-biswedar ka to aise hi chalta hai, jahan mazduri milti hai, ko'i zamin wahan nahin thi, ko'i yahan nahin hai*: meaning thereby, the non-land-owner's fate is like that, only they go wherever they get employment, there also (i.e., in their previous village) they had no land nor do they have any here (in Chhatera). Chhatera, it appeared to Mehar Chand, offered good employment opportunities, because, at that time, there was not a single *Kumhar* household in this village. When Mehar Chand came to Chhatera, he was allowed to live on a plot of uncultivable land belonging to a Jat, named Bojhar. Afterwards, on his request to the village (i.e., the proprietary body), Mehar Chand was allotted a plot of land from the *shamlat* (common land) in the Jogi Sector, where he subsequently built his house.

Important among the wares that are prepared by the *Kumhars* are : *paindha* (a big-sized earthen pot with a medium-sized mouth for storing water), *mungholi* (a smaller-sized earthen pot for storing water and being placed on the *paindha*), *gharia* (a medium-sized earthen pot with a narrow mouth), *karhavani* (earthen pot for boiling milk), *biloni* (earthen pot for churning curds), *baroli* (a medium-size pot in which butter milk is kept for consumption when meals are taken to the fields for those busy working there), *bara* (big-sized pot for storing *ghee* (clarified butter), *map* (earthern jar for measuring wheat), *dhakna* (earthern plates for covering the various types of jars). As the *Kumhars* of Chhatera are not very old residents of this village, they do not work on *jajmani* system. One has to pay the *Kumhar* in cash for any ware purchased from the latter. On the occasion of a marriage, however, if one so likes, he can take from the *Kumhar* whatever earthen wares he needs and leave it for the *gram panchayat* (village council) to decide the amount of money to be paid for these wares.

Some members of these *Kumhar* households have now started

working as agricultural labourers. One *Kumhar* boy is studying in the middle school. All others are absolutely illiterate. The *Kumhars* do not inter-dine or share *huka* with members of any other caste. They belong to Khowal *gotra*, practice *gotra* exogamy and avoid three *gotras* for matrimonial alliances.

JOGI: There are 14 *jogi* households in Chhatera. Traditionally, the *jogis* used to be professional bards and singers. They used to sing devotional songs of chivalry and patriotism, like, *Jaimal, Fateh, Amar Singh Rathor, Jagde Pawar* and *Dulle Bhatti*. They used to go in batches from village to village,[5] camp in a village for five to eight days and perform (in groups of two to three) in front of the *chaupal* (men's community place) and in the sectors inhabited by the 'clean castes'. *Jogis* never performed in the Harijan sectors of any village. The performing groups were rewarded mainly with grains. They would receive the grains and cash collectively and then distribute the same among themselves. This type of singing was their only and exclusive occupation. Only *Jogi* men used to sing, their women did not. In case of illness or spirit possession by any villager, the *Jogis* used to do *jhar phunk* (white magical treatment). Some of them practise it even now, though, due to changed times, villagers feel shy of going to the *Jogis* for this work openly lest they become objects of public ridicule. The *Jogis* do not charge anything for this *jhar phunk* work as such.

In Haryana, *jogis* are considered to be a Backward Class, thereby enjoying certain concessions. The heads of three of the local *jogi* households are the sons of one Jot Ram whose grand-father came here from village Malha Majra at the time Chhatera was founded. They belong to Tur *gotra*. These *jogis* came here on their own and were not invited by the local community. One Sohbat of village Tharaya (a Muslim village near Sonepat) had four sons, two of whom were the sons-in-law of one Jotram Jogi of Chhatera. During the communal riots of 1947 (as a sequel to the partition of the country and the transfer of power), some of the Muslims of village Tharaya were killed while others migrated to Pakistan. The Hindus of Tharaya also left the village in panic and went to nearby villages, wherever they had any relations or connections. Sohbat, along with his sons and grand-children, and also with a couple of his nephews and their families, migrated to Chhatera. The local (i.e., the old) *jogi* residents of Chhatera accommodated these newcomers in their own houses. During the Consolidation of Holdings in Chhatera (in 1956), these newcomers were also given residential plots. Some of them have built houses on their new plots while some others, who, due to financial constraints, have not been able to build their own houses, are still living with their relatives. These *jogis* of Tharaya belong to Pandir *gotra*.

With the other modern means of entertainment like radio, television and cinema coming into existence in the village, or near it, the *jogis* have lost their tradtional profession. No *Jogi* in Chhatera owns any agricultural land, but four of them work as share-croppers. Some of them work on daily wages and are not attached to any particular agriculturist as such. Previously also the *jogis* were not on *jajmani* system and used to pay cash for anything they purchased or any work they got done from anyone, in or outside the village. One *jogi* is running a small provision shop in his house while another has become a milkman who collects milk from the village and sells it in Delhi. Three *jogis* are working as tailors in the village.

Jogis are not allowed to sit with the Brahmans or to share food or smoke with them. These days, some of the Jats, at times, eat with the *jogis*. But this act of the Jats is not appreciated by the villagers. *jogis* do not inter-dine with the Harijans. They do not accept water from, nor do they share *huka* with, the Harijans. *Jogis* practice *gotra* exogamy and avoid three *gotras* - one's own, his maternal grandfather's and that of his father's mother's father.

SUNAR: There are three *Sunar* households in Chhatera. Two of them - real brothers - came here from village Nahra (four kms. away) about two decades ago. The third household, which is that of the son-in-law of one of these old *Sunar* households, came to Chhatera only about five years ago. The *Sunars* are traditionally goldsmiths. But members of one of the *Sunar* households of Chhatera are in service in Delhi and those of the other are running busines in the nearby town of Sonepat.

According to their own version, the two households shifted to Chhatera because of its nearness to the Rathdhana Railway Station. But according to authentic reports from other sources, they had a serious social problem in village Nahra (the village of their previous residence) so they wanted to leave that village. A cousin of these *Sunars* had been running a goldsmith shop in village Nahra and had a number of clients in Chhatera. With the help of these contacts, the two households shifed to Chhatera. Many of their other agnatic relatives are still living in village Nahra. After shifting to Chhatera, these *Sunars* started living in rented houses. One of the brothers got a house plot, free of cost, from one Rupe Jat and built a *pacca* house on that.

The other brother was allotted a house plot on the periphery of the *tausih abadi* (extension of the inhabited area) at the time of Consolidtion of Holdings in the village in 1956. The third household is living in a rented house. He is running a cycle-repair and goldsmith shop. He works on cash payment basis. *Sunars* neither own any agricultural land in Chhatera nor did they have any in Nahra. The *Sunars* have never worked on *Jajmani* system, they had always been working on cash basis.

There are two groups of *Sunars* - *bagri* and *deswali*. The *Sunars* of Chhatera are *deswali* and their original *nikas* (place of origin, exit) is from somewhere in the State of Rajasthan. *Sunars* practise exogamy in respect of three *gotras*. In principle, the *Sunars* can inter-dine with the *Jats*. But because the *Sunars* of Chhatera are not the original members of the local community, as such, social interaction between them and the rest of the Chhatera community is highly restricted.

CHAMAR: *Chamar* is the village tanner. There are 14 *Chamar* households in Chhatera. Two *Chamar* cousins, Sialak and Mohla, came here from village Malha Majra at the time Chhatera was founded. Most of the present *Chamars* of Chhatera are the direct descendants of these two persons, i.e., of Mohla and Sialak. About a decade after the arrival of Sialak and Mohla in Chhatera, one Nanah *Chamar*, of the neighbouring village of Kheri, migrated to Chhatera. A few years after that, one Harnath *Chamar* (who was a son-in-law of Nanah) of village Loe Majra (near Bahadurgarh) also came to Chhatera and settled down here. One Badlu *Chamar* of village Holumbi, (about 15 kms. away) who was a *sala* (wife's brother) of Juglal *Chamar* of Chhatera, lost both his parents while he was very young. His sister brought him to Chhatera with her. Badlu has now settled in Chhatera permanently. About four years ago, one *Chamar*, popularly known in the village as *Baba*, came to Chhatera from Salaspur, a Delhi village, accross the river Jamuna. During those days a road was being constructed in that area passing through *Baba*'s native village, Salaspur. A number of houses in village Salaspur were being shifted elsewhere as the land under these houses was being acquired for the road. *Baba's* house also fell in the line of alignment of the proposed road. *Baba* was having contacts with one Ishwar *Chamar* of Chhatera, so he approached Ishwar and shifted to Chhatera along with his family. For about a year, Baba's family stayed with Ishwar's household. After that, *Baba* purchased a house plot from one Rupe Jat and built his own house on it.

Traditionally, *Chamars* are leather workers. They used to prepare *jot* (leather ropes for tying the plough to the bullocks), repair shoes and remove the skins of dead animals of their *kisans* (farmers). They used to remove the dead cattle (for removing the skin and eating the flesh) to the *hadwari* (literally meaning, a place for bones) near the *mata* (a deity worshipped by the villagers) in the *gora* (community place for cattle). An old *Chamaran* (woman of *Chamar* caste) acts as midwife during almost every child-birth in the village. The *Chamars* of Chhatera had been working on *jajmani* system. A *Chamar* used to get about one-fortieth part (i.e., 2.5 per cent) of the grain produce of his *kisan* and also whatever grains were left in the *pair* (thrashing ground) after *barsawan* (winnowing). One Attar *Chamar* of Chhatera used to collect about 125 to 150 quintals of grain every year. A few of these *Chamars* were so well-to-do that at times even some of the Jats having small land-holdings used to borrow money and/or grains from them.

According to the Revenue Settlement Report of Chhatera (1910), *Kar begar deh khet mein kam karan va kam bojha, asbab, puhnchane ka jab ko'i mulazam ga'on se dusre ga'on tak. Chaliswan hisa kar begar ka milta hai. Aur daswan hisa murdar chamar se kharkrob ko milta hai. Chamre se kuchh wasta nahin hai* – meaning thereby, that the *Chamars* used to do some odd and menial jobs in the fields, used to carry the luggage and loads, etc., of *kisans*. Whenver any Government servant was going from one village to another, the *Chamar*, who used to work in turns, had to carry the luggage of the former. They used to get one-fortieth part of the agricultural produce for these odd jobs. One-tenth of the flesh of dead animal was given to the *Bhangi*, but the *Bhangi* had no share in the hide. Later on, these *Chamars* stopped working on *Jajmani* system and switched over to cash payment system. During the past four decades or so, the situation has changed considerably and none of the *Chamars* of Chhatera is presently following his traditional occupation. Some of them have joined service outside the village, mostly in Delhi, while others work as casual labourers. For about two decades, some of the *Chamars* had been cultivating lands on *batai* (share-cropping). But due to the changed situation, resulting from successive implementation of the progressive land legislations, the land-owners now apprehend troubles in giving their lands to the *Chamars* on *batai*. Most of the *kisans* now do not give anything to their *Chamars*. A few of them, of course, still give grains, etc., to their *Chamars*. But in such cases, the quantity has been reduced considerably and is not fixed. Some of these *kisans* give grains to *Chamars* in order to maintain their own status, while others do so with a view to get votes at the time of elections to bodies like the *gram panchayat* (Village Council).

Among *Chamars*, literacy is very low. For the last few years, however, small children have started attending the local school. The *Chamars* eat meat and drink liquor freely and frequently. They are subject, of course, to economic constraints in this respect. The descendants of Sialak and Mohla belong to the same *gotra*, namely Bahmaniya, while those of Nanah, Harnath and Baba belong to different *gotras*. The practise *gotra* exogamy and avoid four *gotras*. The *Chamars* also ave their *purohits*, locally called *Chamarva pandat* (literally, the *Purohits* of the *Chamars*). Such *Purohits* are few in number and are paid very well by their *jajmans*. The *Pandat (Purohit)* of the *Chamars* of Chhatera lives in village Dasor Kheri, near Bahadurgarh. While the higher castes do not mix with the *Chamars*, the *Chamars*, in their turn, practise severe segregation against the *Bhangis*.

BHANGI: In the village the sweeper is known as *Bhangi*. There are 22 *Bhangi* households in Chhatera, all of them being the direct descendants of two brothers, Phatan and Sehat, who came here from village Malha Majra soon after Chhatera was founded.

Traditional occupation of the *Bhangis* is scavenging. The *Bhangan*, (female of *Bhangi* caste), every day cleans the place where the cattle of her *kisan* (farmer) household are tied. She pats the *gobar* (cow-dung) into *gosas* (cow-dung cakes) and spreads them for drying, and dumps the other refuse into the *kurri* (manure pit at the periphery of the village *abadi*) of her *kisan* for getting converted into *khad* (compost manure). The *Bhangi* has also to clean, every day, the portion of the *gal* (street) in front of his *kisan*'s *ghar* (residential house), *gher* (enclosure for cattle), as well as *baithak* (men's sitting place). In case of a childbirth in a *kisan* household, the *Nainrn* gives bath to the newborn child and the *Bhangan* throws away the dirty water and even removes the night soil, etc. During a marriage in the household of *kisan*, the *Bhangi* cleans the *gal* and does other cleaning jobs like removing the *juth* (left overs) after the feast. The *juth* is collected by the *Nai* from the place where the guests are eating and dumped at another place some distance away, located 'outside', from where the *Bhangi* takes it away. Whenever a *kisan* sells any cattle, his *Bhangi* will escort it to the village of the purchaser and come back to his own village on foot. The *Bhangi* would not be paid anything for this. Cleaning of the Jat *chaupal* (men's community place) has been entrusted to one Ram Sarup and that of the Brahman *chaupal* to his nephew,

Bawaria.

A *kisan* gives to his *Bhangi* 30 to 40 kg. of grain at the time of harvest. Every day, the *Bhangan* collects two *rotis* (breads) and some *lahsi / sit / chhachh* (butter-milk) from each of her *kisan* household. When any people come to Chhatera for the engagement of 'their' daughter with some boy of Chhatera, they pay a rupee to the *panchayat*. This money is handed over by the *panchayat* to the *Bhangi* of the household of the boy. Similarly, when the *mama* (mother's brother) of a girl getting married gives *bhat* (presents of cash, clothes, etc.) to his sister, he gives one rupee to the *panchayat* which is handed over to the *Bhangi* who cleans the *chaupal* (men's community place) where the *barat* of that girl is lodged. According to the records of the revenue department (Settlement Report of Chhatera 1910), the *Bhangi* had to do the common work, governmental as well as other, like running errands, etc. If there was a visit to the village by the *thanedar* (Station House Officer of Police) or any other similar government functionary, the *Bhangi* on duty would bring fodder from the jungle for the horse/mare of the visitor, provide (free of cost) eggs and chicken for the visiting official and carry *basta* (official papers and files tied in a red cloth, also called *lab*) and other luggage of the visitor to the other village. The *lambardar* (headman of a village or of a sector of it, responsible for collection of land revenue for the government) used to make a list of the *Bhangis* on duty on different days. One *Bhangi* would be on duty every day. In case of need, the *chawkidar* (village functionary appointed to take rounds of the village at night, to assist in the collection of land revenue and for other similar works) would find out from the *lambardar* as to which *Bhangi* was on duty on that day and would call him. The *Bhangi* on duty had to render this service during the day and at night, whenever required. After escorting the visitor to the other village (his destination) and leaving his luggage there, the *Bhangi* would return to his village on foot. According to the revenue records, the *Bhangi* is also entitled to the skin of the (dead) horse, mule, poney, donkey and camel of the *kisan*.

With increase in their population, the *Bhangis* have also taken to some of the other non-traditional occupations. Twenty-five of them are in the service of the Delhi Municipal Corporation, three are in the army and a few others are in other organizations in and around Delhi. In fact, from the very beginning, some of them have been working in the army as sweepers. Some of the *Bhangis* of Chhatera have started working as casual labourers while some others have switched over to dairying, though on a small scale only. Previously, they used to keep sheep, pigs and hen only. One Ram Sarup *Bhangi* of the village is even now having 40 heads of sheep. Some of the young *Bhangi* boys have started attending the local school, but majority of those who go to school do so irregularly and leave it half way.

The *Bhangis* don't have any fixed *Nai* and previously they used to help each other in this respect. They have a purohit in village Malha Majra who is also a *Bhangi*. They say *pag bandh di thi* – meaning that they had tied a turban on his head – a ceremony symbolising the acceptance of one as a teacher, preacher etc. All the *Bhangis* of Chhatera belong to Dolgat *gotra*. For striking matrimonial alliances they avoid three *gotras* in marriages. *Bhangis* marry off their children at an early age. Previously, they often used to do that soon after the birth of a child and at times even before that. Though the situation has changed now, but not completely. The custom of dowry is also gradually creeping into the *Bhangi* community and widow re-marriage is prevalent among them. Meat eating and consumption of liquor are quite common among them and these practices are in no way looked down upon. They are the most down-trodden section of village community. They are not allowed to inter-dine or to share *huka* with the members of any other castes. The *Bhangis* cannot sit on a *khat* (cot) belonging to a person of any other caste, even when none else is sitting on it. They cannot sit in close proximity to members of any other caste. Even the *Chamars* do not mix with them, although both the sects belong to the Scheduled Castes. This inter-sectional segregation is often more serious and severe even than the inter-sectional ones. Segregation against the *Bhangis* is clearly reflected even in the location of their residential quarters in the village. During the freedom movement, a new name - Balmiki - was given to them by Mahatma Gandhi. But this term still remains confined mainly to the official jargon, or to be utilized very sparingly on formal occasions in the villages.

SAKA: There was an old Muslim family also in Chhatera, that of water-carriers. Muslim water carriers are called *Saka*. There was one Sultan *Saka*, son of Yadgiri. It is not clear as to when and under what circumstances this family came to Chhatera.

Sultan used to draw water from the village well with the help of a leather bucket and carry this water in a big leather bag, called *mashak* to the *ghars* of the Jats, who used it for preparing fodder for their cattle and for similar other purposes. This water was never allowed to be taken into their *ghars* nor would it be consumed by any human being in the *baithaks/ghers*, because it suffered from ritual pollution; first, because it was carried in a leather bucket and, secondly, it was drawn and carried by a Muslim. Brahmans would not even touch this water. Other castes, except the Baniyas, were economically as well as socially incapable of affording this luxury.

One peculiar and noteworthy point in this connection is that while the lower castes were not allowed to climb the village well, no such limitation was put on the *Saka* in spite of the fact of his being a Muslim. Sultan used to draw water in this bucket and pour it (from a distance) into the vessels of the Harijans waiting there. In fact, there were three distinct places for drawing water at the well. One of these was reserved for drawing water for irrigating the *khets*, the second to be used by women, and the third for Sultan *Saka*.

After the death of Sultan some 40 years ago, no new *Saka* ever came to Chhatera. In fact, after the partition of the country (into India and Pakistan) in 1947, Muslim households in villages in the region shifted to Pakistan. Moreover, with increase in the number of wells (in the village *abadi*) from one to seven dispersed in different caste sectors, installation of hand-pumps in the *ghers* and tube-wells in the *khets*, now even the need for such a person does not exist.

PATHAN: In the small adjoining village of Ladpur which forms a part of the Chhatera *Panchayat* (for details please refer to 4.7.1) there was a Pathan, a Muhammadan from the North-Western Frontier Province (now a part of Pakistan). This Pathan used to work as an agricultural labourer with one of the Jat households of Ladpur.

Due to his very long stay in Ladpur and exemplary behaviour, this Pathan was quite popular in the village and accepted almost as a member of the village community. He had left his native place virtually for ever and after his death, as desired by him earlier, his body was buried in Ladpur itself. There was no other Muslim family in Ladpur although a number of them lived in the neighbouring villages of Akbarpur Barota and Rathdhana.

An analysis of the circumstances under which some households belonging to the various castes moved into Chhatera, after it had been initially inhabited, throws some light on the possible ways in which the outsiders are accepted in the local community in the villages in this region.

The complete self-sufficiency of any Indian village is a myth in more than one ways. There is no village which has some inhabitants of each of the ethno-linguistic group existing in the region. At the same time, the number of those villages none of whose inhabitants renders any service to any household of any other village is very small. The following are some of the castes living in the surrounding villages in the region but no member of whom lives in Chhatera : *Teli* (oil-man), *Dhuniya* (Carder), *Dholi* (drummer), *Chhipi* (tailor), *Jhimar* (basket-maker), *Banjara* (whose male members sharpen the grinding wheels and females work as vendors of items of general merchandise of interest to women), *Khatik* (weaver) and *Maniyar* (vendor in glass bangles for women). Members of the following castes, however, visit the village at frequent intervals : *Banjara*, *Maniyar*, Punjabi, *Sabjiwala* and *Jhimar*. In addition to these, people belonging to some other professions (which have come up recently and hence do not belong to any caste group as such), like those who repair the locks, those who give glass utensils in exchange for old rubber shoes, also visit the village frequently. There also exists a group of specialized people known as *rakhwalas* who look after the wild cattle herds.

Banjara is a caste group whose menfolk move in groups to villages and sharpen the grinding wheels and grinding stones, etc. *Banjara* women sell goods and general merchandise used almost exclusively by women. The *Banjaras* are not on *jajmani* system. They sell things on cash basis. Transactions on credit and barter exchange are, of course, common. Chhatera is catered by a *Banjara* woman from the neighbouring village Akbarpur Barota. There are a number of households of *Banjara* caste in Akbarpur. They all live in a close group housing cluster and lead a sort of well-knit group life.

People of *Maniyar* caste sell *churis* (glass bangles for women). *Churis* have great importance in the life of women of all the caste groups living in the Chhatera region. Every married woman, whose husband is alive, must wear *churi*. *Churi* is the symbol of *suhag* (husband). So, widows do not wear *churis*. When a man dies, his wife (if she is alive) breaks down all her *churis* and never wears any again. Brahman and Baniya women are very particular about the *churi* etiquette, Jats are not so particular. Chhatera is served by one Surja *Maniyar* of village Gadhi. Surja has many villages under him but he cannot cover all of these. He does not visit Chhatera. So he has allowed one Kartar Singh, a *Maniyar* of village Rathdhana, to cover village

Chhatera. There are tweleve *Maniyar* families in village Rathdhana. In addition to Chhatera, Kartar Singh serves village Jatheri also. Kartar Singh comes to Chhatera two to three times a week. He goes round in various *gals* (streets) of the village shouting "*churi*". Those women who need *churis* call him and purchase the same. The *Maniyar* generally sits at one place in the *gal* and women of neighbouring houses assemble there and purchase *churis* from him. At times, some women take him into the *pauli* of their *ghar* and transact the business there. The *Maniyar* does not work on *jajmani* system. He sells *churis* on cash basis. But whenever any marriage takes place in Chhatera, the concerned household keeps four 'annas' (25 paise, i.e., one fourth of a rupee) for the *Maniyar*. When the *Maniyar* visits the village next time, this money is given to him.

A cloth vendor comes to the village almost on alternate days. He is a displaced person from West Punjab (now in Pakistan) and is, therefore, popularly called 'Punjabi'. This Punjabi has been visiting the village since 1947. He lives in Sonepat and moves from village to village on his bicycle with bundles of cloth on its carrier. He sells cloth on money basis. Cases of barter exchange (cloth in exchange for grains) are quite common, especially during the few months following harvest. He also gives cloth to many on credit basis. Majority of his customers are women. So, he keeps mainly those varieties of cloth that are needed by women and children. The Punjabi generally moves in the *gals* (streets) though sometimes he sits in the *paulis* (front-rooms) of the *ghars* (residential houses) of his clients for selling the cloth. This person has won the confidence of the Chhaterans in such an abundant measure that he is consulted by many of them in many matters. He leaves his bicycle and cloth wherever he is at dusk and walks down to Rathdhana railway station to catch a train for Sonepat. Next morning he comes to Rathdhana by train, walks down to the village where he had left his bicycle and cloth the previous evening, and starts on his beat.

Chhaterans do not grow much vegetables except tomatoes in winter and *tinda* in summer. A *subjiwala*, literally meaning the one with vegetables, visits the village almost every day. He also comes from Sonepat but on a poney. The *subjiwala* goes into the various streets of the village and sells vegetables and 'not-so-expensive' fruits of the season, mainly in exchange for grains.

JHIMAR: One Chandgi Ram, a *Jhimar* (basket maker) by caste, from Village Huleri near Sonepat visits Chhatera every winter and remains there for two to three months (Please see plate 4.3). Every farmer household needs a number of baskets for its various agricultural operations. Most of the agriculturists grow a few mulbery trees on the boundary lines of their fields called *thauls*. The twigs and branches of these trees are used for basket making. The twigs of mulbery tree are known for their flexibility, strength and durability. Those agriculturists, who do not own any mulbery trees, purchase the branches and twigs of mulbery from other farmers. Chandgi *Jhimar* stays in the *ghers* (cattle-sheds) of a few selected households who have spacious open accommodation where he can carry out his work. He spends most of his time in the *gher* of one Kirpa Ram Brahman. (see plate 4.4). Chandgi is paid in cash per basket made by him. He is also provided food by the household for whom he is working on particular days.

4.3 FAMILY, LAW OF INHERITANCE OF PROPERTY AND FAMILY PARTITIONS

The discussions contained in this chapter about the family, the process of its fissioning, the law of inheritance of property and family partitions are mainly confined to one ethnic group in Chhatera - the Jats. This is so because the Jats form a dominant group in Chhatera and the detailed discussions about *ghar* and other elements of habitation described in the subsequent chapters are mainly for the Jats. It is observed that some of the observations made here are quite applicable also to other caste groups in Chhatera.

4.3.1 *Family*

Family in Chhatera is patriarchal, patrilocal and patrilineal. The observation of Madan (1965:57) about the Pandits of Kashmir that "the male members of the *chulha* are closely related agnatic kinsmen : grandfathers and grandsons, fathers and sons, uncles and nephews, siblings and cousins. The female members, if married, are usually the spouses of the male members and, if unmarried, their agnates... only in exceptional circumstances is the core group of agnates less in number than the conjugal members of the household", is very appropriately applicable in the case of the Jats as well as Brahmans of Chhatera. The authority of a father over his sons is complete. His wife has a similar control over the female members of the household.

Plate 4.3: Chandgi (*Jhimar*) making *tokris* (baskets) in the *gher* of a Brahman family

Plate 4.4: A big *gher* (also including *baithak*) of a Brahman household built on the periphery of the village *abadi* in the late sixties. Mark its huge size and wide facade as well as the non-traditional style and construction materials

The Jats as well as the Brahmans of Chhatera region practise *gotra* exogamy. They avoid three *gotras*; one's own (i.e., of father), his maternal grandfather's and his father's maternal grandfather's, colloquially called, *apna, nana ka aur dadi ka*. The Jats of Chhatera and those of the surrounding villages practise Jewish levirate. A widow is generally married to the younger brother of her deceased husband. Although in principle there is no bar on her marrying the deceased's elder brother, no such case has occurred in Chhatera so far. The range within which the levirate can be practised includes the deceased's own brother, his father's brother's son, his paternal grandfather's son's son, etc. Similarly the Jats practise sororate also, and there too the range of potential second husbands for a widow is quite wide. Brahmans and Baniyas do not practise levirate.

The wife has to veil her face before all the elder brothers and other older relations of her husband, but not before the younger ones. Elder and younger being, of course, a matter of geneological degree and not of age. Nor may she ever mention the name of any of the elder ones, or even of her husband.

As everywhere in rural India, in Chhatera also the complex households[6] have a strong hold. About two-third of total households in the village are complex ones while one-third are simple. It is reported that previously in Chhatera there used to be very large extended complex households - some of these have had 60 persons or even more living together and taking food from a common kitchen. But now these large households have given way to smaller ones. Joint living is still the ideal but the unwieldy size of the household, the conflicting interests of its members and other such forces become too big to be contained. At present, there is not a single instance in Chhatera where four generations or even two brothers with their married sons are living together.

The authority of the father over his sons is a great binding force for keeping the household together. In some cases the eldest male member in a complex household during his life-time itself partially relinquishes the responsibility of the headship of the household.[7] In such an event one of his brothers, if they are living jointly with him, or one of his sons if his brothers are not living with him, is chosen to take over the responsibility of headship of the family. The most intelligent and shrewd male member - who is generally somewhat educated also - is chosen to look after accounts and management of the household. In fact, he is in-charge of his houshold as a unit of production, as a unit of consumption and also as a group for social interaction. Such a person is called *murabi*. A household whose *murabi* is honest and efficient generally continues to remain joint for a long time. In cases where the *murabi* proves to be dishonest or insincere, or inefficient, the fissioning process of the household gets expedited.

Till the end of his life a man prefers to keep his entire property in his own name. One explanation offered for this is that if the property is formally transferred to his sons, they may not respect him or look after his interests properly. In many cases, during the life time of a person himself his lands are divided among his sons. But it is only an informal arrangement. In the eyes of law his lands are partitioned and registered (in the revenue records) in the names of his sons only after his death. In the memory of the elderly residents of Chhatera there has so far occurred only one case in the history of the village where a person - Amrit Singh *Lambardar* - during his life time itself voluntarily got his lands transferred into the names of his sons. This incident also, it is reported, caused surprise among the villagers as well as among revenue officials. Even the *tehsildar* advised Amrit Singh to reconsider his decision. During the very recent past due to the fear of legislations regarding ceilings on land holdings, a few Chhaterans having large agricultural holdings have formally transferred parts of their lands into the names of their sons. These cases are too recent to be studied for their implications.

4.3.2 *The Fissioning Process*

Soon after the marriage of the sons of a man some sort of *khat-pat*, i.e., trouble, starts. In a large number of cases the complex household does not remain to be a smooth going affair after that. The women (i.e., the *sas* and her *bahus* or the wives of different brothers) start levelling accusations against each other - silently and stealthily to begin with, becoming quite vocal and open eventually. These accusations are like; one's child is not getting good food and similar treatment as the other children in the household, one is being made to do more or harder or dirtier types of work than other women. Women also, it was reported, have the habit of praising their own parents in terms of the treatment and presents, etc., they get from the latter, and also of speaking in a derogatory tone about and making satires against the parents of other women in the household.

It is commonly said in the village that all dissensions in any household start from women. After his marriage the loyalties of a man get distributed. On the one hand, he has loyalties towards his parents, brothers, sisters, etc., and, on the other, he has loyalties to his wife and to her natal family. In fact, it is this duality of loyalties and interest that creates problems. But so long as the father is alive all these conflicts remain passive and sort of dormant and life in the household moves on somewhat smoothly. After the death of the father the eldest brother assumes the role of the head of the complex household. When authority is exercised by a brother this is not relished by the younger brothers, especially by those whose age difference from the head is not much. Similarly, after the death of their *sas* the wives of brothers do not like to remain under the authority and control of the wife of the eldest brother. The unquestioned and spontaneously accepted authority of the father is something unique which has no substitute.

It is generally the younger brothers (especially those who are very much younger in age to their elder brothers) who try to get the household partitioned. This is so, partly because of the excessive authority exercised by the elder brothers and their wives, and mainly due to the consideration that a major part of the expenditure of the complex household is incurred on the children of the elder brothers especially on the marriage of their grown up children. Younger brothers apprehend that by the time their children will grow up and come of age, the complex houshold would certainly have got partitioned. They cannot remain together till then and they would not be able to get the benefits of jointness. So, they want separation. But it is not infrequent, rather such cases are many, where the household is partitioned at the initiative of the eder brother/s and/or their wife/s. As mentioned earlier, initially the bickerings, dissensions and conflicts in a household start from women. But it would not be correct to say that partitions of households always take place primarily due to differences among women. Majority of partitions actually take place only when the brothers themselves start thinking that way. So long as the brothers are on good terms with each other they continue to ignore the suggestions of their wives for partitions and sometimes even rebuke them for this. Some women, (of course, very few) are so quarrelsome, obstinate and stubborn in this respect that even if they are rebuked and/or beaten by their husbands, they do not give up their pleadings for partitioning the household. In such cases, their husbands agree even against their own wishes to ask their brothers for partition. But in such cases the partition generally takes place only in the *ghar* while the *khets*, etc., remain joint. Sometimes two or more *chaukas* are established in the same *ghar*. In such cases, as a unit of production they remain together, i.e., the household continues to be complex, but as units of consumption they are separate. It is, however, also correct that in some of the cases when a man himself is interested in the partition of the complex household, he would encourage his wife to continue creating troubles. The man would use this as a pretext for asking his brothers for partition. This is so because although after a man's death it is the right of his sons to ask for partition of the household, the complex household is still highly valued by the community.

Economic factors are gradually becoming more important considerations for partitioning of households. The fact that a large number of persons from Chhatera are working in Delhi and elsewhere has also got its own implications for the household system in the village. Those members of a complex household who are daily commuters, after retaining some money for meeting their travelling and other related petty expenses, pool their remaining income into the joint purse of the household. They also help their families in agricultural and other works in the mornings, evenings, as well as on Sundays and other holidays, and when the rush of agricultural work so demands even by taking leave from their office. Except the very few who are holding some senior and responsible positions in their office, these service holders attach only secondary importance to their jobs in the city, while their primary allegiance is to agriculture back home. In some of the complex households, persons who are working outside the village and are not even daily commuters, are managing their complex households back in the village as *murabis*.

Those who start living outside the village, after meeting their normal expenses at the place of their stay, pool the rest of their income in the joint purse of the complex household. During the agriculturally busy seasons, they take leave from their respective offices and come to the village to assist their household members. So long as this attitude sustains the household continues to be a complex one. But now the trend among the office-goers is more towards liking white-collar works, i.e., many of them avoid working in the *khets* and doing "dirty" jobs related to farming. Moreover, the type of work requiring very hard labour, like ploughing, etc., can be done only during day time and that too by men who are physically quite strong. Even among those who bring their wives and children to the city, many continue (though functionally only) to be members of their complex households. But when a person starts retaining an unreasonably big part of his income with himself and makes very small contribution to the joint purse of the complex household (back in the village) then the other members, who are engaged in agriculture also similarly take out their own share from the agricultural income and put only the remaining amount in the joint purse of the complex household. This tendency starts the fissioning process of the complex household.

So far as the complexity or otherwise of the household is concerned, this particular factor, i.e. some of the household members working away from the village, has a double-edged implication. Whereas in some cases it has hastened the partitioning of complex households, in some others it has worked the opposite way. Those who live in the city know that if they break off from their complex households it would not be possible for them to look after their *khets* profitably, because in agriculture there must be at least one man living whole time in the village. So, had these city workers (who are at present members of complex households) been depending on agriculture alone and had been living in the village, perhaps a sizable percentage of them would have parted from their complex household by now.

4.3.3 *Inheritance of Property*

Traditionally, in Chhatera the property of a man is equally inherited by all his sons. In principle, no distinction is recognized between his sons in the distribution of property. The only situation where a man is not entitled to a share in the property of his father is that of a *khadehlar* or *gaihlar*. Because a *khadehlar* or *gaihlar* is not his son in the true sense of the term and his name is never entered into the concerned records of the revenue department. *Lambardari* goes by inheritance and it always goes to the eldest brother. When any *lambardar* dies his eldest son becomes the *lambardar*.

Jats practise *pag-wand* and not *chunda-wand* system of inheritance of property. According to the customary law of the village, a daughter has never had a share in the property of her father excepting what is given to her and to her in-laws at the time of the various ceremonies connected with her marriage. After her marriage a woman is given 'enough' by her father in the shape of *chhuchhak* at the time of each child birth to her, and in the shape of *bhat* at the time of the marriage of each of her children, and also on a number of other occasions during her life and also after her death. Even otherwise, whenever a woman visits her parent's village, depending upon the economic condition of her father, she is given presents of cash, clothes, ornaments, etc. Since the passing of the Hindu Succession Act in 1956, a daughter also has the right to an equal share in the property of her parents just like her brothers. But, in practice, no case of a daughter having claimed a share in her father's property has occurred in Chhatera so far. If after the death of her parents a woman is not treated by her brothers properly then her father's brothers (or their sons) consider it to be their duty to look after her like their own daughter/sister.

In cases where a man's land is divided among his sons during his life time itself, a share is retained for him and the rest of the land is divided equally among all his sons. If the father is still active and chooses to live separately from all his sons, in that case, after his death, his share of the land goes to his wife (if she be alive). According to the Customary Law of the region, a woman has only the right of maintenance from her husband's property. She cannot inherit absolute rights as such in the property. After the death of the mother, her share is also equally divided among all her sons. If at the time of partition among brothers their father is already dead but their mother is alive, a similar share is retained for her, which after her death, is divided equally among all her sons. After a man's land has been partitioned among his sons, if he chooses to live with one of them then that son cultivates his father's share of land also and supports his parents. That son also meets all the other social obligations of his parents. In such a case, even after the death of the parents their share of property, unless specifically bequeathed otherwise (which is seldom done here), is also distributed equally among all their sons. In the history of Chhatera, there has been no case of an unmarried son seeking partition from his parents. The separation of an unmarried daughter, of course, is absolutely unthinkable.

A couple not having any son generally adopts one. A man who does not have any son, but has a daughter, would normally adopt one of the sons of his daughter. A man who does not have even a daughter would generally adopt his sister's son. Some issueless men in Chhatera have adopted their brother's sons also. The Jats do not keep their *damads* as *ghar-jamais*. A widow gets (for her life time) maintenace from the property of her deceased husband. In case her deceased husband be sonless, after her death this property would be equally divided among all his brothers. In fact, the case of a widow, especially of an issueless widow, living separately, is a very rare phenomenon. Because, as mentioned earlier, the Jats practise levirate and, therefore, in a vast majority of cases the widow gets re-married to one of the brothers of her deceased husband.

The main difficulty is for those elderly persons who are not economically well off. Cases have also occurred in Chhatera where poor elderly widows, not cared for by their sons, have lived with the families of their (own or of their husband's) brothers, or with such other relatives. If the old man, especially a widower, does not have any son, he lives with one of his brothers or their sons. If a widow has no son, she may live either with her husband's brothers, or their sons, or she may return to live with her natal family. But it is primarily the duty of the brothers of her deceased husband (and their sons) to look after her. The way it was expressed to me, it is so because it is they who, after her death, would inherit her property. In the event of a man dying sonless, his property is inherited by his nearest agnatic kin on the male side, i.e., it goes to his brothers/ brothers' sons, and if he does not have even any such relative, then to his nearest next kins in that line. In other words, the obligation to look after the social responsibilities of a person rests on those who are in the line of succession to his property, the degree of his responsibility, in this respect, being dependent upon one's position in the line of succession and inheritance of property.

If a couple dies leaving behind minor children or even if a man dies leaving behind his young widow, with or without children, then if the brothers of the deceased do not help his dependents, they go to wife's brother and are looked after by him. Even if the widow and/or her children remain in their own village, the *mama* helps them by sending money and/or goods to them in their village and, in some cases, even by occasionally visiting them in their village and assisting them in cultivating their lands.

4.3.4 *Partition*

In a majority of cases, soon after his marriage a man develops loyalties of interests and loyalties which get manifested in the form of troubles in the household. But it is not in good taste for one to demand partition of the household soon after his marriage. Partition is generally a slow process. Similarly, after the death of a man, his sons do not separate immediately. In some cases, married brothers remain together for considerable periods of time after the death of their father. Although the mother also enjoys a place of respect in the family and wields considerable influence in family affairs, in matters of partition, her influence is very insignificant compared to that of her husband. The presence of a widowed mother does not delay partition to any significant extent. Paritions in the life time of widowed mothers are markedly more common than in the life time of father. The presence of a step-mother in a household does not always accelerate the partitioning process among brothers. It is certainly an important factor but there have been cases where men having step-mothers lived jointly with their father. There are cases where a man has two living wives and they pull on well, both living together. Even married brothers with two mothers have been living jointly for long periods.

When partition of property of a household takes place, it is not necessary that each of the brothers should start living completely separately. Sometimes, one or more brothers separate, while others remain together. An unmarried brother does not set up a separate household, he lives with one of his married brothers and it is only after his marriage, that he asks for partition - though not always soon after his marriage. However, instances of permanent bachelors separating and setting up separate households to have *mauj-masti* are not totally non-existent. Similarly, an unmarried sister lives with one of her married brothers till she gets married.

When partition of a household takes place among brothers, the land, etc., i.e., all the immovable property is equally divided among all the brothers. Cash and other such movable wealth is also divided equally. But in a few cases, some portion of it is kept seprately and retained for the marriages of unmarried brothers and sisters. No such provision is ever made for the marriages of the grown up children of brothers.

Among the Jats, both types of partitions - partial as well as complete - are common. For example, in some cases the *ghar* is partitioned but not the *gher* or the *baithak*. In some cases all the three residential structures, viz., *ghar, gher* and *baithak* are partitioned but the *khets* are not partitioned. But once the *khets* have been partitioned, the *gher*, etc., cannot remain joint for long. It is a different thing that two or more separate households may continue to live in the same *ghar*. But they do so as separate households and not as a joint one. In the Jat society there are no factors or causes which prevent complete partition of economic jointness among the brothers. Among the Jats, partitions of households are generally complete.

Let us now examine as to what happens at the residential level when a complex household splits up. There are a number of alternative ways in which such a sitution is met, a few important ones being:

(a) the partitioned households may continue to live in the same *ghar*
  (i) with partitioning walls, or
  (ii) by just coming to an oral understanding about the division of the building without making any structural changes in it,
(b) each separated households may occupy separate structures owned by the complex household,
(c) the complex households may be having some *safaid zamin* and one of the households may put up a structure on this *safaid zamin* and shift there,
(d) the erstwhile complex household may be having some old dilapidated building lying in disuse. This structure may be got repaired, or it may be pulled down and a new structure put up in its place, and one of the new simple households may shift into it,
(e) the complex household may purchase a new plot of land and a structure may be put up on it for one of the separated simple households, and
(f) if the complex household has an acute shortage of space and can find no other alternative, then it may even request the *gaon* for a new piece of land.

In a majority of cases the troubles end after partitioning among brothers. Chhaterans say that *rair se bar achhi*, i.e., it is better to have hedges to separate the *khets* than to use raised mud lines for the purpose, meaning thereby that in case there are continued troubles while being joint, then it is better to put an end to these troubles and establish happiness and peace in the household by a complete partition. When brothers are on good terms, even after they have separated from each other consequent to the partition of the complex household, they continue to share each other's joys and sorrows. They lend agricultural implements and other things to each other. In this respect, a story is commonly told in Chhatera and nearby villages. Two brothers got their household partitioned under unbearable pressures from their wives. But in their hearts they remained united. When their wheat crop had been harvested and the grains were lying in the *pair* the younger brother put 20 maunds of wheat from his own heap into that of his elder brother, thinking that his elder brother had grown up children of marriageable age and his need was greater. When the younger brother was away, the elder brother put 20 maunds of wheat from his own heap into that of his younger brother thinking that the younger brother was like his son and that during his parents' life-time also the younger brother had not been able to enjoy life as much as the elder brother did. The lesson of the story is that although the two brothers loved each other and tried to sacrifice for and help each other, in the ultimate analysis none was a looser.

There have been cases of re-union of partitioned households. But such cases are very few. Once partition of a household takes place, it is very seldom that the partitioned groups unite again. In Chhatera, one Hukmi and his brother's son - a minor at that time - got partitioned after the death of Hukmi's brother. But again, after some time, they united and lived jointly for about ten years. After the death of the mother of the nephew, i.e., Hukmi's *bhabi* they again got partitioned. Similarly, in a neighbouring village - Jagdishpur - also a *kaka* and his *bhatija* remained separated for about a year and then again they united and have now been living together as a complex household for the last twelve years.

4.4 KUNBA

Villages in this region are generally established by people belonging to particular clans/tribes. Chhatera, for example, was founded by Chhatar Singh - a Jat - and Kewal Ram - a Brahman. Most of the Jat and Brahman households of Chhatera are the direct descendants of Chhatar and Kewal, respectively. A Jat household, therefore, does not usually live in isolation in a village. Its natal members have patrilineal kin living with them in the same village, albeit in another or other households. All such agnatically related households taken together constitute a *kunba*. *Kunba* is actually an Urdu word meaning family.

Although in its strict sense the term *kunba* should include all such agnatically related households, in practice if the number of such households in a village is very large and their common ancestor was many generations away, i.e., many generations earlier, they do not include all these households in their *kunba*. Normally grown up persons in the village, when questioned, include in their *kunba* households having a common ancestor three or four generations above (i.e., earlier to) them. Even those households who migrate to other villages do not loose their membership of their original *kunba*. *Kunba*, therefore, is strictly speaking not a territorial group.

Members of a *kunba* share their joys and sorrows with each other. A death or birth in any household in the *kunba* pollutes all the members of that *kunba*. All the members of a *kunba* consider their prestige to be common. Any good deed or achievement by a member of a *kunba* enhances the prestige of all its members. Likewise a misdeed by any member of the *kunba* brings bad name to all of them. Members of a *kunba* help each other in times of need although the most harmful type of jealousies also develop within the *kunbas* themselves, i.e., *intra-kunba* jealousies are much more harmful than *inter-kunba* ones.

4.5 RELIGION AND COSMOLOGY

4.5.1 *Religion*

Chhatera is a Hindu village. The Jats are by and large not the staunch followers of any religion. They do believe in God but then it seems to end there. There is not much beyond the fact that they recognize God's existence and his omni-powerful influence. They generally remember God only when in distress. The reason given by the Jats themselves for their lukewarm attitude towards religion is that, being agriculturists, they are too busy and otherwise also cannot observe much rituals, etc. They are less ritualistic than all other caste groups in this region. "The religion of the Jat is Hinduism; but he does not know very much about it. He talks about *Parmeshwar*, and the more intelligent men say that they believe in only one God..." (*Gazetteer of Delhi Distrtict* N.D.:56).

The Jats of Chhatera and of adjoining villages are specially devoid of the finer aspect of the detailed manifestations of the religious attitudes. Mukerji has made the following observations in this regard:

> The most striking fact that emerges out of a study of these Jat villages is the absence of temples. The absence of temples is striking because an Indian village without a place of worship is a rare phenomenon and obviously hides some clue to certain historical processes..Jats in the first period of their history have been nomads and wanderers, hence their minds, always occupied with the planning of the new move, could never have time or intelligence to work out a system of religion. It was only when the Jats finally and

> firmly set themselves down in the northern sector, they inherited some of the religious ideas of other Hindu castes and began to worship, sometimes or other, the Hindu Gods and Goddesses. Since it was not an element inherent in their own culture but was taken from outside and assimilated within, the religious tendency has never become an important social force in the community organisation of the Jats... But being intensely tribal in spirit, the Jats have an unconditional respect and sentimental attachment for their ancestors and their heroic deeds. Ancestral achievements are the nuclei of many of the Jat folk tales and folk literature. Ancestor worship is thus an important element in Jat culture.
>
> As we move towards the east we find more of Brahmanical orthodox ideas coming into play in the cultural make-up; hence are found the temples built by landlord Jats and usually given to some mendicant (Sadhu).. Almost always these temples are situated outside the village proper's habitations (1957:24-25).

"Hindu and Muslim agriculturists of Rohtak are alike exceedingly indifferent observers of their religion; the Jats will drink water brought up in a skin from the tank or well; the Baniyas are stricter....." (Purser and Fanshawe, 1880:65).

Previously (till about 1920 or so), these people were comparatively more religious minded but the Arya Samaj movement also had a deep impact on their minds. The *bhajniks* used to come to the village during the agriculturally slack seasons, stay there for a few days and perform at the village *chaupal*. These performances were a source of recreation for the villagers as well as agents of reinforcing religion in the minds of the villagers. But towards the beginning of the second quarter of the present century, when the Arya Samaj movement caught momentum, some *parcharaks* from the *gurukul*, especially one Pandit Basti Ram, started visiting the villages, staying there for days together and performing *bhajans* and *updeshas* to remove the deep-rooted folk beliefs and orthodox views (which they called *pop lila*) from the minds of the villagers. Chhatera being close to Delhi and finding a good response here, the *parcharaks* somewhat intensified their activities in this village. All this resulted in a change in the religious beliefs of the Chhaterans, especially of the male population. Jats, therefore, do not have any particular place in their *ghars* exclusively marked for worship, etc.

Women of Chhatera, as of everywhere else, are the custodians of religion. Moreover, due to village as well as *gotra* exogamy (individual village and even groups of villages called *khap* being inhabited by those belonging to a particular *gotra*), the wives of Chhaterans (the *bahus* of the village) are from distant villages where the influence of Arya Samaj has not been so pronounced as in Chhatera and the villages around it. So, the women of Chhatera are comparatively more religious minded than their male counterparts, and the former devote some time every day for worship etc. To use the words of Kiran Prem :

> Most of them are exceedingly indififferent observers of their religion. They have their women folk to pray for them; and they have each their family Brahman or *Purohit* to whom they are *Jajman*. On them they can rely for instruction in the countless ceremonies that should be observed not only in the more important affairs of life but also in the matter of building a house, the correct day for making a journey or starting to plough...There are many to whom all that is involved in these ceremonies has no meaning, and who have broken with the traditions of their fathers (1970:59).

In some of the households women reserve a place for worship, one of the *alas* or *alis* in their *ghar*. This *ala* is generally either in one of the *aobras* or in the *sal* and, in some cases, even in the space under the *parkala*, the idea being that children and cattle may not easily reach there and spoil the sacredness of the place. In every *ghar*, women burn *jot* in this *ala* and offer prayers every day, especially on the occasion of festivals. In the Brahman *ghars*, in some of these *alas* there are photos of Hindu Gods and Goddesses, like, Ram, Krishna, Vishnu, Parvati and Lakshmi. A few have idols of these Gods made of earth, paster of Paris or even in plastic. Any *ala* facing south is never used for religious purposes.

In some of the villages in the region some land outside the *abadi* is earmarked and a structure is put up on it. Such a place is called a *bara*. If there are a number of trees also around such a structure then it is called a *kutiya*. If the structure is quite a substantial one, i.e., big-sized built with expensive and durable materials, it is called *asthal*. Usually a *sadhu*, locally called *bawaji*, lives in each of these places (i.e., in every *asthal*). If architecturally this structure is like an Hindu temple then it is called a *mandar*. A *pujari* - the man who offers prayers to Gods and is in-charge of all the religious activities there - always lives in a *mandar*. The general practice in the region is that provision for a *bara* or *kutiya* is not made at the time of founding a village. *Bawaji bhraman karte hain*, i.e., mendicants keep on wandering from village to village. Whenever during his stay in a village a *bawaji* likes the place and wants to settle in the village permanently, he expresses this desire to the village community. Such requests are generally granted. After that, a piece of land from the *gaon shamlat* outside the *abadi* is marked by the village elders, and a structure is put up on it with contributions from the villagers.

Chhatera has had a *kutiya* and a *bawaji* used to live in it. The then *bawaji* of the Chhatera *kutiya* died about 30 years ago. Although, from time to time, many *bawajis* have been visiting the village and staying in the *kutiya* for short periods, none decided to live here permanently. About a decade ago, a big drain, called drain No. 8, was constructed by the government. The *kutiya* of Chhatera fell in the line of alignment of this drain and, therefore, had to be demolished. Since then there is no *bara* or *kutiya* in this village. There is, in fact, no place for community worship here.

Plate 4.5: *Mandir* recently constructed by the Harijans in Chhatera

The Harijans of the village have recently built a small *mandar* in their sector of the *abadi* (please see plate 4.5). But this *mandar* has been built by the *Bhangis* mainly with a view to improve their social status. It is an imitation of the ways of the caste Hindus, a reflection of the process of Sanskritization.[8] Moreover, it has been possible for the Harijans to build this *mandar* only because of the encouragement from the Jats (i.e., the *biswedaran*) of the village. It is not the result of a sincere desire to build a place of worship. In fact, it was a piece of *shamlat* land under dispute, and in order to play up the situation, the dominant community encouraged the Harijans to build a *mandar* on it.

4.5.2 *Cosmology*

The Jats are not much conscious about cosmology. Till about a century ago, they were more ritualistic in religion and had a different type of folk beliefs about many things. After the Arya Samaj movement (as mentioned in 4.5.1) the outlook of the Jats has changed and they term all folk beliefs about mythology and cosmology, as well as the intricate ritualistic kind of life, as *pop-lila*. When questioned about their cosmology, the reply given by most of the Jats is that when they were born they found the world to be the same as it is today, and it will be the same also when they would leave it. So, for them, they say, there is no question of trying to know about the origin of the world and about cosmology, etc. But at the same time some of the Jats say that previously, i.e., before the Arya Samaj movement, the Jats did have some folk beliefs in respect of cosmology.

They say there are three *tals* : one above us where God Indra and others live; the *tal* on which we the human beings live; and the one below ours called *patal* where, according to some people, the dead live, while according to others Lord Krishna and Arjun went to the *patal* asking Daropadi to cook for them, but they never returned back from there. After every 14,000 years, they say, two types of destructions of the world take place alternatively. These destructions are called *parlay*, i.e., the dooms day, and *maha parlay*, i.e. the great dooms day. They further believe that during the *maha parlay* every thing in the world gets destroyed. There is water, water everywhere. Then there appears a lotus flower. From this lotus flower is born Lord Brahma - the creater of this universe. All the human beings are subsequently, in turn born out of Lord Brahma. Man, the Jats believe, is made of earth, water, air, sun and fire. All these five elements are

Gods. After his death man goes to the south. This is the direction of the dead.

4.6 DAILY LIFE

So far as the daily life of the Jats is concerned, the following observations of Ibbetson are as valid today as these were a hundred years ago:

> The daily life of the ordinary able-bodied villager is one of almost unremitting toil. He rises before dawn, eats a little stale bread, gets out his bullocks, goes to the fields and begins work at once. About 8 O'clock his wife or child would bring him a damper (bread cake of the country), often stale, and a bowl of butter milk, or milk and water (*lahsi; pakki* or *kachi*). At noon he has a hearty meal of fresh damper and a little pulse boiled with spices (dal), or some boiled vegetable (*Sag*); in the cold weather he goes home for it, and does not begin work again till 2 p.m. In the evening he comes home and, after feeding his cattle eats his dinner, the grand meal of the day.
>
> The women of the family have all the grinding, cooking, cleaning the house, and spinning to do. The Jat women also help their husbands in the *khets.*
>
> The life is a terribly dull one. The periodical fair or mela or the occasional wedding forms its chief relief; together with the months of sugar pressing, when everybody goes about with a yard of cane in his mouth, and a deal of gossiping (as well as a deal of hard work) is done at the press. But the toil is unremitting; and when we think about a mud hovel in a crowded village innocent of sanitation must be in July and August, we can only wonder at the marvellous patience and contentment of the villager (1883:122-123).

4.7 THE PANCHAYAT

4.7.1 *Gram Panchayat*

The *gram panchayat* (a statutory body) of Chhatera - which consists of six elected members and an opted one - runs the village administration of both Chhatera and an adjoining small village Ladpur[9]. The *gram panchayat* deals with almost every aspect of the village administration and development. It has the power to settle petty judicial cases and impose a fine on the guilty up to Rs. 20.00 only. The sources of revenue for the *gram panchayat* are : the *chulha tax* of Rupee one per year; ten per cent of the land revenue collected from both the villages - Chhatera and Ladpur; such returns as accrue from leasing the *panchayat's* 50 acres of common land called *gaon shamlat*; and the grants from the government.

4.7.2 *Multi-Village Panchayat*

Whenever there is a breach of norms of the village community of a nature that is too serious to be decided by the *gram panchayat*, or if the matter involves or effects people of more than one village, or when the person concerned does not care for the *gram panchayat* and flouts its authority, then efforts are made to bring other pressures on him. In all such cases, a multi-village *panchayat*[10] is summoned. Besides this, if a general discussion or decision on any important matter is required, or need is felt by the community for some social reforms, even in such situations a meeting of one of these multi-village *panchayats* is convened. The level at which any particular matter shall be taken up depends upon the merits of the individual situation. There are *panchayats* at the levels of four villages (*chaugama*), eight villages (*athen*), 12 villages (*bariha*), 24 villages (*chaubisa*) and 40 villages (*chalisa*), respectively. These are nesting series. Chhatera is member of a *chaugama, bariha, chaubisa* and a *chalisa*.[11]

The *chaugama*, of which Chhatera is a member, includes the contiguous villages of Malha Majra, Kheri Manajat, Akbarpur Barota and Chhatera Bahadarpur (including Ladpur). This *chaugama* is headed by village Majra. These four villages have a very close affiliation with each other. They participate in each other's affairs, joys and sorrows. They have close relations of *bhai-chara*, i.e., brotherhood. They give and accept *ulahna* (complaint) among each others, i.e., they listen to each other's complaints and grievances. If some important action is to be taken against some outside individual or group of persons, some other village or villages by any member-village of this *chaugama*, the other three villages are consulted by it. Every defence or boundary problem is discussed jointly. Even when making some major donations on village basis, they (the four villages) consult one another. They practise *chaugama* exogamy. Just as for certain purposes social relations are at least equally imporant as the biological relations, the territorial proximity is also sometimes as meaningful as the genealogical closeness among individuals and/or groups. Every village is a member also of a small group of all those adjoining villages with which some parts of its boundary is in common. Exogamy is practised even within this kind of groups. They share many other common interests and understandings, privileges and obligations. This is called *sim-jor-ki-biradri*, i.e., the brotherhood of the common boundary. These are ego-centred overlapping groups. The Jats of Chhatera, of course, maintain a special relationship with those in the *pauli thola* of Majra.

NOTES

1. For details please see Chandhoke, S.K. 1978d.
2. The most important part of a marriage ceremony among the Hindus is the rituals performed by the "couple-in-the-making" while circumbulating round the sacrificial fire with one end of their respective head gears tied together.
3. Of these two brothers, Ishwar and Dayanand, one is in the army. So, practically there is only one household in the village now carrying out the profession of Nai.
4. For the service caste people, their clients are their main possession/wealth/property. Just like the division of landed property among the various co-parceners (of the land-owning sections) at the time of fissioning of the family, among the service caste people there is division of the *jajman* households. So, these *jajmans* are inherited, transferred, transferred back, sold and even mortgaged almost in the same fashion as any of the landed property.
5. The *Jogis* of Chhatera had under their jurisdiction villages Gadhi, Malha Majra, Chhatera, Ladpur, Barhi Fatehpur and Machhri.
6. The terms Household, Simple Household and Complex Household have been used here by me exactly in the same sense as by Shah (1973).
7. In most of the cases, I was told, this is done due to the old age and/or failing health of the eldest male member.
8. Sanskritization is the process of a low caste rising to a higher position in the caste hierarchy by adopting the Sanskritized way of life. To quote Srinivas (the scholar who coined the term) himself in this connection, 'The caste system is far from a rigid system in which the position of each component caste is fixed for all time. Movement has always been possible, and especially so in the middle regions of the hierarchy. A low caste was able, in a generation or two, to rise to a higher position in the hierarchy by adopting vegetarianism and teetotallerism, and by Sanskritzing its ritual and pantheon. In short, it took over, as far as possible, the customs, rites and beliefs of the Brahmans, and the adoption of the Brahmanic way of life by a low caste seems to have been frequent, though theoretically forbidden. This process has been called "Sanskritization" (1962:42).
9. Ladpur is included in this *panchayat* to fulfil the legal requirement that there must be a minimum population of 1,250 under a *panchayat*.
10. For details please refer to the article on the topic by Chandhoke, S.K. in the February, 1983 issue of *EKISTICS*, Athens
11. Baden-Powell, B.H. (1913) has also given information about the origin of groups of 24,42 and 84 villages locally formed.

FIVE

PHYSICAL ASPECTS OF THE VILLAGE

5.1 THE KHAP

THE LOCAL term for a group of villages belonging to people of the same *gotra* is *khap*. Villages in the region are not alone, these are generally one of a cluster of villages (Figure 5.1) covering an area having traditions of a common origin and descent (Opler, 1956:5). In certain matters the *khap* acts as a unit of social interaction. Just as it is sometimes said that such and such caste has so many villages, similarily, it is said *Dahiya ki khap man chalis gam sain* – meaning thereby that the group of villages inhabited by the Jats belonging to the Dahiya *gotra* consists of 40 villages. A *khap* always has a common leadership, common code of conduct and sanctions. For certain purposes, the residents of a *khap* treat themselves to be an 'in-group' and act with a 'we-feeling' identifying all the villages (and their inhabitants) to be in the *khap* (Chandhoke, 1983:30). Every *khap* has a *panchayat* also which performs certain special functions. The Jats of Chhatera belong to Jun *gotra*. There is no other village of Jun *gotra* in this region. But the Jats of Chhatera treat themselves as members of the *Dahiya ki khap*, and the Dahiyas also recognize this relationship.

5.2 PATTERN OF VILLAGE LAYOUT

5.2.1 *General description*

Villages in this region are strictly of nucleated type. Not only there are no hamlets, there are no field houses even. The residential area is located at one place, called *abadi*, with green fields all around (Please refer to figure 5.2). The only private structure (individual property) outside the *abadi*, a small room here and there, is to protect the tube-well, where a couple of *khats* and on rare occasions some agricutural in-puts are kept for very short durations.

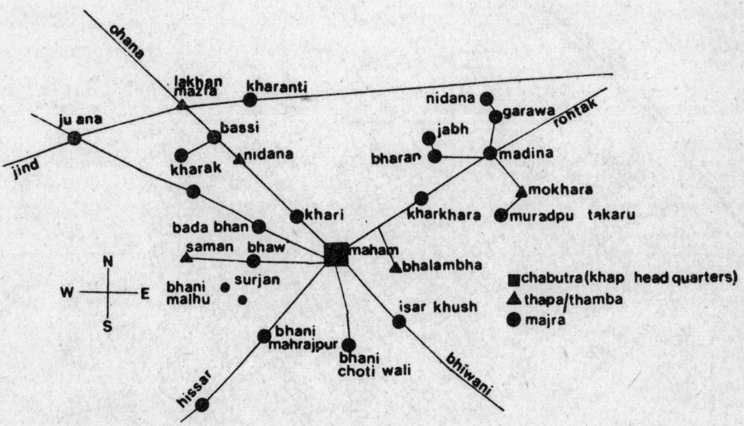

Figure 5.1: Plan of *Chaubisi* Meham *Khap* of Chopra Jats (District Rohtak, Haryana

The *abadi* is always located on the land higher than the surrounding fields. There is a proverb, *ghar uchan khet nichan*, meaning thereby that the houses should always be at a higher level and the agricultural fields at lower level.

Villages in this area have since long time been nucleated, and there is absolutely no tendency towards dispersal during the last century. To quote Purser and Fanshawe in this connection :

> Looking at the large area of the villages, Mr. Tomason hazarded a guess in 1845 A.D. that the Settlement which has just expired would be marked by the foundation of many outlaying hamlets. This has not been the case and is not likely to be so.
>
> ...the people seem to be quite content to plod long distances daily to and from their work - a habit born no doubt of the days

when they might be compelled next moment to take refuge from the fields within the fortified villages.

A ditch nearly always surrounded a village itself, and the outer walls of the dwellings are completely closed towards it (1880:10).

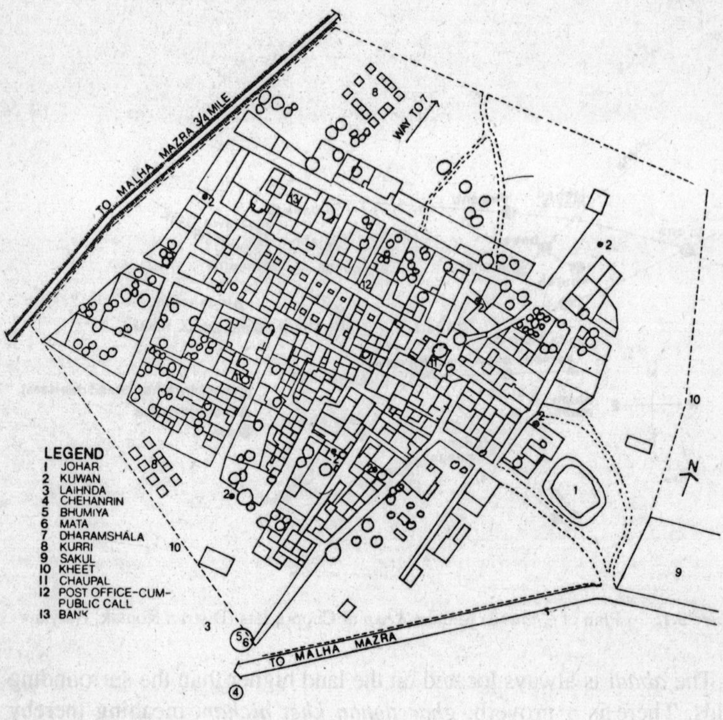

Figure 5.2: Existing Plan of Chhatera

The following observations of Ali, H.A. about Mewat villages in the adjacent region is fully applicable to the Chhatera region also:

> The plains are studded with villages here and there - each presenting the appearance of a low mound varying in dimensions according to the size of its population. The height of these mounds partly represents the age of the village. A high ground was originally selected, partly for protection against water logging and partly to serve as vantage point to see approaching foes. But this high

ground has become higher by the accumulating debris of successive mud houses (1970:47).

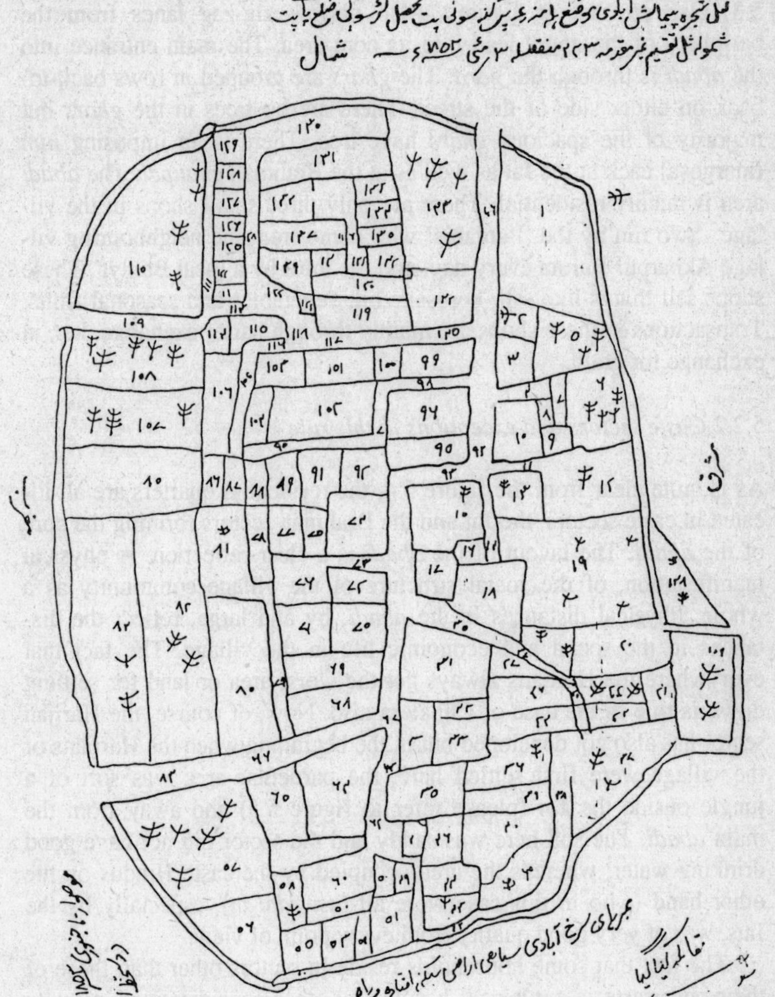

Figure 5.3: Plan of Abadi of (Adjoining) Village Malha Majra As on 3rd May, 1853 Depicting the Tight Character of the *abadi* with a Wall around it Having very Few Openings - typical Character of Villages in the Region

The village is an agglomerated amorphous cluster of houses with dead walls facing the *khets* around. The *abadi* has an introvert, i.e., inward-looking character in its physical aspect (Please refer to figure 5.3) also see list of figures. Also narrow zig-zag lanes from the periphery of the *abadi* lead into its core area. The main entrance into the *abadi* is through the *gora*. The *ghars* are grouped in rows back-to-back on either side of the street. There are no trees in the *ghars* but majority of the spacious *ghars* have tree. There is an imposing *nim* (margosa) each at the Jat as well as at the Brahman *chaupal*. The *abadi* area is mainly residential. There are only three small shops in the village - two run by the 'Punjabis' who come from the neighbouring village Akbarpur Barota every day, and the third by a local Baniya. These shops sell things like salt, kerosene oil, vegetables and seasonal fruits. Transactions in these shops are mainly through barter exchange, i.e., in exchange for grain.

5.2.2 *Caste sectors and exceptions to this rule*

As is quite clear from the figure 5.4, the residential quarters are all located in caste sectors, the Jat and the Brahman sectors forming the core of the *abadi*. The layout of the *abadi* is a clear reflection. A physical manifestation, of the social structure of the village community as a whole. Physical distances in the *abadi*, by and large, reflect the distances in the social and economic life in the village. The fact that everywhere the Harijans always get the worst area or land for settling down is true in the case of Chhatera also. Now, of course, the Harijan sector has also got developed but in the beginning when the Harijans of the village were first settled here, the particular area was sort of a jungle ouside the *kot* (please refer to figure 5.5) and away from the main *abadi*. The soil here was sandy and the sector did not have good drinking water, whereas the area occupied by the caste Hindus on the other hand (who in this case were all *biswedaran*), especially by the Jats, was of very good quality from every point of view.

The fact that some households reside in sectors other than those of their own caste is explained, besides by other considerations, also by the stage of the development process of the village at which a particular family migrated into Chhatera, partly by the nature of the relationship of that family to its *jajman/kisan* and mainly by the fact that some of the members of the proprietary body have their lands scattered in almost all parts of the *abadi*. Whenever any *be-biswedar* leaves the village, the ownership of the plot under his house, etc., reverts back into the proprietary body. According to the oldest settlement report of the village (1880) available with the revenue department, *gairmalkan* cannot mortgage, pawn or sell the residential house and without the permission of the *malkan* they cannot make houses on the demolished site in the area. They cannot remove *malba* or use debris if they move to another area. So long as they and their heirs live there, the *malkan* cannot dispossess them. They can take wood from the trees for making houses, etc., but cannot sell the wood.

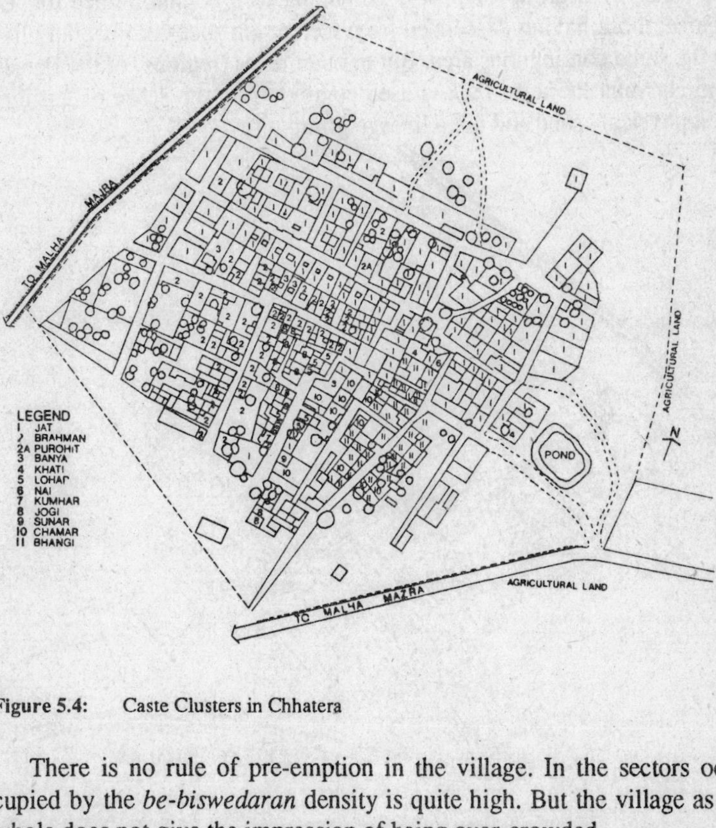

Figure 5.4: Caste Clusters in Chhatera

There is no rule of pre-emption in the village. In the sectors occupied by the *be-biswedaran* density is quite high. But the village as a whole does not give the impression of being over-crowded.

Some of the streets had been brick-paved and cambered to the middle for being used for surface drainage. But, in course of time, partly due to constant use and the vagaries of nature and partly due to the lack of civic sense among the villagers, parts of these pavings have gone down under mud and dust - at places three to four feet deep. The streets are used not only for circulation but also for many other activities spilling out of the house.

Although in the revenue records of the village its sectors are mentioned as *thola-Jatan* and *thola-Brahmanan* (because Jats and Brahmans are the only land revenue paying groups in the village), in actual practice, the village not being a big one, there are no divisions like *tholas*, *patis* and *panas*. In some of the nearby big villages, however, such divisions do exist. The Chhaterans sometimes use the term *thok* in the sense of a group of people belonging to a common ancestor. Of course, those having descended from a common ancestor generally live in the same continguous area. But in other areas (regions) of the Punjab and Haryana the term *thok* is used commonly in the sense of territory or a physical space and not a lineage group.

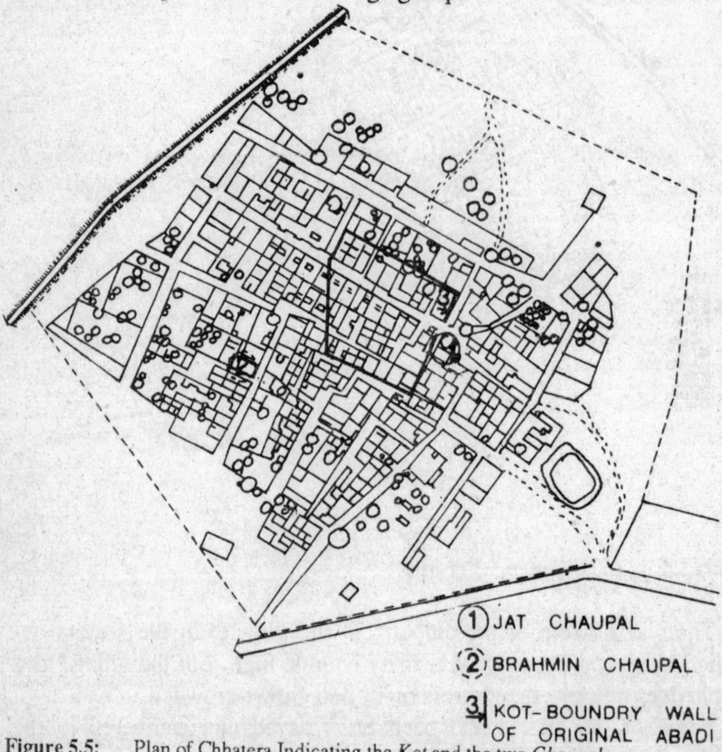

Figure 5.5: Plan of Chhatera Indicating the *Kot* and the two *Chaupals*

While talking to outsiders or speaking in a formal tone, Chhaterans use terms, like, *gali-Jogiyan* or *gali-Brahmanan*, etc., although the *Jogis* have more than one *gals* now. While talking among themselves, if the Chhaterans want to call somebody, then for an easy identification they say *bhai Brahmanan men se bula laiya phalan ke*, meaning, thereby, brother call so and so from the Jats/Brahmans depending upon the caste to which the person to be called belongs.[1] If, however, in the same caste there are more than one person bearing the same name then the name of the father of the person to be called is also added. Of course, there are nick-names for almost every individual and for every family in the village.

5.3 BAKHAL/BAGAR, i.e. CLOSED HOUSE CLUSTERS

5.3.1 *Reasons for and advantages of this pattern*

From the law and order point of view, the Chhatera region had some of the very disturbed times in history. There was, therefore, naturally a great emphasis on giving a very closed and tight character to the habitations at the macro- as well as micro-level. "...Nearly every conqueror who invaded India from the north or attacked the Moghul royal city from the south, extended his ravages in all probability to Rohtak, and it is not surprising, therefore, if the vestiges of many destroyed villages are to be found..." (Purser and Fanshawe, 1880:10).

To use the words of Kiran:

> The Rohtak district...is strategically situated in the passage from the north-west through the Delhi Gateway to the broad Ganga plain. The routes from Peshawar and Multan to Delhi converge here. The area, as a whole, witnessed some important historical events and movements...lying in an area of much political activity it could survive and maintain its identity because its inhabitants were verile people... (1970:20).

There are two main routes (now National Highways as well as main railway lines) from the north leading to the capital city of Delhi – one, Delhi-Ferozepur route which extends up to Multan, Karachi, etc. (now in Pakistan); and the other, Delhi-Amritsar route which extends to Lahore, Rawalpindi, Peshawar, etc., (also in Pakistan) and further to Kabul (in Afghanistan). The invading armies used to come through

both of these routes. Before a final assault on the capital contingents coming through the two routes used to join together and re-organize themselves in the area presently forming the Rohtak district, particularly in the small sub-region in which Chhatera falls.
Purser and Fanshawe have mentioned this point thus:

> From the time of increasing quarrel which began in 1817 on the death of Bahadurshah, the successor of Aurungzeb, the Moghul empire fell rapidly to its ruin. The Jats, Marathas, Sikhs and the English all fought here and invaded it during different periods. During all this time of turmoil and bloodshed the district was profoundly affected. It formed the eastern region of Haryana, a tract which gained its unenviable reputation for murder and robbery at this time...Encouraged by the weakness of their rulers the people began to refuse to pay revenue and adopted a warlike and independent spirit, which set those who set to coerce them at defiance (1880:31).

Due to this kind of disturbances as well as considerations of privacy and the close kinship ties, houses used to be constructed in close lanes in villages which themselves comprised of a number of such lanes packed with houses clustered together closely. Writing about the Jat habitations in general, Mukerji remarks :

> A complete block of houses belonging to families tracing their origin to the same source are often found within one compound. Such a compact family block is locally known as Bakhal. Bakhal is not a caste-feature but a family-feature. When the property of a family is divided and the house is divided within, one-roomed houses are created each having its separate door but the original house as such remains intact externally. The different houses in a Bakhal are occupied by several families tracing their origin to a near and immediate ancestor. Jats and other communities have their separate Bakhals so that in a limited area only one community has its residences (1957:23).

A similar phenomenon that was very much prevalent in the past, some remnants of which still exist in the region, was locally called *bagar*. But in Chhatera only the Harijans and some of the other *be-biswedaran* used to live in the *bagars*. The *biswedaran* had their residences within the *kot*, i.e., the village wall. Moreover, their *ghars* are also of a fort-like construction. The Harijans of Chhatera even now live in *bagars* (please see plate No. 5.1). *Bhangis* have two *bagars* - *urla-bagar* and *parla-bagar*. Similarly, *Jogis* also live in two *bagars*. Some of these *bagars* have had as many as 30 to 40 *gnars* in each of them. More or less similar observations have been made by Chandhoke and Singh (1969:4) about the Saharanpur region (Uttar Pradesh, India) also. The explanation for the existence of *bakhals* among the Harijans and Muslims, as reported by Chandhoke and Singh, is that of acute shortage of space and "their clinging together is also an attribute of their weak position in the society, the closely knit structure and physical proximity of families affording them a psychological sense of security, enabling them to face the hostilities of powerful individuals and groups". Among the higher castes, however, this *bakhal* system is absent in the region, because they neither have scarcity of land nor do they feel insecure. The reason for the presence of *bakhals* among the higher sections of society in some of the regions is their fear from outsiders which is non-existent in this region these days.

Plate 5.1: A get-together in a Harijan *bagar* Child enjoying *huka* Tired man with legs up relaxing on *khat* in the background

Writing about the Bharatpur region of Eastern Rajasthan, India, Chandhoke and Singh observe that (Please refer to figure 5.6):

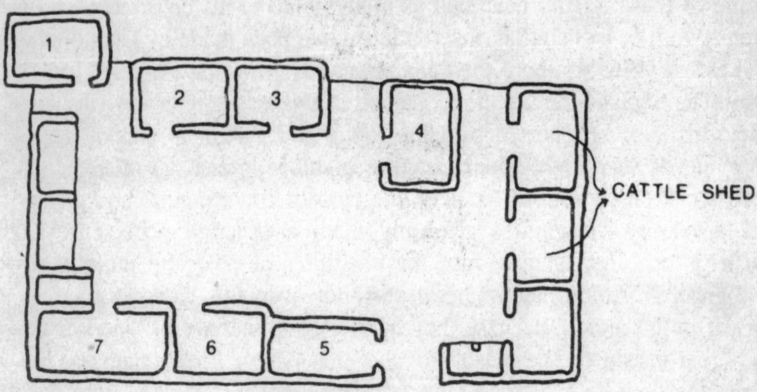

Figure 5.6: Plan of a *Composite House*

There is a marked contrast between the houses of the well-to-do and the rest of the villagers. The well-to-do generally have separate buildings for the house proper, the male living quarters and the cattle sheds. Almost 60 per cent of the households in the region have to make do with a single bare room, while 1.5 per cent of the households have no regular room at all. These people tend to live jointly on a single plot accommodating several distinct dwelling units (composite houses). In these Composite Houses, the cattle sheds are often grouped in one corner of the plot, though separate structures may be possessed by different households. The houses are found to be grouped in three different ways: (1) along both sides of narrow and winding streets constructed in a continuous row; (2) around a closed street; (3) grouping of closely related households around a common open area with access restricted to a single point, where common cattle sheds are provided.

COMPOSITE HOUSES: A composite house is a well-defined and enclosed complex comprising a number of dwelling units belonging to closely related families. The access to the complex is normally at one point. The individual houses are one or two-roomed. Generally all the dwellings are of the same size and design (1974:68,69,70).

The main advantage of this pattern of house groupage was that if one door was closed the whole *bagar* was protected. Only those persons who had business there needed to enter a *bagar*. If there was a single man, woman, or child present there he could keep an eye on the entire complex. The pattern also promotes co-operation among the households and helps maintain and strengthen social control. Residents of a *bagar* form such a close-knit group that it has been observed that even the dogs belonging to a *bagar* recognize the people living there and those who visit the *bagar* frequently. If any stranger comes there the dogs immediately start barking and raise an alarm. Besides that, this kind of a house groupage pattern is also advantageous internally (as stated earlier). A *bagar* is named after its eledest male member. When naming somebody, for easy and quick identification, people say (so and so from such and such *bagar*.)

The open space (between the *ghars*) in a *bagar* is also called *bagar*. This is the reason that at the micro-level, i.e., in the individual structure (it may be *ghar, baithak* or *gher*) also, except in the *chaukband* type of *ghar* where the central open court is called *chauk*, the open space is called *bagar*.

Besides, other similar situations have also been recorded by Chandhoke and Singh (1974) about Rajasthan villages, by Forde (1963) about the Blackfoot tribes of Africa and by Rohit Singh (1972) about the Manipuri villages in general and those inhabited by the Purums in particular. Writing about the Yoruba tribe, Forde observes :

> The houses of related families are usually built in continuous groups of four or more to enclose a square compound reached through a single gateway. On the outside they present a blank expanse of clay walling, and their entrances and the verandahs, stretching continously from one house to the next, face the compound (1963:152).

About the tightly grouped clusters of houses in general, with special reference to those of the Savaras - a row of houses which have a common plinth and a common roof and which look like one single house - Karve has made observations which seem to be quite appropriate in the case of the *bakhals* of Chhatera also:

> There are different ways of arranging and building houses in which the houses unit cannot be defined merely by the 'gestalt' as ap-

parent to the eye but a reference is needed to the internal structure, sometimes to the number of cooking places and separating walls and sometimes to families and lineage (1957:20).

About the Purum houses, Rohit Singh observes thus:

> All the houses are built on raised one to two feet high mud platforms. The house grouping presents a pattern which facilitates working of kinship obligations across households of closely related kins. The fissioned households of close patrilineal relatives tend to stay in close proximity using a common same courtyard. The members of the group share in common different aspects of living and avail of the benefit of social coverage under one experienced and older person. (Such a group is always named after a family surname . . . (1972).

5.3.2 *Changes in the pattern*

Although any pattern of human habitation, once formed, has a tendency to perpetuate itself, no pattern, however tenacious, can go on resisting the winds of change indefinitely. For the last 35 years or so, as a result of the changed law and order situation and due to the operation of a number of other factors, this pattern of house groupage is on the way out very fast. In cases where the amount of land owned by a family within the *abadi* is too small, but the numerical strength of the household has increased considerably and the family has consequently fissioned out (resulting in the partitioning of property, etc.), in course of time, the new house groups have acquired somewhat the character of *bagars*. Although these new *bagars* do not have *barnas* (doors/gates) at the point of entry, these are otherwise still very much retaining the character of the old *bagars*. This shows that because of disappearance of insecurity this particular element has disappeared (from the *bagars*) otherwise this pattern of house groupage has not completely outlived its utility, and also that the shortage of space has not ended for these people. There is no easing of the situation in this respect. In such a *bagar*, the common court - also called a *bagar* - is treated as the front court of each of the *ghars* in the *bagar*, although a particular *ghar* may be situated far away from the *gal*. For all ceremonial, religious as well as social purposes the part of the *bagar* that abuts the *gal* is treated as their *barna* by each of the *ghars* in the *bagar*.

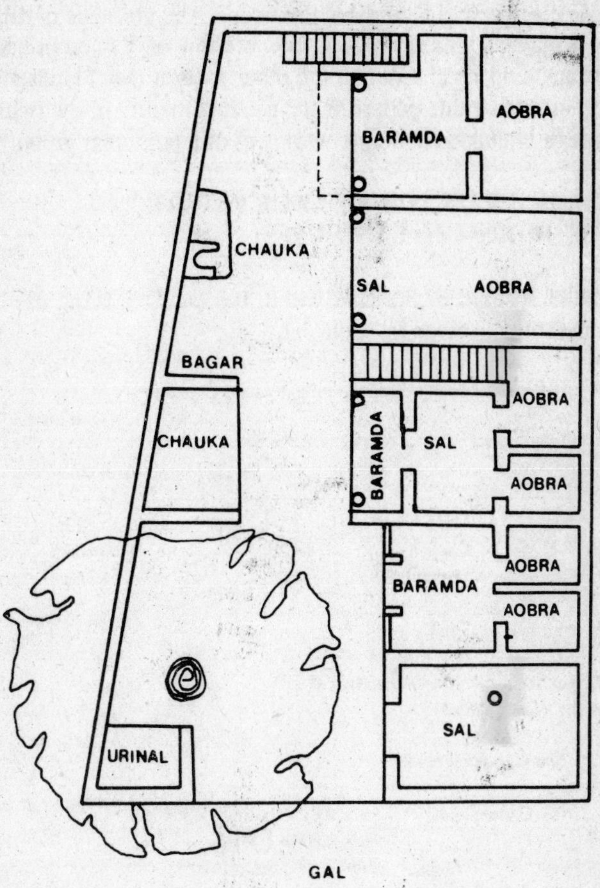

Figure 5.7: Layout Plat of a Brahman *Bagar*

Since there is not much congestion within the *abadi* of Chhatera, and almost all the *biswedaran* households have reasonably spacious *ghars, baithaks* and *ghers*, etc., with open spaces therein they do not feel need for any sort of enclosed open spaces at the group level. Their level of community life is different. In the Brahman sector of the village, of course, there are two house clusters called *bagars* (please refer to figure 5.7 and plate 5.2). Actually these are not truly *bagars* in the sense they exist in the case of the depressed sections of the community. It is a notable point that none of the *bagars* has even a single *baithak* within it. All the houeholds living in these *bagars* have their *baithaks* elsewhere, i.e., outside the *bagar*. The presence of this type of house groupage pattern among one section of the proprietary body (Brahmans) and its absence in the other section (Jats) lends support to the argument that this pattern is the product mainly of the twin factors; shortage of land and economic weakness of a particular group.

5.4 BREAK-UP OF THE VILLAGE ESTATE ACCORDING TO LAND-USE

A detailed account of the land within the *lal dora* being used for different purposes is given in Table 5.1.

TABLE 5.1: Land-use break-up of the village estate Chhatera

(total area = 742 acres)

S.No.	Use	Area (in acres)
1	*Abadi*	13.0
2	*Khets*	666.5
3	*Shamlat deh*	62.5
	Total	742.0

Source: Records of the *gram panchayat* at and the village *patwari*

Note: *Shamlat deh* includes :

(a) *Charagah* = 12 acres (including *chehanrin* = 1 acre), and

(b) *Johars* = 2.5 acres

5.5 THE DENSITIES

5.5.1 *Densities and land-use within the* abadi

Because the *lal dora* was considerably extended in Chhatera at the time of consolidation of holdings in the village in 1956 and a sizable amount of land was earmarked for *tausih abadi*, a lot of space is still lying vacant within the *lal dora*. There is, therefore, no congestion within the *abadi*. To quote Lewis Oscar in this connection :

> At each Settlement the limits of the habitation area are fixed. The habitation area or the residential section of the village is excluded from the revenue system, and is, therefore, tax free, in distinct contrast to the house tax found throughout much of the world. Since the area is tax free, there is no necessity for the *Patwari* to maintain a record of the invidivual site holders. It is said that the individual sites were plotted on a map during the settlement of 1880, but at present there is no exact record of these holdings. Traditionally it is a type of common land which differs from the others in that houses are constructed on it, as well as coutyards and other enclosures... (1958:96).

Plate 5.2: Afternoon activities in the *chauk* of a Brahman *bagar*. Young women making *semi* (vermicelli), old woman spinning *charkha*. Bedding spread for drying on the terrace parapet

Break-up of the land within the *lal dora*, according to use, is given in Table 5.2.

TABLE 5.2: Break-up of area within the *lal dora* of village Chhatera according to use

(Total area = 13 acres)

S.No.	Use	Percentage to total area within the *lal dora*
1	Residential	44.8
2	Under roads and foot-paths	20.8
3	Commercial	0.3
4	Public and semi-public use like *chaupal*	1.2
5	Other uses like cattle-sheds	5.3
6	Area vacant at present	27.6
	Total	100.00

Source : Ghosh and Kulsreshtra 1973.

5.5.2 *Densities in the various caste sectors*

Jats and Brahmans occupy major part of the *abadi* land. Their sectors are located side by side. In fact, in the old village, i.e., in the beginning when the village was founded and for quite some time after that, it is only the Jats and the Brahmans who had been living within the *kot*. About the villages of Rohtak district in general, Purser and Fanshawe (1880:120) have observed that "The proprietors, Baniyas and Brahmans, live in the centre; the menials on the outskirts of the village". It is also interesting to note that the outer belt (as if serving as the first line of defence) consists mainly of the out-houses of the Jat families and residences of low and Scheduled Caste families. The central cell consists of Jat residences (Mukerji, 1957:24).

Ownership in the *abadi* being in proportion to one's share in the agricultural lands and the *be-biswedaran* being at the mercy of the *biswedaran*, land with the non-agriculturists is very meagre. This has naturally led to different densities and varying degrees of congestion in the sectors inhabited by the different caste groups. While in the sector inhabited by the Jats density is hardly 50 persons per acre, in the Brahman sector it is as high as about 150, while in the sectors occupied by the non-land-owning sections of the community it is all the more high. This is so in spite of the fact that during the last consolidation of holdings in the village the non-proprietors were given a lot of land in the *tausih abadi*.

5.5.3 *Densities in the core and in the periphery*

The core of the village *abadi* is compact and thickly populated with a density of over 150 persons per acre. The peripheral areas are sparsely built, having a density of less than 50 persons per acre. Although no out-houses or field-houses have come up in Chhatera so far,[2] the *abadi* has now developed a tendency for an outward movement. Formerly, villagers preferred to live in the inner parts of the *abadi*. But now the choice is more in favour of the outer parts. This is evident from the behaviour pattern of the villagers at the time of partition of property among different brothers, and other agnatic kins due to fissioning of the family, and also from a careful look at the details of the mutual exchanges of property in the village during the last couple of decades or so.

TABLE 5.3: Housing conditions in village Chhatera

(Total = 138 houses)

S.No.	Type of Housing	Percentage
1	In good condition with life expectancy of about 20 to 40 years	47
2	In fair condition with life expectancy of 10 to 20 years	30
3	Fit for demolition	23
	Total	100

Source : Ghosh and Kulsreshtha 1973

5.6 FACILITIES, UTILITIES AND SERVICES IN THE VILLAGE

The village is deficient in facilities, utilities and services. Water supply in the *abadi* is by wells and hand-pumps, locally called *barmas*. There is no sewage disposal system in the village. A couple of latrines have now been constructed but even these are not used. Surface drainage is very poor. One often finds pools of water stagnating at places.

5.7 HOUSING CONDITIONS IN THE VILLAGE

An idea about the condition of the existing housing stock in the village can be had from Table 5.3.

5.8 APPENDIX TO CHAPTER Five

Local Organization of Tribes

Source : Ibbetson (1883:120-121)

The primary sub-division of the tribe is into *thapas* or *thambas.* A tribal community having obtained possession of a tract, in course of time it would be inconvenient for them all to live together, and a part of the community would found a new village, always on the edge of a drainage line from which their tanks would be filled. This process would be repeated till the tract became dotted over with the villages all springing originally from the one parent village. The people describe the facts by saying that, of several brothers, one settled in one village and one in another; but this no doubt means that the part of the community that migrated consisted of integral families or groups of families descended in one common branch from the ancestor. In this way many villages were divided known by the same name, with the addition of the words *kalan* and *khurd* (big and little). This by no means implies that *kalan* is larger than *khurd*, but only that the older branch settled in *kalan*; in fact the old records always use the word *buzurg* (elder) instead of *kalan*.

The group of villages so bound together by common descent from a *thapa*, and are connected by sub-feudal ties which are still recognized, the village occupied by the descendants of the common ancestor in the eldest line being, however, small and reduced in circumstances, still acknowledged as the head. To this day, when a headman dies the other villages of the *thapa* assemble to instal his heir, and the turban of the parent village is first tied on his head. When Brahmans and the brotherhood are fed on the occasion of deaths, etc., (*mel jor*), it is from the *thapa* villages that they are collected, and the Brahmans of the head village are fed first and receive double fees. So among the menial castes, who still retain an internal organization of far greater vitality than the higher castes now possess, the representative of the head village is always the foreman of the caste jury which is assembled from the *thapa* villages to hear and decide disputes. In old days the subordinate villages used to pay some small *Chaurayat* to the head village on the day of the great Diwali. The head village is still called the "great village", the "turban village", the "village of origin", or the "*thika* village", *thika* being the sign of authority formally impressed in old days on the forehead of the heir of a deceased leader in the presence of the assembled *thapa*. In one case a villager told me he had changed his thapa, because there were so many Brahmans in his original *thapa* that he would find it expensive to feed them. I sopke to the original *thika* village about it, and they said that no village could change its thapa. "*Put kuput hosakta; magr ma kuma nahin hosakti*". "A son may forget sonship; but not a mother her motherhood".

NOTES

1. This shows how individual persons are identified with physical places that are patterned caste-wise.
2. An agriculturist family of village Bindroli - two miles north-east of Chhatera — has purchased some agricultural lands in village Ladpur (under Chhatera *panchayat* itself). This land adjoins that of Chhatera. As this new family does not own any land in the *abadi* of Ladpur it has built a small house in its agricultural fields. Some male members of the family stay in this out house, especially during the agriculturally busy seasons. An elderly woman of the family comes from Bindroli every day and cooks for those staying in the out-house and returns home to Bindroli every evening. Some cooked food is brought from Bindroli itself.

SIX

ECONOMIC ASPECTS

CASTE SYSTEM has traditionally been exercising a very strong influence on the life and style of the Indian people. In spite of its having lost some ground during the last three-four decades, this institution still holds a considerable sway in the country side. In this system, the caste of a group and its occupation almost invariably go together as occupations are caste-prescribed. Besides, there is the famous *jajmani* system - a mechanism through which the roles and rights of various caste groups are very meticulously, though at times intricately, worked out and laid down. These roles and rights are recognized and accepted by all sections of the village community.

The social and economic aspects of caste and *jajmani* systems are quite inextricably interwoven with each other. So, a lot of information and data which throw light on the economic life of Chhaterans have been covered along with the social aspects. Therefore, though, in the first instance, it may apparently appear to the reader that enough information on the economic aspects of the life of Chhaterans has not been given in the present chapter, a careful second thought would remove this misconception because a lot of information which one may expect to find in this chapter has already been given in a preceding one on Social Structure.

6.1 OCCUPATIONAL PATTERNS

The main occupation of the Chhaterans, quite naturally, is agricutlure. However, during the decade 1961-71, the percentage of workers engaged in the primary sector declined from 91.8 per cent to 65.5 per cent of the total workers. Mechanical farming, higher literacy rates, fewer employment opportunities in the village and its proximity to

Delhi being the major factors accounting for this shift. Some eight per cent of the total workers are engaged in their traditional occupations, a little over seven per cent have seen a complete change in their occupation, while 19 per cent work mainly as agricultural labourers.

Over one hundred Chhaterans are working in the Delhi Municipal Corporation, Posts and Telegraphs Department, Delhi Electric Supply Undertaking, the Sales Tax Department and in the various ministries of the Government of India, in Delhi Administration, Delhi Development Authority, etc. Most of them commute to and from the city every day. About 20 of them working in the Delhi Transport Corporation, Delhi Police, Fire Brigade, etc., visit the village on week-ends or even more occasionally. A number of Chhaterans are serving in the army also.

6.2 AGRICULTURE

According to the revenue records in 1972, there were 54 agricultural holdings in the villages; 41 per cent of these being less than five acres, 36 per cent between five and 15 acres, and only two holdings were more than 25 acres each. Since then the number of holdings have increased and the average size has, consequently, gone down. Traditionally, the main agricultural crops in the region have been wheat, *bajra, jawar*, gram and pulses. Though farmers in some of the neighbouring villages sometimes used to grow paddy also on small plots, this crop was never grown in Chhatera. Sugarcane and oilseeds were also grown in small quantities only.

In 1971, the village had seven tractors, 25 tube-wells, two crushers, 20 threshers and a large number of other big and small agricultural implements.

In 1970, the total agricultural produce of the village was estimated to be 2,875 quintals. About 60 per cent of this produce was estimated to have been consumed in the village itself, while the 40 per cent surplus was sold in Narela and Sonepat *mandis* (Ghosh and Kulsreshta, 1973). During the same year there were 126 draft animals in Chhatera. There were also 202 milch animals and 34 other animals (including sheep, pigs, poultry head, etc. kept exclusively by the Harijans), and the daily sale of milk in the village was about 130 litres (Please see plate 6.1).

Plate 6.1: *Bitoras, bungas* and *kurris* in the village *shamlat* (common land) at the outskirts of the *abadi*

6.3 INCOME AND EXPENDITURE

According to the same source (i.e., Ghosh and Kulsrehtha, 1973), the per capita income in the village was estimated to be Rs. 402.00 in 1970. Castewise, among the Jats, Brahmans and Harijans it was Rs. 510, Rs. 337 and Rs. 301, respectively. The per capita expenditure during the same year was estimated to be Rs. 300. About 33 per cent of the households in the village were reported to be under debt, the amount of loan taken by them during the year being Rs. 1,40,000 only. About 50 per cent of this loan was spent on non-productive purposes like weddings, etc., while the rest was invested in land, house, tractor, vehicle and agricutlrual implements.

6.4 SOME RECENT CHANGES

6.4.1 *Agriculture*

A perceptible change in the fields of agriculture and animal husbandary started in Chhatera about six seven-years ago, i.e., around 1980-81. Never before in the history of the village had paddy been ever grown. As a result of the continuous efforts of the staff of the Agriculture Extension Department of the State Government and partly because of the villagers' contacts with the outside world, in 1979 some of the farmers of Chhatera for the first time sowed paddy in some of their fields. In the beginning, due to lack of experience with this crop they were not able to rear it properly. As a result, their per acre yield was 12 to 14 quintals only. After two-three years, the villagers had gained some experience and carried out sowing as well as transplanting operations properly and in time. They have also adopted new strains of paddy like, Sathi, Parmal No. 106, Jaya, Punjab Basmati No. 1 and Gaurav. As a result of all this, the per acre yield of paddy in the village has risen to about 25 quintals.

During the 1985 rabi season, about 65 per cent of the total cultivated land in the village was under wheat, 10 per cent under vegetables and the remaining 25 per cent was used for growing a variety of other crops like mustard, *barseem* and gram. The main source of motivation for the large-scale shift in favour of the cultivation of paddy is very high net per acre profit fetched by this crop. At the present level of prices, according to the version of the agricuture department, for one acre self-cultivated plot of wheat, the in-puts cost about Rs. 1,200, while the gross income is between Rs. 1,500 and Rs. 1,600, thus leaving a net margin of only between Rs. 300 and Rs. 400. The cultivation of paddy, on the other hand, fetches as high a profit as rupees 1,500 per acre, or even more.

The per acre yield of wheat has also considerably increased during the last few years. This has been achieved due to the adoption of new strains like, DWL 5023, HD 2285, HD 291, HD 2281, WH 283, Raya Prakash and Raya Indra, as well as by the use of weedicides, like tolken. Previously, between 50 and 60 per cent of the wheat crop used to get eaten away by a wildly growing weed called flarish minor (locally known as *balori*). But now with the use of tolken, this problem has been taken care of.

As a result of the steep fall in the demand and price of sugarcane in 1980, the Chhaterans have totally abandoned the cultivation of this crop. Among the vegetables, previously the major varieties grown for marketing were tomato in winter and *tinda* in summer. For the last five to six years, farmers in Chhatera have also started growing brinjals (which last several months in the year) and *torai* (cucurbita). About the economic advisability of prefering the cultivation of vegetables over wheat, paddy or other similar crops, the villagers are still in doubt. This is partly so due to the fact that the cultivation of vegetables is a labour-intensive operation, the landlords not being able to arrange enough labour from within their own families have to hire labour which has become quite expensive and not-so-reliable. Moreover, vegetables constitute a very delicate crop the proper growth of which requires at least very favourable, if not ideal, weather conditions, the chances of which are roughly estimated to be only once every three-four years in this region. So, the villagers lable the cultivation of vegetables as *sata* (speculation). Besides that, the system of distribution in our country being what it is, the actual grower does not gain in the same way as the vegetable seller or the middle-man. A major portion of what the utlimate consumer is made to pay is quietly cornered away by the different categories of middle-men. But on one point they are quite convinced and it is that the cultivation of vegetables at least assures them of continuous in-flow of cash throughout the season.

As a result of all these changes, the concept of crop rotation has also picked up in Chhatera and the average intensity of cropping in the village as a whole, which was definitely less than 100 per cent till a few years ago, is conservatively estimated to have risen to around 150 per cent. All this shows that in this village agriculture has now become labour-intensive. But along with these changes, the villagers have also started taking help of more mechanical devices. During the last five years, the number of tractors as well as tube-wells in the village has increased considerably. In addition to the very wide use of mechanical thrashers for harvesting wheat, the harvesting combines have also appeared on the village scene. During the harvesting season, farmers from the neighbouring State of Punjab bring these machines here and operate the same on rent basis. In order to finish the harvesting operations quickly - partly to avoid taking any chances with the uncertain weather and partly because of the non-availability of an adequate amount of labour, at reasonable rates, during those days - the farmers prefer to go in for these mechanical devices despite the fact that in this process a lot of *tura* (straw) which forms a substantial part of the cattle feed round the year goes waste and whatever little quantity of it is obtained, it is not relished by the cattle because of its different size, shape and perhaps taste also.

Any chances of the Chhaterans going in for the cultivation of vegetables in the near future on a scale large enough to generate a potential force for a trend towards dispersal of their habitation, or even to lead to the coming into existence of some farm houses, are not yet visible.

6.4.2 *Improved Breed of Cows*

Incidentally, at about the same time as these changes in the field of agriculture started in the village, a stage was also set in Chhatera for radical changes in the field of breeding and rearing of cattle. In the initial stages, work in this sphere was started through the Village Welfare Organization - a non-political voluntary body (constituted of a group of Chhaterans themselves) working here. The National Dairy Research Institute (N.D.R.I.), Karnal, extended to Chhatera its scheme of supplying Jersy breed cows to the villagers.

In 1976-77, a non-governmental organization, called Action For Food Production (AFPRO), selected Chhatera as one of the villages under its programme and extended its activities there. The AFPRO gave a grant of Rs.1,60,000 for the development of activities falling within their frame of reference. A plot of *panchayat* land measuring about eight acres, located far away from, and towards, the North of the village *abadi* (residentaial area), was leased in by the Village Welfare Association. This undulating and sandy piece of uncultivable waste was got levelled and a tube-well was installed there for growing green fodder to be sold to Small and Marginal Farmers at no-profit-no-loss basis. But this venture did not succeed, partly because the land being sandy - having considerable deposits of the Jumna sand - was not suitable for growing fodder and partly because the villagers did not like to go to such a distant place for buying fodder. So, within four years of its start, the venture had to be called off. The land was handed back to the *panchayat* and its lease got mutually cancelled. A veterinary dispensary was also established in the village in 1977-78 with money from the AFPRO grant. The main function of this centre (dispensary) is to promote artificial insemination of local cows for the improvement of their breed. About five years ago a local young man was trained by the N.D.R.I. in the field of animal diseases especially in artificial insemination work. He is now very successfully managaing this work in the village. To improve the breed of local cows, the N.D.R.I. gives to the village free supply of semen for artificial insemination. A part of the AFPRO grant was also utilized for buying a Nitrogen Container for preserving this high quality semen. For running this Nitrogen Container, the N.D.R.I. supplies liquid nitrogen to the association free of cost.

All this has helped in bringing about a considerable increase in the yield of milk among cows in the village and in nearby villages. As a result of artificial insemination, the offsprings of the cows, whose daily yield used to be two to three litres only, started giving 10 to 12 litres of milk per day, while in the next generation this yield increased to 18 to 20 and in some cases even up to 22 litres.

There is hardly any household in Chhatera today which does not have one ot two cows of the improved breed. Even those caste groups which had not been keeping milch cattle previously have now entered this field. One reason for this is also the easy availability of financial assistance for this purpose from the nationalised banks. A branch of the Syndicate Bank having been opened in Chhatera itself, this work has received great impetus. The number of cows of the improved breed in the village today is more than that of the *desi* (local) variety. But Chhatera has a large population of buffalloes also, and these buffalloes together with the *desi* (local) cows still outnumber the cows of the improved breed. This change (i.e., the trend towards owning cows of the improved breed) has increased the income of household owners and is bringing about perceptible changes in their life styles, at least in the case of those falling at the lower rungs of the economic hierarchy.

It is hoped that the changes which are presently taking place in the village in this respect may, after some time, also result in some sort of an obliteration of the very sharp line of segregation among the sexes and in the discrimination of the respective areas, spaces and structures – to be used by them as well as by others.

6.4.3 *Trends of Change in Habitation*

The age-old preference among the villagers for living in the core areas of the *abadi* (residential area of the village) is gradually weaning out. Now the trend is to move towards the periphery. In those cases where fissioning of families has taken place in the recent past, this trend has come out very conspicuously in terms of preferences shown by the different parties. Even otherwise, a few households owning quite substantial and spacious *chowk-band* (central-court) as well as other types of structures, within the core area, have locked the same and moved into some modified *ghars* (residential houses) or *baithaks* (men's sitting places) or even *ghers* (enclosures for cattle) on the periphery. Some of these households are using both the structures, i.e., the ones in the core and the others towards the periphery. But the use to which the structures in the core are put has also changed. These are generally being used for storage and related purposes.

Another important factor very forcefully operating on the village scene is the installation of a large number of hand-pumps for water in the *abadi* (residential area) - both in the sectors inhabited by the *biswedaran* as well as the *gair-biswedaran*. The few hand-pumps that were previously confined to the *ghers* (enclosures for cattle) located mainly at the periphery are now, as if it were, moving to the *ghars* (residential houses) in the core also. Where a household does not find sufficient space (for the installation of a hand-pump) within its house/plot the same is unhesitatingly installed outside (i.e., in the street), on its own or even public land. For this purpose, the spaces created by the set-back or tappering lines between adjacent buildings are found by these households to be very handy. Factors responsible for such a great increase in the requirement for water are like the increase in the number of cattle - especially cows of the new breed which require more water - slight change in the sense of hygiene among the villagers and desire among them to look clean and well-dressed resulting in more frequent washing of clothes, etc.

The installation of a number of hand-pumps has made an increased amount of water easily available near the place of its consumption. The quantity of waste water has also increased proportionately. This phenomenon has affected the space under the street in more than one ways; first, a lot of space is taken by the people and pitchers around these pumps, and, secondly, the mud and slush is created through the entire length of the street.

Some idea of the form that this problem will eventually take will be clear only after a few years. Whether the individual households themselves or the village *panchayat*, or both of them, will pay any attention to this problem (of the improvement and proper maintenance of the drainage system) and will improve the drainage. Women, who have to shoulder the entire responsibility of drawing and bringing, water are also now beginning to look at such hard-work as 'drudgery' and have started to have a desire to get it lightened as much as possible. In course of time, this new developement may also considerably alter the age-old division of labour (among the sexes) in this respect.

The traditional rigidity in terms of the design and form of houses is gradually mellowing down. Previously, for the residential structures, people preferred *chowk-bandi* (central-court design). Even those, who, due to one reason or the other, could not make that and had to go in for some other form had to choose from a very limited variety of traditional designs. The choice in this respect was highly restricted. Even after having built a house on one of those patterns, the ultimate desire and goal of the villager invariably used to be to have a *chowk-band* (central-court) *ghar* (residentail house). But the houses built in the village during the last five to six years show that villagers now tend to adopt some non-traditional designs. They are gradually developing a liking for living in ventilated houses located in comparatively open and clean surroundings.

The way human-cattle segregation has been traditionally achieved in Chhatera is also undergoing changes. Though villagers are becoming conscious of the utility of achieving this object, the form (i.e., the way) in which this new thinking will be manifested in the use of spaces remains to be seen. The extent of these changes and the exact form that they will take can be expected to become somewhat clear only around the end of the present decade.

A careful analysis would reveal that these changes are coming (i.e., taking place) not only because of the changes occurring in the economic life of the villagers, or due to their exposure to the urban ways of life. Previously, development and expansion of the *abadi* (residential area) used to take place in an organic, natural and gradual way. But now this process is taking place in a sudden, rapid and direct manner. It is expected that after some years discernible changes would perhaps be visible not only in the designs and forms of individual structures but even in the pattern of habitation at the level of the village (i.e., in the village layout) itself. A careful and deep probing into the nature and extent of these changes and the related changes in other spheres of life of the villagers may prove to be fruitful if conducted at the close of the present decade.

SEVEN

THE GHAR

7.1 PLACE OF GHAR IN THE LIFE OF CHHATERANS

HOUSE OCCUPIES a very important place in the life of any community. It is not only a shelter but it also gives, to its possessor, a sense of security and helps him to attain social status. As a local proverb goes : *maya se pyari chhawa hai*, meaning thereby: shelter is dearer than wealth.

The ideal of the dreams of every Chhateran is a *chaukband ghar*. This is the ultimate desire or goal of every villager in general and that of agriculturists in particular, irrespective of the consideration whether one may or may not be able to achieve it till the end of his life. Although *chaukbandi* is an old pattern and, perhaps under the changed circumstances, has outlived some of its utility, it appears to have been an ideal solution to the human need of shelter, or an ideal compromise between the culture of these people and their physical environment, during the period of history when this pattern was evolved, flourished and was finalized. Once formed, a pattern or design has a tendency to persist and perpetuate itself. It changes only under the unbearable pressure of very extreme or revolutionary kind of situation. The pattern once formed does not give way easily. This is a characteristic especially very typical of vernacular architecture.

To borrow some ideas from Rapoporat (1969), the simpler a society the more uniform or identical the dwellings of its members. The vernacular design process is one of models and adjustments. There is, of course, individual variablity and variation or differentiation. The model itself is the result of the collaboration between the builders and the users of houses responding to particular physical and social situations and circumstances. This is what is meant by tradition. Tradition has the force of law honoured by everyone through collective assent. Respect for tradition gives collective control, which acts as a discipline. Without tradition there is no longer the reliance on accepted norms, and there is a beginning of institutionalization.

Every one does not have the land and other resources to build a *chaukband ghar*. So they have to make do with slightly different patterns, and after living in these houses many people have even realised that the new design have many advantages over the *chaukband* type. *Chaukandi* is considered to be an ideal total solution and it gives a considerable social status to its owner. I have had the occasion to discuss this matter at length with some of the highly educated young men in the village. Even they cherished this desire. One of these educated young men who was desirous of going to Canada, when asked by the author, "What will you do Joginder with the lot of money that you will amass in Canada and bring here with you when you return back home?" spontaneously he replied : *bas ab zindagi ki aek hi tamana baki raih gai hai Chandhoke Saheb, gaon mein ake chukband gar dunga* meaning thereby, "Only one desire of my life remains to be fulfilled, Mr. Chandhoke, on my return I will install a *chaukband ghar* in the village (i.e., in Chhatera)." The place occupied by house in the life of a community is also sometimes reflected in its folklore. This is especially so in the case of India (Crooke, 1918). The following stanza from a song the young house wives of Chhatera often sing reflects this: *mere sasur ki chunsath pauri re main to charhti utarti hari*, which means, the stair-case in my father-in-law's house has 64 steps, and I get tired climbing it up and down.

7.2 UTILITY OF STUDYING A JAT GHAR

The present study covers mainly the Jat *ghar*, because the *ghars* of the *be-biswedaran* are very small and are somehow built wherever these people are given plots by the *biswedaran* of the village. Moreover, the *be-biswedaran* are non-agriculturists and they have not been keeping much cattle. So, their *ghars* are not elaborate ones. The *ghars* of the *biswedaran*, on the other hand, are substantial ones built according to elaborate plans. These houses, therefore, offer a very good opportunity to study house as the reflection of the way of life of those who inhabit it. Among the *biswedaran*, again, Jats hold the major share in the village proprietary body. Moreover, in the surrounding villages; Brahmans are generally *be-biswedaran*. Whereas a study of the Jat house can throw light on a wider region, that of the *ghar* of any other section of the local community would not be able to reveal so much and will also have a restricted area of validity. It is, however, not intended to deny the utility of undertaking similar studies of the *ghars* of other castes. In fact, it is the technique developed for the present study, rather than the study itself, which is more important.

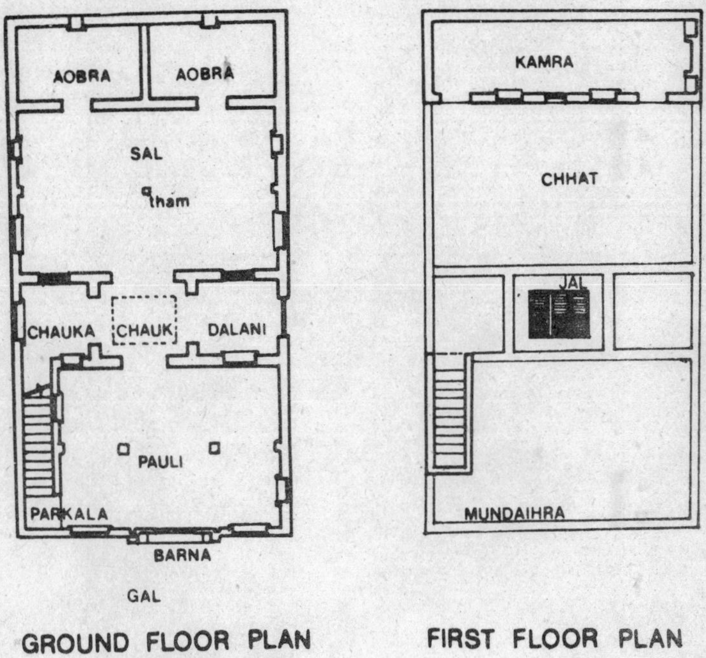

Figure 7.1: Plan of a *Chauk-band* Jat *Ghar*

7.3 DESCRIPTION OF A JAT *GHAR*

The *chaukband ghar* of a Jat is invariably built on an oblong plot of land, with one of the shorter sides abutting the street (Please refer to figure 7.1). The Jats do not like, rather they have folk beliefs against building *ghars* on square plots and also against building square rooms. A *chaukband ghar* is a substantial pacca structure made of burnt bricks, generally exposed outside and plastered inside. In many cases, a

Plate 7.1: Front facade of a *chauk-band* Jat *ghar*. Mark the arch on the enterance, *sar-dar* (the big plank on the top side of the door frame, *chauntris* (stone seats for sitting) on the either of the door, the small openings (for ventilation) placed high in the walls and the ornamental brackets under the eaves

portion of the external wall near the entrance is plastered to emphasize the entrance. It is also, sometimes, decorated with folk murals. In the old *ghars*, one also finds liberal use of stone elements like *thams*, *tadras*, slates and the steps of the stair cases, etc. Most of the *ghars* have decorated arches at the entrance and richly carved doors with *chauntris/sahmchis* (small stool-like stone platforms for sitting) on both sides of the entrance.[1] (Please see plates 7.1 and 7.2).

Plate 7.2 *Barna* of a Jat *ghar* with men sitting on *Chauntris*. Mark the staggering line of the openings to achieve visual privacy

The roofs of *ghars* are invariably *katcha* supported by wooden rafters called *karis* and the roof is finished with mud *phaska* and rammed earth. There is hardly any *ghar* in Chhatera with a completely *pacca* roof. The floors are also generally all *katcha*. At the most, one may sometimes come across a *pacca* flooring in the *chauk* (court) of a *ghar* (Chandhoke, S.K., 1978 c: 234). Mukerji (1957: 20) has also made a similar observation about the houses of Jats in general "...in more prosperous houses the flooring of the courtyard is made of stones".

A *ghar* constructed on an ideal (i.e., with an optimum size and shape) plot has a typical design. Safety, security as well as privacy are the overriding considerations in the design and construction of a *ghar*. The depth of the plot is divided into six parts (Please refer to figure No. 7.1). In other words, a *chaukband ghar* is a six-bay deep structure. The first two bays in the front, i.e., those on the side abutting the street, comprise of a big *do-kariya* (i.e., with a span covered by two *karis*) hall, called *pauli*. On one side of the *pauli* is the *parkala* (stair case). The next (i.e., the third) bay of the *ghar* consists of an open court, called *chauk*, and two covered spaces, called *dalanis*. The width of this third bay (excluding a width equal to that of the *parkala* in the *pauli*) is divided into three parts. The two *dalanis*, each equal in width to one of these three parts, stand on the left and right side of the *chauk*, respectively. The third part in the centre is an uncovered (open to the sky) space. Besides this third (i.e., one-third) part of the third bay, the space equal in width to that under the *parkala* (on one side in the *pauli*) is also included in the court. So, the open court in the centre, called *chauk*, is bigger than each of the *dalanis* on its sides, the difference being equal to that of the *parkala*.

This type of division of spaces is done partly with the intention of attaining (visual) privacy in the *ghar* because, in this way, the *barnas* in the various covered spaces are staggered and do not all fall in one line (Please refer to Figure 7.1 and plate 7.2). Every *barna* is invariably placed by the Chhaterans in the centre/middle of a covered space. A man standing in the *gal* cannot have an inside view of the whole *ghar*. This point will become very clear when one looks at the plan of the Jat *ghar*.

Under the fourth and fifth bays falls a big family hall, called *sal*, while the sixth bay is divided into two store rooms called *aobre*.

A *chaukband ghar* generally has a couple of rooms on the first floor which are reached by the *parkala* (stair). The remaining space on the first floor is an open terrace, called *chhat.*

A look at the descriptions of Jat *ghars* given in some of the old documentary sources (attached at Appendixes IV and VI) would perhaps help in having a more clear idea of the same and it also confirms one's impression that the house design of a people is a well-considered and matured reaction of their culture to the physical environment in which they live, and that the house design is not an off-hand product of an individual's mind.

7.4 HARIJAN HOUSES

The Harijan dwellings are not only grouped separately from others, they are also significantly different in a variety of ways - plinth area, number of rooms, domestic facilities, frontage of the plot as well as the use of building materials. Harijan houses are single-storeyed and *katcha.* These are separately located, often opening to the brick-paved path and are grouped around a square. (Please see plates 7.3 and 7.4).

Plate 7.3: A group of *katcha ghars* in the Harijan Sector

A Harijan dwelling consists of a large multi-purpose room, one or two small stores and sometimes also a kitchen and a courtyard. The courtyard, if any, is formed by the boundary wall and is often a mere extension of the path. There is always one entry to a dwelling and not a single window opening into the *gal*. The window, if provided in rare cases, is abnormally small. The Harijan houses are constructed of 18" thick mud walls, finished on both sides with a coat of cow-dung. The roof, made of rammed earth placed on wooden joists, is covered with bamboo, wooden planks or twigs and leaves, and finally plastered with cow-dung. The floor is *katcha* - mud plastered with cow-dung.

Plate 7.4: Old and new side by side. See the old wooden *thamb* and *shaihtir* still in position

NOTE

1. Whenever any male member of the household comes to the *ghar*, if he finds the outer *barna* of the *ghar* locked, he can sit on the *chauntri* and wait till the person (generally a woman) who has the key, comes. Sometimes, during sunny winter afternoons and during summer days when there is cool breeze outside, men folk or children sit here to enjoy the same. This author has also observed some elderly males enjoying their meals on the *chauntris* of their *ghar* under the above said conditions. This is especially so in the case of *haweli* where the *chauntris* are quite big-sized ones.

EIGHT

OTHER CUTLURAL ASPECTS RELATED TO HABITATION

8.1 SENSE OF PRIVACY AND HOUSE DESIGN IN CHHATERA

NO DOUBT the importance of physical factors in shaping any human habitation cannot be undermined; nevertheless the social heritage, myths and folk beliefs of a community play an important role in this spehere.

The particular sense of privacy, that the Jats have, is achieved in their *ghar* partly by the placing of the *barnas* in a particular manner. The main *barna* (in the wall abutting the *gal*) is never placed in the middle of the wall. It is always staggered a little. If there is a *parkala* in the front covered space, i.e., the *pauli*, then the *barna* is shifted to the other side of the centre by a distance equal to the width of the *parkala* (Please refer to figure 8.1). As one enters the *pauli*, the space on one side (generally on the right) is more than on the other. One reason for this difference is also that efforts are made to see that there is a minimum of nine feet wide covered space available on at least one side. This is so because of the requirement of space for the cattle that are to be tethered there. If on one side of the *pauli* there is an *aobra*, then it is the front of the *pauli* and not that of the total house plot that is taken into consideration for placing the *barna*.

The *barna* between the *pauli* and the *chauk* is always placed in the centre of the *bhit* (wall). In the last (i.e., in the rear most) bay of the *ghar*, since there are two *aobras*, their *barnas* are naturally on the two sides of the central line of the *ghar*. So, the *barnas* of a *ghar* are not all in a straight line. This type of division of space is done partly with the intention of achieving (visual) privacy in the *ghar*. A person standing in the *gal* in front of the *barna* of a *ghar* cannot have a clear view of all the spaces inside the *ghar*. While placing the main *barna* in a *ghar*, consideration is also given to the location of the main *barna* of the *ghar* across the *gal*. The two are preferably staggered, though not necessarily completely.[1] References to the orientation and placing of the doors in a house are found even in the *Griha Sutras*.

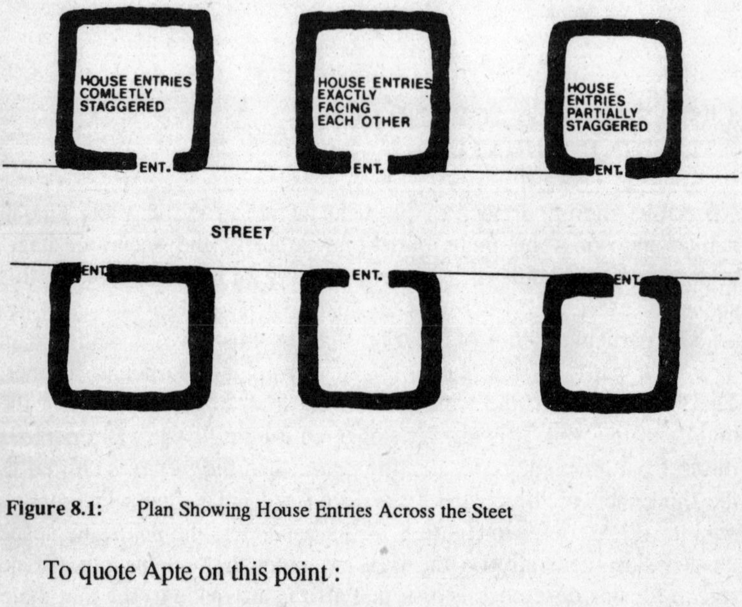

Figure 8.1: Plan Showing House Entries Across the Steet

To quote Apte on this point :

> The back-door should not face the chief house-door. The chief house-door should not face the door of another house, and should be so constructed that the house-holder should not be seen by unholly persons while performing religious acts or while dining in his house and passers-by should not be able to see the valuables in the house. The frequent reference to the 'Threshold' indicates strong door-frames with a strong sill (1954:141-142).

In Chhatera, no important *barna* in any structure has ever been fixed with only one *pala* (leaf). Sometimes, in a *kotha*, or in some very ordinary and temporary enclosure, some people fix a single leaf. In such a case, there is no fixed, or even a preferred side (i.e., right or left, or in terms of the cardinal directions or in any other sense) for fixing the hinges to this leaf. The only consideration in this matter is the availability of space inside for opening the leaf.

Even from the point of view of the partitioning of a *ghar* at a future date, when the household fissions out, it is necessary that the main *barna* in any structure should not be placed in its centre, because the partitioning wall has to be built in the centre in order to make equal divisions of the structure. In old days, even in very big *hawelis*, the Chhaterans used to fix only one main *barna* (i.e., entrance to the structure). (Please see plate 8.1). The very beautiful, substantial, expensive and functionally built structures turned into very ugly and useless (dis-functional) portions when partitioned. This can be seen from figure 8.2.

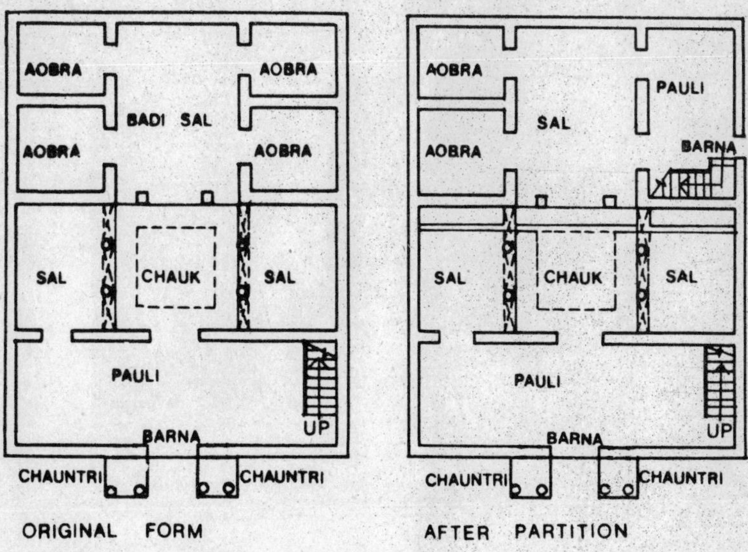

Figure 8.2: Plans Showing a Jat *Haweli* before and after partition

This stately mansion has been divided into two portions by erecting a high wall in its middle running from left to right. The erection of this wall, besides entailing avoidable expenditure, has resulted in the wastage of some very useful space in the most important part of the structure. It has further deprived both the poritions, especially the one at the rear, of light and air.

Plate 8.1: *Haweli* - a visual study. An imposing mansion on the Mughal architectural style

At the time of partitioning, feelings among brothers and/or other agnatic relatives are such that no body is prepared to forgo even a square centimeter of land even in cases where such a small sacrifice may considerably help in retaining the functional utility of the original structure.

In the process of partitioning, the dividing line between the two *aobre* on the right hand side at the rear has been removed and this total space has been converted into a *sal*. An entrance to this newly-created *sal* has been provided by puncturing the wall towards the right side and fixing a *barna* in it. Even this could become possible because luckily there was a *gal* on that side also. Normally, in nucleated villages most of the house plots open on one side only.

A *parkala* has been constructed in this *sal* leading to the first floor. This has deprived the *sal* of a lot of useful space and privacy.

The damage done, by this partitioning, at the first floor of this originally stately mansion is all the more serious.

About the habitations of the Jats in the Punjab, Mukerji has written thus :

> The construction of the house is done with the object of maximum strength and security. The thickness of the walls (*asar*) is nearly one yard while their height (*bheet*) is nearly 5 yards. The walls being made of mud and being thick are very strong...Among the Chehils, the largest Jat tribe in Punjab, no openings are made in the roof, even to this day. The reason ascribed being the historical fact that once Chahil, the son of Raja Kang and founder of the tribe, saw some fairies bathing in a tank. He at once seized their clothes and only restored them on the condition that one of them became his bride. One Ichcharam was given to him on the condition that he never abused her and she bore him a son, but one day he spoke harshly to her and she disappeared through an opening in the roof. Hence to this day the Chahil Jats of Punjab do not make any opening in the roof. We know that the districts of Patiala, Ludhiana, Ambala, Amritsar and Gurdaspur are terribly hot places during the summer, the temperature shooting as high as 100°F, which would have necessitated an opening in the roof as well. Thus the openings are necessary but due to the perpetuation of a historical myth the peculiarity in the make-up of the roof persists to this day. This clearly proves that in many cases it is not the geographical conditions but the social heritage that becomes the determinant of the elements of geographical reality. Upper storeys are rarely constructed primarily because the mud walls and the roofs are not so strong as to support the weight of the upper storey. Upper storeys are often tabooed as well; for example, the Najar Jats of Ludhiana

district think an upper storey brings bad luck. Thus, superstitions too play a signficant part in the form and the build of the houses. It is always unlucky to build a house broader in front than at the back. Such a house is called *Sher Dhana* (tiger-mouthed). A house to be lucky should be cow-mouthed or broader behind than in front. Houses are also, to be luckly, to contain an even number of sides preferably four, six or twelve sides. A southern aspect of a house is believed to be unlucky. If in a house there is a door on the southern side, another house with a north-facing door is built just in front of the former to counteract the evil effect of the south-facing door. In Gurgaon a house should, if possible, face towards the south. The explanation of this superstition is to be found in the Hindu mythological idea acccording to which south is the direction dominated by *Yama Raj* or the God of Death (*Swastika,* the most pious and representative symbol of Aryans, manifests *Yama Raj* through its southern limb). It might also be interesting to note here that the southern sector of the village is the main residential area of the families belonging to the Scheduled Castes. The house very often faces east (the direction of the Sun-rise or *Suryodaya*) or north (the direction of the Himalayas). The geographical factors are also discernible. A house facing south would always be most exposed to the heat of the Sun. Little rainfall permits the construction of broad and flat roofs. Clay bricks also keep the rooms cooler during the hot summer and the larger surface of the roofs allow a quicker and greater amount of back radiation of heat during the night (1957:19).

8.2 ORIENTATIONS

Every community has got some preferences as well as avoidances for certain cardinal directions. Depending upon the physical conditions of the habitat of the community, and the folk beliefs of its members, certain orientations are preferred by them while a few others are avoided. These preferences and avoidances vary on a scale of continuum and are not applicable with the same degree of rigidity in all the matters.

8.2.1 *Orientation of the ghar*

Regarding the orientation of the *ghars, ghers* as well as *baithaks* in Chhatera, east is the most preferred direction. Next is west and then north. South, of course, is the most avoided direction. This attitude of not orienting a structure towards the south is applicable in the case of *ghars, baithaks* and the *ghers* alike. East is considered to be the direction of the *dewtas* (Gods). According to the history of Hindu religion, all the religious acts, or acts of religiousity, have taken place in this direction. The villagers say that all the places of pilgrimage for the Hindus lie towards the east of this (i.e., of the Chhatera) region. Being worshippers of the Sun God, if their house is facing east, they can have a *darshan* (holy view) of the *Surya Dewta* (Sun God) every morning.

In the planning of any human habitation, due regard has to be given to the micro-climate of the region also. The Chhatera region being a hot one, if a house is oriented towards the east it will not get so hot in summer. Moreover, in this region, almost throughout the year the wind blows mostly from the east, and it is, therefore, called *purwa*, i.e., easterly. A house facing the east would, therefore, get a lot of fresh air which is very essential for human beings as well as for preventing the grains (which the villagers being agriculturists store in large quantities) from getting spoilt, especially because the *ghar* has a fort-like closed construction where the chances of the breeze otherwise entering are very poor. South is avoided because of its being regarded as the direction of the *rakshasas* (demons). *Lanka* (Ceylon), considered to be the symbol of sin (because of its assoication with the *Ramayna* Epic), lies to the south of India. Moreover, after one's death his spirit, it is believed, goes to the south. When Lord Mahadeva's son Lord Ganesha was beheaded, an elephant's head (which was transplanted on Lord Ganesha's neck and he was revived to life) was also brought from the southerly direction. Moreover, they say the slope of the earth is towards north-east and all the rivers and other water courses in this region flow from the south-westerly direction. So, from that point of view also, it is not advisable to face a house towards the south. A dying person is placed with his head towards north and feet towards south. Even on the *chitah* (pyre) he is placed in the same way. References to this aspect of human habitations are found even in the *Sutras*. "G. says that he who is desirous of fame or strength should build his house with its main door to the east. The door should be to the north if one is desirous of children or cattle, and to the south if one desires all these things but it should not be to the west" (Apte, 1954:141-142).

An archaeologist has observed: "The experience of many genrations has proved that they (plans of villages) were the best for the purpose of defence, and gave the most healthy, pleasant and most practical layout for the Indian village or town. The Easterly axis of the plan ensured that the principal streets were purified by the rays of the Sun sweeping through them from morning till evening; while the intersections of main streets by shorter ones running north and south provided a perfect circulation of air and the utmost benefit of the cool breezes" (Havell, 1915:9). A large number of studies throw light on the folk beliefs held by various communities in respect of their houses, etc. Roy, for example, reports thus:

> As for houses, when an Oraon begins to build his house, he must commence with one of the two walls running east to west, although a portion, however small, of all the four walls of the house, must be erected the very first day he begins the building.
>
> An Oraon or a Munda will not, if he can avoid it, have an extension to his house made towards the south, nor remove his house further to the south of his old house site. Even migrating southwards from one village to another is considered ominous. When a Munda or an Oraon is obliged to do so, he does not go straight in southerly direction but proceeds first a mile or more in another direction and then turns southwards towards his real destination.
>
> The Munda and Oraon believe that a south-facing house brings ill-luck; and if they can manage to do so, they will construct their house with the face either to the east or the west. North-facing houses are, however, sometimes built as being less objectionable than a south-facing one.
>
> It may be noted that Hindu castes in Chotanagpur and in some parts of Bihar, as in several other parts of India, generally observe similar restrictions about the construction of houses, especially in the villages. In Chotanagpur I have seen some Hindus in the villages, in order to avoid the necessity of having a south-facing house, construct an enclosed veranda in front of the southern door of the main house so as to have the other entrance to the house either on the eastern or the western wall of the veranda.
>
> The two totem-huts that I have seen, the one at village Amboa and the other at village Jamgain, both, however, open towards the east, and so do all the Dhumkurias or bachelor's dormitories amongst the Oraons (1915:279-280).

Roy has analysed the basis of this attitude in the following way:
The east appears to be regarded by the Mundas and the Oraons,

who form the principal inhabitants of Chotanagpur, as also by their Hindu and semi-Hinduised neighbours as the most auspicious point of the compass, and the south the most inauspicious. Perhaps the reason for this is to be sought in the fact that most of the Chotanagpur tribes identify the Sun with their Supreme Deity (the *Singbonga* of Mundas and the *Dharmes* of the Oraons) and that at least some of these tribes believe with the Hindus that the souls of the dead go southwards to the land of *Yama*. ('*Jom-Raj*' or 'the Devouring King', as some Mundas call him (1915:277).

Roy (1920) has made certain similar observations about the Asur habitations (of Chotanagpur) also. Another interesting observation in this connection is that by Rapoport :

> The Hogaku system of orientation in Japan determines the location of Japanese houses with regard to topography, while in India houses on hillisides are strictly oriented to the East so that the doors face up to the slope. In Gibralter and Ellice islands houses are oriented to the forces of the universe rather than to the topography, as was also the case in China... Non-use of land through the reservation of graves, groves of trees, historical tree sites and sacred water sources is an important general aspect of the influence of site on house placement - but site in the spiritual, not the physical, sense (1969:28-29).

One may then ask that, is it that there is no structure in the village oriented towards the south?[2] In fact, the layout of every village is evolved in a very natural manner. No artificial solution to the problem is attempted. The physical factors also play a very important role, the gradients of land being one of them (Srivastava, 1962).

Unlike their urban counterparts, the ruralites neither have the resources nor the skills and, above every thing else, they have the least of intentions and/or pretensions to find out artificial solutions to such-like problems. But while planning a new village or a *tausih abadi*, efforts are made, so far as possible, to design the layout in such a manner that southerly direction is avoided to the maximum possible extent.

In fact, the subtle point (which to my mind appears to be a compromise between the philosophical and practical aspects) is that the main entrance to a structure (and with that, of course, the orientations of all the doors and windows and all other points are fixed, because the house has to rigidly follow a model) should not be "clearly" facing the south. The term "clearly" means that there is no obstruction or cover in front of the main *barna* of the structure. If there is any structure across the *gal* facing the one under reference, then the *an* (i.e., the defect or the inauspicious element) is broken, its negative effect is cancelled. According to the Hindu astrology related to the human habitations, it is felt that the real entrance is the entrance to the *abadi* at somewhat a macro-level, and that is always through a lane. If a house is facing south then the entrance to the lane, in which this house is located, is from the east or the west. So, this situtіon is not objectionable. Even if there is no built-up structure across the street, but if plots on the opposite side of the street have been earmarked and the street has been demarcated, the objection is no longer valid. In other words, in such a situation the plot becomes free from that drawback.

As is well known to every student of human habitations, the *abadi* (at the level of the total *abadi*) in a North Indian nucleated village is invariably inward-looking or "introvert" (in the physical sense) in character. So, the chances of any plot having its orientation toward the south, and not having any structure across the street, are practically negligible.[3]

8.2.2 *Orientation of elements of the ghar and of some other important things*

Some of the other things which should not be oriented towards the south are : *chulha, khat, khor*, bullocks under the yoke when stopped for rest in the *khets*, the *hali* (i.e., the man behind the plough) while taking rest in the *khet* for a puff at the *huka*, a person while taking meals, *tijori, bitora, bitora* opening, *thapas*, (among the Brahmans the *thapas* should not be put on any side of a wall running north-south), the *jot*, the person sitting for any religious or life-cycle ceremony or for performing any auspicious act.

The *shaihtir* in the roof of any part of a structure should be in a perpendicular direction to the wall which has the door to that part of the structure. For example, if the entrance to a covered space is form the east, then the *shaihtir* must be placed north-south and not east-west. One explantion given by the villagers for this rule is that if the *shaihtir* is placed east-west then the *karis* would have to be placed north-south and this is an inauspicious direction. Some villagers argue that if in this case the *shaihtir* is placed east-west then the entire weight of the roof will come on the *barna*, which is structurally not a good solution. Besides this, in such a case, the *thams* under the *shaihtir* would obstruct the circulation in that space. The direction of the *shaihtir* is important also because the use of space below it is more or less fixed. A person sleeping on the *khat* should not have the *shaihtir* passing across his chest, or above his body cutting it right to left.

Besides houses, some of the other things in respect of which these rules are strictly observed in the Chotanagpur area, Roy (1915:278) mentions, the direction in which a corpse is placed on the pyre, a stone called *kundi* stone (by the side of some stream, near which the earthen jars containing the bones of a dead person collected after his funeral, are broken before the bones are consigned to the water), *bidi-diri*.[4]

8.3 OTHER FOLK BELIEFS ABOUT THE GHAR

The Chhaterans have a folk belief also about the number of *karis* in any covered space. Even the books on Hindu astrology, related to human habitations, contain various solutions. Chhaterans avoid numbers eight, 16, 20, etc. Moreover, the number should be odd but not 13. They count the *karis* in the sequence *ind, yam, raj, ind, yam, raj, ind, yam, raj.....* The total number of *karis* in the roof of any individual covered space should be such that counting should end at *ind* or *yam* but not at *raj*. About the direction of the *shaihtir*, it is the house-owners who are very particular, while about the number of *karis* it is the *raj* (mason) who is very rigid.

Three, 13 and nine are not considred to be good numbers and are, therefore, avoided. The villagers say *nau, terah, tin, ke ta pawepari na awe chhin*, meaning thereby, nine, 13, three; either one will readily get something (as if it was lying there for him), or he will loose. Which means, it is sort of a gambling to use these numbers or be associated with them. These numbers will either make one's fortune or completely mar it. So, the Chhaterans never make three *alas, alis, almaris, aobras, janglas*, etc., in any wall. Even in those rare cases where there are three *aobras* in the same line the *barnas* in these three *aobras* are invariably four, i.e., in one of the *aobra* they would fix two *barnas*. To take a practical view, perhaps this also helps in achieving symmetry in the building. Three *dats* (with two *thams*) are common; but four *dats* (which would normally require three *thams*) are very rarely found. In a Jat *ghar* in Chhatera, where the *sal* has four *dats*, the house-owner has provided four *thams* also (by having two, instead of the normal one, in the centre).

Chhaterans prefer oblong house plots rather than square ones or of any other shape. A plot with all its angles at 90° is highly preferred. Same is true in the case of individual spaces also. A *sherdhana/ sanp mukha* (lion-like / snake-mouthed, i.e., with a broader front and narrower rear) plot is never accepted for construction, while a *gaudhana* (cow-like, i.e., with a narrower front and a broader rear) is considered to be auspicious. Even when one does some consturction which is not having its sides at right angles, he would cover up the defect in walls and all the inside covered spaces are always kept at right angles. *Is bat ki sankhya mante hain*, i.e., the villagers consider it to be inauspicious. A *bhujkat* (literally, armless, meaning thereby, a plot with less than four sides) is never accepted for construction. Although a plot with more than four sides is also generally avoided, some structures on such plots do exist in Chhatera and surrounding villages.

The front part of a plot should be entirely built upon, i.e., the front part of a building should always be a built space. It must be a *chhawa* (covered space) and not an open space, because the villagers believe that if the front portion is an open space then a death is bound to take place in the family of the owner of that building in the near future. Writing about the folk beliefs of the Jats of Karnal district, from where the ancestores of the Jats of Chhatera originally came, Ibbetson remarks:

> Of course, the superstitions of the people are innumerable. Odd numbers are lucky... But three and 13 are unlucky because they are the bad days after death so that *tera tin* is equivalent to 'all any how'. And if a man, not content with two wives, wishes to marry again, he will first marry a tree, so that the new wife may be the fourth, and not the third. So if you tread upon a three-year old part of cow-dung you loose your way of certainty The preference for number 5, and less markedly for 7, will have been apparent throughout the foregoing pages. An offering to a Brahman is always 1 1/4, 2-1/2, 5, 7-1/2 and so on, whether rupees or seers of grain. The dimensions of walls and parts of walls and their gear, on the other hand, are always fixed in so many and three-quarter hands; not in round numbers. The tribal traditions of the people and those concerned with the numbers and areas, with chief's wives and sons, and with villages swarm with the numbers 12, 24, 16-1/2, 52, 84 and 360 (1883:155).

The villagers also believe in the "evil eye". Sunday and Friday are considered to be good, i.e., auspicious for starting construction of a house, etc., for sending a *beti* to her *susral* for the first time, for bringing a *bahu* home from her parents' place, as well as for starting sowing or harvesting operations. The open space in very structure - especially that in a *ghar* - is always preferably kept in the middle. Even when a *ghar* is not of the *chaukband* type, efforts are made to keep the open space in the middle. Rear open space can sometimes be had in a *gher*, or even in a *baithak*, but never in a *ghar*. This rule is relaxed only in cases where the shape and size of the plot do not at all permit the open to be kept in the middle.

8.4 VARIOUS LEVELS OF LIVING IN THE VILLAGE

There are three different levels of living in the village. The first level is that of the household, and it consists of *ghar, baithak* and *gher*. A major part of the life of all members of every household is lived at this level.

The second level is that of the village *abadi*. When an important guest is coming to the village, he is received and seen off at the *gora*. The *barat/janet* in a girl's marriage is received at the *gora*, some ceremonies are performed here and then the *barat* is escorted to the *chaupal*. Even when a *barat* is not received at the *gora* by a big gathering, at least the *Nai* and a few elderly male members from the bride's side go to the *gora* to welcome the *barat* there and then escort it to the village *chaupal*. After a marriage in the girl's village, when the *barat* is leaving for the boy's village, it is seen off at the *gora*. It is at the *gora* that the mother of the girl puts *thapas* on the chest of the boy's father. The village lanes being narrow and zig-zag ones, the transport of the boy's party has generally to be parked at the *gora* and, therefore, the ceremony of putting water on the wheels of the carriage (to carry the bride) by the women of the bride's family is also performed at the *gora*.

On the occasion of the death of a person, when the dead body is taken out for funeral, the corpse is first stopped at the *gora* and some ceremonies are performed there. From the *ghar* of the deceased up to the *gora* there are four *kandhiyas* (pall-bearers) all the time. These four *kandhiyas* also keep on changing. In fact almost every person accompanying the dead body wants to have his turn as a *kandhiya*. From *gora* to *chehanrin* there are only two *kandhiyas*, and those who take their turn at the *gora*, the same two carry the corpse up to the *chehanrin*. After crossing the *gora*, the *kandhiyas* are never changed. Women never go to the *chehanrin*. When men carrying a dead body have moved 50 to 100 yards away from the *ghar* of the deceased, the women folk also follow them, but they stop at the *gora*. Women stay at the *gora* for some time, fill in the *paindhas* with water from the *kuwan* and return back to the *ghar* of the *deceased*. When men return to the *gora* from the *chehanrin*, they wash their hands, legs and faces with the water in the *paindhas* at the *gora* and then return to the *abadi*.

The third level of living in the village is that of the *sim*, i.e., the boundary of the village estate. When a very honoured guest is coming, or when a person is returning to his village after a great achievement, pilgrimagè, a long absence, or if he is coming from a very distant place, he is received at the *sim*. A *bahu*, when returning to her own (in-laws') village after visting that of her parents, is also always received at the *sim*. A *beti* is received at the *sim* throughout her life. Previously, on such-like occasions the person returning to his village used to pick up some earth from the field on the *sim*, put it on his/her forehead and bowed in respect at the *sim* facing towards the *abadi*. Similar rules were observed in the case of an outward journey also. With the modern means of transport taking the place of the old slow-moving *gadi* or *tonga*, etc., the position in this respect has somewhat changed. When a person travels by train, sometimes the railway station assumes the position of *sim* in this respect.

One comes across mentions of this type of practices even in the *Griha Sutras* :

> When a person leaves his village on journey, he mutters 'Free from danger may we be. May the village entrust me to the care of the forest, and looks at his house and says 'Do ye both, *Mitra* and *Varuna*, protect this house for me'. When he enters the village on his return at the end of his journey he should mutter 'May the forest entrust me to the care of the village', and should not enter it without carrying something with him such as fuel, flowers, etc. The words with which he addresses it while approaching it and looking at it before actually entering it are touching and show us how the house had become the rallying point and centre of material prosperity in the eyes of the house-holder. 'House do not tremble, I come back to thee, rejoycing in my mind. That of which the traveller thinks, that in which dwells much joy, that I call the

house'; 'Here are invited cows, goats and sheep and friends, the sweet companionship of friends. May our dwellings always be unharmed, with all our men. Then he enters the house with the formula 'To thee I turn for the sake of safety and peace. O blissful one, O helpful one'. Similarly the love or respect that the house (symbolical of his family or social relations) inspired in the mind of the house-holder is seen from the instructions (H.G.S.) that he should avoid all quarrelling on the day on which he has arrived and should utter auspicious words and then accept water for washing the feet. A definition of the 'Home' is implicit in these *Mantras* (Apte, 1954:144-45).

A similar observation by Baillie about a U.P. village is quoted by Ahmad, Enayat thus :

> Village gods are supposed to reside on the outskirts of the village. 'The Deohar' or village gods form a very distinct group, to whose honour in almost every village, petty offerings are made at appointed seasons at the mounds (*than*) sacred to each almost in every village in the Province. A villager usually does not dare cross the protected jurisdiction (1952:233).

About the Bhil villages, in Deccan, Karve writes :

> Most of the villages have boundaries which are marked by some kind of stones or trees or streams. Sometimes there are temples of Bhairi or Bhairoba, Naruti Devi (the mother goddess), etc., to mark and to protect the boundary. Though in the extremely scattered villages it is difficult for a casual observer to see the boundaries, they are well known to all the villagers.
>
> Among the many Gods which the Bhils worship there is always the Hirva or Shirva Dev. Shiv or Hiva is the boundary and Hivara and Shivara Dev seems to be the guardian of the boundary. Among the Warlis there is a Hirva Dev which probably is the same as the Bhil's Hivara Dev (1957:87).

There is no occasion in a year or in the life of an individual person when the village boundary may come in for ceremonial treatment as reported by Shah (1955:71-72) about the Bhil villages of Panchamahals, and by Karve (1957:87) also about the Bhil and Warli

Plate 8.2: Street entrance in the village. Mark the rope tied to the house tops on either side of the *gal* symbolizing *rok* observed as a quarantine against diseases among human beings as well as cattle

villages of Deccan. Perhaps the main reason for the absence of any ceremonial treatment of the *sim* in a manner like those observed by Shah and Karve is that Chhatera is a very tightly nucleated village while those referred to by Shah and Karve are of the hamletted type. There is, of course, one occasion when ceremonial treatment is given to the area of the village under actual habitation (which is different than the *abadi* land as per the revenue records). In fact, this is sort of a quarantine treatment. This function is organized whenever some cattle disease breaks out in a village or in the surrounding villages. All the approaches to the inhabited area of the village are sealed with a symbolic tying of a rope (made of the locally available hemp) on the street corners (which can be seen in the plate 8.2). For 48 hours, no person is allowed to enter or go out of the sealed area. During this period, all the persons who are inside this area take only non-cereal meals. Religious singing and prayers go on almost incessantly. This ritual is called *rok, tham or rokna*, meaning stoppage, blockade and checking.

NOTES

1. This practice is at a little variance than what the author, in course of his fieldwork for another study (Chandhoke & Singh, 1968) observed in some villages of Bayana tehsil of Bharatpur District, Rajasthan. In the Bharatpur region, especially among the Brahmans, the main doors of two houses facing each other, across a street, must either lie exactly in the same line or be staggered away completely (i.e., the two doors should not cut each other as this causes what is locally called *an* which, it is believed in this region, is inauspicious and brings calamities to both the households, particularly to the one which has constructed its house earlier. This can be seen in figure No. 8.1. This comparison of different practices leads one to the conclusion that while the practice in Chhatera region is based on the objective criterion of privacy (although privacy itself is a very subjective concept), the one prevalent in the Bharatpur region is based on folk beliefs and orthodox ideas, which cannot be explained by simple reasoning.
2. I was told by a master mason of the area that, in fact, the human greed and lust for land sometimes overpowers a man. At times, with some people, the economic benefits weigh more heavily than all the other considerations, especially than those based merely on folk beliefs, etc. There have been some instances (though none in Chhatera so far), the master mason continued, where, because of some land lying vacant towards the south of a plot owned by some person, he made his house facing the south in order to be able to quietly grab that extra land. After some time, when other people in the village had forgotten that incident (of land grabbing) the orientation of the house was changed, to avoid the ill-effect of the southerly orientation.
3. There was one such case in village Nangloi (about ten miles away) in Delhi. At first the plot owner was very hesitant. But when his *purohit* suggested him to sink a well in front of the plot and plant a *pipal* tree near this well before starting construction on the plot and after planting the tree to go ahead with the construction, the *jajman* (i.e., the plot owner) did not take much time to start the process. The family has now been very happily living there for the last few

decades and is prospering.

4. Sometimes the relatives of a deceased Munda (particularly if the latter was an important personage in his village, or died at the ripe old age), in addition to burying his remains or his effigy in the family graveyard under a flat stone-slab, also erect a memorial stone which is known as *bidi-diri* or a 'standing-stone' because it stands upright on the ground like a pillar. This memorial column must face east.

NINE

ELEMENTS OF PATTERNS OF HABITATION AT THE MACRO-LEVEL

THE MAIN elements of the pattern of habitation (at the macro-level) in Chhatera and other villages in the region are as follows:

9.1 JOHAR

The water tank called *johar* has an important place in village life. In fact, the digging of a *johar* is the first thing to be done at the time of founding any new *abadi*. The entire habitation process starts with the digging of a *johar*. The earth so dug is used for raising the *Kot* around the *abadi*. Writing about the village tanks during Panini's times, Agarvala (1953:137-138) observes that "...why the moat was built first can be understood from the fact that the earth so obtained was utilized for raising the mud-rampart or for moulding bricks for the city-wall or as Kautilya says for ramming in the hollow masonry". Some of the big villages in Chhatera region have more than one *johar* also. "...the tanks (called *johars*) form a special feature of the district; round the longer villages as many as seven or eight will be found, and some are exceedingly fine" (Purser and Fanshawe, 1880:10). Chhatera itself has three *johars* covering a total area of two-and-a-half acres. Two *johars* are in the *shamlat deh* and the third is in the *shamlat thola* of five-six households. But for all practical purposes, the third *johar* is also common to the entire village, i.e., it is open to use by all sections of the village community without any distinction. *Johars* are used by human beings for bathing and for washing clothes, and by cattle for bathing and drinking. Cattle also relax in the *johar* (Please see plate 9.1).

Plate 9.1: *Johar* in (adjoining village) Bankner with cattle bathing in it. A *kuwan* can be seen on the right side

No separate places are marked at any *johar* to be used exclusively by any of the various castes, i.e., in theory, there is no segregation of castes here. Similarly, in theory there is no segregation of sexes on any *johar*. But, in practice, whenever any man goes to a *johar*, he avoids the place being used by women at that time, if any, and remains at a distance from them (Chandhoke, 1978:230).

The *johars* get filled up with rain water. Villages, which have some canal or its tributary flowing nearby, use canal water also for filling their *johars*. Along with rain-water, mud and many other things also get swept into the *johars*. The *johars*, thereby, get silted and filled-up every few years. Whenever such a situation arises, the entire village community gets together to clean the *johar*. For the last few years, the main *johar* in village Chhatera has dried up because of silting and, therefore, needs cleaning. The village community is not bothered about it and no efforts are being contemplated to clean and deepen the *johar* because the *biswedaran* do not have much difficulty about water now. Quite a few of them have got hand-pumps installed in their *ghars*, and many of them also have tube-wells in their *khets*.

The function of the *johar* for drinking of water by the cattle, while under the guardianship of the village *pali* during the day, is now served by drain no. 8 (mentioned earlier). Cattle relax in the bed of this drain and drink water from it. Presently, the main difficulty on this score is being experienced by the *be-biswedaran*, especially by the 'untouchable' castes. They don't have *khets* and, therefore, no tube-wells. Their house plots being small and congested, with no arrangement or even possibility of proper disposal of waste water, the *be-biswedaran* cannot conveniently install hand-pumps. Moreover, financially also it is not easy for them to make this provision. Hence, this blessing (of tube-wells and hand-pumps) for the *biswedaran* has this side effect of a curse for the *be-biswedaran*.

9.2 KUWAN

The drinking water well, locally called *kuwan*, is not only an important landmark in the rural scene but also plays an important role in the life of the village. In fact, the very location of the *abadi* and its pattern at the macro-level (i.e., the village layout) are to an extent determined by the availability and location of the drinking water source. Discussing specifically the Jat habitations, Mukerji (1957:111) writes "... The digging of wells and well irrigation also had a lasting influence on the coming together of the population and thus creating an agglomerate and clustered settlement. The well always was dug first and then the habitations were constructed around it. The seed of clustering was thus the well within the village. In general, in all the villages, the central and the most used well is as old as the first habitation itself".

Kuwan plays such an important role in the life of these villagers that it is revered by them almost to the extent of being worshipped. About five weeks after the birth of a male child in a household, the mother is taken to the *kuwan* from which the family draws water. Women of the household and female near relatives of her husband's family accompany the mother to the *kuwan*, singing all the way. A *puja* (worship) called *jalwa pujan* is performed there.[1] It is only after the *jalwa pujan* ceremony that the mother is allowed to do any work in her house. On the occasion of *Diwali* festival, members of every household place a *diwa* on the *kuwan* from which its members draw water.

Drawing and bringing water from a *kuwan* are a woman's job. If a man, whose wife is unwell, is seen by others while taking water from the *kuwan*, he becomes an object of ridicule to his friends and others.

There is hardly any other meeting place for women to gather in the village. Besides, they are too busy otherwise to find time to gather at a place. The *kuwan* plays the role of a club, a community centre, or a women's *chaupal*, if one may call it so. It is here that news, views and pleasantries are exchanged, questions are raised and answers given. It is a good place of outing for the women folk. Although during the past decade or so, some of the well-to-do households among the land-owning sections of the village community have also installed hand-pumps in their *ghers*, still the main source of drinking water in Chhatera is its seven *kuwans*. Before the installation of hand-pumps, *kuwans* were the only source of drinking water in the village.

Plate 9.2: Visitors from Delhi observing women drawing water from the *Chamaron-ka-kuwan*. See the *chhatri* (canopy) and the *nim* tree above

All the seven *kuwans* are located at the outer periphery of the *abadi*: four – *Gore wala, Ratti Ram Ka, Hukmi aur Badle ka* and *Rattan Master ka* – are located in the Jat sector; while there is one *kuwan* each in the sectors inhabited by the Brahmans, *Chamars* and *Bhangis*, respectively. (Please refer to figure 5.2 and plate 9.2).

In terms of segregation of castes, the position is different on the *kuwans* than that on the *johars*, where no caste distinction is made. The *Chamars* and *Bhangis* can use only their own respective *kuwans*. From the other five *kuwans*, members of any of the 'touchable' castes can take water. But in practice, because of their own convenience, even among the 'touchables', people take water only from the *kuwan* nearer to their *ghar* / *gher* / *baithak*, etc., wherever the water is required.

As their very names indicate, some of the *kuwans* were constructed by individual persons or individual families, while others by the entire caste group or *gram panchayat*. Previously, every *kuwan* used to be maintained and also, therefore, controlled by those who built it. Even all the members of the 'touchable' castes could not take water from whichever *kuwan* they liked. When a person or a household was not on good terms with the owners of a particular *kuwan*, no member of the former household could take water from that *kuwan*. Since the last consolidation of holdings in the village in 1956, all the seven *kuwans* in Chhatera have come under the control of the *gram panchayat*.

In the beginning, when the village was founded, there was only one *kuwan*, *Gore Wala*, in the village. As its very name indicates, this *kuwan* was located in the *gora deh* of the village. It is not fitted with a persian wheel. At that time water from this *kuwan* was used for domestic consumption as well as for irrigational purposes. In fact, there were three clearly marked portions on this *kuwan* : one used by men-folk for drawing water for irrigational purposes; the second to be used by women for drawing water for domestic consumption and the third used by a Muhammadan *saka* (water carrier) named Yadgiri. All the three portions of the *kuwan* had their separate pulleys, etc., so that these could all be used simultaneously. In addition, there were a couple of in-built cattle troughs forming a part of this structure. A major portion of water spilling from the vessels, or otherwise falling on the well-platform, would automatically go into these troughs while, at times, some people drawing water from the well would themselves put some portion of it into these troughs. Cattle returning to the *abadi* from the *khets* or *charagah* used to drink water from these troughs.

When the *Bhangis* and *Chamars* did not have their own separate *kuwans*, any member of their caste who needed water used to wait at a little distance from the *kuwan* till some caste Hindu woman came to fetch water for herself, would, with her own bucket, throw water from a distance into the Harijan's vessel. Whenever Yadgiri was at the *kuwan*, he would draw some water and pour the same into the utensils of the Harijans waiting near the *kuwan*. This fact is clearly mentioned in the Settlement report of Chhatcra (1910). Hindus and Muslims, the report says, could draw water from this *kuwan* without any distinction.

Plate 9.3: Cattle strolling in the *gora*. In the foreground heaps of *gobar* collected by the *pali*

9.3 LAIHNDA / GORA DEH

Every village has a large cattle population, colloquially called *gora*, in this region. The cattle cannot be confined to the *ghars, ghers,* or *gitwars*, of their owners throughout the day. They need to be taken out for a stroll, for grazing in the open fields and for relaxation in the *johars.* This need is all the more greater during the summer season. At the time of founding a new village, so also at the time of every (revenue) Settlement or Consolidation of Holdings and the consequent extension of the *lal dora*, some land is earmarked for the above purpose. In the terminology of the revenue department, this land is called *gora deh*, but the colloquial term for it is *laihnda. Laihnda* is always adjacent to the village *abadi* and is on the road or a passage whereby one enters or leaves the *abadi. Laihnda* is under the managerial control of the *gram panchayat*. There are also always a number of *rukhs* in the *laihnda* which provide shade for the cattle as well as for the human beings who, on certain occasions, sit there (please see plates 9.3 and 9.4).

Plate 9.4: Sheep returning to *ghar* after grazing in the jungle. Harijan owners escorting through the *gora*

It is neither possible nor economical for any household to spare a person for the whole day (every day) to take out their cattle for grazing, etc. So, for this work, an arrangement is made on community basis. Every morning, almost all the villagers leave their cattle at the *laihnda*. The cattle are taken by the *pali* to the *charagah* or even to the *khets*, when there are no crops standing, and then to the village *johar*. In the afternoon, the *pali* brings back all the cattle to the *laihnda* and from there the cattle itself return to its respective homes. This being an every day routine the year-round, the cattle also know the paths leading to their respective places (please see plate 9.5).

Charagah or *charan* is the land earmarked for cattle-grazing at the time a village is founded. Some trees are grown on this land and, at times, one finds some grass here. Nothing else is ever grown on this land. The *charagah* of Chhatera covers twelve acres of land (which includes one acre under *chehanrin*). This area under the *charagah* can neither be divided (among the proprietors of the village) nor diverted to any other use. On the occasion of *holi* festival every year, women of the village go to the *laihnda* singing. They take some fuel with them.

Plate 9.5: Cattle relaxing in the *gora*

Since the *laihnda* is quite an open space located close to the *abadi*, *Holika* is burnt there. *Dussehra* festival is arranged by every village in its *gora*. Effigies of the demons *Rawana*, *Kumbhkharna* and *Meghnath* are also erected and burnt here. In the month of *phalgun* (February-March) every year, the boys of the village play the game of *kabadi* (an Indian game in which two teams participate at a time) in the *laihnda*. Now, of course, with the coming up of the schools, the venue of games is also gradually shifting to the school grounds (please see plate 9.6).

The *laihnda* being an open space, quite a few activities can be undertaken there. "...The space immediately around the village is called *goira*; and here the cattle stand to be milked, ropes twisted, sugar presses erected and all the opertions conducted for which free space is necessary..." (Ibbetson, 1883:120). In a boy's marriage, after the *ghor charhi* ceremony the procession is taken to the *gora* and from there to the *baithak* of the household. In a girl's marriage, the *barat* is received and seen off at the *gora*. All important guests, of individual households as well as of the entire village or a section of it, are received as well as seen off by their hosts at the *gora*. Even a dead body, while being taken from the *abadi* to the *chehanrin*, is stopped at the *gora* for some time. Some ceremonies are performed here and the *kandhiyas* change for the final part of the last journey of the departed villager.

Plate 9.6: Fire wood collected in the *laihnda* for *holi*

9.4 CHEHANRIN/MASANRN

At the time of founding a village, some land is earmarked for the disposal of its dead. The place where the dead are burnt is called *chehanrin* or *masanrn*. The place where the dead bodies are buried is also locally known by the same name, i.e., *chehanrin*. But in the terminology of the revenue department the burial ground is called *qabristan* while the cremation ground is described as *marghat*.

At present, no section of the Chhatera community adopts any other method than cremation for the disposal of its dead. There is only one *masanrn* in Chhatera. It is about two furlongs away and towards the south of the village *abadi*. It is a one acre plot of just open land without any enclosure or structure on it. The *masanrn* is located near the main *johar* of the village, so that after burning the dead at the *chehanrin*, the mourners can go straight to the *johar* and wash themselves (an essential ritual they must perform in order to get rid of the ritual pollution) before they can re-enter the *abadi*. Women and children never go to the *chehanrin*. After the menfolk carrying the dead body have moved about a hundred yards from the *ghar* of the deceased, the women also move towards the *chehanrin* but stop at the *gora* and wait there for some time. In Chhatera, as in most of the other villages in the region, there is a *kuwan* in the *gora*. Women fill water in the *paindhas* from the *kuwan*, leave the *paindhas* there and come back to the *abadi*. When the men-folk return from the *chehanrin*, they wash temselves with this water and then return to the *abadi*. Presently, no segregation (on caste basis) is practised in the *chehanrin* of Chhatera. This is contrary to the position existing in some of the south Indian villages, where the classical division of castes is observed even in the cremation grounds (Sivertsen, 1963:33).

In the Chhatera region the *chehanrin* in every village is invariably located towards the south of the *abadi*. There is a folk belief that south is the direction of the dead and that after his death everyone has to go there. Moreover, in this region, the wind generally blows from the easterly direction (*purwa*) or from the westerly direction (*pachhiya*), seldom from the north and practically never from the south. So, if the *chehanrin* is located towards the south of the *abadi*, foul smell of the burning of dead bodies will never come towards the *abadi*. Previously the *chehanrin* of Chhatera was towards the north of the present *abadi*. At the time of Consolidation of Holdings in 1956, that plot was converted into agricultural land and a new plot towards the south of the *abadi* was earmarked to be used as *chehanrin*. Being the followers of Arya Samaj, the Chhaterans did not object to the conversion of the old *chehanrin* into agricultural land.

When Chhatera was founded, the *Bhangis* and *Jogis* used to bury their dead. All the other castes have (from the very beginning) always been burning their dead. But the dead bodies of children of these castes (dying before the age of seven or eight) also used to be buried in a burial ground of the *Bhangis*. Now, of course, the dead bodies of children dying only a few months old are buried, all others are burnt. Although a drift towards not burying the dead started some time earlier, there has not been even a single case of burial in Chhatera since India got its independence in 1947. In the settlement report of the village (1880) *chehanrin* and *qabristan* have been shown separately. The 1910 settlement report, however, indicates that dead bodies of the Hindus were burnt in a plot of land, measuring three *biswas*, and the dead bodies of the *Chamars* were also burnt in a corner of this plot. It further states that the dead bodies of the *Bhangis* were buried in *khasra* (plot) No. 347, measuring 18 *biswas*, and the dead of the *Jogis* were also burried in the *marghat*. There was no plot of land marked as *qabristan*. The funeral and the burial grounds were located towards the north and south, respectively, of the village *abadi*. At the time of the Consolidation of Holdings in the village in 1956, all these were combined into one plot.

9.5 BHUMIYA / MATA

Although, as stated earlier, the Jat villages are conspicuous by the absence of temples, there is a tribal institution which is a cult of ancestral worship. To quote Mukerji in this connection:

> In sharp contrast to the tribal Jathera is the *Bhumia* in the south-east Punjab. Here, when a new village or colony is founded, the first thing to be done before the houses are actually built is to raise a mound of earth on a spot near the proposed village and plant a Jand tree in it. Houses are then built. The first man who dies in the village whether he be a Brahman or Jat or *Chamar* is burnt or buried on this mound and on it is built a masonry shrine which is named after him. The fortunate man is deified as *Bhumia* or Earth-god and worshipeed by Hindus of all classes in the village, being looked upon as its soul guardian deity (1957:24-25).

Every village in the Chhatera region has a *bhumiya*. In addition to the *bhumiya*, the villagers make a *Mata*. *Bhumiya* and *Mata* are always made near the *laihnda* (Please see plate No. 9.7). The villagers have reverential fear for the *Mata*. Whenever anyone in the village falls into trouble, they say that he has not offered *parshad* to the *Mata*. On the *saten* (seventh day) of the month of *Chait* (March-April) women and children go to the *Mata* at about 7.00 a.m. They wash the *Mata* and place some *basaure* - balls of cooked *daliya* - there. Every new born child is taken to the *Mata* a few days after his birth. On the occasion of the marriage of a boy, after the *ghor charhi* ceremony in the *gal* in front of the *banra's ghar*, the *banra* is taken to the *Mata* in a procession and he offers some coin there and *hath jor den* (pays his respects). On the day, after the return of the *barat* to the *banra's* village, the *banra* and the *banri* (with the ends of their respective head gears tied to each other) go to the *Mata* accompanied by the women of the *banra's* household singing all the way. Whenever anyone in the village suffers from 'pox', after he or she has recovered, he or she is taken to the *Mata* and a *puja* is performed there. *Patashe* are offered to the *Mata* and *hath jor den*. These *patashe* are distributed among children. There is a tradition of *manauti* at the *Mata*. Some people come to the *mata* and pray to her to grant their desire, and also promise that when their desire is fulfilled they would visit the *Mata* again and make such and such presents.

9.6 DHARAMSHALA

It is not very long ago that the means of transport in the countryside were very slow. Even today, the vehicles, like, *tonga* and *bailgadi*, that are used in villages, are slow moving ones and cannot always complete their journeys during the course of a single day. Moreover, in summer the journey cannot be undertaken during the day time. The villager has to travel in the morning, rest during the day, and then again resume his journey after the Sunset. So, the travellers need a place near some *abadi* where they can spend the night in safety, and can also, if need be, get some of the things required by them. Therefore, many road-side villages in this region have a place where travellers can stay for some time and relax. Such a place is known as *dharamshala*. During the last century, such rest houses were not so common in the Rohtak district in general, "There are usually no large *sarais*, used by traders and merchants. Carts and camels usually journey all night along with their loads" (Purser and Fanshawe, 1880:11). But villages in the Chhatera region have been having this kind of facility since long.

Chhatera has one such *dharamshala* situated on a main road at the outer periphery of the village estate, about three furlongs from the *abadi*. It is a two-roomed *pacca* structure with a *kuwan* in front of it. There are a number of mango and *jaman* (common black plum, Java plum) trees around the *kuwan*. When this *dharamshala* was originally built in 1922-23, this place was at the crossing of two very important roads; the *Badshahi Sarak* (i.e., the King's Road) running from Baghpat to Kharkhauda and the one running from Sonepat to Majra side. Amrit Singh, a big landlord and the then *lambardar* of the village, got the *dharamshala* constructed on his land with his own funds. During his life time, every summer, Amrit Singh used to run a *piyau* (a kiosk for free distribution of drinking water) for the travellers. The *lambardar* used to appoint a person to man the *piyau* and pay his entire salary from his own resources. With the introduction of faster means of transport, like, trucks, buses and tempos, etc., these *dharamashalas* have ceased to have much of their utility. Though the *dharamshala* in Chhatera is still there, because of its being practically in a state of complete disuse, it gives the appearance of a deserted place.

Plate 9.7: *Mata* (right) and *bhumiya* (left) under *jal* trees in the *gora*

9.7 KURRI

Manure is one of the most important farm in-puts. Although farmers of Chhatera have now very well taken to chemical fertilizers also, but, partly because of its own peculiar qualities and partly because the organic manure costs the farmer practically nothing, organic manure still continues to play a very important role in agriculture in this region. Almost all round the village *abadi*, outside the *lal dora*, separate pieces of land (from the *shemlat deh*) have been allotted to individual agriculturist households for digging manure pits. These pits are called *kurris*. The main concentration of *kurris* is, of course, near the *laihnda*. The villagers have not obtained the approval of the revenue department for this allotment. In the latest revenue records, therefore, there is no mention of these *kurris*. Like *gitwars*, *kurris* are also generally allotted to each household in the sector near its *gher*. So *kurris* are also [illegible]ated caste-wise (plates 6.1 and 10.2).

The entire refuse, waste and sweepings (including the waste *gobar*) from the *ghar*, *gher* and *baithak*, of every household is everyday dumped by the women of the household, or by the *Bhangan*, of those who have engaged one for the purpose, into its *kurri* and allowed to rot there till compost, locally called *khat*, is ready for use in the *khets*. Whenever a household needs *khat* in its *khets* this is taken from its *kurri* (generally by men) and spread over the *khets*. The following observations of Ibbetson in this connection are worth noting:

> The dung-heap (*kurri*) is started when the rains are over. A great hole is dug in the ground, and straws, cattle-beddings, sweeping of horse and cattle-sheds, and all sorts of refuse are thrown into it. During the rains the cow-dung is too wet to be patted up into fuel-cakes, and is all thrown on to the heap. The rain is allowed to fall freely upon it, and it is periodicaly turned over and worked up by the sweepers. As soon as the rains are over it is fit for use. It is taken to the fields in carts (1883:164).

9.8 **SAKUL** (SCHOOL)

With the increasing emphasis on educating the rural masses as a part of the vigorous rural development efforts by the government since Independence, the village *sakul* has also come to occupy an important position in the life of every rural community and has become an important landmark in every rural habitation. Chhatera has a *sakul* located to the north-east, just outside the village *abadi*. Established in 1946 as a co-educational institution, it is one of the oldest *sakuls* in this region. For about two and a half decades, it had been imparting instructions up to the primary level only. As a result of the intensive development work initiated in the village after its having been adopted by the *Hindustan Times*, this *sakul* was raised to the middle standard in 1972. It is a co-eductional *sakul* with about 200 students and nine teachers. About 75 per cent of the students come from Brahman and Jat households, while the rest belong to the Harijan families. Besides serving Chhatera, this *sakul* caters to the needs of a number of neighbouring villages also.

The *sakul* is located on a plot of land measuring about one acre. This plot was earmarked for the purpose at the time of the Consolidation of Holdings in the village in 1956. Prior to that, the *sakul* was located near the village *johar* (towards the south of the *abadi*). The site of the old *sakul* has since been converted into *khets*. The primary section of the *sakul* is housed in a *pacca* building block (comprising of five classrooms, a staff room and a store) built in 1969 with monetary contributions and *shramdan* (voluntary labour) by the villagers, and some grant from the State government. The middle section of the *sakul* is housed in, more or less, an identical building block put up on the other side of the plot facing the old block. There is a hand-pump in the *sakul* and children do gardening here. The *sakul* has a play ground which is reasonably good from the village standards. In a corner of the *sakul* compound there is a septic tank latrine. It was built with the hope that it would act as an extension agent and, in course of time, this new idea in the field of public health would spread from the *sakul* to village homes and help in improving the physical environment in the village. As a partial fulfilment of the essential requirements for a middle *sakul* to be sanctioned by the government, in 1971-72 a twin set of staff residential quarters was built in a corner of the *sakul* compound. This structure was also put up with the villagers' own resources and a matching grant from the Development Department of the Haryana Government.

Besides the *sakul* serving the educational needs of the community, its compound is used for some other community purposes also. Games, like, *kabadi*, especially on occasion of festivals like *holi* (an activity which has traditionally been performed at the *laihnda*), Independence Day celebrations and other functions in the village are organized in the *sakul* premises. Whenever any important dignitary visits the village and the gathering is too large to be accommodated at the village *chaupal*, or if the *chaupal* is not free, the function is organized in the *sakul* compound. Previously, all such functions used to be arranged at the *chaupal*. The *sakul* is a common and neutral place. So, all such general functions which concern the village community as a whole, and for which a lot of space is required, can be, and are often, organized in the *sakul* compound (Please see plates 9.8 and 9.9).

9.9 KHET

The most precious wealth of any agriculturist family is its agricultural land, locally called *khet*. *Khets* are the mainstay of the economy of any village where the predominant means of livelihood is farming. The *khets* of Chhatera are located all round its *abadi*; almost 50 per cent of these lying across drain No. 8 (mentioned earlier). Although a Consolidation of Holdings had been completed in the village in 1956, almost two decades have passed since then and the commonly prevalent problem of sub-divisions and fragmentations of holdings in Indian villages has appeared on the Chhtera scene again.

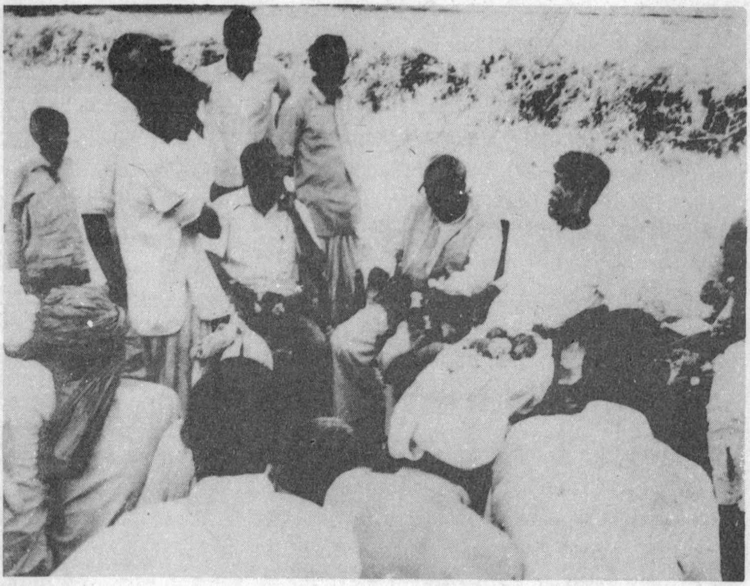

Plate 9.8: Housing minister of India discussing with the villagers in the *sakul* compound

Almost throughout the year, a considerable part of the life of the male members (in the working age group) of every agriculturist household is spent in its *khets* preparing the fields, sowing, harvesting, and carrying out a number of other agricultural operations in between. During agriculturally peak seasons, some of the men-folk sometimes stay in their *khets* for days together. Women and children of every agriculturist household help their men-folk by working in the *khets*, supplying food, etc., and running errands. During the slack agricultural seasons, women often go to their *khets* to collect vegetables, sugarcane and other field products for domestic consumption; and sometimes just for an 'outing' also. Every agriculturist household carries out most of its agricultural operations in its *khets*. *Bitoras* and *bungas* are often made here. Dead cattle are burried by the agriculturists in their *khets*.

For attending to natural calls, the villagers have to go to their *khets*. Since the installation of tube wells in their *khets*, men often go there for bathing and women for washing clothes

Plate 9.9: *Paindha* (pitcher) race among girls organized in the village *sakul*

9.10 ABADI

Villages in this region being strictly nucleated ones, the residences of all the inhabitants of any village are concentrated at one place. This area, reserved for residential uses, is called *abadi*. In Urdu, the term *abadi* also means population. When used as a verb, 'to *abad*' means 'to Inhabit', or 'to populate'. Therefore, the *abadi* of any village means its populated area, or the area where its population lives. The limits or boundary of the *abadi* are known as *lal dora*. The area inside the *lal dora* is exempt from land revenue. The only tax levied here is the *chulah tax*. This is levied by the *gram panchayat*. So, the revenue records, which are maintained exclusively for revenue collection, obviously do not contain details of the *abadi*. The entire *abadi* is treated as one holding and is given one *khasra* number. Inside the *abadi*, no bye-laws, or any other statutory restrictions are applicable.

In every village, at the time of each Revenue Settlement, the requirements of *abadi* land are assessed in the light of the increased population and its changed circumstances. The *abadi* area is extended accordingly. The new extension of *abadi* is known as *tausih abadi*. The last settlement in Chhatera took place in the year 1910. But the *abadi* was again extended in the village at the time of Consolidation of Holdings here in 1956. The *abadi* of Chhatera, measuring 13 acres, is located almost at the centre of the village estate. Important elements of space around the *abadi* are : *ghars, ghers, baithaks, chaupals, kuwans, gitwara*, etc. (For details please refer to Chapter 5).

9.11 CHAUPAL

Every village and, for that matter, every human habitation generally has some common place where community life can be lived, and where the activities, connected with any particular section or entire local community, are carried out. In rural areas, there are no hotels or rest houses or dak bungalows for catering to the needs of visitors and officials from outside the villages for their various functions. The following remarks of Hongiman (1954) show that this kind of space, specially for the males, is almost a universal phenomenon among rural settlements :

> Buildings occupied or used primarily by man have an extensive distribution around the world. According to Hoebell, similar facilities for women remain far less developed, primarily because family demands leave women little freedom compared to men, and because in many communities the importance of males is emphasized. Such emphasis on males congenial to and maintained by activities, like rituals, that occur in men's houses.
>
> Roughly speaking, such houses fall into two classes. In the first group are those structures that serve for routine activities including overnight use as sleeping places by village bachelors and guests. In the second class are so-called "club houses" primarily associated with special functions, like the performances of large-scale ceremonies, storage of ritual paraphernelia, meetings of sodalities and esoteric instructions. Actually, the latter buildings seem to occupy one end of a continuum and in a particular instance it may be difficult to know where to classify a community's men's house. The distinction rests on an increasing number of uses, mainly ceremonial in character, characterizing the "club house" versus the

"dormitory".

In the Jat villages of Haryana the respective rough parallel of a dormitory and the club house are the *baithak* and the *chaupal* (Chandhoke, 1977:24).

The old origin of this institution

Chaupal plays a very important role in the village life and serves a very useful purpose. This institution has, therefore, always been there and one finds its mention even in some of the very old texts and revenue records. Writing about rural habitations in India, Jha (1955) remarks thus:

> The centre of the village was full of activities. At the inter-section of the two main streets was the recognized meeting place for the meeting of the elders. A *banyan* or *pipal* tree or a mound, sufficed for the mote-house or assembly hall, except when the village was big enough and could afford a mandapam or a salam. The village 'Salam' was pillared pavillion, sometimes made of bricks, though in general of wood. It was provided with 'phalaka' or block-tables, jars of water and oil-lamp. It was an attractive place, surrounded by a wall with a gate.
>
> Besides being a seat of delineation for the village politics, the 'Salam' served the purpose of a rest house for the guests, both the lay and the clericals. This village hall served the function of the modern village school. Important religious preceptors and other important persons were invited to come to the village and to deliver public lectures to the villagers in this rest house. There was an arrangement for giving dinners to the guests and constant supply of water. It was matted, white-washed, strewn with grass and smeared with cow-dung. This hall was like the modern *Dharamshala* with this peculiarity that there was provided not only free lodging but free board also.
>
> The village mote-hall served the purpose of a public kitchen and on the occasion of festivity the villagers took their meals together there.
>
> This hall was under the supervision of the headman and he looked to its maintenance. Any body seeking admission into it had to take his permission and nobody could go in without getting his

feet washed.

The villagers jointly built mote-hall (Salam), constructed reservoirs, feeding travellers (*sattra*), places where water was supplied freely to the travellers..... Everybody contributed his mite towards the success of a common thing.

Chhatera:

The village of Chhatera has two *chaupals* - one in the Jat sector and the other in the Brahman sector. These are, therefore, called Jat *chaupal* and Brahman *chaupal*, respectively.

Plate 9.10: Jat *Chaupal*. Mark its high plinth, imposing *nim* tree and the vast village square in front of it

In every village, the *chaupal* is always built on a grand scale, i.e., much better and different than individual *ghars*. "Fine village rest houses (called *paras*) built of masonry ... are to be found in the well-to-do villages in the canal tract..." (Purser and Fanshawe, 1881:9-10). The Jat *chaupal* of Chhatera is the village centre. It is a focal point in the village. It is an imposing structure marked by high plinth and an imposing *nim* (margosa) tree. It has a big verandah with two rooms on one side and a spacious platform in the front. There is an open space or the village square in front of the Jat *chaupal* (see plates 9.10 and figure 9.1).

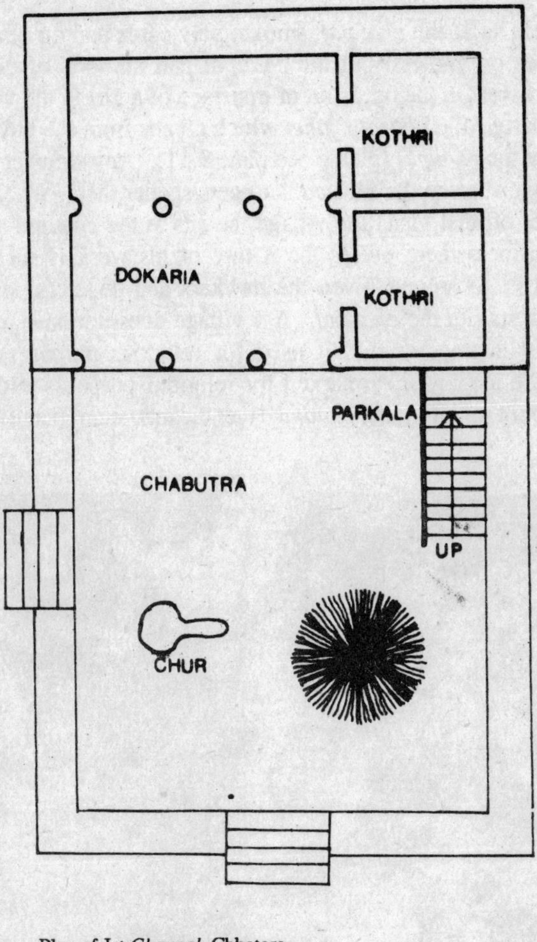

Figure 9.1: Plan of Jat *Chaupal*, Chhatera

Functions

Chaupal is a common and neutral place for the entire village. Any work, related to the village community in genral is done here. Meetings of the *gram panchayat* (elected body of villagers to run village administration), as well as of the multi-village *panchayat* are held at the *chaupal*. Whenever any person is to be reprimanded for the breach of village norms or for committing any serious offence, it is done at the *chaupal*.

Villagers sit at the *chaupal*, smoke, play cards and do other things. Gossip goes on endlessly at the *chaupal* and all sorts of discussions take place here. On the occasion of marriage of a girl in the village, the marriage party called *barat* / *janet* which comes from the boy's village is lodged at the *chaupal* (please see plate 9.11). Any stranger or visitor to the village stays at the *chaupal* and gets shelter there. Whenever any government official visits the village, he sits at the *chaupal* and transacts his business there unless the nature of his work is such that requires him to go around. Even the hawkers and peddlers, visiting the village, can stay in the *chaupal*. If a village does not have any *kutiya* (structure with trees around it used for religious purposes) or *bara* (land outside the *abadi* earmarked for religious purposes with a small structure built on it), any *sadhu* (mendicant), *sant* (saint), *bawaji*

Plate 9.11: *Barat* staying at the Jat *chaupal*. Old and young in various noods *Hukas* and *task* (cards) - a must in every *barat*

(religious person), *faqir* (mendicant, generally a Muslim), or such other persons, visiting the village stay at the *chaupal.*

In the Settlement Report of the village it is stated that : "The *lambardars* of the village purchase things in consultation with members of the proprietary body from any one shop they wish. No particular supplier is fixed for the purpose. On every harvest, this money is realized from members of the proprietary body along with land revenue and paid to the contractor / supplier. Repair of *chaupal*, oil for *chaupal* lamp, food, etc., for the travellers staying at the *chaupal*, and help rendered to the *faqirs* are some of the items, expenditure on which is met by the villagers jointly".

Plate 9.12: Village meeting at the Jat *chaupal* Author explaining to villagers the problems of physical environment in Chhatera. Big laddle-shaped *bhati*, called *chur*, in the centre used for boiling water for *barats*

Most of the teachers in Chhatera school are from outside the village. Until recently there was no residential accommodation in the school for the teachers. So, these school teachers stay in the *chaupal*, which, besides being a common place, also being located in the heart of the village *abadi*, has many advantages.

Chaupal is the centre of all administrative, social, cultural and recreational activities in the village. The community television set is also kept and played at the *chaupal*. Any cultural programme organized in the the village by the Chhaterans and/or outsiders is always performed at the *chaupal* (please see plate 9.12). All the public functions like the programmes on the Independence Day and Republic Day are organized at the *chaupal*.

The village square - called *chauk* - is very handy on the occasion of functions with large gatherings. Only sports events are organized in the school compound because the school has good grounds and the space in and around the *chaupal* is not sufficient for such purposes. Even the *bhajniks* (those who sing *bhajans*, i.e., religious and devotional songs) organize their activities and functions at the *chaupal*. *Jogis* also used to perform mostly at the *chaupals*. Now-a-days, even the political parties organize their functions at the *chaupal*.

Masculine Place

Traditionally, the *chaupal* is a 'masculine' place. Women have nothing to do with the *chaupal* and do not even go to it. Even when no male member is present there, some of the orthodox women pull down their *ghunghat* (veil) while passing near the *chaupal*.

In 1972, when a team of specialists from the All India Institute of Medical Sciences, New Delhi, visited the village, they camped at the *chaupal* and examined the patients there. Some of the women patients (majority of them being quite elderly) refused to climb the *chaupal* to get themselves examined. At the tactful intervention of the author, one of the Lady Eye Surgeons came down from the *chaupal* and examined these orthodox ladies in the *baramda* of a *ghar* across the *gal*. So very rigid are the attitudes of the villagers in respect of the *chaupal*.

The Wind of Change

Recently, change has started in the village in this respect. During television shows, some of the women do come to the *chaupal*, while some others, who do not come to the *chaupal* proper, occupy vantage positions near the *chaupal*. In fact, the first incident which set the trend for this change was the visit to the village by Mrs. Indira Chakravarty (wife of the Governor of Haryana) in 1970. Mrs. Chakravarty was seated at the *chaupal*, since, according to the local custom whenever any honoured guest or high dignitary visting the village is to be accorded a grand reception, this is done at the village *chaupal*. Since Mrs Chakravarty was a lady, at the instance of the government officers, accompanying her, the village elders had to call some of the village women to the *chaupal* to sit with her.

Such incidents occur in any village very rarely. The elderly male folk of the village were constrained under very special and exceptional circumstances to take this 'unpleasant decision' which broke an age-old tradition.

Cost and Maintenance

The present structure of the Jat *chaupal* was put up about 85 years ago with contributions from the entire village, though mainly from the Jats. The Brahman *chaupal* was built about 35 years ago with contributions mainly from the Brahmans of the village. Prior to its existing structure, the old structure of the Jat *chaupal* which was a *katcha* (a thing which is not quite durable), stood at the same site. Some trees standing on *shamlat* (the village common) land near the *abadi* were sold out by the village to some charcoal manufacturers. In a geneal body meeting of the village community, the villagers resolved to spend this amount on the construction of a *pacca chaupal*. But the sale proceeds of these trees were not sufficient for the purpose and hence the Jat households in the village had to make additional contributions. The old structure was demolished to make place for the new *pacca chaupal*. Only one Jat in the entire village did not contribute for the construction of the new *chaupal*. But, as a village *chaupal* is always a *sanjhi jagah*, or a *shamlat* (a common place / a joint property) of the entire village community, he has also always been allowed to use it. Although major contributions for the construction of any *chaupal* may be made by a particular community, there is no restriction on accepting donations from others. In fact, in the neighbouring small village Ladpur, money for this purpose was collected from even outside the village. So, everyone has an equal right to use a *chaupal*.

There has never been any dispute about the use of the two *chaupals* in Chhatera. Even thc meetings of the *panchayat* have been held sometimes in the Jat *chaupal* and sometimes in the Brahman *chaupal*. Being bigger in size and centrally located, the Jat *chaupal* is used more often. Therefore, some people in the village say that it has become a *panchayat ghar*[2] though in reality it is not so. But whenever anybody simply says *chaupal*, it signifies the Jat *chaupal*. The Brahman *chaupal* is always called the Brahman *chaupal*. The two *chaupals* in Chhatera can be used by the Jats, Brahmans, Baniyas, *Khatis, Lohars, Nais* and *Jogis*; in short, by all the 'clean castes' in the village. The *Chamars* and *Balmikis*, or *Bhangis* cannot use these *chaupals*. In some of the nearby villages, the Harijans have managed to build their own *chaupals*. The Harijans of Chhatera are also making serious efforts in this direction.

Whenever a meeting of any multi-village *panchayat* is convened in Chhatera, it is held at the Jat *chaupal*. A multi-village *panchayat* meets at the Brahman *chaupal* only if the Jat *chaupal* is not free. When a Brahman *barat* comes to the village, even if the Brahman *chaupal* is vacant, members of the bride's family prefer to lodge their *barat* at the Jat *chaupal* as, according to them, 'it has the shade of a big *nim* tree and a bigger place'. But, in reality, what they have in mind is the prestige value that the Jat *chaupal* has acquired due to several reasons.

In any village, the particular section of the community which constructs a *chaupal* has the preferential and not exclusive right to use it. For instance, if on a particular day two *barats* - one of the Jats and the other of the non-Jats - come to the village, the Jat *barat* will stay at the Jat *chaupal*, while the other one will have to be lodged elsewhere. The same is true of the Brahman *chaupal* also. Sometimes, more than one *barat* are simultaneously lodged in the same *chaupal*, provided all these *barats* are of the same caste.

The village sweeper - *Bhangi* - cleans the *chaupal* everyday. Whenever a *barat* stays at the *chaupal*, this *Bhangi* gets one rupee and a *patal* of food (i.e., food for one person served on a tree-leaf plate called *patal*). While a person is giving *bhat* (i.e., making presents) to his sister on the occasion of the marriage of her son/daughter, one rupee is taken out of the presents and kept in a fund for the maintenance and repair of the *chaupal*. This money is not deposited with the *panchayat* but is kept with a person specially nominated by the village community for such works. There are similar rules for the Brahman *chaupal*. This shows that although so far as the right to use the *chaupal* is concerned there is no distinction between various castes, in reality, at least to a certain extent, the two *chaupals* belong to two separate groups. In practice, therefore, these *chaupals* are the property of the particular caste groups. Hence, the liability or obligation of these groups to repair and maintain their respective *chaupals*.

Original Location of the Chaupal

Among the elderly people in this region, the *chaupal* is also commonly known as *paras*. But this term is so out-moded that a majority of the middle-aged persons are not at all aware of it. The word *paras* seems to be a distorted version of the Hindi word *purush*, meaning male. Probably it is so because *chaupal* is a male's place. Writing about the villages of Rohak District, Purser and Fanshawe have recorded that, "...The village rest house (called *Paras*) are to be found situated outside the walls or in the middle where several roads meet. Before it, on the platform are beds and cooking pots for use by the travellers on whom the barbers and *Chamars*, whose turn it is, wait. In some of the villages the rest house is merely a large open shed. But in most it is handsomely laced with wood-work and part of the walls are brick-built; while in many the rest houses are made of masonry throughout, and the plastered walls are decorated on their exterior with pictures of tigers and horses, elephants and railway trains, Hindu Gods and British soldiers" (1880:60). Similarly, Ibbetson has reported about the Jat villages of Karnal thus " Every village keeps open house to the country side. A traveller (*bateo*) who has no friends in the village puts up as a matter of course in the common room (*Chaupal* in the north, *paras* in the south) of the village and receives food and tobacco free; though he will, if possible, choose a village inhabited by his own tribe. Every government servant passing through the village is fed in like manner" (1883:106).

In any village, whenever a *chaupal* is constructed in the earlier stages of the founding of the village, in the first instance, it is located outside the *abadi*, or at least outside the area already inhabited at that time. Of course, in old villages already having an old *chaupal*, if the new structure is also put up at the same site, it may now become a part of the *abadi*. Likewise, the *chaupal* in Chhatera, when originally built, was outside the *abadi* and the *kot* (boundary wall around the *abadi*) (Please refer to figure 5.5).

Some of the elderly residents of Chhatera and of nearby villages also call the *chaupal* as *jangal-was*, meaning 'the house in the jungle'. But a deeper study reveals that the *jangal-was* is not the same thing as the *chaupal*. In fact, *jangal-was* does not have any structure. When a *barat* comes to the bride's village (according to the old custom, which, in some cases, is even now being partially observed), it would stop at the *jangal-was*, a place in the *gora* near the village approach-road, completely outside the *abadi*. The bride's party would come there to receive the *barat*. After completing preliminaries, like, the formal introductions and presentation of gifts here, the *banra* would be escorted to the *banri's ghar*. Elderly villagers put it colloquially as "*Jo barat a'ye karti use pahle bahar jangal mein thaihraya karte, cha'y pani pila kar pancha't chaupal par le a'ya karti*, meaning the *barat*, on its arrival, used to be lodged in the jungle outside, and after entertaining it to tea, the *panchayat* used to escort it to the *chaupal* (in the *abadi*). Describing the functions that performed when a *barat* arrives at the *ghar* of the bride, Ibbetson (1883:130) remarks, "... The girl's and boy's relations then fight for the stool on which the boy stood, and the boy's relations win, and carry it off in triumph to the *jandalwasa*, which is the place fixed for the residence of the guests. This should, in theory, be outside the village; but for convenience sake it is, generally, in the *Chaupal*..."

As mentioned earlier, with the changing social conditions, the role of *chaupal* is no doubt getting modified. But as the needs which this institution basically satisfies are of a fundamental and permanent nature, *chaupal* still continues, and shall continue, to enjoy an important position in the life of the rural community as an integral and prominent part of their habitat.

9.12 GITWAR

Besides the *ghar, baithak* and *gher*, another important place for every agriculturist household is the *gitwar*. A *gitwar* is an open plot of land, practically vacant, with slightly raised mud boundary lines for the demarcation of the plot. One or two trees are often planted here to provide shade for the cattle. Presently, all the *gitwars* in Chhatera are inside the *lal dora*. Before the extension of the *lal dora* in 1956, most of the *gitwars* in the village were outside the *lal dora*, but these have now come within the *tausih abadi*. In course of time, due to pressure on land, some new *gitwars* will again come up outside the extended *lal dora*. *Gitwars* located inside the *lal dora* are always on the land owned by the respective individuals themselves, while most of those outside the *lal dora* are on the *shamlat* land.

Fuel wood and cow-dung cakes, called *gose*, are stored by every household in its *gitwar*. *Bitoras* (heaps of cow-dung cakes) are often made here. Sometimes, even *kups* (straw stacks) are made in the *gitwars*. During the rainy season and also in summer (depending upon the weather conditions), sometimes the cattle are kept in the *gitwar* during certain parts of the day. Some of the poorer households, who do not have separate *ghers* for their cattle, keep their cattle in their *gitwars* during day time and in their *ghars* at night. Whenver the *bailgadi* (bullock-cart) is not in use, it is parked in the *gitwar*. At harvest time, the *gitwar* is often used as a *khalihan* (thrashing ground). *Pair* is often made here and women do winnowing. Heavy agricultural implements are also stored there. During the thrashing operations, the place becomes a *pair*. Otherwise it is not called a *pair*. That time it is called a *gitwar*. During the *gur*-making season, the *kolhu* (cane-crusher) is also often installed here (please see plates 9.13 and 9.14).

Plate 9.13: *Bungas* and *bitoras* of *Brahmans* in *gitwar* at the outskirts of *abadi* near *gora Gose* spread for drying in the foreground

Gitwar is an extremely useful place for the agriculturist household. It is commonly said in the villages that a *zamindar* can do without a *ghar* but he cannot do without a *gitwar*. These days even some of the Harijan households in the village have got some sort of *gitwars*. Actually, these are house plots allotted to them, which, for the time being, are being used by these households for tying cattle and for stacking fuel, etc. Sometimes, a *gitwar* can also be turned into a *ghar* or *baithak*. In that case, a *gitwar* is made in the *khet*, or the person has to obtain a new piece of land, either by purchasing, or in exchange for some other land, to shift his *gitwar* there. This happens during the course of the growth of the village *abadi*.

Plate 9.14: *Bajra* winnowing in a *gitwar* in the *tausih abadi*. Tractor in the background *Bails* busy thrashing in (two other) nearby *pairs*

In addition to being used by its owner, a *gitwar* is often used by others also. A *gitwar* near one's *ghar* / *gher*, although it may belong to some one else, is used by a person for thrashing operations. A *gitwar* is not used by those who are not on good terms with its owner household. Similarly, a household can also build a *kup* on a nearby *gitwar*, belonging to someone else. In some of the *gitwars* one finds *kups* belonging to three or four different households. A *gitwar* located far away from the *ghar* / *gher* of its owner household can be freely used by other households living near it. But as and when the owner household needs its *gitwar*, it can use it in any manner it likes. The ownership right of a household in its *gitwar* is absolute and remains fully intact even after its having been used by other people for long number of years.

Gitwars are located almost all around the periphery of the village *abadi*. Like the *ghars* and *baithaks*, the *gitwars* are also located in caste-wise sectors. The *gitwars* of a caste group are always found near the sector where its *ghars*/ *ghers* are located. Jats and Brahmans - the only land-owning castes in the village - have their respective *gitwars* at one place each while the so-called *gitwars* of some of the other caste groups have got mixed up (please see plate 9.15).

Plate 9.15: A village open showing the style and pace of life

9.13 KUP / BUNGA

After harvesting their wheat and gram crops, the farmers get a lot of straw, locally called *tura*, which forms a sizable part of the cattle-feed and is needed the year round. Therefore, it needs to be stored carefully. Every household stores some *tura* in its *ghar* or *gher* for immediate consumption. For long-term storage, big conical-shaped stacks of *tura* are made, covered on all sides with woven *tura*. These heaps are then tied with the *bajra ki puli* (bundles of *bajra*), or with *kapas ki lakri* (sticks, i.e., stems of cotton plants). Such a heap is called *kup* or *bunga*. In order to protect the *bungas* against cattle, thorny bushes are placed around them. Some exceptionally big-sized *bungas* are these days protected with barbed-wire fencing. Making a *kup* is a man's job and only a few men in each village possess this skill. Those not proficient in the art of *kup* making take the help of other skilled persons in the village.

When *tura* is required by the owner of the *kup*, a small opening at the ground level is made in the *kup* through which *tura* is taken out by women. A *kup* is also opened, or removed, when the *tura* is to be sold. Sometimes a *kup* may remain unopened for long periods of, say, three to five years.

Kups can be made in the *khets* as well as in the *gitwars*. One can make a *kup* even in someone else's *gitwar* located near one's own *ghar* or *gher*. Some of the *gitwars* have a number of *kups*. The size and number of *kups* in a *gitwar* brings prestige to the owner/s of these *kups* as well as the owner of the *gitwar* on which these have been made.

9.14 **BITORA**

The cow-dung cakes, locally called *gose*, (sometimes in the presence of outsiders, some of the villagers also use a sophisticated term, *uple*) are an important fuel for villagers. *Gose* have a place and importance of their own in the life of the villagers. By and large, the villagers do not purchase any fuel, at least not for their domestic consumption. They use whatever they get free, like, the stems of cotton plants, wood and trimmings of their own trees.

Gose are used in the kitchen and also for keeping the fire simmering continuously in the *baithak* and/or in the *pauli* of the *ghar*, and elsewhere for the *huka* (hubble-bubble). Women of every household collect *gobar* from the place where the cattle of the household are tied and carry it to their *gher* or *gitwar* where it is mixed with *tura* and patted into cakes which are spread on the ground or stuck against the walls for drying. The well-to-do households get this work done by their *churhi*. When the *gose* have dried, these are stacked in heaps which are then plastered on all sides with cow-dung. These heaps are called *bitoras*. *Bitoras* are of different forms (shapes); cubical, conical, pyramidical, etc. Making the *gose* and also the *bitoras* is a woman's job. To protect a *bitora* from rains, a straw cover, called *chhapri*, is made over it after the *Mawas* in the month of *Jaith* (May-June).

Only *gose* can provide the type of fire best suited to the life style of the inhabitants of Chhatera and surrounding villages. It keeps on simmering for long periods of time, without either flaring up or getting completely extinguished by itself. *Gose* fire is readily available round the clock and can be instantly used for the *huka*. It also quite suits the food habits and cooking methods of these villagers. Every household uses a number of earthen vessels which cannot stand very intense heat.

Moreover, for boiling milk, and for slow cooking of *sag*, *daliya* and many other similar dishes, relished and commonly consumed by these villagers, it is only the *gose* fire which is suitable. In addition, the cooking process goes on almost un-interrupted even in the absence of the housewife (from the *ghar*), at times for hours at a stretch, when she is away to the *kuwan* for fetching water, or to the *khets* to help her husband there, or doing other similar work. The housewife is neither worried that the fire may get extinguished leaving the food half-cooked (and thus spoiled), nor has she the least of apprehension of the fire becoming intense enough to burn the contents of the pot. So, with the *gose* fire, the housewife can rest assured about the 'pot luck'.

Bitoras are made in the *gitwars* or in the *khets*. Households having specious *ghers*, can make *bitoras* even in their *ghers*. Like *bungas*, *bitoras* can also sometimes be constructed in another person's *gitwar* near one's own *ghar* or *gher*. The observations of scholars in this respect, a century and a quarter ago, are fully valid to this day. "...Close round the skirts of the village are placed the enclosures for fodder and fuel (*gatware* and *bitore*); strongly fenced with thorns, resounding in the morning with the noise of the chopping of fodder, and at times full of women arranging the cakes of dried fuel, or preparing to carry them off in the baskets to houses..." (Purser and Fanshawe, 1880:6). When *gose* are required, a small opening at ground level is made in the *bitora* by the women of the household and *gose* are taken out by them for daily consumption and carried to their *ghar*, *gher*, or *baithak*, wherever required. A household which does not make any *bitora*, stores all its *gose* in its *ghar* or *gher*.

NOTES

1. Behind this *puja* is a common belief that *jal* and *ag* are the abodes of *dewtas*. Once, when a child was in her mother's womb, he said, 'O God, please take me out of this hell'. Feeling pity for the unborn child for the torture he was undergoing, the *jal dewta* (the Water God) stood surety for the child and the child was delivered. It is because of this reason that whenever a childbirth is about to take place, a *lota*, filled with water, is placed near the woman who is to deliver, and five weeks after the childbirth the *jalwa pujan* ceremony is performed as a mark of gratitude to the *jal dewta* for his having blessed the child to come out safely from his mother's womb and relieved of the agony.
2. With the coming into existence of the Statutory *Panchayats* as a result of the implementation of the three-tier system of *Panchayati Raj* in the country, in many villages, *Panchayat Ghars* have been constructed with a major financial

grant from the State Government. The uses and functions of these buildings are somewhat different from those of the traditional *chaupals*. Some of the villages now have both the facilities - a *chaupal* and a *Panchayat Ghar*.

TEN

ELEMENTS OF PATTERNS OF HABITATION AT THE MICRO-LEVEL

10.1 THE THREE MAIN PARTS OF A HOUSE

IN VILLAGE Chhatera, every built-up space is called *chhawa*. The term *makan* is not commonly used here. But whenever it is used, it is done so interchangably with the term *chhawa*.

The Chhaterans practise segregation among sexes in such an extreme form that they build separate structures to be used by men and women, called *baithak* and *ghar*, respectively. There is also a third structure where part of the everyday life of the villagers is lived. This is the cattle shed, locally called *gher*. Almost every *biswedar* (landholder) in the village has land for *ghar*, *baithak* and *gher*, separately, though not all of them have constructed all three structures.

The *baithak* and *gher* are generally located on the same plot. The well-to-do households have constructed separate portions to be used as *gher* and *baithak*, respectively, while those who cannot afford it (and such households constitute a vast majority of the total population) have both *ghar* and *baithak* together, so that the total space is used interchangably. Such a space is generally called *gher*. Only two households in Chhatera have their *ghar*, *gher* and *baithak* each located in a separate plot. These households have three independent structures each for the purpose of living. Fifteen households, seven Brahman and eight Jat, are such that each of them has its *ghar*, *gher* and *baithak* all located on one and the same plot. In the case of about an equal number of households, the *ghar* is on one plot and there are separate constructed portions on another plot to be used as *gher* and *baithak*, respectively. In this case the total structure is called *gher* or *baithak*, depending upon the fact that as to which part is more prominently and substantially built. If the structure has a very wide gate to allow a tractor, etc., inside, it is called *darwaja*, literally meaning gate (please see plate 10.1). Each of the remaining households has a *ghar* on one plot, and the *gher* and *baithak* are together on another plot and are used interchangably. The total structure in such a case is generally called *gher* (please refer to figure 10.1).

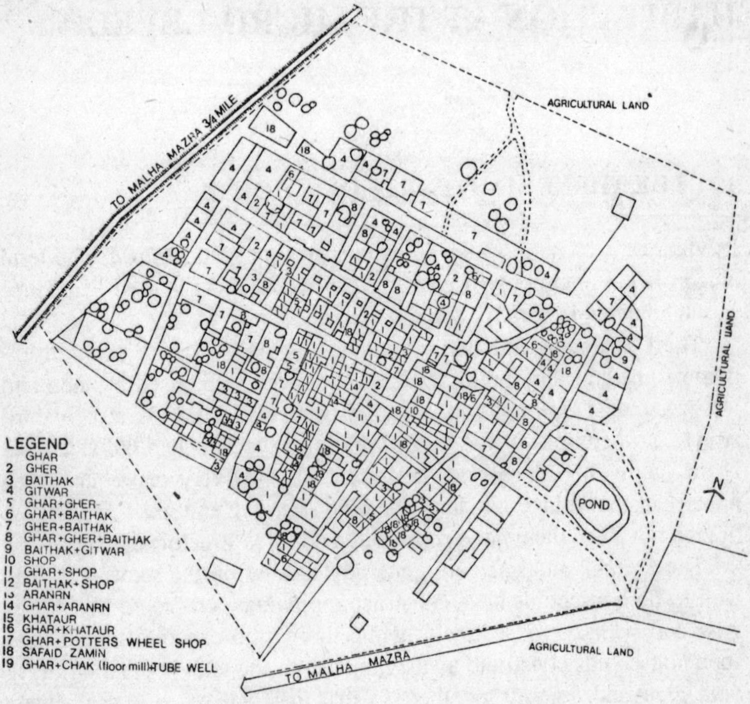

Figure 10.1: Plan of village *Abadi* showing use of structures at the residential level, *Chhatera*

10.1.1 *Ghar*

Regular activities in the ghar and the participants: The term *ghar* exclusively is used in a general sense to mean home or dwelling as against the *gal, chaupal*, etc. Cooking in every household is always done by the women and they always cook in the *ghar*. Normally, all meals are taken by all members of the household in the *ghar*. In fact, the grown up male members of the household go to their *ghar* mainly for taking meals. Other than that, they go to their *ghar* only when they have some specific work to do there. Even male guests of a household, who are lodged in its *baithak*, are taken for meals to its *ghar* by the male members of the household. Only when some people are working in the *khets*, their food is taken there by women or children of the household. Some of the elderly male members of every household, especially widowers, visit their *ghar* very rarely. Most of the time these elderly males remain in their *baithak* and their meals are taken to the *baithak* by the children or grown-up male members of the household. Milk and tea, when not served with meals, are served to the male guests at the *baithak* itself. Not even all the male members of a household itself always go to their *ghar* for taking milk and tea. One of them, generally a younger person, brings it from the *ghar* and serves it to those present in the *baithak*.

Plate 10.1: A recently constructed *gher* with a wide entrance. Tractor parked in the portico. A trolley and a thrasher can be seen in the *bagar* in the rear

During a marriage in a household, a *bhati* is installed in its *gher* and sweets are prepared there by the *halwai*. After the sweets have been prepared, these are carried by the male members of the household to the *ghar* and stored in one of the *aobras* there. If a household does not have a *gher*, the *bhati* is made in the *gher* of one of its relative or friends household located nearby. On the occasion of the *tewa* ceremony, in connection with the marriage of a boy (held generally in the *gal* in front of the *ghar* of the household), after the necessary ceremony is over, selected male guests are taken inside the *ghar* and fed there. In a girl's marriage, members of the *barat* as well as guests of the *banri's* household are served with meals in the *ghar* of the *banri*.

The *ghar* of every household is the place for the safe-keeping of its valuables and the storage of its goods and property. On every harvest, after the necessary disposal, i.e., after giving their stipulated share to the *kamins* working on *jajmani* system, and selling, if necessary, some portion of it, a major part of the remaining food grains and other agricultural produce are stored in the *ghar*. The clothes, beddings (except those needed in the *baithak* everyday), utensils and, in fact, every thing, which is not specifically needed in the *baithak*, is kept by every household in the *ghar*. Every household, particularly when it has shortage of accommodation in its *baithak* and/or *gher*, keeps some of its agricultural implements in its *ghar*.

During winter nights and rains, whenever there is shortage of space in the *gher*, some of the cattle, especially the milching ones, are kept in the *ghar*. During pregnancy, as well as illness, the cattle are preferably kept in the *ghar*, so that it can get the constant care from the women of the household. These are, generally, that cattle whose milk is consumed by the household itself. Cattle kept in the *ghar* get a special food and better care than those tied in the *gher*. Cattle in its lactation period are treated preferentially over that of its dry periods. During winter, or rains, if a household receives guests from outside the village who have brought cattle with them (which they often do) and accommodation in the *gher* of the host household is not adequate to accommodate all the cattle, i.e., his own and also of the guests, some of these cattle are tied in the *ghar*.

Ghar, often called by the Chhaterans as *rahayshi ghar* (residential house) or *raihne wala ghar* (the house for living), is the main residential place for every household. It is the nest where the entire family life is lived in and develops. All intimate activities are always performed by all members of every household in their *ghar*.

The chief occupants of a *ghar*, during the diurnal period, throughout the year, are the women and children of the household. Almost the entire daily life of the women of every household is lived in their *ghar*. Small children remain in the *ghar* most of the time everyday under the supervision of their mothers and other female members of the household. All the children of every household are always brought up in the *ghar*. Among the grown up males, the newly-weds visit their *ghar*, especially at night, more frequently than others. Particularly during winter some of these newly-weds spend almost the entire night in their *ghar* with their wives. Procreation always takes place in the *ghar*. Every woman must always deliver her each child in the *ghar*. If, under some special circumstances, a woman delivers a child in her parents' village, there also, she must do so in the *ghar*.

Whenever the *Banjaran*, the *Maniyar*, the *Punjabi*, the *sabji-wala* and similar other service caste people visit the village on business, they visit the *ghars* of their clients and transact the business there in the *pauli* or in the *gal* in front of the *barna* of the *ghar*. It is mainly on the occasion of a marriage in the family of his *jajman* that the *Nai* visits the latter's *ghar* to perform his functions (detailed at 4.2) there. Beggars invariably go to the *ghars* for begging because in a village people seldom dole out cash to the beggars. Beggars are given grains or cooked food which are kept in the *ghar*. Moreover, serving food in Chhatera is a woman's job.

All female relatives, friends, guests and visitors of a household, whenever they arrive, are received by the women of the household in their *ghar*. These female visitors are also always lodged and entertained in the *ghar*. Whenever a married woman visits her parents' place, called *mayka* (literally meaning mother's place), even when she is accompanied by her husband, she stays in the *ghar* of her parents while her husband is lodged in the *baithak* and visits the *ghar* only when invited and escorted to the *ghar*, generally, for meals. Whenever a man visits his married sister in her *sasural*, he is also basically lodged in their *baithak*. But the housewife's brother, called *sala*, is allowed to go to her *ghar* frequently and move about there freely. This special privilege enjoyed by the *sala* is not extended to any other male relative of the household.

The ritual centre for all the members of a household is their *ghar*. Worship by everyone, except when one is on a pilgrimage or in the temple, etc., is always performed in his *ghar*.

Whenever a new cattle is purchased by a household, it is decorated with *tums* (silver ornaments) and gay clothes and brought in the *gal* in front of the *barna* of the *ghar*. Women of the household, standing in the *pauli* of the *ghar* (across the *daher*) perform *arta* of this cattle. After its *arta*, if the cattle is to be kept in the *pauli* of the *ghar* it is brought inside, otherwise it is taken to the *gher*.

Occasional activities in the ghar: All the members of every household always perform all the important religious, social and life-cycle ceremonies in their *ghar*. On the second or third day after a childbirth, the new-born is given a bath by the *Bhangan* of the household in the *aobra* and women of the household sing songs outside it. This ceremony is called *nahan bar*, literally the 'day of bathing'. For the first ten days after a childbirth in a household, the *Bhangan* is allowed, rather she is taken, inside the *ghar*. After the tenth day, she is not allowed there and the normal restrictions, on her entry and movements in the *ghar*, become operative once again. On the sixth day, a function called *chhati* (literally meaning 'the sixth day') is celebrated in the *ghar*. It is believed that on this day the 'Goddess of Fortune', called *bemata*, visits the place where the childbirth has taken place and writes the fate of the child. The period of first six days after a childbirth is considered to be dangerous, both for the new-born and for the woman who has delivered. Particularly the sixth day is a very critical stage for them and members of the household keep a strict round-the clock vigil on both of them. Close relatives and friends of the family gather in its *ghar* on this occasion. Among the Brahmans, *lapsi* is fed to those assembled while among the Jats, *gungni* and *patashe* are distributed. The child is dressed in a new shirt and the child's mother distributes clothes among the girls of the household and those of the closely related ones. On this occasion, the *purohit* is given *sukha sidha* (dry rations). In the event of the birth of a male child, the *mishrayn* puts *thapas* on the walls of the *ghar* of the household and on the outer walls of the *ghars* of all the close agnatic relatives of the child in the village. On the tenth day after the birth of a male child, the entire *ghar* is cleaned and *lepai* is applied on its floors. On this day, all the cotton clothes of the household are washed, the utensils are cleaned and all the earthenwares are replaced by new ones. All the members of the household, as also some of their relatives and friends, gather on this occasion. *Hawan* is performed by the *purohit* of the household while the women keep on singing. The well-to-do, locally called *Bhagwan*, households feed the entire village on this occasion. On this day, *sutak nikal jata hai*, i.e., the polluting effect of the family disappears. It is only after this function that any outsider may accept any cooked food from any member of the household and from their close agnatic relatives. When the child is six months old, his/her hair are shaved. This ceremony, called *mundan*, more important in the case of a male child than female, is also performed in the *ghar*.

On the occasion of a marriage in a household, starting a few days before the actual day of marriage, every day the *Nai/Nainrn* of the household applies *batna* on the body of the *banra/banri* and after that gives a bath to him/her. This ritual is performed in the *ghar*. On these days, women of the household and some of their female relatives and friends sing songs in the *ghar* of the person getting married. The *mama* of the person getting married comes to his sister's village with presents of cash, clothes and ornaments, called *bhat*. The *bhati* (person who brings the *bhat*) comes to the *ghar* of the person getting married. He stands in the *gal* in front of the *barna* of the *ghar* and his sister, standing in the *pauli* (across the *daher*), performs his *arta*. After the *arta*, the *bhati* delivers the *bhat* he has brought in his sister's *ghar* and then goes to the *baithak*.

On the occasion of a childbirth and also marriage, a *pipli* [leaves of *pipal* tree (ficus religiosa; wisdom of the Buddha) tied like a garland string] is tied on the *sardar* of the *barna* of the *ghar*. During a boy's marriage, all ceremonies before the departure of the *barat* take place in the *ghar*. A decorated *ghori* is brought in the *gal* in front of the *barna* of the *ghar* of the *banra*. The *banra*, with his *mukat* on, is seated on the *ghori* here and his mother puts her *chuchi* in his mouth. The procession proceeds to the *gora*. After paying respects at the *Mata*, it goes to the *baithak* of the *banra*. This ceremony is called *ghor charhi*. After the *ghor charhi* ceremony, the *banra* is allowed to re-enter his *ghar* only when he returns with his *banri* after his marriage with her in her village. Women do not accompany the *barat* to the *banri's* village.

When the *barat* reaches the *banri*'s village, after reception at the *gora* and the *chaupal*, it is taken in a procession to the *ghar* of the *banri*. The *banra* stands in the *gal* outside the *barna* and the *banri*'s married elder sister, standing in the *pauli* (across the *daher*), performs his *arta*. After the *arta* ceremony, the *banra* goes back to the *chaupal* where the *barat* has been lodged. The *banra* and his father are not allowed to enter the *ghar* of the *banri* till it is about the time for the *phere* to start. *Phere* are always performed in the *ghar* of the *banri* in an 'open-to-the-sky' place. All the other intimate and sacred ceremonies connected with marriage are also performed in the *ghar*.

When the *barat* is about to leave the *banri*'s village, the *doli* is brought in the *gal* in front of the *barna* of *ghar* and the *banri* gets into it there. Elderly women of the *banri's* family put water on the wheels of the *doli*, an act considered to be a good omen and a well-wishing that the *banri* may reach her *sasural* safely and may get a warm welcome; and a pleasant atmosphere and treatment there. When the *doli*, with the *banri* in it, starts moving away, the *banri's* mother implants a *thapa* on the chest part of the the shirt of *banra's* father and his other relatives in that category, i.e., *banra's* father's brothers, etc., called *samdhis*. In case, however, the *doli* cannot come into the *gal* in front of the *banri's ghar*, it is parked at the *gora*. In that case, the ceremonies of putting water on the wheels of the *doli* and of implanting *thapas* are also performed at the *gora*. When the *barat* returns in the *banra's* village, all the members of the *barat* first go to the *ghar* of the *banra*. The *banri* is made to stand in the *gal* in front of the *barna* where women of the *banra's* family and their female relatives, standing in the *pauli* (across the *daher*), perform *arta* of the *banri*. After the *arta* ceremony, his own as well as cousin sisters of the *banra* block his entry into the *ghar* and demand presents of cash, clothes, ornaments, etc., from him. They allow the *banra* and his *banri* to enter the *ghar* only after they have received the presents. All ceremonies subsequent to the *arta* are performed inside the *ghar*.

Whenever any man falls seriously ill, he is brought to his *ghar* so that he may be looked after properly as some of the grown up family members are always there. Chhaterans always try that the death of every human being must take place in the *ghar*. This is so arranged, partly because death is a *samskar* (life-cycle ceremony) and all the life-cycle ceremonies and rituals, from one's birth to death, must take place in his *ghar*, and partly because of the reason that the dying person can have a nice time in the company of his/her children and other close relatives and can pirvately pass on to his sons, and to others he wishes to, all the secrets and information he wants to convey including those regarding his property. The dead body is given a bath and draped in new clothes by the members of the household, close relatives and friends. In case of the death of a woman, this work is done by the women folk. The dead body (wrapped in a coffin) is taken out of the *ghar* on the shoulders of the deceased's brothers, if it be a man, and on those of her husband's brothers if it be a woman, and taken (on its last journey) to the *chehanrin* for funeral. In many cases, immediately after the dead body has been taken out of the *ghar*, women of the household fix a nail in the *chaukhat* of the main *barna* of the *ghar*. This is done particularly in the event of the death of a young person, or a woman in her pregnancy, or at the time of delivery. Because, in such cases, it is locally believed, chances of the departed soul not getting salvation or re-incarnation, for quite some time, and consequently its keeping on haunting that *ghar* are very high. By fixing an iron nail in the *chaukhat* of the main *barna* of the *ghar*, the villagers believe, the entry of the departed soul (i.e., the soul of the deceased) to the *ghar* is barred. At least the soul would not come to that *ghar* and trouble its inmates. Women and children never go to the *chehanrin*.

After the funeral of the dead body at the *chehanrin*, men folk return to the *abadi* and assemble in the *gal* in front of the *ghar* of the deceased. One of the members of the household, almost invariably a woman, who has not accompanied the dead body to the *chehanrin*, stands in the *pauli* of the *ghar* and sprinkles water on them, after which the mourners disperse. Some of them move to the *baithak* of the deceased while others go to attend to their own work. At that time, women mourners assemble in the *ghar* of the deceased. All the death and post-death ceremonies of every member of every household are always performed in the *ghar*.

On every *sankrant*, all members of every household get up early in the morning. Women clean the *ghar*, everyone takes bath earlier than usual and they all pray in their *ghar*. Some special dishes, particularly sweet ones, are prepared on this occasion. On every *mawas*, women of the household clean the *ghar* and apply *lepai* on its floors. Members of every household get up early in the morning and take an early bath. On this day, many of them go to Delhi to have a dip in the holy river Jamuna. *Khir* (rice pudding in milk) is cooked in every household and at least one Brahman, preferably the *Purohit*, is fed by the women in the *chauka* of the *ghar*. If the *tham* in the *sal* is a wooden one, women of the household annoint it with mustard oil. If it be a stone *tham*, it is painted. *Banso-ke-phul* are spread in the *sal* of the *ghar*. On every *mawas*, bulls are given complete rest. They are not yoked in the *bail gadi*, or in the *hal*, or used for any other purpose, get special care and treatment on this day, *Khuraihra* is applied and oil massage is given to them. Some of the households even give a special food to their bulls on this day. On the occasion of *makar sankrant*, i.e., the first day of the month of *makar* (November-December) each year, every *bahu* of a household (particularly the newly-married) presents blankets to her *sas* and to other senior female relatives on her husband's side. The *sas* poses as if she has gone angry with the *bahu*. This ceremony is celebrated in the *ghar*.

According to the Bikrami calendar, every month consists of two *pakshas* (fortnights), the *paksha* with darker nights being known as *Krishna Paksha* and the one with brighter nights as *Shukul Paksha*. On the *puranmashi* (last day of the *Shukul Paksha* with the brightest night in the month) in the month of *Bhadon* (August-September) every year falls the festival of *salono*, popularly known as *raksha bandhan* in the urban areas of North India. On this day, women in every household write (in Devnagri script) *Ram, Ram, Ram...* (above the *chauntris* near the *barna*) on the outer wall of their *ghar*. When any male member of the family comes to the *ghar* for meals, his own and/or his father's sister ties *paunchi* (a piece of coloured thread) on his wrist. As a mark of reciprocity for her having tied *paunchi* on his wrist, the man gives her a present of cash, ornaments, cattle, etc. This ritual of tying a *paunchi* is a symbol of reminding her brother, by the sister, that in case of need he owes the duty to come to her rescue and protect her. Elderly Jat males generally do not go to their *ghar* even for taking meals. In that case, or if due to some other reason even a young man does not come to his *ghar* for meals, when his meals are taken to the *baithak/gher*, his sister / father's sister also goes there and ties the *paunchi* on his wrist.

Janam Ashtami (birth day of Lord Krishna) falls in the month of *Bhadon* (August-September). Men and women, particularly the latter, remain on fast the whole day. Women and girls, sing songs in their *ghar* during the day and at night wait at the *chhat* of their *ghar* for the moon to appear. When moon is visible, they offer *aragh* (offering water as a symbol of welcome to the new comer, a form of worship) to it. Those who have fasted can eat only after offering *aragh* to the moon. The villagers also make offerings to their *Purohit* and give something in charity to the beggars on this festival, which is always observed by every member of the household in his/her *ghar*.

Holi (the festival of colours) falls in the month of *Phalgun* (March-April) every year. Water colours are played in the *ghar* as well as in the *gal* in front of the *ghars*. Men and women celebrate *holi* together. One noteworthy point here is that, although the Chhaterans exercise a considerable degree of segregation on the basis of sex and also on the consideration of 'born-in' and 'married-in', on the occasion of *holi* it is the *bahus* who play with the male members while the *betis* only help the revellers by drawing water from the *kuwan*. *Betis* do not play *holi* with men, i.e., women do not play *holi* with the menfolk of their parents' village. Men throw coloured water on women while the latter beat up the former with *koras* (whips) and *dandas* (sticks). Previously, when the population of the village was small, members of all the 'touchable' castes used to play *holi* together while all the 'untouchables' of the village used to play *holi* separately in another group. But now, with the population of each of the castes in the village having grown considerably, this festival is celebrated on the level of individual caste groups, and, in fact, within each caste on the level of the *kunba*. At times, some persons belonging to a particular caste may also go to some other caste sector and play *holi* with some persons of that caste. But this inter-caste mixing for playing *holi* never takes place at the level of any caste group as such. Moreover, this mixing is restricted in the sense that membrs of a 'touchable' caste can go and play holi with the members of only some other 'touchable' caste. Inter-group mixing among the 'touchable' and 'untouchable' caste groups is not permitted even on the occasion of *holi*.

On the occasion of *holi*, special dishes are cooked in every household. A special significance of this festival is that from the day following *holi*, villagers start harvesting their rabi crop, just as in the Punjab, the festival of *baisakhi* is celebrated on the day preceding the day of the start of rabi harvesting there.

Hoi (the festival of children) is also celebrated by every household in its *ghar*. As *hoi* is celebrated for the welfare of children, households not having any children do not celebrate it. Women with small children fast on this day. Women clean the *chauka* of their *ghar* and apply *lepai* on its floor. Women paint *hoi* with *geru* on the wall near the *chulha*. *Chityan ki taswir kadhya karen geru te*, i.e., they make pictures of animals with *geru*. *Khir* and rice are cooked on this occasion. Though men-folk generally do not participate in this function, they are not forbidden from doing so.

On the *chauth* (fourth day) of the month of *Kartik* (November-December) every year, every married woman whose husband is alive celebrates a festival, called *karwa chauth*, for the welfare of her husband. Women take bath early in the morning and fast the whole day. At about 4 O'clock in the afternoon, each of these fasting women fills a *karwa* (small earthen pot) with water and perform *puja* after which they break their fast. This festival is also celebrated in the *ghar*. Traditionally, in Chhatera and surrounding villages, *karwa chauth* used to be celebrated by women of Baniya and Brahman castes only. This new adoption is primarily a cultural drift from some of the other sections of the Jats themselves, particularly from those living in distant villages across the river Jumuna, rather than an immitation of the women of other caste groups living in Chhatera and surrounding villages.

Food grains and other agricultural, products, like, chillies, are dried in the *ghar*, so that in case of rain, or other inclemencies of weather, the same can be quickly removed to some covered place by the women of the household. Charkha spinning and other similar activities, like, needle-work and quilt threading, are carried out by the women of every household in their *ghar*.

Activities that are never carried out in the ghar: Male strangers and those with a doubtful character are never allowed by the members of any household into their *ghar*. When such persons are lodged in the *baithak* of an household, even their meals are taken by the male members of the household to their *baithak* and served to these outsiders there.

The elderly male members of every household visit their wives in their *ghar* at night less frequently, and, whenever they go there, they do so in a kind of sneaky manner and spend very little time there, much less than the comparatively younger men. A visit by a very elderly male member, particularly if he be a widower, to his *ghar* at night is something completely out of question.

If any person, especially if it be a male, meets with an accidental death outside the village, particularly if the dead body has been subjected to a post-mortem examination, his dead body is preferably cremated outside the village itself. If at all the corpse is brought to Chhatera, it is straightaway taken to the *chehanrin*. In such a case, the corpse is not brought to the *abadi*, at least not to the *ghar*.

Activities that can be carried out in the ghar and also alternatively in other places: Although food is normally taken by every member of a household in his *ghar*, sometimes it is also taken at other places, like, (a) the *baithak*, if the man is elderly or there are some male guests whom the members of the household do not want to bring to their *ghar*, or when it is not one of the main meals, i.e., when they are taking tea, milk or some snacks, etc., and (b) the *khets*, when these people are working there and it is not convenient and advisable for them to come to their *ghar* for taking meals.

Households not having any separate *baithak*, sometimes use the *pauli* or *chaubare* of their *ghar* as their *baithak*. But the male members of a household not having a *baithak* generally themselves spend a considerable part of their spare time in the *baithaks* of their friends or relatives. Moreover, it is only the well-to-do households who can afford *chaukband ghars*, and the question of the non-existence of *baithaks* in such cases is generally a remote possibility.

After attaining the age of six-seven years, children of every household come to their *baithak* and / or *gher* during the day time to play. At night, they sometimes sleep there also at the *chhat* during summer, and in the *aobras* during winter. Sometimes, children also come there to study under the supervision of some educated male member of the household. This is so because literacy among men is much higher than among women and, most of the time, men remain in their *baithak* / *gher*. During a marriage in a household, if there is shortage of space in the *ghar*, the male guests are sometimes served their meals in the *baithak*. In case of an acute shortage of space, the space and the situation permitting, cattle can be tied in the *baithak*.

Although every household normally stores its grains and other agricultural products in the *ghar*, there is no restriction on storing the same in the *baithak* also. In fact, men always have an apprehension that if grains are stored in the *ghar*, a part of the same may be given by the women of the household (without the knowledge of the former) to the *Punjabi* and/or other vendors for purchasing clothes and other things for themselves and for the children. So, the wise men intentionally store some of their grains in the *baithak*. Although fuel is stored by every household in its *gher*, a part of it is always kept in the *ghar*, especially during the rainy season. In case of an acute shortage of space in its *gher*, a household can keep some of its milching cattle in the *ghar* also. Sometimes, even bullocks are tied in the *ghar*. In fact, the circumstances permitting, there is no restriction even on parking a *gadi* there, though it is not possible in a *chaukband ghar*.

On the festival of *salono*, a woman can tie a *paunchi* on the wrist of her brother/brother's son in the *ghar*, *gher* or *baithak*.

What happens at other places when some activity takes place in the ghar?: During a marriage in a household, *mithai* is prepared by the *halwai* in the *gher* of the household. But after it has been prepared, the *mithai* is carried, by the male members of the household, to the *ghar* and is stored in one of the *aobras* there. *Mithai* is ultimately served in the *ghar*.

On the occasion of *beah*, in connection with a boy's marriage, the *Purohit* from the *banri*'s side first comes to the *baithak* of the *banra*. From the *baithak*, the male members of the household take the *Purohit* to their *ghar* and feed him there. Food is served by the women of the household. On the occasion of *tewa*, the invited men gather in the *baithak* of the *banra* while women gather in his *ghar*. *Nai* of the *banri*'s side first comes to the *ghar* of the *banra*. After delivering the presents there, carrying the *tewa* in his pocket, he goes to the *banra's baithak*. On his arrival at the *baithak*, the men assembled there move towards the *ghar* of the *banra* and sit in the *gal* in front of the *barna* of the *ghar*. On this occasion, women remain singing in the *pauli* inside the *ghar*. The *ghor charhi* ceremony is performed in the *gal* in front of the *barna* of the *banra's ghar*. But after being taken to the *gora* in a procession, the *banra* comes to his *baithak* and remains there till the departure of the *barat* for the *banri's* village.

Every young married woman, on the occasion of the *makar sankrant* every year, particulrly on the first one after her marriage, presents blankets, etc. to her *sasur* and to other male relatives in that category. This ceremony is performed in the *baithak*, but a similar ceremony, wherein she makes presents to her *sas* and other female relatives, is performed in the *ghar*. As soon as a couple arrives in the wife's village, they part their ways on the periphery of the village. Husband goes to the *baithak* and wife to the *ghar*. Throughout the stay of the couple in that village, they stay at those two separate places.

All the death as well as post-death ceremonies of every member of every household are performed in the *ghar*. But during the mourning period, for the daily mourning sessions, women assemble in the *ghar* of the deceased while men assemble in his *baithak*.

10.1.2 *Baithak*

Regular activities in the baithak and the participants: Literally speaking, the term *baithak* means 'sitting place'. Although some persons have defined '*baithak* as the men's sitting place', in reality, it is practically the 'men's only' place. *Baithak* is the symbol of masculanity. If we observe any *baithak* over a period of 24 hours, during any part of the year, we will find that its chief occupants are men, i.e., grown up males. Throughout the year, a major part of a man's daily life is spent in the *baithak*.

A boy, from the age of 12 or 13, starts visiting the *baithak* (his as also of his relatives and friends nearby) during the day time more frequently and spends more time there. After attaining the age of 15 or 16, he becomes a regular member of the *baithak*. Unlike in the dormitories among the tribals, or similar institutions among some of the other communities elsewhere, there is no formal ceremony to mark the initiation of a person into the *baithak* fraternity. After entering a particular age-group, a boy simply starts spending more time in the *baithak* and taking more interest in its activities regularly, actively and unhesitatingly without any inhibition or shyness. Moreover, all the other members of the *baithak* fraternity start considering him to be a full-fledged member of their group.

Although there is no formal membership of any particular *baithak* or of any group of *baithaks*, every individual generally sits among a particular group of people and, therefore, in particular *baithaks*. The following observation of Mayer (1960:135) about sitting places in a village in Central India are quite appropriate in Chhatera's context also: "The sitting place is the spot where one thinks of looking for a particular person, and the membership, though loose, is predictable enough to predict this..."

Plate 10.2: Men making ropes on the terrace of a Jat *baithak*. Old man relaxing on *khat* with *huka* by his side

Except those activities that can be carried out only at other specific places, like, the major agricultural operations in the *khets*, marketing operations in the *bazar*, all the activities (daily as well as seasonal) of men take place in the *baithak*. Whenever they are free from the *khets* and other outdoor work, men everyday remain in the *baithak*. They smoke, gossip, play cards, make ropes and do all such other works in the *baithak* during day and also at night. During the slack agricultural seasons, the *baithaks* are humming with life (please see plates 10.2 and 10.3).

Plate 10.3: Group of Jats engrosseed in playing *tash* (cards) in the *baramda* of a Jat *baithak*

Females above the age of eight to 10 visit the *baithak* only for a work, like, fetching water from the hand-pump, washing clothes at the pump, cleaning and sweeping the floors of the *baithak* and applying *lepai* on the same and to fill water in the *paindhas* to be consumed by the men-folk. Women come to the *baithak* to do the above-said works because, according to the local customs, all such works are to be done by the women only. Even for doing these works, the women prefer, and try, that they should go to the *baithak* at such times when men are likely to be away from there, but if any male member is present in the *baithak* at that time, women pull down their *ghungat* (veil) to cover their faces, hurriedly finish their work there and leave the *baithak*. So long as women remain in the *baithak* doing these works, they move about there in a manner as if they have nothing to do with the life in the *baithak* and whatever goes on there.

Sometimes, when only family members and close male relatives are in the *baithak*, the *betis* of the family go there and talk to their father, brothers and other close relatives like *chachas* and *taus*. Otherwise they never participate in any of the activities going on in the *baithak*. In fact, many of the things which the *betis* want to discuss in confidence with their father, brothers and other close male relatives they do so in the *baithak* because of the presence of their *bhabis* and other such women relatives in the *ghar*.

All the male guests, relatives, friends and other visitors are always received by their male hosts at their *baithak* and are entertained and lodged there. Whenever a son-in-law of the family, called *damad*, visits his *sasural* (in-laws' place), he is also lodged in the *baithak*. A *damad* and his relatives, called *batyau*, are always highly respected. But whenever they are in his *sasural*, the *batyaus* are supposed to observe very strict discipline and code of conduct particularly their movements are very much restricted and they do not move about without being invited and escorted.[1] All the parental male relatives of the housewife, except her brother, whenever visting her *sasural*, are treated by her in-laws just as their other male guests. These relatives do not enjoy the same freedom in that village as that enjoyed by the *sala*.

Whenever the *Nai*, *rakhwalas* (keepers of wild cow herds) and other menials visit their *jajman*, on business or otherwise, unless they have some specific function to perform in the *ghar* of the *jajman*, they visit him in his *baithak*. All those visiting the village on business, like, for purchasing grains and cattle, always come to the *baithak* of the villagers concerned and transact the business there.

Every *baithak* always has at least one *huka* in it. The *chilam* (top earthen part of the *huka* in which fire is kept) has to be re-filled at intervals and the male members of every household, therefore, always keep *gosa* fire simmering in a *hara* in their *baithak*. All the *pacca baithaks*, and even some of the *katcha* ones, have built-in *haras*. Even a 'not-so-well-to-do' household always keeps in its *baithak* at least two or three *khats*, one or more *paindhas* containing drinking water and one or more tumblers and/or *lotas* with which men in the *baithak* drink water from the *paindhas*. Some of the *baithaks* have tables and chairs, some have crockery and radio sets also, while a few can boast of even electric fans. Every household generally keeps its English (Europen style) furniture (generally got in dowry), if any, in its *baithak*. This furniture is, of course, sometimes kept in the *chaubare* (rooms on the first floor) of the *ghar* also.

Occasional activities in the baithak: On the occasion of *sagai* (betrothel) in connection with a boy's marriage, close male relatives and male friends of the family are invited to the *baithak* of the *banra*. Women are not invited on this occasion. *Tilak* (red auspicious mark) is applied on the forehead of the *banra* by an elderly male member from the *banri*'s side. On the occasion of *beah* (a ceremony held one or two months before the actual day of marriage), *Purohit* of the *banri*'s side brings *tewa* (a paper containing certain information about the marriage date, etc.) to the *banra's* village. This ceremony is also held in the *baithak* of the *banra*. After the *ghor charhi* (riding the mare) ceremony, once the *banra* goes to his *baithak*, he remains there till the departure of the *barat* for the *banri*'s village. On the occasion of a marriage, all the male guests stay in the *baithak*. If the household does not have a *baithak* or if accommodation in the *baithak* of the household is not enough, these male guests are accommodated in the *baithaks* of the relatives or friends of the household.

On the occasion of *makar sankrant* every year, every young married woman, accompanied by other woman members of her husband's household, goes to the *baithak* and presents blankets to her father-in-law and to her husband's elder brothers.

Activities that are never carried out in the baithak: The chhaterans do not observe the same degree of restrictions in the matter of allowing the kind of people into their *baithak* as they do in the case of their *ghar*.

No valuables are ever kept in the *baithak*. No social, religious, or life-cycle ceremony, or ritual, is ever performed in the *baithak*. Food is never cooked in the *baithak*. In some solitary cases, one observes cooking being done in the *baithak*. This happens generally when the men are cooking meat, etc., which (the Jats and Brahmans of Chhatera being vegetarians) is not cooked in the *chauka* in the *ghar*. Moreover, because their women folk do not agree to cook non-vegetarian dishes. But the food cooked in a *baithak* is not taken into the *ghar*, nor is it eaten by the women. It is not a *shudh* (free from ritual pollution) food and cannot be used for any rituals, etc.

No woman ever participates in the activities that take place in the *baithak*. This rule is all the more strictly applicable in the case of *bahus* than in the case of *betis*. A *bahu* would never sit in a *baithak* or discuss anything with her husband or with any other grown up man there. Procreation never takes place in the *baithak*, at least a childbirth is never arranged there. All possible efforts are made by the members of every household to ensure that no member of the household, especially a young one, may die in the *baithak*.

Activities that can be carried out in the baithak and alternatively in other places: Food is usually taken by all members of every household in their *ghar*. At times, some elderly male members and strangers are served their food in the *baithak* also. Sometimes, people who are busy working in their *khets*, take their meals there itself. Food is always cooked by women of every household in the *ghar*. But if a household ever wants to cook a non-vegetarian dish, it is cooked in the *baithak* or *gher* by the men-folk.

Beggars generally visit the *ghars* for begging. But at times they visit the *baithaks* also.

Some of the households store a part of their agricultural produce in their *baithak*. This is done primarily as a measure of control over its spending in barter exchange by the women of the household. In case of shortage of space in the *gher* of household, some of its cattle are tied in *baithak* also. Sometimes men and catttle share the same space in the *baithak*.

What happens at other places when some activity takes place in the baithak?: All the death and also post-death ceremonies of every member of every household are always performed in the *ghar*. But when women gather in the *ghar* for mourning sessions every day, men gather in the *baithak*. Similarly, although every life-cycle ceremony as such is always performed in the *ghar*, all the male guests who come on the occasion from outside are lodged in the *baithak* and they come to the *ghar* only at the time of the specific ceremony or for meals.

Children of those households whose *ghers* are attached to their *baithaks*, especially if the *baithak / gher* has a spacious *bagar* (court), go and play there during the day and study under the supervision of male members. During summer nights, children sometimes sleep at the *chhat* of the *baithak*. Women generally do not go to the *baithak*, but sometimes, when only her father, brothers or other very close male relatives are in the *baithak*, a *beti*, irrespective of her age, can go there and discuss things with them. On the occasion of *salono* festival, if a man does not come to his *ghar*, his sister / father's sister goes to the *baithak* and ties the *paunchi* on his wrist there.

On the occasion of *beah* in connection with a boy's mariage, the *Purohit* from the *banri's* side first comes to the *baithak* of the *banra*. After the necessary ceremony at the *baithak*, the *Nai* is escorted by the male members of the family to the *ghar* and fed in the *sal* there. On the occasion of the *tewa* ceremony, the invited men gather in the *baithak* of the *banra* while women gather in his *ghar*. On the arrival of the *Nai* at the *baithak*, these men shift to the *gal* in front of the *barna* of the *banra's ghar*. At that time, women sit in the *pauli* (inside the *ghar*) and keep on singing there. All the male and female guests are fed inside the *ghar*.

The *ghor charhi* ceremony is performed in the *gal* in front of the *barna* of the *banra's ghar*. But after being taken to the *gora* in a procession, the *banra* comes to his *baithak* and remains there till the departure of the *barat* for the *banri's* village. As soon as a couple arrives in the wife's village, they part their ways at the periphery of the village itself. He goes to th *baithak*, and she to the *ghar*. Throughout the stay of the couple in that village, the husband and the wife, respectively, stay at those two separate places. On the occasion of the first *makar sankrant* after her marriage, every new *bahu* presents blankets, etc., to her *sasur* and other senior male relatives of her husband in the *baithak*. A similar presentation ceremony for her *sas*, and other senior female relatives, takes place in the *ghar*.

Till recently, no Harijan of Chhatera, or of any other village in the region, possessed any *baithak*. As all the Harijans are *gair-biswedaran*, they had no ownership rights in the land. Besides, the plots of land on which these people were allowed (by the *biswedaran* of the village) to build their *ghars* were very small, and the Harijans did not have the ownership rights even in respect of these plots. So, the question of the construction of a *baithak* by any Harijan simply could not arise. Since Independence in 1947, the situation in this respect has changed. At the time of the Consolidation of Holdings in the village in 1956, the Harijans were given bigger plots of land in the *tausih abadi*. Moreover, the ownership rights of these plots also now vest in the recipients. Many of the *Bhangis* of the village have taken up jobs in Delhi (some of them have even purchased *mohallas* there) and a few have got jobs in other urban centres as well as in the army. As a result of all this, the economic condition of the Harijans of the village has improved considerably and four of them have constructed sort of small *baithaks*.

10.1.3 *GHER*

Literally speaking, the term *'gher'* denotes an enclosed space or an enclosure. *Gher* is the place for cattle. The predominant use of this place is for tying cattle. Throughout the year, a major part of the life of the cattle of every household is lived in its *gher*. All the cows and bufalloes (barring those, who, being sick or expecting, have been kept in the *ghar*), except from morning to afternoon, when these are taken by the *pali* to the *laihnda* and then to the *charan* or *johar*, are always in the *gher* during the day as well as at nights. For the bullocks of every household, *gher* is the resting place. The bullocks are taken out of the *gher* only when needed in the *khets* or *gitwar* or to be yoked in the *gadi* (bullock-cart).

Every agriculturist household has to keep bullocks for drawing the plough and for other agricultural operations. In addition to that, it has to keep milching cattle also. Therefore, every agriculturist household needs a *gher*. Even those *biswedaran* (land-owners) who have not done any construction for the *gher*, have set apart *abadi* land for the purpose. A *gher*, as compared to a *gitwar* (which is also sometimes used for tying cattle during the day time), is comparatively a permanent place marked for cattle. A *gher* invariably has some covered space attached to it which is used by those who attend on the cattle, prepare fodder and also sleep there at night to guard the cattle.

Gher is used for keeping fuel and fodder also. *Bitoras* and *kups* are often made in the *ghers*. The *gandasa* (chaff-cutter) is generally installed by every household in the *gher*. Chaff-cutting can be done by men, by women and also by both of them jointly. Women of every household go to their *gher* in the afternoon and cut the fodder there. Space in the *gher* permitting, at times, some of the minor agricultural operations like thrashing of small amount of grain are also performed there.

Traditionally, the Jats have not been performing *Lakshmi Puja* (worship of the goddess of wealth). Their *Lakshmi* (wealth) being their cattle, they perform *Gordhan Puja*. As the legend goes, once upon a time *Gordhan* was the *pali* (cowherd). Every agriculturist household performs *Gordhan Puja* in its *gher*. On the day of *mawas* in the month of *Kartik* (October-November) every year, a *gordhan* of *gobar* is made in the open space on the floor of the *gher* (near the place where the cattle are tied) of every agriculturist household. *Gordhan* is made by the *Bhangan* of the household who cleans that place every day. A *khat* is placed on the *gordhan* and a *saur* (quilt) is spread on the *khat*. A *musal* (pounder) is placed near this *khat*. On that day, villagers bring *gandas* from their *khets* for the first time during the season. Each household brings five *gandas*, called *panchganda*. One of these five *gandas* is placed near the *gordhan*. On the evening of the *mawas* day, all members of every household perform *puja* near the *gordhan* in their *gher*. At the time of *puja*, members of the household place some cash (say rupees five to ten) near the *gordhan*. Afterwards, this money is removed and spent on purchasing some 'good' food for the cattle. On the following day, women of the household make *gose* of the *gordhan* and place the same for drying on the walls of the *gher*. Since these *gose* are considered to be very auspicious, when dried up, these are placed at the bottom of the *bitoras* and are not consumed immediately. In fact, these are the last ones to be consumed.

On the occasion of a marriage in a household, a *bhati* is made in its *gher* where the *halwai* prepares *mithai*. Some of the reasons for preparing the *mithai* only in the *gher* (in spite of the fact that, when prepared, it is stored in the *ghar* and consumed there) are : (a) generally, there is not much space in the *ghar* for making a *bhati* (big-sized hearth); (b) whatever space is there, it is full of women and children, women cooking food there; and (c) the *halwai* being a male, and that too an outsider, cannot be allowed inside the *ghar* for so many days.

No social, religious or life-cycle ceremony is ever performed in the *gher*, the only exception to this rule being the *Gordhan Puja* which is always performed in the *gher* because of its association with cattle.

Although basically the place for cattle is the *gher*, in case of shortage of space or when some cattle are ill, or pregnant, these can be kept in the *ghar* and / or *baithak*. During the day time, some of the households tie their cattle in the *gitwar* also.

After the children have somewhat grown up, they come to their *gher* during day for playing and also to study there. In the households having a *gher* attached to their *baithak* with a spacious *bagar*, particularly where the *baithak* / *gher* has a *parkala* (staircase) also, children play in the *bagar* or at the *chhat* during the day and often sleep at the *chhat* during summer nights.

On the occasion of a marriage, sweets are prepared in the *gher*. After these have been prepared, the sweets are carried to the *ghar*, stored there and are served there also.

10.2 THE BASIC UNIT OF HABITATION - GHAR

10.2.1 *The main spaces*

Pauli: The very first covered space on entering the *ghar* through its main *barna* from the *gal* is called *pauli*. The term is sometimes applied in the case of the first covered space (abutting the *gal*) in the *baithak* also. But our discussion here shall be confined to the *pauli* of the *ghar*.

The *pauli* is generally a big-sized *do-kariya* (two-bay deep) room with the *barna* to the *ghar* from the *gal* through it. A *pauli* has small windows (called *janglas*) placed high on the wall on both sides of the *barna*. The old *ghars* also have very small laddle-shaped openings placed high on the wall abutting the *gal*. A *pauli* has one or two *haras* (fire places) on the floor level on both sides of the *barna* where a *gosa* fire is always kept simmering for the *huka* - the life-blood of the *Haryanvis*. Every *pauli* has one or two *paindhis* for keeping *paindhas* (big earthen jars) for storing drinking water to be consumed by those in the *pauli*. Some of the *paulis* have *almaris* also. But due to security considerations these *almaris* are not made in the outer wall. Every *pauli* has one or more *khors* (cattle trough) also.

Actually, the term *pauli* is used for some place outside the *ghar* proper. When a villager sitting in the *pauli* needs something, he would often say *ghar se le aiye yeh chiz*, meaning thereby, please bring such and such thing from the *ghar*. This indicates that the *pauli* is sort of a semi-detachable part of the *ghar*, and that *ghar* proper, in fact, starts only after the *pauli*. Though occupying an important position in the *ghar* and serving a useful purpose there, the *pauli* is an element that can perhaps be removed from there. If a household, not having a *pauli* in its *ghar*, has a *baithak* nearby, many of the functions normally performed in the *pauli* can without much difficulty be shifted there. It would, however, be a misconception to think that the *pauli* is a superfluous part of the *ghar*. The *pauli* is like a transitional space between the inner part of the *ghar* (often referred to as *zanana*, meaning "for women"), on the one hand, and the *gal*, on the other. It is like a 'twilight zone', a buffer or a frontier between the sacred and profane. *Pauli* is the threshold of the *ghar* just as *daher* is the threshold of the *pauli*.

Pauli is primarily a men's place, especially for those households which do not have separate *baithaks*. It is because of this reason that the *paulis*, especially the *pacca* ones, have *haras* for keeping fire for the *huka* used (at least openly) by men only. A *pauli* can be used jointly by human beings as well as by cattle. There is no complete division into halves, sometimes (for example, during rains or if some outsiders have come and their bulls have also to be accommodated in the covered space) the entire space in a *baithak* is used by the cattle while on some other occasions, the cattle are removed elsewhere (outside the *ghar*) and the entire space in the *pauli* is used by human beings.

Whenever a Harijan visits the *ghar* of a twice-born, on business or otherwise, he is allowed up to the *pauli* only. When cattle are tied in the *pauli*, the *Bhangan* has to go there for removing *gobar* and cleaning the place. *Gobar* is removed from the *pauli* by the *Bhangan* of the household for making *gose* while the entire other refuse is taken away by her from the *pauli* and dumped into the *kurri* for making *khad*. Even when a Harijan is to be given food by a twice-born household, it is given in the *pauli*. On the occasion of a marriage, or any other similar function in a caste-Hindu household, Harijans are fed in the *pauli* of the *ghar* of the household. Even there, the Harijans have to remain near the main *barna*, i.e., in the portion of the *pauli* nearer to the *gal*. On the occasion of a childbirth in a household, the *Bhangan* and the *Chamaran* of the household are required to go beyond the *pauli* of the *ghar*. The *Bhangan* goes there for cleaning purposes while the *Chamaran* acts as a midwife. After these Harijan women have left, the *ghar* is cleaned and purified by the women of the household.

Beggars are allowed up to the *pauli* only. Shoes are also not allowed beyond that place. Brahmans generally remove their shoes in the part of the *pauli* nearer the *gal*. Transactions by the women of the household with persons like the *Maniyar*, the *Banjaran*, the *Punjabi* and other similar service caste people are often carried out in *pauli*. Due to these reasons a *pauli* is not considered to be a *shudh* (i.e., pure and free from ritual pollution) place. Chhaterans have the habit of eating while sitting on the floor. Because the *pauli* is not considred to be *shudh*, and there is lack of privacy in it, food is seldom served or eaten there. Because their *bahus* have to observe *pardah*, the eldrly male members in the Jat households generally do not go inside their *ghar*. Such elderly male members, even when they come to their *ghar*, remain in the *pauli* most of the time. Sometimes their food is also served in the *pauli*.

Practically no social, religious or life-cycle ceremony is ever performed in the *pauli*.

Whenever any male outsiders, guests (friends or others) are allowed into the *ghar*, they are entertained by its male members in the *pauli*. Only those male outsiders whom the members of the household consider to be very intimate are allowed beyond the *pauli*. A household, which does not have a separate *baithak*, uses the *pauli* of its *ghar* as its *baithak* also, though, in such a case, the male members of the household would, for most of the time, go and sit in the nearby *baithaks* of their close relatives and friends.

The *pauli* is not completely 'out of bounds' for the women of the household and for their female relatives and guests. In a household, having a separate *baithak*, when the male members are not in the *ghar*, the *pauli* is used by the women, first, because it is the most airy part of the *ghar*; secondly, being on the outer side of the *ghar* it provides a sort of a 'window' to the outside world; thirdly, villagers want to make intensive use of the available space. Sometimes, women of a household receive and entertain their female guests in the *pauli* of their *ghar*. Transactions by the women of the household with persons like the *Banjaran*, *Maniyar*, and the *Punjabi* are often carried out in the *pauli*.

Most of the households have now provided double doors in their *paulis*. In the *barnas* of the *pauli* opening into the *gal* and the *chauk*, respectively, besides wooden leaves, additional leaves with iron bars have also been fixed. When cross ventilation is required, women of the household spread *khats* in the *pauli* and lie down there. In winter, when sunshine comes into the *pauli* through the *jal* in the *chauk*, small children, after being given a bath, are put in the *pauli*. The main fuel used by the Chhaterans is *gose*. So, whenever they are igniting fire in the *ghar*, it creates a considerable amount of smoke in the *chauka* and *sal*. At that time, women in the *ghar* go to the *chhat* (terrace at the roof top) or move into the *gal*. But if there is a new *bahu* in the *ghar* (as she has to observe a more severe degree of *pardah* and is also given a preferential treatment) she is seated in the *pauli* and its doors are closed. Women sometimes spin *charkha* in the *pauli* (please see plate 10.4). When a *barat* comes back with the *banri* to the *ghar* of the *banra*, after the *arta* of the *banri* some of the 'not-so-intimate' ceremonies are performed in the *pauli*.

No member of any household ever keeps any of his valuables in the *pauli*.

Chauk: Every *chaukband ghar* has a central court called *chauk*. The third bay of the *ghar* consists of an open court, called the *chauk*, and two covered spaces called *delanis*. The width of the third bay (excluding a width equal to that of the *parkala* in the *pauli*) is divided into three parts. The two *dalanis*, each equal in width to one of these three parts, stand on left and right of the *chauk*, respectively. The third part in the centre is an uncovered (open to the sky) space.

As is well known, "The location of the courtyard is inseparable from the question of privacy and security..." (Mitra 1966:6). So, when a *ghar* is not of the *chaukband* type, efforts are made to keep the open space in the middle. If the open space in a *ghar* is not in its centre, it is called a *bagar*. A parallel example recorded by Grierson has been quoted by Mitra (1966:95) thus :

Plate 10.4: Old woman spinning *charkha* in the *pauli* of her *ghar*. Mark openings in the various bays and *thapas* and religious writings on the walls above the *chauntris* on both sides of the *barna*

In listing the parts of houses, Grierson in his "*Bihar Peasant Life*" gave the first place to the courtyard known generally as *Angan*. The term *Angan* is used for the open space provided inside the house between structures on two sides or on four sides. Often space is provided in the front or back of a house in which case it is known as *Aguar* or *Pichuar*. These being provided in addition to the *Angan*.

The *chauk* is covered with a *jal* (an angle iron frame with iron bars in it) at roof level and has openings on all the four sides with either *chaukhats* of wood or *maihrabs* in brick and stone masonry. Such a court is called *chauk*. The *jal* is fixed for allowing light and air inside the house without being a detriment to its security. It is known as *chauk-ka-jal* or *jal-gagan-wala*.

Sometimes, cooking may also be done in the *chauk*, in that case smoke easily goes out through the *jal* above. It is the corners of the *chauk* near the *sal*, and not the ones near the *pauli*, which may be used as *chauka*. The most preferred part of the *chauk* in this connection is its corner near the sal and the *chauka*. If cooking is done in the corner of the *chauk* near the *pauli*, then any body coming from outside may bring in his shoes and thereby pollute the place. *Hara* (removable hearth) for hot water is always kept in the *chauk* while the *hara* for boiling milk is invariably kept in the *chauka*. During extremely hot evenings, Jat households temporarily place the *hara* for milk also in the *chauk* so that it may not get spoiled. On such hot evenings, the Jats, at times, take their meals while sitting on *khats* (bedsteads) spread out in the *chauk*. During a marriage, at times, food for some of the male guests is served in the *chauk*. After churning milk, the *biloni* (earthen pot for churning) and the *rai* (churner) are placed in the *chauk* for drying. In the *chauk*, being an airy and sunny place, the odour of the *biloni* and the *rai* disappears easily. *Ukhal* (mortar for pounding grains, etc.) and *musal* [pounder for husking *bajra* (Indian corn, pearl millet)] are used in the *chauk*.

Utensils are cleaned by the women of the household in the corners of the *chauk* near the *pauli*. Chhaterans, in fact, do not mind cleaning their utensils in the *gal*. But because of the *pardah* system, whenever any elder male passes that way, the young woman cleaning the utensils has to pull down her *ghungat* (veil) with her dirty hands, and in the process she spoils her costly *aorhni* (the head gear). Women, especially of households not having any *chaubare* in their *ghar*, at times place a *khat* in a corner of the *chauk* and bathe under its cover. Women in every household often use *charkha* in the *chauk* of their *ghar*. During the mild seasons, i.e., when it is neither very hot nor very cold, women and children, and even their female guests, sleep in the *chauk*. The *chauk* also serves as a small playing ground for the children of the household. During rainy season, grains are spread in the *chauk* for drying during the day because if spread on the *chhat*, the grains may be spoiled by the pigeon, peacocks and similar other birds. Moreover, as soon as the showers come, women of the household can immediately remove the grains from the *chauk* and put the same under cover. Women often spin *chaybba* in the *chauk*.

Among the Jats, after a childbirth the *hawan* on the *chhati* is also at times performed in the *chauk*. In a girl's marriage, *phere* (circumambulations) are invariably performed in the *chauk* of the *banri's ghar*, because *chauk* is 'open-to-sky', this being one of the rigidly laid down conditions for any space to be used for the *phere* ceremony. When the *phere* are in progress, men sit in the *chauk* and women in the *sal*, while children and some young women go to the *chhat* of the *ghar* and observe the ceremonies through the *jal*.

Among the Baniyas, the central court of the *chaukband ghar* is called *saihan* - an Urdu word. During a marriage in a Baniya household, *bhati* for preparing *mithai*, etc., is also generally made in the *saihan* of the *ghar*.

Dalan / Chauk : Covered space on either side of the *chauk* is called *dalan* when big in size, and *dalani* when small. Strictly speaking, the *dalans* and *dalanis* exist in the *chaukband ghars* only. In some of the *ghars* of other types also people fix a *chaukhat* near the open space in the *ghar*, and the open space inside this *chaukhat* is labelled as *dalan* or *dalani*. But actually, the terms *dalan* and *dalani* are reserved for such spaces in the *chaukband ghars* only.

One of the *dalanis* is used as a cooking space and is called *chauka*. Milk is always kept in a *hara* in the *chauka*. *Paindhi* for keeping *paindhas* (earthen jars) containing drinking water, *tandi* for keeping clean *basan* (utensils) and the *garar* (grinding wheel) for grinding flour for human consumption are all in the *chauka*. Food is always cooked in the *chauka*. Sometimes, food is also eaten in the *chauka*. The *Purohit* is always served food in the *chauka*. *Thekas* (big jute bags used for storing grain) are often made in the other *dalani*. This *dalani* is also sometimes used for storing *chun* (wheat flour) and other stores related to the *chauka*.

When two adjacent *ghars* belong to two brothers, a door is often kept in the common wall between the *dalanis*. This opening enables the residents of the two *ghars*, especially their women folk, to conveniently have private conversation freely and privately

The most sacred part of a *ghar* is its *chauka*. Every household performs some of the ceremonies and festivals, especially those relating to women and children, in the *chauka* of its *ghar*. Every year, on the *gyaras* (eleventh day) of the month of *Kartik* (October-November), women make *har narayan ka thigna* near the *chulha* in the *chauka*. They also print foot impressions of the children near the *chulha*. *Hoi*, a festival of children and celebrated for their welfare, is also performed in the *chauka*. Women draw *hoi* with *geru* on the wall behind the *chulha*.

In no *ghar* are the dirty utensils ever cleaned in its *chauka*, *chilam* and shoes are never allowed there and nobody ever sleeps in the *chauka*. Till about a couple of decades ago, no Brahman household ever used to allow even its own children to enter the *chauka*. Some of the households have two *chaukas*. Whenever there is a pressure of work, due to the presence of a large number of guests in the household or any other reason, both the *chaukas* are used simultaneously. This second *chauka* is made either in the *chauk* or in the *sal*.

Sal : In a *chaukband ghar*, the covered space in front of the *aobras*, located in the rear part of the *ghar*, is called *sal*. It is a big family hall under the fourth and fifth bays. In a *ghar* which is not of the *chaukband* type, the location of the *sal*, depending upon the size and shape of the house plot, may be different than in a *chaukband ghar*. But in all cases the *sal* is located very close to the *chauka*, so much so that in some of the small-sized *ghars* a part of the *sal* itself is used as *chauka*. *Sal* which is sort of a verandah, is generally *do-kariya* (two-bay deep). The roof of the *sal* generally rests on a wooden *shaihtir*. In some of the recently constructed *ghars*, iron girder has replaced the *shaihtir*. The wooden *shaihtir* is supported by a vertically placed wooden log, while a steel girder is generally supported by a brick masonry column. In both the cases, the vertical element supporting the roof is called *tham*.

Sal is the living room wherein during all parts of the year, a major part of the life of women and children in every household is lived. *Sal* is also used as a dining space by all members of every household. Even the male guests of the household, who may be lodged in the *baithak*, are escorted to the *ghar* for meals and are fed in the *sal*. On the occasion of various functions in connection with a marriage ceremony, meals for the *barat* and for other quests are preferably served in the *sal*.

Some items of movable property of every household, like a *tijori* (iron-safe) for keeping valuables, a large steel trunk (made by the village *Lohar*) called *almari* for storing bedding and the ceremonial clothes for occasional wear of women, the big wooden box called *sanduk* for storing *logar* (home-spun cotton yarn) and *dolra* (the big jute cloth used for agricultural purposes) are all kept in the *sal*. *Charkhas* are kept, and often used by the women, in the *sal*. A major part of the utensils of the household are kept there. *Garars* for making flour, particularly those used for grinding the animal feed, are kept and used in the *sal*. Grains and other food stuffs, both, cooked as well as uncooked, are generally kept in the *sal*. Grains are stored in the *sal* in *thekas* (very big jute bags) and *kothis* (big containers of mud or brick). *Khats* are stacked in the *sal* and the cycle is placed there (please see plates 10.5 and 10.6).

Plate 10.5: Proud owner of the *ghar* sitting on a *khat* in the *sal*. See *shaihtir*, *karis*, *tham*, *almaris* and *alas* in the *sal* and also *barnas* and *roshan-dans* of the *aobras*

Plate 10.6: *Gur* bags hung from a hook in the ceiling of the *sal* - a measure of protection against rodents and dampness. *Thekas* containing wheat (with a *Swastik* mark) in a corner having two women with *ghungat* standing on the either side. Mark the small *roshandan* high up in the wall (on the right) for light and air for health of human beings as well as of the stored grains, etc.

Every household keeps all its valuable articles in the *aobras* of its *ghar*. The most valuable articles, like cash, ornaments and important documents, are always kept in the *tijori*. But a *tijori* is never kept in any *aobra*. It is always placed in the portion of the *sal* near the *chauka*. Being very heavy, a *tijori* cannot be easily removed by any outsider. Therefore, it can be safely kept in the *sal* where it remains under the constant vigil of the members of the household. Even when there is a single woman in the *chauka*, from there also she can keep an eye over the *tijori*. Being a status symbol, *tijori* has a prestige value. If a *tijori* is kept in one of the *aobras* of the *ghar* hardly anybody, other than the members of the household themselves, would know about its existence. But it has to be displayed since the presence of a *tijori* in a *ghar* indicates that the household is an 'Old Rich' one. Moreover, as every *tijori* contains *lachhmi* (wealth), it is an object of veneration and *puja* (worship) especially during the festival of *Diwali*. Since all *pujas* in every household are performed in the *sal*, if the *tijori* is kept at some other place it cannot be easily brought to the *sal* for *puja*. Therefore, a *tijori* is kept in the *sal* partly because the *sal* is a sacred place and partly because *sal* is the place where most of the *pujas* are performed by the household.

Sal is a private portion of the *ghar* mainly for women and children. Only close male relatives and very intimate male guests are taken by members of the household to the *sal*, that too generally only for meals. Female members of every household receive and entertain their female relatives and guests in their *sal*. During a major part of the year, women and children of every household sleep in the *sal*. Male strangers, outsiders, those coming to the village on business and people with doubtful character are never allowed into the *sal*. This restriction on the entry of outsiders to the *sal* is due to the dual consideration of privacy and security.[2]

All the life-cycle ceremonies, from birth to death (and even post-death) of every member, are performed in the *sal* of the *ghar*. *Raihnrn wale gharan mein, jahan chulha chauka howe, uske as pas jahan manrnsan ke raihne wala ghar howe*, meaning thereby, in the residential *ghar* where the hearth and kitchen are located, it is the *ghar* for human habitation. In terms of sacredness, *sal* is next to the *chauka*. Almost all important social and religious functions and ceremonies are performed in the *sal*.

Procreation takes place near the *sal*. From *homa* (on the *chhati*) after a childbirth to his death as well as the post-death ceremonies are all performed in the *sal*. *Chhati, homa, mundan*, tying of *mor* on the *banra's* forehead, as well as ceremonies performed on the arrival of the new *bahu* and *damad* are all performed in the *sal*.

On the sixth day after every childbirth in any household, the *Mishrayn* makes *setiya* with *gobar* on the *tham* in front of the portion of the *ghar* where the childbirth has taken place. As every childbirth almost invariably takes place in one of the *aobras* in the rear part of the *ghar*, so *setiya* is made in the *sal*.

On the occasion of a boy's marriage, when the *Nai* from the *banri*'s side comes to the *banra's ghar*, whatever presents he brings with the *tewa* are taken to the *sal*. On this occasion, women make *bel* with *geru* on both sides of the entrance to the *sal*. On the occasion of a girl's marriage, immediately after the *phere* ceremony the couple gets up and implants *thapas* on the rear wall of the *sal*. *Thapas* are implanted for the *barhautri*, i.e., increase in their progeny. After a marriage in the *banri*'s village when the *barat* arrives back in *banra's ghar*, after the necessary ceremonies like *arta* at the *barna* and *thapas* in the *pauli*, the *banri* is taken to the *sal* and seated there. All the intimate ceremonies on this occasion are performed in the *sal*. When a person is about to die, he is brought, by the members of his household, to the *sal*. The dead body is bathed in the *sal* and new clothes are put on it here before it is taken out for its last journey.

All important festivals are celebrated in the *sal*. On the occasion of *Diwali, homa* and *puja* are performed in the *sal*. On the occasion of *salono*, a sister ties *paunchi* on the wrist of her brother when he comes to the *sal* to take his meals there. On the *makar sankrant* every year, women in every household spread *banson-ke-phul* in the *sal*. Only those festivals that are connected with children and cattle, like *hoi* and *gordhan*, are celebrated at other fixed places connected with children and cattle, respectively. The *tham* in the *sal* is more important than all the other *thams* in the *ghar*. The status enjoyed by this *tham*, among other elements of the *ghar*, is like that of a *batyau* among the members of the host *kunba*.

Cattle, *huka, chilam* and shoes are not allowed into the *sal*. Some of the households, who have small non-*chaukband* type *ghars* and no other structure, have sometimes to accommodate some of their cattle in the *sal*. This they do very reluctantly and very unpleasantly. In such cases also, there is a mental demarcation of the portions used for *sal* and non-*sal* functions, respectively. This distinction is generally reflected in the different types of plastering treatment given to the two spaces by the women of the household.

In some of the *ghars* at times, one finds cooking being done in the *sal*. This happens only when a household gets a large number of guests and the *chulha* in the *chauka* cannot cope with the rush of work. In such situations, some women of the household start cooking in the *sal* while others continue cooking in the *chauka*.

Aobra / kothri / kotha : Aobras are generally the rear rooms in a *ghar*. The last bay in a *ghar* is turned into *aobras*, generally two in number. In some of the *ghars*, of course, *aobras* are also located on the sides of the *sal* or the *pauli*. In any case, an *aobra* is an end room in the *ghar*. When an *aobra* is located behind, or on one side of the *sal*, then entrance to it has to be through the *sal* alone. When an *aobra* is located on the side of the *pauli*, the entrance to it, depending upon the shape of the house plot and the layout of the *ghar*, may either be through one of the *dalanis*, or the *pauli*. Sometimes, a small room on the first floor of a *ghar*, when used mainly as a store, is also called *aobra*. But invariably every household tries its best to store all its goods on the ground floor of its *ghar*, and the terms *aobra*, *kotha* and *kothri* are almost exclusively used for such rooms on the ground floor of a *ghar*.

Aobras are closed dark rooms having dead walls all-around. The only opening in an *aobra* is the *barna* for entering it, and one or two very small-sized ventilation openings placed high in the wall in the inner part of the *ghar*. These small openings, generally located above the *barna*, are called *roshan dans* (ventilators). *Roshan dans* are provided for light and air to enter the *aobra* so that the grains (with a very high percentage of moisture content) stored in it may not get spoiled. The circulation of fresh air helps the grains to dry up quickly and properly. This closed character of the *aobras* is due to the fear of thefts, as these are the main store-rooms in a *ghar*, another reason for this being privacy.

Aobras are the main store-rooms in a *ghar*. They are used for storing foodgrains, *tura* (straw of wheat or barley), other dry fodder and other items of agricultural produce. After harvesting, grains are stored in the *aobras*. About 50 per cent of the *pacca ghars* in Chhatera have *pacca bukharis*, made mostly in the *aobras*, for storing grains. In those *ghars* which do not have *pacca bukharis*, women of the household make *katcha* ones themselves. *Saurs* (quilts) and clothes are kept in the *almaris* and/or *sanduks* kept in the *aobras*.

During severe winter nights, some of the women and children sleep in the *aobras* of their *ghar*, but, generally, the *aobras* are used only for sleeping by the newly-married couples. Every childbirth in a household is invariably arranged in one of the *aobras* of its *ghar*. But no *aobra* whose entry is through the *pauli* is ever used for this purpose, because *pauli* is primarily a man's place and is not such a private part of the *ghar*.

One of the *alas* (niche in the wall) in an *aobra* is generally used for worship by the women of the household. Some photos or idols of Gods are kept in this *ala*, and a *jot* (cotton-wick dipped in clarified butter) is lit every day. On the occasion of a marriage in a household, *mithai* prepared by the *halwai* in the *ghar* is brought by the male members of the household to the *ghar* and is stored in the *aobras*. On the occasion of *Diwali* every year, every household keeps a *diwa* burning the whole night in one of the *aobras* in the *ghar*.

Chhat: The unbuilt area on the first floor of a *ghar* is called *chhat*. *Chhat* is reached through the *parkala* (staircase) and, in turn, leads to the *chaubare* or *kamre*, if any.

During summer nights, women and children, or young couples, often sleep on the *chhat* of their *ghar*. In households not having separate *baithaks*, sometimes even the male members of the household and their male guests sleep on the *chhat* of their *ghar*. In that case, women do not sleep there. During day time in winter, especially after bathing and washing their hair, women and children sit in the sunshine on the *chhat*. Children play on the *chhat* most of the time. After washing the clothes, women spread them on the *chhat* for drying. Similarly, chillies and grains are also spread on the *chhat* for drying. At night, everyday, these are removed into the *chaubare*. Some fuel is also stored by every household on the *chhat* of its *ghar*.

During a marriage in a household, if there is shortage of space on the ground floor of the *ghar*, at times the male guests are served meals on the *chhat*. At night *kharar* (big-sized thick cloth woven from hand-spun cotton yarn) is spread on the *chhat* for women and children to sleep on. During certain festivals also the *chhat* is used by the members of the household. A case in instance is the sighting of moon on the *janam ashtami* festival.

Chaubare / Kamre : A *chaukband ghar* generally has a couple of rooms on its upper floor which are reached by the *parkala* (stair). Such a room is called *chaubara*, or *chaubare* (if plural). If there is also a *baramda* (verandah) in front of these first floor rooms, then these rooms are called *kamre*, or *kamra* (if single).

Chaubare are generally used by young couple in the household. The English (European) style furniture (generally received in dowry) is kept in the *chaubare*. Some of the households store some of their beddings, especially the *saurs*, and other 'not-so-often-needed' and 'not-so-costly' clothes in the *chaubare* of their *ghar*. During rainy and winter nights, at times, some of the women and children sleep in the *chaubare*. At times, women take bath in the *chaubare*. Grains being dried at the *chhat* during the day time are removed into the *chaubare* at night by the women and children of the household.

A household, not having a separate *baithak*, may sometimes use the *chaubare* of its *ghar* for accommodating its male guests. But the *chaukband ghar* being an expensive one, only the well-to-do households can afford it. So, it is very seldom that the owner of such a *ghar* may not own a *baithak*. No member of any household ever keeps any of his valuable or costly things in the *chaubare*.

Parkala : Every *pacca ghar* has a *parkala* (staircase) that connects the ground floor with the first floor. At the ground floor, the *parkala* is through the *pauli*, while on the first floor it opens into the *chhat*. On the first floor, there is a bigger landing which has a *barna* so that the *parkala* may be locked. Similarly, on the ground floor also, there is a *barna* through which one enters the *parkala* from the *pauli*.

Parkala is to be used for going up and down only. But due to shortage of space in the *ghar*, some of the households keep earthen jars (containing *bajra, jawar*, etc.) in the *parkala*. At times, some of the agricultural implements, like drills and ropes, are also kept in the *parkala*. In *ghars* where the space below the *parkala* has a *barna* in it, it is generally full of earthen jars (of various sizes and shapes) containing various grains, *ghee, sugar*, etc.

No function, ceremony or other similar activity is ever performed in the *parkala*.

Atari : The last landing of the *parkala* at the exposed *chhat* level is called *atari*. This is slightly larger in area than the average landing of the *parkala*. There is a *barna* in the *atari* so that the *parkala* can be locked. Actually, the *atari* is a landing place only, but, at times, some grains are also kept there during rains or at night.

Gal: The street, on both side of which the *ghars* stand, is called *gal*. Most of the *gals* in Chhatera, especially those in the sectors occupied by the *biswedaran*, are *pacca* (brick-paved) ones. In a way, the portion of the *gal* in front of a *ghar* is also a part of the the *ghar* because the entire life of the members of no household can be lived inside the *ghar* itself. Therefore, no description of the various spaces in a *ghar* can ever be complete without a mention of the *gal* in front of it, and of the various uses to which it is put.

Elderly women sometimes sit in the *gal* in front of their *ghar* and spin *charkha* there. The *Banjaran, Maniyar, sabji-wala* and a number of similar service caste people come and sit in the *gal*; women from the nearby *ghars* assemble and transact their business in the *gal*. (please see plate 10.7).

Plate 10.7: Afternoon activities in a *gal*. Young girls making *semi* and children playing around

A few days before the marriage of a boy, the *Nai* from the *banri*'s side brings *tewa* (paper containing the date of marriage and other similar information). The *Nai* first goes to the *baithak* of the *banra*, where male members of the family and male guests have already gathered. On the arrival of the *Nai* in the *baithak*, the men-folk, who have already gathered there and the *Nai* move towards the *ghar* of the *banra*. Men-folk sit in the *gal* in front of the *ghar* and the necessary ceremonies are performed there. The *ghor charhi* ceremony is performed in the *gal* in front of the *barna* of the *banra's ghar*. *Arta* of the *bhati* (maternal uncle of the person getting married), of the new *damad* (son-in-law) and of the new *bahu* (daughter-in-law) is performed while they stand in the *gal* in front of the *ghar*. On the death of a person, the portion of the *gal* in front of the *ghar* of the deceased is often used for the gathering of mourners, especially males.

During the *Holi* festival every year, men and women play colours mainly in the *gals*.

10.2.3 *Important elements in the ghar*

Barna : The main entrance to a *ghar*, i.e., the door through which one enters the *pauli* from the *gal* is called *barna*. On the top side of the *barna* there is a wooden plank (for decoration) called *sardar*. Although every door in a *ghar*, or for that matter in any structure, is called *barna*, whenever no specific mention is made, the term *barna* means the main door of a *ghar*[3] (please see plate 7.2).

Barna is the point where the first entry of every living being (human and animal alike) into the house and, through it, into the household is registered. On the occasion of the marriage of a girl, when the *barat* reaches the *banri*'s *ghar*, *arta* of the *banra* is performed at the *barna*. The *banra* and his father are not allowed to cross the *barna* of the *banri*'s *ghar* till it is actually the time for the *phere* ceremony. When a new *banri* arrives at her *banra*'s *ghar*, her *arta* is also performed at the *barna* of the *ghar*. On the occasion of a marriage when the *bhati* (the *mama* of the person getting married) comes with the *bhat* (presents), his sister performs his *arta* at the *barna* of her *ghar*. Whenever a new cattle is purchased by a household, it is decorated with *tums* (silver ornaments) and gay clothes and brought in the *gal* in front of the *barna* of the *ghar*. Women of the household standing in the *pauli* (across the *daher*) perform *arta* of this new cattle. After the *arta*, if the cattle is to be kept in the *ghar* then it is brought into the *ghar*. Otherwise it is taken to the *gher*. It is not essential to bring every newly-purchased cattle inside the *ghar* after its *arta*.

Whenever any household constructs a new structure (*ghar*, *gher* or *baithak*, especially a *ghar*) or puts up an extension to an existing one, the *betis* of the household hang a *tota* (parrot) made of green cloth and filled with rags, from the *sardar* of its *barna*. The *tota* is, of course, sometimes hung from the *shaihtir* also. This ceremony of hanging the *tota* on the *barna*, or on the *shaihtir*, is performed as a symbol of well wishing for the household owning the structure. The *betis*, who tie the *tota*, are given presents, generally in cash, by the elder male members of the household.

Whenever a household makes any alterations in its *ghar*, or whenever any *ghar* is partitioned, the main *barna* in it is never closed (i.e., filled-in). Rather, if need be, an additional *barna* is fixed. Although, due to certain folk beliefs, people in the village say that filling-in the *barna* means that the progeny of the household has stopped, actually closing the old *barna* would aesthetically look odd, technically it would be difficult to do so, especially at the level of technology available in the village, and economically it would be expensive.

On the occasion of a *chhati* after a childbirth, women sing songs sitting near the *barna*. On this occasion, *thapas* are also put on the outer wall of the *ghar* by the side of the *barna* as well as near the *barnas* of the *ghars* of the close agnatic relatives (of this household) in the village. In the month of *sawan* (July-August), women of every household write *Ram, Ram, Ram,*[4] ... (in Hindi) with *geru* on the wall on both sides of the *barna* of their *ghar*. On the occasion of *salono* every year, women of every household make salono, write *Ram, Ram, Ram* ... and put a piece of thread of the *paunchi* and a little cooked food on the *barna* of their *ghar*. On the *Diwali* festival every year, women in every household put *haldi* (turmeric) mixed with mustard oil on the *barna* of their *ghar*, and place a *ghee ka diya* (lamp burnt with clarified butter) on the *barna* of their *ghar*.

Daher : The threshold, i.e., the lower side of the horizontal member of the *chaukhat* of the *barna* is called *daher*. The main *barna* of a *ghar* is the dividing line between the *ghar* - the protected place - and the *gal* - the world unknown. The *daher* of the *ghar* symbolizes the transitional line. *Daher* is the point where all entries to the *ghar* are registered. So, *daher* enjoys a special position among the various elements in a *ghar*.

Daher is considered to be dangerous/sacred. To sit on the *daher* as such is not a taboo. But no function is to be performed by any person while sitting on the *daher*. Nobody eats any thing while sitting on the *daher*. Beacuse, to do so is taken to imply that this person has no place inside the *ghar* - an advance indication of the ensuing ruin and bankruptsy of that person. Behind this taboo is the history of the life and death of King Harnakashyapa. King Harnakashyapa was a very religious-minded and learned person. Pleased with his spiritual achievements and the severe penances undertaken by him, the Gods blessed him with a *vardan*[5] that he would neither die during the day nor at night, neither would he die inside the *ghar* nor outside it, he would neither be killed by a man nor by any animal and would neither die on the floor (i.e., on the ground) nor in the air or sky and would neither be killed with an *astra* nor a *shastra*.[6]

After obtaining this *vardan*, the mind of King Harnakashyapa changed, he became proud and started feeling himself to be the greatest of everything in this world. He declared himself to be the God and asked, rather forced, every one in his kingdom to worship him like a God. As a result of these misdeeds the Gods felt that somehow he must be finished. But the above-said *vardan* enjoyed by him was coming in the way of his removal from the world. So, to finish Hirnakashyapa, the Gods created a very peculiar creature. This creature was neither a complete human being nor completely an animal. The *rakshasa* (demon) placed the head of Harnakashyapa on the farmer's thigh and the rest of his body on the *daher* of the latter's place, and killed Harnakashyapa with his claws. This incident was enacted at a time when it was neither day or night, it was twilight period. This is the background of the particular type of feelings attached by the Chhaterans with the *daher*.

Tham : The pillars supporting a roof are called *thams* (single *tham*). A *tham* may be of stone or brick or even of wood. If the roof rests on *dats* then the *thams* are made of stone, or of brick, if the *chhat* is supported by a wooden *shaihtir*, or by a steel girder, then the supporting *tham* is generally of wood, although in some of the recently constructed structures brick masonry *thams* have been provided to support even a *shaihtir*.

Thams enjoy an important position in every *ghar*. This seems to be a legacy of the period when the level of technological development and, therefore, of the house design, used to be such that the entire load of the super-structure was borne by the pillars and everything was dependent upon the *tham*. The idea of the 'Central Post' which, in the Sanskrit literature, is known by various names, like, *griha-stambha* and *mul-stambah*, and the tree-shaped houses help in understanding this point very clearly. Even among the various *thams* in a *ghar*, the ones in the *sal* and, all the more so, the one in that part of the *sal*, which is nearest to the *chauka*, are the most cared for. The Chhaterans often say that the position enjoyed by this *tham* nearest to *chauka*, amongst the various parts of a *ghar*, is like that of a *batyau* among the members of the host household. If the main *tham* in a *ghar* is a wooden one, occasionally, and especially on festivals and social or religious ceremonies in the household, women of the household anoint it with *ghee* or with mustard oil. If it be a stone *tham*, it is painted on such occasions. Similar treatment is given to the *kauliya* / *satun* (i.e., the pilaster) also.

10.3 DOMAINS OF THE MAN AND THE WOMAN IN TERMS OF SPACE

The division of space into man's and woman's domains is only a relative, and not an obsolute, one. It is only a difference of degree in the man's and woman's presence, at the various places and spaces on different occasions to perform various functions. There is only one place in the village which is reserved exclusively for the use of only one sex and where the members of the other sex cannot go at all. This is the village *chaupal*. There is no parallel place, within or outside the *ghar*, which may be used exclusively by women, and which may be 'out of bounds' for the masculine sex.

Among the rest of the places, the two extremes are the *baithak* and the *chauka*, the former located away from the *ghar* or completely detached from it and the latter very much in the heart of the *ghar*. In the *chauka*, man goes only for his meals. In the *baithak* the woman comes only for a work. Here again, the emphasis is different at the various stages of the life-cycles of the males and the females. Besides the factors of age and sex, as stated earlier, the fact whether one is 'born in the family' or is 'married into the family' is an important consideration at both the places – *ghar* as well as *baithak*.

A boy below the age of 12 or 13 does not visit the *baithak* so frequently, Most of his time is spent in the *ghar*. Between the age of 12 and 16, he visits the *baithak* more frequently and spends more time there.

This indicates that man keeps on moving from *ghar* to *baithak* and from *baithak* back to *ghar*. In other words, the proportion of time that he spends in the *ghar* and the *baithak*, respectively, goes on changing along with changes in the stages of his cycle.

From the age of 15-16 he becomes a regular member of the *baithak* and spends very little time in the *ghar*.

Whenever man needs to be closer to the woman (mother, wife, etc.), he spends more time in the *ghar*, otherwise he is in the *baithak*.

After his marriage, again, the young man starts spending more time in the *ghar*, especially during the night, although he does not sever his relationship with the *baithak*.

In his childhood he needs to be looked after by his mother, needs her close and constant attention. As he grows along he starts drifting away from the *ghar* towards the *baithak*. till a stage comes when he drifts very much away from the *ghar* After his marriage this emphasis shifts back towards the *ghar*.

As his married life reaches an advanced stage, especially after his younger brothers have got married and the *bahus* have to observe *pardah* from him, this person starts spending less time in the *ghar*, and more and more time in the *baithak*.

As he gets elderly, particularly if he becomes a widower, he starts spending all the more of his time in the *baithak*. Among the Jats even a stage comes when the fellow practically stops visiting the *ghar*. Even his food is brought to the *baithak*.

As he starts loosing interest in the woman, he again starts drifting away from the *ghar* towards the *baithak*.

For his death, of course, he is brought to the *ghar*.

It is his fast approach in or imminent death, clearly visible in the immediate horizons, which brings him back to the *ghar* thus bringing to an end the drama of his life at the very stage where it began.

NOTES

1. One of the important winter agricultural produce in Chhatera is red chillies, locally called *marcha*. During the author's stay in the village, he observed that during the day time *marcha* are spread in the sunshine on the *chhat* or in the *bagar* of the *baithak/gher*, and removed into some covered space at night. Exactly the same treatment was meted out by the Chhaterans to their *damad/jamai* and his relatives (all called *batyau*) also. During day time, *khats* are spread on the *chhat* of the *ghar* or in the *bagar* of the *baithak/gher*, 'good' (preferably new) beddings are spread on these *khats* and the *batyaus* are seated on these. The *batyaus* can sit, gossip, play cards, lie down, smoke, relax or even sleep there. Tea and milk, etc., are served to them there itself. One or more *hukas* are always kept ready there for the *batyaus*.

   Moreover, just like *marcha*, the *batyaus* also do not move from their place by themselves. They move about only when requested to and escroted by their hosts. The new *batyaus* do not even go to the *khets* to ease themselves unless requested and escorted. At night, just like *marcha*, these *batyaus* are also placed (i.e., lodged) in some covered space. The *batyaus* have to observe a very strict code of conduct, so much so that the author sometimes joked with the Chhaterans: *Chawdhrisaheb ap log to batyauon ko marcha ki tarah sukhne dal dete ho*, meaning thereby that you people (the Jats) place your *batyaus* for drying up exactly the same way as you spread your chillies.
2. Once, the *Purohit* of the Jats of Chhatera took a stranger to the *sal* of his *ghar* and served food to him there. While taking food in the *sal*, this stranger visually surveyed the place and, a couple of days later, a burglary took place in the *ghar* of the *Purohit*. In the course of investigations it was discovered that the same stranger who had been fed in the *sal* of the *ghar*, had committed the burglary.
3. According to the masons in this region, the main barna in a *ghar* is also called *dar*. But the villagers here seldom use this term.
4. Ram is the name of an important Hindu God who was the main hero of the epic Ramayan.
5. Blessing in the shape of a word of honour.
6. *Astras* are those arms which the user keeps on holding while hitting the enemy, whereas a *shastra* has to be thrown at the enemy, manually or mechanically.

ELEVEN

SETS AND PATTERNS

11.1 THE STRUCUTRE OF CLASSIFICATION

AS STATED earlier, there are three different levels of residential living in the village, viz., (a) *ghar* and *baithak*, (b) *abadi* or the area within the *lal dora* and, (c) *sim* or boundary of the village estate. This distinction at the macro-level is a Centre *versus* Periphery one, i.e., the more we move towards the central areas, the more important, intimate and 'good sacred' the areas become. And the more we move towards the peripheral areas, the less significant, less intimate and more secular, or profane, these tend to be. When we take the two main divisions at the first level, viz., the *ghar* and the *baithak*, it is found that the *baithak* is considered to be an outer part as it is outside the *ghar*. *Ghar* is considered to be the central and most important place in the home and all other places are viewed in relation to it.

11.2 THE RELATIONS

In fact, this centre *versus* periphery relation should not be treated as an isolated dimension which may be properly understood all by itself. This relation is a part of the bigger system consisting, besides the above, also of certain other relations or sub-systems of classification. The most important relations can be listed as follows:

1. Centre *vs* Periphery
2. Inner *vs* Outer
3. Front *vs* Rear
4. The Cardinal Points N = S == E = W
5. Coverd Space *vs* Open to Sky

6. Clear *vs* Transitional or Marginal
7. Human *vs* Animal
8. Male *vs* Female
9. Ourselves *vs* Strangers
10. Natal *vs* Conjugal or In-married
11. Living *vs* Dead
12. Upper *vs* Lower
13. On the Earth *vs* Off the Earth
14. Right *vs* Left
15. Closed or Enclosed *vs* Open
16. Katcha *vs* Pacca
17. Head *vs* Foot
18. Entrance *vs* Exit

For a realistic understanding of the bigger system, it is indispensable to clearly explain each of these sub-systems and relate them to each other.

11.2.1 *Centre vs Periphery*

The most important and one of the major relations, or sub-systems of classification, in the life of the Chhaterans is the Centre *versus* Periphery one. As discussed earlier, the distinction between the three levels of residential living in the village is a Centre *versus* Periphery one. The *abadi* is the centre with *khets* and all other spaces located around it. The *abadi* is also more sacred than other places. Within the *abadi*, the *ghar* is at the centre while other spaces, like, the *gher*, *baithak* and *chupal*, are on the periphery. At the same time, *ghar* is more sacred than all these other places. Within the *ghar* itself, the *chauka* is at the centre and it is also the most sacred part of the *ghar*. The *abadi* is also safer than the places outside it. Similarly, *ghar* is safer and more secured than other places within the *abadi*, and so on.

Women almost always remain at the centre while men remain at the periphery. It is the men who cross the *sim* much more frequently, while women remain within the village estate. Within the *sim*, again, women mostly remain inside the *abadi*. Although they do go out of the *abadi* to help their husbands in the fields, etc., they go out much less frequently than their men-folk. Women do not cross the *gora* so often. Within the *abadi* also, women are mostly confined to the *ghar* and move out much less than men, whereas men remain more in the *baithak, gher* or *chaupal*. At the time of the marriage of a boy, the *banra* becomes the centre and women are on the periphery. It is on occasions like the birth of a male child, sickness and death, that a man comes to the centre and women shift to the periphery. When a man is ill or about to die, he is kept in the *sal* of his *ghar*. Similarly, a sick or expecting cattle is kept in the *ghar* and becomes the centre of attention. This shows that the point of attraction is always at the centre. A thing which is vulnerable is at the centre while others are at the periphery.

Members of the proprietary body of a village live in the core of its *abadi* while others generally reside at the periphery. This distinction is all the more sharp in the case of 'untouchables', i.e., the contrast between 'touchables' and 'untouchables' is very conspicuous at the level of the total *abadi*. The 'untouchables' are the 'fringe' people, or the people at the periphery, not only in the physical sense of the term but also in the social, cultural and economic matrix of the village life. At the level of the total *abadi*, the quarters of 'untouchable' castes are located at the periphery or the outskirts. Before the demolition of the *kot* in Chhatera, when the main village was inside the wall, the sectors inhabited by 'untouchables' were outside it. Within the *abadi*, in the area inhabited by 'touchable' castes, the Harijans are allowed to move about more freely in the *ghers* and *baithaks* than in the *ghars* proper. Within the *ghar* of a 'touchable', again, Harijans are allowed only up to the *pauli* and not in the portion beyond. Again, within the *pauli* itself, Harijans, preferably, remain in the outer part of it nearer the *gal*, i.e., in the portion used by the cattle. The place for community life of cattle is the *gora*. When cattle come to the *ghar* they are allowed up to the *pauli* only, i.e., the periphery of the *ghar*. *Garar* for making animal feed is kept in the *sal* while the one for grinding floor for human consumption is always kept in the *chauka*.

Biswedaran : Be-biswedaran : : Centre : Periphery : Intimate life is lived in the central part of the habitation while ceremonial aspects are on the *sim*, or the periphery. All production takes place at the periphery while storage and consumption are at the centre. The distinction between the intimately known persons and others is exercised at various levels in the village. Those who are complete strangers to the village are lodged in the *chaupal*, which, as a rule, is located outside the *abadi*. It is a public area. In Chhatera also, when the *kot* existed, the *chaupal* was outside the *kot*. To those staying at the *chaupal*, food has always to be supplied by the village community. There is a mention of the detailed arrangement for it in the *Shart Wajib-ul-arz* and the

Misal-e-hakiyat in the "Settlement Report of the Village" (1880). Those who are somewhat related - biologically, sociologically or in terms of business dealings - are brought to the semi-public, semi-private residential area (the *baithak*). Those who are friendly, familiar and intimate are taken to the *ghar* (a private area). Within the *ghar* again, only those who are really close and intimate are taken into the *sal*; others remain in the *pauli*.

11.2.2 *Inner vs Outer*

The Inner *vs* Outer relation is visible in various parts of the ghar. For example, the *pauli*, which is the outer part of the *ghar*, is profane. *Pauli* is non-sacred or less sacred than the *chauk*. Even within the *pauli*, the portion nearer to the *gal* is less sacred than that nearer to *chauk*. Further, the *sal* is more sacred than the *chauk*. All important religious functions and life-cycle ceremonies are performed in the *sal*. Food is also eaten here. *Aobras* are the farthest from the *barna* or the *gal* part of a *ghar*. But *aobras* are not considered to be so sacred although these cannot be said to be non-sacred because, during marriages, sweets made in the *gher* are stored here. *Ala* for keeping *jot* is also in the *aobra*, and sometimes photos and/or idols of some of the gods are also kept here. Thus, it would not be realistic to make a very general statement that, the inner a part of the *ghar*, the more sacred it is, and vice versa. This supports the view that no single relation can alone explain all the variations in a situation. One has to take into account the entire network of relations in order to fully understand the total structure of classification of any community.

Inner vs Outer: The two dimensions: The *dalanis* are considered to be more sacred than the *chauk*. This is so inspite of the fact that the direct distance between the *dalani* and the *gal* is the same as the distance between the *chauk* and the *gal*. But direct distance is not the only consideration, it has to be qualified by approachability and the circulation pattern in the *ghar*. The approach distance from the *barna*, or the *gal*, to the *chauk* is less than that to the *dalani*. So these are two different dimensions of the same aspect.

Clean utensils in a *ghar* are kept 'inside' in relation to the place where cooking is done. It may be 'inside' in terms of the distance from the *barna*. If cooking is done in the *chauk*, clean utensils may be kept in the *dalani* although the direct distance between the *tandi* and the *gal* may be less than the direct distance between the *chauka* and the *gal*.

Cleaning of utensils is, on the contrary, done on the 'outer' side. Clean utensils are brought from the *tandi* 'inside' and used for meals. After meals, utensils are cleaned (with *rakh* taken from the *hara*) in an 'outer' corner of the *chauk*. After having been cleaned, the utensils are again placed on the *tandi* 'inside' while the used *rakh* is put on a place still more 'outside'. Here again, the position and the concepts of 'inside' and 'outside' are to be understood in the light of the above-mentioned two dimensions of physical distance and approachability.

The *gal* is seldom used by women in any other way than as an artery of communication, except on occasional transaction with the hawker or spinning of *charkha*, that too only by elderly women. The *gal* is invariably used by men for sitting out, especially on ceremonial occasions, and for parking their *gadi*, etc. When men-folk are in the *pauli*, women remain inside the *ghar*. When men are away, women (whenever they need) come out into the *pauli*, sit, spin, transact business and even entertain their guests there. Women also look after the cattle (if any) kept in the pauli. So, this equation of *Man : Woman* and *Outside : Inside* is reduced to, 'presence of males *versus* their absence'. Thus, it is the presence of man that pushes the women 'inside'. Moreover, on certain ceremonial occasions, when women need to come to the *pauli*, men-folk move out of the *ghar* into the *gal*. Women even sing and perform other ceremonies in the *pauli*. Similarly, when women need to come into the *gal*, men-folk move a little away from there, i.e., they move into the outer portion of the *gal*. Therefore, though men and women live in 'outer' and 'inner' compartments, respectively, this moving inside by the latter is not always a one-sided affair; it is a two-way process; but the positions are never reversed.

The use of *aobras* also changes with change in their location. When an *aorba* is behind, or on the side of the *sal*, it is used for storing; (a) grain, *tura, bukharis* and other similar items and agricultural implements, etc., and (b) *saurs*, clothes, etc., *almaris* and/or *sanduks*, sweets (during marriages) and such other things. But if an *aobra* is located on a side of the *pauli*. the articles mentioned in the first category are stored there but not those mentioned in the second. The *saurs* to be used in the *pauli* are, of course, kept in such an *aobra*.

The location of *aobra*, whether near the *sal* or the *pauli*, has three implications: (a) the one near the *pauli* is not so safe, (b) women cannot freely go to such an *aobra* because entrance to it is through the *pauli* and (c) because all sorts of people come to the *pauli*, therefore, this space is neither safe nor sacred.

Every childbirth in every household is arranged in one of the *aobras* of its *ghar*. As the services of a *Chamaran* and a *Bhangan* are required at the time of childbirth, the more convenient place for a childbirth would be an *aobra* situated by the side of *pauli*. Even otherwise, the *Chamaran* and the *Bhangan* are freely allowed up to this place. So, they can very easily go to *aobra* attached to the *pauli* without causing any disturbance to other parts of the *ghar*. But this is never done, i.e., a childbirth is never arranged in such an *aobra* partly because of the presence of men-folk in the *pauli* and partly because being easily accessible from the *gal* it is an unsafe place. When *aobras* in a *ghar* are by the side of the *pauli*, even cattle are sometimes kept there. But when these are near the *sal*, cattle are practically never kept there except by those few who do not have any separate *gher* or *baithak*. This is so because, while going to an *aobra* near the *sal* cattle have to pass through the entire *ghar* thereby reducing its sacredness. The use and status of a space is not automatically determined by the name it bears, but it changes with any change in its location. It can be thus stated:

Inside : Outside :: Private : Public
Inside : Outside :: Women's Place : Men's Place
Inside : Outside :: Intimate : Not Intimate
Inside : Outside :: Sacred : Profane

Grown-up males remain mostly in the *baithak*. Even when they come to the *ghar*, they generally remain in the *pauli*. But a newly-married man spends a lot of time in his *ghar*, especially so at night. While in his *ghar*, he remains with his wife in the *aobra*. So, it can be concluded:

Inner : Outer :: Special Functions : General Functions
Inner : Outer :: Intimate : Not so intimate

In a marriage, after the *phere*, the new couple implants *thapas* in the *sal* of the *banri*'s *ghar*. When the *barat* returns back to the *banra*'s *ghar*, the new couple puts *thapas* in the *pauli*. Thereafter, all the public functions are over and they put *thapas* in the *sal* also. When two adjacent *ghars* belong to two brothers, generally an opening is kept in the common wall through which the residents can visit each other's *ghar*, or, at least, can talk to each other easily and in privacy. This opening is invariably kept in one of the *dalanis* and never in the *pauli*, since, being in the inner part of the *ghar*, a *dalani* is an intimate place and the opening is used mostly by women.

11.2.3 *Front vs Rear*

Another relation, of course, every close to that of Inner *versus* Outer, is the Front *versus* Rear one. The real meaning of the two terms, 'front' and 'rear', depends on as to how *ghar* is viewed. These terms have been used here as seen by a person standing against the rear wall of the *ghar* (i.e., against the rear wall of its *aobra* behind the *sal*) and looking towards the *gal*. In other words, the person should be having his back towards the rear wall of the *ghar* and his face towards the *gal*. When the terms 'front' and 'rear' are defined in this sense, it would be observed that:

Front : Rear :: Man : Woman
Front : Rear :: Untouchables : Touchables
Front : Rear :: Cattle : Human
Front : Rear :: Outsiders : Ourselves
Front : Rear :: Public : Private
Front : Rear :: Ceremonial : Intimate
Front : Rear :: Profane : Sacred

The discussion on the Inner *versus* Outer relation is, by and large, applicable in the case of Rear *versus* Front one also.

11.2.4 *Cardinal Points*

Cosmology has always played a very important role in the life of every community. Whatever the cosmology of a community, it is the cardinal points which are the immediate indicators of the orientation of physical spaces. The Chhaterans consider east to be a very auspicious direction; the direction preferred next to it is west, and then comes north. South, of course, is the most avoided direction. For a *ghar*, *baithak*, as well as *gher*, east is the most preferred orientation.

Orientation is important not only in the case of a structure but also of a *chulha*, *khor*, the wall on which *thapas* are put, the *ala* for *puja* or for placing a *jot*, for spreading a *khat*, for placing a *tijori*, making a *bitora*, a *bitora* opening, for giving rest to bullocks in the *khet* while under the yoke, for the *hali* to take rest in the *khet*, for one to be seated for taking his meals or for performing any religious or life-cycle ceremony. Orientation is also important for placing a dying person on the floor as well as for placing the dead body on the pyre. Even for locating the *chehanrin*, in relation to the *abadi* in a village, the orientation is very important.

These orientations are guided by the fact that east is the direction of the rising Sun. Sun is treated as a God and is called *Surya Dewata*. Another factor is the direction in which the winds generally blow in this region. There are also prevalent folk beliefs that east is the direction of *punya* (virtuosity) and all the important places of pilgrimage for the Hindus are located towards the east of the Chhatera region, while all the major sinful acts, such as brawls and fights between groups following the respective paths of virtuosity and otherwise (as enshrined in the legends of the local community and the Hindu scriptures), have always been performed in the south. *Lanka* (Ceylon) - the land of *rakshasas* - is also in the South. The slope of the earth is itself towards north-east, and the orientations of many things are adjusted accordingly. In the Sanskritic scriptures also, there are prescriptions about the orientations, especially about those related to human habitation (Apte, 1954:141-142). Details about cosmology as contained in the *Agni* and other *Puranas* also guide the orientation in the various walks of life, including habitation, of every Hindu community (Shastri, 1967).

11.2.5 *Covered Space vs Open to Sky*

The covered spaces are considered to be more sacred than the ones that are open to the sky. On the occasion of *sagai*, the main ceremony is performed in a covered space. The *tewa*, *beah* and all other ceremonies connected with marriage, except that of *phere* (where it is essential that the space must be open to sky) are all performed inside coverd spaces. Even *homa* on *Chhati* after a childbirth is performed in a covered space. In fact, all the life-cycle ceremonies (right from birth to death) of every individual are performed in covered spaces. All *pujas* and other religious ceremonies are performed in covered spaces. Food is preferably cooked as well as eaten in a covered space. In every *ghar*, *chauka* is considered to be the most sacred part. Closest to *chauka* lies the *chauk*, but *chauk* is not so sacred as the *sal* which is not close to the *chauka*. This is partly so because *sal* is a covered space. It can, therefore, be concluded that :

Covered Space : Open to Sky :: Private : Public
Covered Space : Open to Sky :: Sacred : Profane
Covered Space : Open to Sky :: Intimate : General

11.2.6 *Clear vs Transitional or Marginal*

All important works are done in places falling under clear-cut categories, i.e., either inside the *ghar* or outside it, either on the ground floor or on the first floor, either in one space or in the other, etc. Functions are performed either in the *gal* or in the *pauli*. The *barna*, being a transitional place, nothing important or significant is ever done on the *daher*. Similarly, no function or ceremony is performed in the *parkala*. Due to shortage of space, at times, some people put some of their not-so-valuable things like earthen-wares or agricultural implements in the *parkala* of their *ghar*. But actually the *parkala* is not meant to be used for such purposes. *Parkala* is to be used only as a connecting link between the ground floor and the first floor. Similar is the case with the *daher* also (discussed earlier).

No important work is done during twilight period. The story of King Hirnakashyapa mentioned earlier (while discussing the *daher* at 10.2.3) is relevant here. So, it can be concluded that :

Clear : Transitional or Marginal :: Auspicious : Inauspicious

Clear : Transitional or Marginal :: Sacred : Non-sacred Dangerous

11.2.7 *Human vs Animal*

All over the world, every community has always been observing distinction between human beings and animals and has been giving a differential treatment to the two. In the structure of classifications in the life of Chhaterans also, there is a complementary pair of relations to this effect. Although it is generally said that, in the interest of public health, village houses must provide segregation between human beings and cattle, in reality, to a certain extent, it is already there. Women and children live in the *ghar*, men in the *baithak* while the cattle live in the *gher*. Compared to the *ghars*, *ghers* are located more in the outer parts of the *abadi*. Where *baithak* and *gher* are located together on the same plot, different parts are earmarked to be used by cattle and human beings, respectively. Whenever, due to any reason, cattle have to be kept in the *ghar*, these are in kept in the *pauli*. In a *chaukband ghar*, cattle are never allowed to go beyond the *pauli*. Within the *pauli*, again, the portion on one side of the main *barna* is marked for cattle and on the other for human beings. Segregation of human beings from cattle is so complete that even festivals (like *gordhan*) connected with cattle are celebrated in the *gher*, while those connected with human beings are celebrated in the *ghar*. Similarly, at the level of the whole village, just as there is a *chaupal* for men, there is a *laihnda* for *cattle*.

Although the folk beliefs of the Chhaterans are related to the behaviour pattern of human beings as well as cattle, these are not so rigid in the case of the latter. Details of land-use mentioned in the "Settlement Report of Chhatera" (1910) show that there were 12 acres of land in the *laihnda*. In the same report, it is subsequently stated that this 12 acre plot included the *chehanrin* also which was one acre. The structures for human beings are superior in design and specifications than those for cattle. Moreover, the proportion of *pacca* structures among those for human beings is considerably higher than that among the structures for the cattle. These, as well as earlier discussion in this work, lead one to conclude that :

Human : Animal :: Centre : Periphery
Human : Animal :: Inner : Outer
Human : Animal :: Superior : Inferior
Human : Animal :: Rear : Front
Human : Animal :: *Pacca* : *Katcha*

11.2.8 *Male vs Female*

As stated earlier, segregation is practised in Chhatera, besides other things, on the basis of sex also. The differential behaviour towards males and females is reflected in almost all spheres of their life including division of labour and use of spaces. For example, the woman has to do household work while the man looks after agriculture, etc. The woman no doubt helps man in agriculture, but bringing water (for domestic use) from the *kuwan* is exclusively a woman's job. If, under any circumstances, a man is seen bringing water from the *kuwan*, he would become an object of ridicule by his friends and other villagers. Cooking is a woman's job, done in the *ghar*. But if any non-vegetarian dish is to be cooked, this is done by man, and that too, outside the *ghar*.

Huka is the life-blood of the Haryanvis. Every Jat household has got at least one *huka*. In Chhatera, about 50 per cent of women smoke. Although no social stigma is attached to smoking by women, they do not smoke openly and it is not in good taste for a woman to smoke publicly. Even life-cycle ceremonies, like *chhati* and *mundan*, are celebrated more elaborately in case of a male child. In fact, at the time of childbirth itself, it is the arrival of a male child which is the cause of happiness and rejoicings while a female child is received casually - sometimes even with a negative attitude. A male child is considered to be an asset for the family. Among the Jats, property is inherited through the male line, and after a man's death, it is his son who can offer to the *Purohit* certain things which, it is believed, would reach the soul of the dead person. Jats are partiarchal, partri-local and partilineal. There is dominance of males among the Jats.

Ghar is mainly the woman's domain while man spends most of his time, throughout his life, in the *baithak* or in the *gher*. Even within the *ghar*, man remains mostly in the front, i.e., in the outer part of the *ghar*, especially in the *pauli*, while the part of the *ghar* beyond the *pauli* - sometimes referred to as *zanana* - is occupied by woman. *Chaupal* is one place in the village which is meant exclusively for men and no woman is ever allowed there. There is no such place in the village meant exclusively for women. One reason for the absence of such a place for women is the male dominance in the community and the fact that because the household chores keep the woman so busy that hardly any time is left with her to indulge in any of such activities which go on at the *chaupal*. A woman is not allowed to accompany a dead body to the *chehanrin*.

Domains of man and woman in terms of space have been clearly brought out at length in 10.3. For Chhaterans, contracting a marriage falls almost exclusively in man's sphere. Unlike in many other patriarchal, patrilocal and patrilineal communities, which assign this work to their women, among the Jats, it is the men who contract matrimonial alliances. For contracting a marriage it is the male members of the household who go out to other villages. Previously, this used to be the role of the *Nai*. The *Nai* and other males would obviously visit the *baithaks* (not *ghars*) of the potential families. On the occasion of a *sagai*, only male relatives and male friends of the household gather in the *baithak* of the *banra*. Women do not gather on this occasion. *Ladus* sent by the *banri's* side on this occasion are distributed among the assembled men.

At the time of *beah* also, the *Purohit* of the *banri's* side comes to the *baithak* of the *banra* and the function takes place there. Afterwards, of course, the *Purohit* is escorted to the *ghar* of the *banra* and is fed there in the *sal*. The main function relating to a marriage is always performed in the *ghar*. All male guests remain in the *baithak* and come to the *ghar* only for main functions. *Mithai* is made in the *gher*. It is mainly from the time of *tewa* ceremony onwards that the association of women, with the newly-contracted relationship, becomes close. Women need to know the date of marriage, number of *bans*, etc. Moreover, immediately after the *tewa* ceremony, a large number of guests have to be fed in the *ghar*.

Matrimonial activities are always initiated from the *baithak*, and as the actual day of marriage starts approaching, *ghar ko ghasakne lagte hain*, i.e., they start drifting towards the *ghar*. Once the marriage ceremonies start in fullswing, these get practically concentrated in the *ghar*. *Raihne wale gharan mein, mansan ke raihne wale gharan mein jahan chuka chulha howe*, i.e., in the residential house for human beings where there is *chauka* and *chulha*. *Ghar* becomes the focus of all activities. It is from this headquarters that all activities are directed.

On the basis of this and the detailed discussions elsewhere in this book, it can be further concluded that :

Man : Woman :: Periphery : Centre
Man : Woman :: Outer : Inner
Man : Woman :: Front : Rear
Man : Woman :: Head : Foot
Man : Woman :: Right : Left

11.2.9 *Ourselves vs Strangers*

There is no human group in the world which does not distinguish between in-groups and out-groups. Even higher animals distinguish between members of their own groups and strangers. Among visitors to Chhatera, those who are complete strangers are lodged in the *chaupal* which is outside the *abadi*. When the *kot* was in existence in Chhatera, the *chaupal* was outside it. Those people who are somewhat closer, or less stranger, are taken to the *baithak*. It is only a few very intimate outsiders who are allowed into the *ghar*. In a marriage, the *banra* (who is the most honoured guest and has almost already got entry into the family of his in-laws) and his father are not allowed to enter the *banri*'s *ghar* before the time of *phere*. After his *arta*, by his *sali*, at the *barna* of his *sasural*'s *ghar*, the *banra* and his *father* go back to the *chaupal*. After *phere*, the *banra* is taken into the *sal* of the *ghar* but other members of the *janet* remain at the *chaupal*.

Of those outside male members who are allowed into the *ghar*, majority goes up to the *pauli* only, only a few intimate men are allowed beyond the *pauli*. Those households who do not have separate *baithaks* but do have *chaubare* (on the first floor of their *ghar*), take these 'not-so-intimate' male guests to the *chaubare*. But on the ground floor of their *ghar* they do not allow them into the portion beyond the *pauli*. Even those outsiders, who come to the village on business regularly, transact their business in the *gal*. Only very intimate ones are taken into the *pauli*. On the basis of this, it can be concluded that:

Ourselves : Strangers :: Inside : Outside
Ourselves : Strangers :: Centre : Periphery

Those strangers who are allowed into the village for some special work are treated very respectfully and as guests. On the basis of discussions in the previous chapters it can be said that :

Ourselves : Strangers :: Foot : Head
Ourselves : Strangers :: Lower : Higher

11.2.10 *Natal vs Conjugal or In-married*

Althrough their lives, the Chhaterans allow more freedom to their *betis* than to their *bahus*. Comparatively, *betis* are always in the front while *bahus* are in the rear. But on the occasion of the festival of *holi*, it is the *bahus* who are in the front while *betis* remain in the rear. The *bahus* play *holi* with men while the *batis* only supply them water from the *kuwan*. It means that on normal occasions the *bahus* are kept away from men, but since during *holi* there may be some laxity in the social norms (not-so-decent jokes are exchanged and men are given some physical beating by women with *dandas*), the Chhaterans consider the involvement of their *betis* in such activities to be out of place. But the *bahus* are allowed to participate in these activities. When men are present in the *pauli* / *baithak*, if there are only family members, or very close relatives / persons, a *beti* can go there for work or she can even sit there and talk, although she would not participate in the activities going on there. But a *bahu* cannot do even that. Even when she has to pass that way, she would pull down her *ghunghat* and hurriedly move away. This clearly shows the distinction between the behaviour of those born-in and those married-in. This conclusion is further supported by the discipline to which the *damads* and *batyaus* of the Chhaterans are subjected.

Another occasion, when one observes a deviation from the normal pattern of male-female inter-action, is the departure of a *barat* from the *banri*'s village for the *banra*'s village. The mother of the *banri* puts *thapas* on the chest of the *banra*'s father and of *banra*'s father's brothers, etc. Putting *thapas* falls within the woman's domain. So, *thapas* have to be put by the *banri*'s mother and not by her father. Since the *banra*'s mother is not present on this occasion - among the Jats, women do not accompany a *barat* party - *thapas* have to be put on the chest of the *banra*'s father. In this relation, sometimes jokes are also cracked. During *salono* festival, men go to their *ghar* to get the *paunchi* tied on their wrists by their sisters. On the occasion of the first *makar sankrant* after her marriage, a new *bahu* goes to the *baithak* to present a blanket to her *sasur*. This shows that, while in the case of a *beti* the man comes to his *ghar*, in the case of a *bahu*, it is the woman who goes to the *baithak*.

A distinction, though in limited aspects, is also made between the wife-givers and wife-takers. This can be seen in the degree of freedom allowed to a person in the village of his sister's *sasural*, especially in her *ghar*, when he visits her there.

11.2.11 *Living vs Dead*

There has always been a distinction between the living and the dead. A living person always tries to sit, or lie off the earth, while a person about to die, as well as after his death, is placed on the earth. It is believed that the human body is made of earth and that after the death of a person his body again merges into the earth. In certain respects, both, a living person and a dead person, are treated alike by their fellow-beings while in certain other respects the two are treated differently. When a dead body is taken to the *chehanrin*, like an honoured guest going away from the village, it is given a send off at the *laihnda*. The ceremonies performed at the *laihnda* also indicate that a dead body is treated like an honoured living guest departing from the village.

The fact that, in a newly-founded village, the person who dies first (without any consideration of his caste) is treated as the *bhumiya*, indicates that the caste system is only for the living beings and not for those who are dead. But it seems that the dead bodies, as such, do not transcend across the caste barriers completely because traditionally caste distinctions have been practised at the *chehanrin* also. When a living being parts from a family, for example, a girl after her marriage leaving her parents' *ghar* for that of her *sasural*, certain rituals are performed at the *barna* of the *ghar*. Similarly, a new entrant into *ghar* (human or animal) is given certain treatment at the *barna* which is not done at the time of the exit of a dead person from his *ghar*.

11.2.12 *Upper vs Lower*

Another relation, or sub-system of classifiction, is the Upper *versus* Lower one. It has been observed that in absolute terms, there is a clear distinction between the two terms, 'upper' and 'lower'. For example, take the distinction between the ground and the first floor. Ground floor is more sacred than the first and subsequent higher floors. All the important functions are performed on the ground floor. All life-cycle ceremonies, from birth to death, are performed here. When a person is seriously ill and his death is considered to be imminent, if at that time he is on the first floor, he is immediately removed to the ground floor. Some of the other intimate functions, like cooking, are also performed on the ground floor. Even in *ghars*, having enough covered space on their first floor, the functions performed on the floor are not so important ones and at least some of these are such that can also be performed in the open or in the *bagar*. A *chaukband ghar* has a semi-fort like construction. The *chauk*, as described earlier, forms only about one-fifteenth of the total area of the *ghar*. Moreover, because of the high wall all around, adequate amount of sunshine cannot reach the *chauk*. During hot seasons, women and children generally sleep in the *chauk* of their *ghar*, but the new couples sleep on the first floor..

On the ground floor itself one finds a slightly different situation. For example, those things which are to be accorded a superior status and are treated as sort of 'sacred' are not kept directly on the ground; rather these are placed on some thing else kept on the floor. The higher the level above the ground, the more "good sacred', respectful and prestigious it is considered to be. Conversely, the lower the level, the more profane, less important and less significant it is thought to be. In every *ghar*, the level of the floor of the *chauka* is always kept higher than that of its *chauk*. Even in those *ghars*, which are not of the *chaukband* type, if due to shortage of space, the cooking space is not provided separately but only as a part of some bigger space, the floor of this part of the space is kept at a slightly higher level. Food, while being eaten is generally kept on a *patra* (a wooden plank with short legs) so that, because of a higher level, it gets a place of respect and importance. Members of every household normally take their meals in the *sal* of their *ghar* (on the ground floor). But during a marriage, at times, meals for male guests are served even on the *chhat* of the *ghar* (which is on the first floor). But even on such occasions, when there is an acute shortage of space in the *ghar*, the *Purohit* is invariably fed in the *chauka*.

Guests and outsiders are normally not allowed in the *ghar*, and when they are brought into the *ghar*, they are taken to the *chhat* or in the *chaubare* - on the first floor. When women and children are on the ground floor of a *ghar*, male members and male guests of the household go to the first floor. But at the time of *phere* during a marriage, when male members and male guests of both the sides are on the ground floor, young women and children go up and watch the ceremonies through the *jal* of the *chauk*. On this basis, it can be concluded that:

Ground Floor : First Floor :: Private : Public
Ground Floor : First Floor :: Intimate : Not-so-Intimate
Ground Floor : First Floor :: Sacred : Profane
Ground Floor : First Floor :: General : Special

When a group of people are sitting together, the level is an important consideration in the sitting arrangement. Of course, besides the level, another factor also comes in here, and that is, the type of furniture used. A person, whom the Chhaterans want to give more respect is seated at a place, or on a thing, which is higher in level compared to the levels of the places or things on which others are seated. For example, if some elders are sitting on *kursis* (chairs), the younger persons would sit on *khats*. If the elders are sitting on *khats* and all the *khats* are full, and at times even when some place on the khats is still vacant, the younger persons sit on the ground. This distinction in the seating arrangement is made not only on the basis of age, but also on that of sex and the fact as to whether one is born in the family/village or is married into it. The distinction in the level of seating is also practised between the guests and the hosts, and also on the basis of the social status enjoyed by a person. The better seat on a higher level is always offered to the guest. The status of the guest is also a consideration for this purpose.

Men and women normally do not sit together; they do not even gather together as a freely mixing group. But whenever they mix, in restricted groups and in a restricted way though, the higher level or better seats are always offered to the males. Even in the absence of anyone else, when a man and wife are alone, if the man occupies a *kursi*, his wife will sit on a *khat*. If the man sits on a *khat*, his wife will sit on something lower in level than the *khat*. Even when both of them sit on the same *khat*, the man would sit on the part of the *khat* considered to be its ''head' and the wife on its 'foot' portion. It can, therefore, be concluded that:

Higher : Lower :: Elder : Younger
Higher : Lower :: Man : Woman
Higher : Lower :: Superior : Inferior
Higher : Lower :: Guest : Host
Higher : Lower :: Sacred : Profane

11.2.13 *On the Earth vs Off the Earth*

As such, the ground is considered to be impure. So, while eating one does not keep his food on the earth. It is always kept on a *patra*. But when food is eaten while sitting in the *chauka*, it is placed on the floor itself.

While about to deliver a child, a woman is invariably made to lie on the floor. When a person in any household is about to die, the floor of the *sal* of his *ghar* is cleaned and purified with *lepai*, and the dying person is placed on it. It is believed that unless one meets his end while lying on the earth itself, he will neither attain salvation nor shall he easily get re-incarnation. The basic idea is that man is born of earth, i.e., he is made of earth and that after his death, he has again to become a part of the earth itself and, for that, one must die while in direct contact with the earth. Earth is something that God has made himself while all the other things are man-made.

11.2.14 *Right vs Left*

The right *versus* left relation is not much in evidence in the life of the Chhaterans. It is reported that till about a quarter century ago, the Harijans were not allowed to sit on the right hand side of the caste Hindus. In fact, the main consideration in the seating of the caste Hindus and the Harijans was the direction of the flow of the wind. Harijans were not allowed to sit in the direction (in relation to the place occupied by the caste Hindus present there) from which the wind was flowing; rather, they would sit in the direction towards which it was flowing. But whenever the wind was stationary and its direction was not evident, the Harijans were not allowed to sit on the right (of the twice-born), as seen by the caste Hindus present there.

When one enters a structure (be it a *ghar*, *gher* or *baithak*) through its main *barna* in the *gal*, the portion of the structure on his left should be more, i.e., bigger than that on his right. If there are *aobras* on one side of the *pauli*, or in the room into which one enters from the *gal* through the main *barna*, then only this space, i.e., the *pauli*, etc., is to be considered for this purpose. The total frontage of the structure is not the actual consideration for this purpose. This rule is applicable only in the case of the space immediately inside the main *barna*, and not in case of other rooms and spaces, etc., in the other bays of the structure. But, somehow, Chhaterans are unable to explain the logic of this practice. Whenever a couple sits together for any religious or life-cycle ceremony, the man always sits on the right while the woman (i.e., his wife) sits on his left. So, one can conclude that :

Right : Left :: Higher caste : Lower caste
Right : Left :: Man : Woman
Right : Left :: Superior : Inferior

11.2.15 *Closed or Enclosed vs Open*

Almost all the important life-cycle ceremonies of the Chhaterans are performed in open spaces. Food is invariably taken in an open space. The enclosed spaces are used mostly for storage, etc., due to reasons of security. Throughout his life, a Chhateran spends much more time in the open spaces than in enclosed ones.

11.2.16 *Katcha vs Pacca*

In the life of the Chhatérans, there is also a *katcha vs pacca* relation, or sub-system of classification. All their folk beliefs and the consequent restrictions they observe with respect to their houses, are applicable much more in the case of *pacca* structures than the *katcha* ones. The discipline of house design, construction and use is not observed with the same degree of severity and rigour in the case of *katcha* structures as in the case of *pacca* ones. This is perhaps so, because the *kata* structures are relatively temporary with a shorter life expectancy. Moreover, even if something is made in a 'wrong' way, it can be rectified more easily in a *katcha* structure than in a *pacca* one.

11.2.17 *Head vs Foot*

Khat, the most commonly used and multi-purpose piece of furniture of the villagers, is used for sitting also. A *khat* can accommodate a number of persons at a time. The more a portion of the *khat* lies towards its headside, the higher is its status or importance. The leg portion of the *khat* being less significant, the position of the person who sits there aslo becomes less significant. Even when a man and wife are sitting on the same *khat*, the man would occupy its head part while the wife would sit on its foot portion. Similar distinctions in occupying parts of a *khat* are also made on the basis of age, status and the guest *versus* host consideration. Therefore, it can be concluded thus:

Head : Foot :: Man : Woman
Head : Foot :: Elder : Younger
Head : Foot :: Guest : Host
Head : Foot :: Superior : Inferior

11.2.18 *Entrance vs Exit*

On the arrival of a new *damad* or a *bahu* at the *ghar* of their *sasural* their *arta* is performed. Similarly, the *arta* of a *bhati* and of a newly-purchased cattle is performed at the *barna* of the *ghar*. So, *arta* is a function symbolizing the entrance of a new member into the household or ceremonial welcome to an honoured guest. But no such ritual or ceremony is performed at the time of the final exit of any member of any household from the *ghar*, i.e., neither when, after her marriage, a bride leaves her parents' *ghar* for that of her *sasural* nor when the dead body of any household member is taken out of the *ghar* for funeral.

This shows the existence of an entrance *versus* exit sub-system of classification, or relation, in the life of the Chhaterans. Entrance is more important and significant than exit - a view which is further strengthened by the fact that after every harvest, when grains are brought to the *ghar* for storage, certain rituals are observed on this occasion while no such ritual is observed when the grains are taken out of the *ghar* for sale, for household consumption, or for any other purpose. Similarly, when after its having been sold out, an animal leaves the *ghar* of its owner, no ritual is performed at that time.

11.3 THE PRIMARY AND SECONDARY RELATIONS

In no structure of classification are all the relations accorded equal value. The various relations have greater and lesser importance in the total structure of classification and have different roles in producing the pattern. They carry differential functional loads and affect the shape or design of the house and habitation in different ways. Some of the relations can be categorized as primary, while others can be called secondary.

From the foregoing discussions, it is evident that the relations: Centre *versus* Periphery, Inner *versus* Outer, Front *versus* Rear, The Cardinal Points, Covered Space *versus* Open to Sky, Clear *versus* Trasitional or Marginal, Human *versus* Animal, Male *versus* Female, Ourselves *versus* Strangers, Natal *versus* Conjugal or In-married, Living *versus* Dead, and the Entrance *versus* Exit, are primary ones, while the rest of the relations carry a secondary load. Of all the relations, the Centre *versus* Periphery one is the most important. This can also be observed in the distinction between the three levels of residential living in term of sacredness, safety, as well as movements and activities of women and also in other respects in different parts of the *ghar* itself. It is also true in regard to the location of residential quarters of the *biswedaran versus be-biswedaran* in the village, in the location of residential quarters and movements of the Caste Hindus *versus* the Harijans, and in the locations and movement of human beings *versus* cattle. Not only that, even the placing of things connected with the human beings and cattle respectively, like *garar*, the movements of intimate persons *versus* strangers, as well as the intimate *versus* ceremonial aspects of life run on the Centre *versus* Periphery basis.

The Inner *versus* Outer relation is visible not only among the various parts of a *ghar* but even within certain individual parts themselves. The sacredness, privacy, intimacy and segregation on the basis of sex and caste, as well as the cattle-human segregation are reflected in the Inner *versus* Outer relation. More or less related to it, and carrying a similar functional load, is the Front *versus* Rear relation.

So far as sacredness and profanity are concerned, the Front *versus* Rear relation has a very great importance in the life of the Chhaterans. Similarly, attitudes of the Chhaterans about the Transitional *versus* Clear categories, especially those related to the performance of any function or ceremony, are also very rigid. The Natal *versus* Conjugal or In-married relation too has a great importance in almost every sphere of life of the Chhaterans and carries a very heavy functional load in terms of shaping the design of their habitations at both the micro- as well as macro-levels. It would, perhaps, not be wrong to say that the life of the Chhaterans almost entirely revolves around the Centre *versus* Periphery, and Inner *versus* Outer relations. The other relations, viz., Upper *versus* Lower, On the Earth *versus* Off the Earth, Right *versus* Left, Closed or Enclosed *versus* Open, *Katcha versus Pacca*, and the Head *versus* Foot ones have a secondary role in their life. These relations carry lesser functional loads in terms of affecting the house designs and the habitation patterns of the people of Chhatera.

Though a higher physical level is considered to be more important, respectful and prestigious, it is qualified by certain other factors also. Similar is the case with the On the Earth *versus* Off the Earth relation. Of all the sub-systems of classifications, or relations, in the life of the Chhaterans, the Right *versus* Left relation has perhaps the lowest importance and hence carries the least functional load in terms of shaping their habitation. More or less similar is the condition of the Closed or Enclosed *versus* Open relation. Similarly, the functional loads carried by the *Katcha versus Pacca* and the Entrance *versus* Exit relations are also not much. Compared to these, the Head *versus* Foot relation is somethat more weighty. On the basis of the foregoing discussion, all the complementary pairs of relations and the total structure of the system of classification (which these pairs of relations constitute), in the life of the Chhaterans, can be put in the shape of a chart that follows. In fact, an ideal situation would be if we can go beyond this and say something about the articulating machanism which combines all these relations together and makes a unified whole out of them. Once we arrive at that, we can understand the philosophy of life of the Chhaterans clearly, and, that too, not merely with regard to their habitation but also several other spheres of their life.

THE HUMAN HABITATION

as a

SYSTEM OF RELATIONS

Habitation and Universe	Man and Nature	Habitation and Itself
SPACE, EARTH AND SKY (COSMOLOGY)	SPACE AND LIVING BEINGS	CON-STRUCTION AND INTERNAL RELATIONS OF SPACE
On the Earth/ Off the Earth	Human/Animal Male/Female	Clear/ Transitional or Marginal Centre/ Periphery Inner/Outer
The Cardinal Points N = S == E = W	Natal/Conjugal or In-married Ourselves/Strangers	Front/Rear Upper/Lower
Right/Left	Living/the Dead	Enclosed/Open
Head/Foot	Entrance/Exit	*Katcha/Pacca*

TWELVE

SUMMARY AND SUGGESTIONS FOR FURTHER WORK

12.1 SUMMARY

THE FOREGOING discussion in this book, motivated by a desire to have an understanding of the character of rural habitations and of the process and mechanism of their origin, growth, change, etc., has clearly brought out the fact that it is the social factors which play a predominant role in shaping the layout of any habitation. I have also studied the limitations of all the existing theories, which, because of their predominant physical bias, fail to get us a realistic understanding of the human habitations.

It has been observed that different villages, in almost similar physical settings, economic circumstances and law and order conditions, have assumed different patterns. At the same time, innumerable instances have also been observed where whole communities or parts of the same, having migrated to different regions, have repeated their old habitation pattern at the new places even though the physical conditions there may be totally different and these habitations, scientifically speaking, may be found to be inappropriate for the climatic conditions of the new region. Observations by various scholars like Karve (1957: 100) that "the way people build their houses, group them and the way arteries of internal and external communication are formed would lend itself to ecological and anthropological analysis"; Mukerji (1967: 102) that "the study of settlements is also the study of human reactions to environmental factors, because settlement is the product of adjustment between the social forces and the physical conditions of the habitat"; Aurrauseau (1920:237) and Bhattacharya and Verma (1956-57:303) that definite groupings of human populations is a conscious human response to, rather than an actual physiographic control by, a number of actors in each region; Mitra (1966:11) that the two different types of orientations of tanks/bunds and *abadis* in villages originally founded by the Hindus and the Muslims, respectively, all lead to one and the same conclusion, namely, that social factors play a very decisive role in shaping any human habitation. Scholars (belonging to different disciplines), studying rural habitations, have generally laid almost the entire emphasis on one or the other individual factor, like, the altitude of the place, availability of water (including rainfall), law and order situation and necessity of the services of village craftsmen. Although, under certain exceptional sets of circumstances, even a single factor may sometimes cause a habitation to develop a particular pattern, it is seldom possible to pinpoint any one factor to be responsible for the formation of any pattern. It is always a group of them responsible for this. It is also always difficult to disentagle/isolate the various factors responsible for shaping a habitation and to determine the exact role played by each of these factors in this process. An attempt should, however, be made to find out as to roughly what pattern a rural habitation is likely to assume under a particular set of circumstances. This itself, if achieved, would be no mean a contribution. The author has some material for the preparation of a Distribution Map of the entire country depicting the locations of villages with various types of layout patterns. Such a map would be quite meaningful when studied in conjunction with, or related to, the other distribution maps depicting various factors, like, the social organization and physiographic conditions.

The present work does not and cannot in any way claim to have unravelled the complicated mechanism of the formation of the habitation of Chhatera, and least at all of the rural habitations in general. But it has certainly proved to be a successful exercise, useful for further work on the subject, and has brought to light various directions along which work must be pursued further in order to understand this process. Of course, no work can claim to provide a ready-made answer to the problems of rural habitations in general. Each village has a unique pattern and mode of life and has, therefore, to be studied as such.

Geographers have studied different types of habitation patterns in different geographical regions and also the geographical spread of the various patterns. The interest of geographers has been confined mainly to the study of physical forms and physical factors related to these forms. They have primarily described the way a village, or a part of it, looks like.

Doxiadis - the founder father of *Ekistics* - has indentified five basic elements of human habitations; namely, nature, man, society, shells and networks. One of the greatest mistakes, according to Doxiadis, committed in the study of human habitations is that of considering them to be consisting of nature, shells and networks only. Thus, the essence of habitations - man and society - have been completely neglected. In doing so, we are making the same mistake as the medical science which for centuries had concerned itself with human body, and studied its structure mainly through anatomy but overlooked its functioning which could be studied through physiology. This continued for centuries until the time when modern medicine established the coordinated study of functions and structures. Ekisticians also seem to have higlighted the shallowness of the existing studies of human habitations, when they say that:

> In actual life we are interested in functions, but since these are not easily expressed physically, therefore, we tend to think of a settlement in terms of its shells even though what really matters is the men who live in it or use it in another way (Doxiadis, 1968:24).

Sociologists and anthropologists have been concerned more with man and society. Besides describing the patterns as such, they have also been trying to understand the hows and whys of these patterns. On the study of human habitations, although the approach followed by sociologists and anthropologists, as compared to that of geographers and others, has been a more realistic one, they have so far been raising more questions rather than finding answers to these questions. For example, scholars like Chauhan (1964:80) have arrived at hasty conclusions of a general nature that where residences for men and animals are separate, an increase in the number of families in the next generation is followed by an extension of the residential area and the area is demarcated for cattle and for storing fodder. Work done for the present study (discussed at 4.3.1 and 4.3.2) helps in understanding this problem more clearly.

In fact, so far as the origin and growth of Chhatera are concerned, this author has collected sufficient data regarding structures (including *ghars, baithaks* and *ghers*) that came into existence when the village was founded at its present site and as to who occupied each of these structures and for what purpose. After that, with the passage of time, when the new generations came up, who shifted where, which new structures came up and what were the uses to which all these structures (old and new) were put. This information has been collected about all the caste groups in the village. But the data is all the more rich with respect to that part of the village *abadi* which falls within the erstwhile *kot*. It is proposed to process and publish this material shortly.

As regards habitations at the micro-level, in the concerned disciplines, either the topic of dwellings is neglected or treated as secondary even when relevant. Whatever studies on this topic are available, these are confined mainly to the physical aspects. The houses have been studied in a typical engineer-like fashion. Cultural geography, for example, has concentrated on listing of house types and description of features. But there is no effort to link these forms to life patterns, beliefs and desires of those who inhabit these houses. Some geographers have studied houses in relation to climate. Some others have confined themselves to the study of form and elevation and at times, even the layout. But they have not studied the house plan at all. There have been some studies of building materials and construction techniques also.

Even in the sociological literature, mentions of houses are mainly descriptive rather than analytical. Most of the sociologists and anthropologists have also been studying the houses in an engineer-like fashion. They talk mainly about the house groupages (Chauhan, 1960, 1964, 1967; Karve, 1957; Stephen, 1960) or different parts of the ancestral estate (Srinivas, 1965). Some of them (Bose and Malhotra, 1965; Lyer, 1937; Opler and Singh, 1948; Singh, R.L., 1957; Srinivas, 1965, etc.) talk about the form or appearance of the house, using such expressions as "Fort-like". A few of the sociologists (Bose and Malhotra, 1965) have described the number of storeys and dimensions of these houses and have also attempted categorizations like *katcha*, *pacca*, etc. A large number of those, who have studied that human dwellings, talk about the building materials used and the construction techniques adopted. Some of these scholars have laid undue emphasis on the description of the various elements in the dwelling. But, in reality, it is the intrinsic structure of a house which is of prime importance while the extrinsic elements have only a secondary value.

Some of the scholars have listed the various spaces in a house, a few of them have discussed the arrangement of these spaces also. Some have listed the uses of these spaces and also the persons who use each of these. Some scholars have described the two main parts of a house, i.e., the one for men and the other for women, while some others have described some of the important uses of these two parts in a bid to bring out the segregation of sexes in the use of spaces in a house. But one special feature of all these descriptions is that the house plan has not been discussed, i.e., the manner in which the various spaces in a house are related to each other and how these all fit into the total plan have not been discussed.

Physical spaces by themselves are not much meaningul, what is of paramount importance is their inter-relationship with each other, culture is important not only for use of space but even for the very concept of space. Even in the classical Indian architecture, there is a great deal of emphasis on this aspect. Just as the various physical spaces have not been related to each other, the inter-relationship of the uses of these spaces - the crux of the problem - has also been neglected.

As the divisions of the house, i.e., the details of the house plan, are more important than its elements, the inter-relationships of the uses of various spaces are more important than the uses of individual spaces by themselves. Moreover, the arrangement of various spaces, and the use of each individual space as well as the inter-relationship of the uses of various spaces, should be able to clearly reflect the culture of its inhabitants. But none of these works has made any attempt to link the life-style of the people with the arrangement and use of the various parts of their house. Perception and use of the spaces is more meaningful. But it is this very aspect which has so far been completely overlooked by all the students of human habitations.

Some of the studies have also described the cattle-human segregation in the house. But they do not explain as to how each of these spaces can be used for the purpose other than the one for which it is primarily meant, i.e. as to how, under certain circumstances, even cattle can be allowed into that part of the house which is primarily meant for human beings and vice versa. The two sets of spaces and their respective uses have been studied in isolation from each other.

Some scholars have also attempted to divide the spaces in a house into sacred and profane. But they have done a very rough and generalized sort of division. Man has always been dividing spaces into sacred and profane, but these are not two watertight compartments. Sacredness and profanity vary on a scale of continuum. One can understand this mechanism clearly only when he studies it against the background of the entire philosophy of life of the people who inhabit it. One scholar has described the Right *versus* Left classification which dominates the entire life of the members of a particular community. He has also tried to relate this sub-system of classification with the house design of those people and with the use of various spaces in the house. But that is too simplified a solution. There never exists a singular system of classifcation in any culture. It always comprises of a number of sub-systems, each carrying a different degree of load in different spheres of life. Unless all these sub-systems, and their inter-relationships (with each other) are clearly understood, it is not possible to understand the problem in its totality or analyze it in its true perspective.

Some studies have mentioned, though in a passing way, the priority that housing enjoys in the life of a community. But unless the priority of other things in the life of the same people is also studied, it is not possible to understand that of the house alone. To sum up, life has to be studied in its totality and only then the house can be related to it. The approach traditionally followed for the study of human habitations and the one developed for the present work are presented in a diagramatic form in the ensuing chart.

I THE TRADITIONAL APPROACH

HABITATION

Constituent parts of elements

↓

Material, Form and Functions

↓

Constituent parts of elements

II APPROACH FOLLOWED IN THE PRESENT WORK

HABITATION

The struc ure of system of relations
established between elements

HABITATION
and itself
↑
Man
&
Nature
↑
UNIVERSE
Cosmology

12.2 SUGGESTIONS FOR FURTHER WORK

On the basis of the discussion in the foregoing Chapters, as well as from other experiences, the author feels that further work on the following aspects of this field, i.e., of rural habitations, may be taken up for further research:

1. Regarding the relations or the sub-systems of classification in the total structure of classification as practised by the Chhatera community, as discussed in this Chapter, further work should be undertaken in this direction with a view to narrow down the number and variaties of the complementary pairs of relations. The ultimate objective being to arrive at more fundamental, precise and specific basis of classification and at the articulating mechanism that combines them all into one system and renders meaning to them..
2. A more pointed and deeper study of the cosmology and folk beliefs of the Jats and others should be undertaken and, with the help of that work, further research on the habitations of these communities should be undertaken on the lines detailed below.
3. Field data collected for the present work helped in crystallising the thinking about the problems and issues raised in my theoretical study. The subject being of a relatively unexplored character, the field data and the experience gained in the present study, as presented in this book, should be utilised for making a deeper analysis of the subject of human habitations and, more so, for a review and understanding of the existing literature on the subject, especially of that contained in the Sanskrit literature (including scriptures). It further needs to be studied if, in view of the rapid social change taking place in the society, these theories and findings still have relevance.
4. During the recent past, there has been some new thinking in the field of architecture also. For example, the works of the Greek Architect - Doxiadis - and others at the Athens Centre of Ekistics and elsewhere have added new dimensions to the existing theories in the field of architecture. These developments have brought about sort of a revolutionary change in the concept of space. More research projects should be undertaken by sociologists and anthropologists to study human habitations with a view to understand and evaluate this new thinking and

derive social meanings.

5. Rural India has been currently undergoing transformation at a pace unheard of in its entire history. These changes have hardly left any aspect of rural life untouched. Though the Jats of Haryana have traditionally been enjoying a reputation of being conservative and rigid in attitudes towards almost all aspects of life, during the recent past, the region in which village Chhatera - the focal point of this study - falls, has been experiencing changes at a rate much higher than that in most of the other parts of the country. A repeat study of the village and the region around it after a reasonable gap (of time), say about two decades, may throw light on the process of change as well as the role played by the various factors, individually as also collectively, in influencing the mechanism of rural habitations. Perhaps the present author may himself undertake this task.

BIBLIOGRAPHY/REFERENCES CITED

A. SOCIOLOGY, ANTHROPOLOGY AND ETHNOGRAPHY

Ahuja, Sarayu (1980). *Socio-cultural dimensions in some Indian villages*. EKISTICS, Athens. 47(283): pp.289-95.

Ali, Amir (1937). Individual differences in Indian villages. Proceedings of the twenty-fourth Indian Science Congress at Hyderabad, Calcutta. pp.335-36.

Ali, H.A. (1970). *The Meos of Mewat*. Delhi: Oxford and IBH Publishing Co.

Ambedkar, B.R. (1948). *The untouchables: Who are they and why they became untouchables*. New Delhi: Amrit Book Co.

Arnold, Van Gennep (1960). *The rites of passage*. Translated by Monica, B. Vizedom and Gabriel, L. Caffe. Introduction by Solon, T. Kimball. London: Routledge and Kegan Paul.

Baden-Powell, B.H. (1898). *The origin of land-tenures in India*. Journal of the Royal Asiatic Society of Great Britain and Ireland, London. Vol. 30.

(1913). A short account of the land revenue and its administration in British India: with a sketch of the land tenures. London: Oxford.

Bailey, F.G. (1955). *An Oriya hill village, in India's Villages*. M.N. Srinivas (Ed.) Bombay: Asia Publishing House.

(1960). Tribe, caste and nation: a study of political activity and political change in highland Orissa. London: Oxford University Press.

Basham, A.L. (1967). *Wonder that was India: A survey of the history and culture of the Indian sub-continent before the coming of the Muslims*. London: Siduick and Jackson.

Bever, Gleen H. (1959). Housing and personal values. Ithaca (N.Y.) : Copwell University.

(1965). *Housing and society*. New York: Macmillan.

Bhandari, J.S. (1936). Kinship, marriage and family among the Korua of Dudhi Mirzapur (U.P.). *Eastern Anthropologist*, Lucknow 16(2): pp.79-106.

Bhattacharya, Vivek Ranjan (1971). *Challenge of village India*. Delhi: Metropolitan Book Company Private Limited.

Bohannan, Paul (1965). Refer to Morgan, Lewis H. 1881.

Bopegamage, A (1957). *Delhi : A study of urban sociology*. Bombay: University of Bombay.

Bose, A.B. and Jodha, N.S. (1967). Some observations on factors influencing settlements of households. *Man in India*, Ranchi 47(4): pp.271-78.

Bose, A.B. and Malhotra, S.P. (1963). Anthropo-geographical study of the settlement pattern of a desert village. *Man in India*, Ranchi 43(3): pp.233-49.

(1965). Residential segregation and housing in a desert village. Journal of Asiatic Society, Calcutta 7(3-4): pp.173-80.

Bose, A.B. Malhotra, S.P. and Bharara, Lajpal. (1963). Socio-economic differences in dispersed dwellings and compact settlement types in arid regions. *Man in India*, Ranchi 43(3): pp.119-30.

Bose, A.B. and Sen, Mohanlal (1963). Spatial aspects of rural living. *Man in India*, Ranchi 43(1): pp.9-26.

Bose, N.K. (1958). Types of villages in West Bengal, a study in social change. *Economic Weekly* (Annual), Bombay 10(4): pp.149-52.

Bose, N.K. and Sinha, S. (1961). Peasant life in India : a study in unity and diversity. Calcutta : Anthropological Survey of India.

Bracey, H.E. (1959). *English rural life*. London: Routledge and Kegan Paul.

Brain, J. Murton (1975). Territorial and resource structure of Tamil villages in 1880: implications for settlement evolution. in W. Brockie (ed.) *Proceedings of the International Geographical Regional Conference*. Hamilton: N.Z. Geographical Society. pp. 219 -33.

(1976) Territory, social structure and settlement dynamics in Tamil Nadu before 1800 A.D. *Pacific View Point*, New Zealand. 17(1): pp.3-22.

Carstairs, G. Morris. (1952). Bhail villages of Western Udaipur. *The Economic Weekly*, Bombay 4(9): pp.231-38. Reproduced in, M.N. Srinivas. (ed.) India's villages.

Chandhoke, S.K. (1963). A study of the functioning of 100 village *panchayats* in Ludhiana district. Conducted by the Graduate students of the Punjab Agricultural University, Ludhiana during the Summer of 1963. An unpublished report.

(1970). Experience in a rural housing project and its sociological implications. Paper presented at a Study Group meeting of sociologists and other social scientists that met in the Lady Irwin College, New Delhi.

(1972). The Tana Bhagats of Chotanagpur (conflict with the existing society). Vanyajati, New Delhi 20 (3-4): pp.128-44.

(1973a). The problem of rural housing - a solution. Sunday World, the *Hindustan Times*, New Delhi. III(32): pp.6.
This article has been reproduced in Rural Plan, Punjab Engineering College, Chandigarh. XV (1-3): pp.1-5.

(1973b). Rural habitation patterns. Seminar presented at the Delhi School of Economics, University of Delhi, Delhi.

(1974a). Types of rural habitation patterns - report on a research in progress. Paper presented at the Twelfth All-India Sociological Conference, Varanasi.

(1974b). Towards facing the housing crisis in village India; an approach. *Civic Affairs*, Kanpur. XXI (11): pp.17-23.

(1976a). Types of Rural Habitation Patterns, Master of Literature Thesis submitted in the University of Delhi, Delhi.

(1976b). Caste segregation in villages, *The Hindustan Times*, New Delhi, April 16, 1976. p. 7.

(1976c). Towards a better rural habitat. *The Hindustan Times*, New Delhi, October 6, 1976. p. 7

(1976d). Review of the book *The Human Settlements We Need*, by C.A. Doxiadis. New Delhi, Tata-McGraw Hill Publishing Company Limited, 1976. Published in *The Hindustan Times* Weekly, New Delhi, October 17, 1976. P. 14.

(1977a). Rural habitat: making villages livable. *Swasth Hind* (English), Special Number on "Habitat". Central Health Eduction Bureau (Ministry of Health and Family Planning, Government of India), New Delhi. February, 1977: pp.34-7.

(1977b). *Chaupal*: The traditional village centre, Haryana, India. *EKISTICS*, Athens. 43(257): pp.221-223

(1977c). *Chaupal* - the men's community place in a Jat vllage of Haryana, India. *Urban and Rural Planning Thought*, New Delhi. 20(1): pp.24-31.

(1977d). *Rural Housing Demonstration Project, Village Bankner*, Delhi 1976-77, (Ed.). New Delhi, Rural Housing Wing, School of Planning and Architecture.

(1977e). Housing conditions in rural India. *India International Centre Quarterly*, New Delhi. 4(2): pp.172-235.

(1978a). Segregation of sexes and use of spaces. Seminar presented at the Delhi School of Ecnomics, University of Delhi, Delhi.

(1978b). Rural housing and village planning in India. Paper presented at the two-day All India Seminar on Role of Technology for Rural Development, organized by the Government Polytechnic, Gorakhpur, on May 17-18, 1978 on the occasion of their Golden Jubilee Celebrations.

(1978c). The habitation pattern of a Jat village of Haryana, India. *EKISTICS*, Athens. 45(270): 229.

(1978d). Haryana village : a study of ethno-linguistic groups. *Urban and Rural Planning Thought*, New Delhi. 21(3-4): pp.122-38.

(1979). The deluge : a social leveller. *India International Centre* Quarterly, New Delhi. 6(4) : pp.341-50.

(1980). The human habitation in India : an anthropological approach. *EKISTICS*, Athens. 47(283): pp.296-300.

(1981). Socio-cultural dimensions of human environment. Paper presented at the International Conference on Environmental Education, New Delhi, December 16-20, 1981.

(1982a). Problem of rural housing in India. Paper presented at the IGU International Symposium on Engery Resources, Environment & Habitat Transformation in Developing Countries. Meerut (India), March 16-20, 1982.

(1982b). The Indian village communities : trustees of unity in the land of diversities. Paper presented at the XVIth All India Sociological Conference, Annamalai University, Annamalai Nagar. December 29-31, 1982.

(1983a). The human environment : role of socio-cultural factors in man's adaptation to physical environment - with special reference to habitat. Paper presented at the XIth International Congress of Anthropological and Ethnological Sciences, Quebec City and Vancouver (Canada), August 14-25, 1983.

(1983b). Importance of forests in tribal life. Paper presented at the Seminar on Forests and Tribals. Organized by the Indian Environmental Society, New Delhi. November 1-2, 1983.

(1983c) The multi-village panchayat - a nesting series in Jat villages of Haryana, India, *EKISTICS*, Athens, 50(298) : pp.29-34.

(1983d). Housing and the weaker sections. Paper accepted for the National Symposium on Anthropology and The Weaker Sections. Ranchi (India). December 31, 1983 to January 2, 1984.

(1985a). Socio-cultural dimensions of heritage conservation. Paper presented at the Workshop on Heritage Conservation. New Delhi, June 5-6, 1985.

(1985b). Environmental impact assessment : some socio-cultural dimensions. Paper accepted for Training Workshop on Environment Impact Assessment, organized by the International Society for Environmental Education (ISEE) in association with the International Centre for Integrated Mountain Development (ICIMOD) in Kathmandu (Nepal). June 9-13, 1985.

(1985c). Human settlements in India in 2000 and beyond with special reference to Delhi - a case study. Keynote Address delivered at the International Seminar on Human Settlements in 2000 A.D. and Beyond, jointly organized by the World Society for Ekistics and the Athens Centre of Ekistics, in Athens (Greece), July 9-11, 1985.

(1985d). The under-privileged sections and their habitation. Paper presented at the National Symposium on the Problems of the Under-privileged Communities, organized by the Indian Anthropological Association and the International Union of Anthropological Sciences, New Delhi. December 30, 1985 to January 1, 1986.

(1986a). Housing and built environment in rural North India. Paper presented at the XIth World Congress of Sociology organized by the International Sociological Association and the Indian Sociological Society, New Delhi, August 18-22, 1986.
(This paper is being printed in a book containing selected papers presented at the World Congress).

(1986b). Housing and planning : cultural factors and innovations. Paper presented at the World Planning and Housing Congress 1986, organised by the Royal Australian Planning Institute, Eastern Regional Organization for Planning and Housing and the International Federation for Housing and Planning, in Adelaide (Australia) September 28 - October 3, 1986.

(1987a). Kuwan : water source and the traditional social centre for women, Haryana villages, India. Paper accepted for publication in a special issue (on women) of *EKISTICS*, Athens.

(1987b). Role of informal (Co-operative) Associations in providing urban/civic amenities - three case studies. Paper accepted for the International Seminar on Housing and Urban Management Through Co-operatives, jointly organized by Kent-Koop (Turkey) and International Co-operative Alliance (U.K.) in Ankara during September 13-16, 1987.

Chandhoke, S.K. and Singh, K.B. (1968). The study of planning pattern of existing houses in villages - Bharatpur Region - (Rupbas and Bayana in particular). School of Planning and Architecture, New Delhi, Mimeographed.

(1969). The study of planning pattern of existing houses in villages - Saharanpur Region - (Roorkee Tehsil in particular). School of Planning and Architecture, New Delhi. Mimeographed.

(1974). Village housing conditions in the Bharatpur region, Eastern Rajasthan, India. *EKISTICS*, Athens 38(224): pp.67-72.

Charles, Green (1965). *House and home*, in David Oakley and K. Raman Unni (ed.) the *Rural Habitat*, New Delhi : School of Planning & Architecture.

Chaudhury, K.N. Shyam (1955). Territorial arrangement, tradition and village organization in Car Nicobar Islands. Bulletin of the Department of Anthropology, Government of India, Calcutta 4(2): pp.1-12.

Chauhan, B.R. (1960). An Indian village : some questions. *Man in India*, Ranchi 40(2): pp.116-127.

(1964). Residential concentrations and caste groupings in rural setting. *Man in India*, Ranchi 44(2): pp.175-81.

(1967). *A Rajasthan village*. New Delhi: Vir Publishing House.

Collin, Roser (1952). A hermit village in Kulu. *Economic Weekly*, Bombay 4: pp.477-82. Reproduced in M. N. Srinivas. (ed.) India's Villages.

Crooke, W. (1918). The house in India from the point of view of sociology and folklore. *Folklore*, London. Vol. 27.

Cunningham, Clarke E. (1964). *Order in Atoni house*. Bijdragen tot taal-land-n-Volkenkunde, Hague 120: pp.34-68.

Desai, A.R. (1961). *Rural Sociology in India*, Bombay : The Indian Society of Agricultural Economics.

Douglas, Mary (1968a). *Purity and danger : A comparative study of concepts of pollution and taboo*. London : Routledge and Kegan Paul.

(1968b). *Pollution.* In New International Encyclopaedia of Social Sciences.The Macmillan Companyand the Free Press, U.S.A. pp. 336-42.

Dube, S.C. (1954). A Deccan village. *Economic Weekly*, Bombay 6(19-20) : pp. 526-29 and pp.553-54.

(1956). *Indian village.* Foreword by Opler, M. E. London : Routledge and Kegan Paul. Second Impression.

(1958). India's changing villages : human factor in community development. London : Routledge and Kegan Paul.

Durkheim, Emile (1965). *The elementary forms of religious life.* New York : Macmillan. First published in 1951.

Durkheim, E. and Mauss, M. (1963). *Primitive classification.* Translated into English, edited and with an introduction by Needham, Rodney. London: Cohen and West.

Ellis, T.P. (1917). Notes on Punjab customs. Lahore : Civil and Military Press.

Emiko, Ohnuki-Tierney (1972). Spatial concepts of the Ainu of the North-west Coast of Southern Sakhalin. *American Anthropologist*, Washington 74(2): pp.426-57.

Fene Genup (1965). *The forest of symbols.* Cornell : Cornell University Press.

Firth, R. (1956). *Human types.* London: Nelson. Revised Edition.

Forde, C. Deryll *1963. Habitat, economy and society.* New York: E.P. Dutton and Co.

Fox, Richard. G. (Ed.) 1970. *Urban India : Society, space and image.*

Gangulee, N. (1935). *Indian peasant and his environment.* With a foreword by Sir Stanley Reed. London: Humphrey Milford Oxford University Press.

Gerald, Berreman D. (1963). *Hindus of Himalayas.* Bombay : University of California Press.

Ghurye, G.S. (1960). *After a century and a quarter : Lonikand then and now.* Bombay: Popular Parkashan Depot.

Gough, Kathleen and Schneider, David M. (1960). *Matrilineal kinship.* California : University of California Press.

Grierson, George A. (1926). *Bihar peasant life.* Patna: Government of Bihar Miscellaneous Official Publications.

Hall, E.T. (1959). *The silent language*, New York : Doubleday.

(1966). *The hidden dimension.* New York: Doubleday.

Honigman, J. (1954). The men's house in West Pakistan (a survey based on three villages). *Eastern Anthropologist*, Lucknow 7(3-4): pp.130-37.

Iyer, Ananthakrishna, L.K. (1928). The Mysore tribes and castes. Mysore: Mysore University.

(1937). An ethnographic survey of the Coorgs. Presidential Address, Section of Anthropology. Proceedings of the twenty-fourth Indian Science Congress, Calcutta : pp.311-32.

Karve, Iravati (1957). *The Indian village*. Bulletin of the Deccan College Research Institute, Poona. Taraporewalla Volume 18: pp.74-106.

Karve, Iravati and Damle, Yashwant Bhaskar (1963). Group relations in village community. Poona: Deccan College.

Khan, C.G. Hussain (1977). Okkar: The basic unit of Kodava organization. *The Eastern Anthropologist*, Lucknow. 30(1): pp.1-14.

Kuper, Hilda (1972). The language of sites in the politics of space. *American Anthropologist*, Washington 74(2): pp.411-25.

Levi-Strauss, Claude (1963). *Structural anthropology*. Translated by Claire Jacobson and Brooke Grundfest Schoepf. London: The Penguin Press.

Lewis, Oscar (1958). *Village life in Northern India: Studies in a Delhi village*. New York: Vintage Books.

Lutt, Jurgen (1987). The village community from Marx to Weber : the Indo-Germanic connection. Paper presented at the International Seminar on Karl Marx and Max Weber: Relevance to Contemporary Society. New Delhi, October 7-10.

Madan, T.N. (1965). *Family and kinship : A study of the Pandits of rural Kashmir*. New Delhi : Asia Publishing House.

Maine, H.S. (1876). *Village communities in the east and west*. London: John Murray.

Malhotra, S.P. and Bharara, L.P. (1963). Socio-economic factors in a desert village. *Economic Review*, A.I.C.C. New Delhi 15(5): pp.23-7.

Malhotra, S.P. Bharara, L.P. and Joshi, P.L. (1966). Impact of land, water and vegetation resources on the economy of a desert village. Annals of the Central Arid Zone Research Institute, Jodhpur 5(2): pp. 219-28.

Masters, A. (1957). Housing in an Indian village. *Population Review*, Madras 13(1-2): pp.52-56.

Mathur, K.K. (1967). *Nicobar Islands.* New Delhi: National Book Trust.

Mayer, Adrian C. (1952). *Land and society in Malabar.* With a preface by Raymond Firth. London: Geofferey Cumberlege.

(1960). *Caste and kinship in Central India.* London : Routledge and Kegan Paul.

(1961). *Peasants in the Pacific: A study of the Fiji Indian rural society.* London : Routledge and Kegan Paul.

Meggitt, M.T. (1957). *House building among the Mae Enga.* Western Highlands, Territory of New Guinea. Oceania, Sydney 27(3): pp.162-76.

Miller, Eric J. (1952). Village structure in North Kerala. *Economic Weekly*, Bombay 4: pp.159-64. Reproduced in M.N. Srinivas. (ed.) India's Villages.

(1954). Caste and territory in Malabar. *American Anthropologist*, Washington 56(3): pp.410-20.

Morgan, L.H. (1881). House and house life of the American aboriginals. Washington: Government Building Office. Volume IV of *Contributions to North American Ethnology.* Reproduced in 1965, with a foreword by Paul Bohnnan. Chicago: Chicago University Press. Classics in Antrhopology Series.

Nath, V. (1962). Village, caste and community. *Economic Weekly*, Bombay 14(49): pp.1877-88.

Nath, Y.V.S. (1954). Bhils of Ratanmal : lineage and local community. *Economic Weekly*, Bombay 6(49): pp.1355-60.

Needham, Rodney (1954). A structural analysis of Purum society. *American Anthropologist*, Washington 56(3): pp.410-20.

1963 Refer to Durkheim, E. and Mauss, M. 1963.

Nelson, Lowry (1952). *Rural sociology.* New York, American Book Co.

Newell, Lowry W. H. (1952). A Himalayan village. *Economic Weekly*, Bombay 4(8): pp.208-20.

(1957). A Gadi house in a Goshen village, Chamba State, North India. *Man*, London 57: pp.24-5.

Opler, M. E. (61956-57). The extensions of an Indian village. *Journal of Asian Studies*, Harward 16(1): pp.5-10.

Opler, M.E. and Singh, R.D. (1948). Divison of labour in an Indian village. In, Coon, Carleton, S. Ed. a reader in *General Anthropology.* New York: Henry Holt and Company. pp.464-96.

(1952). Two villages of Eastern Uttar Pradesh (U.P.) : an analysis of similarities and differences. *American Anthropologist*: Washington 54(2): pp.179-91.

Pandit, Trilokinath (1959). The Gujjars of Kashmir valley : some observations on their ecology and social organisation. *Vanyajati*, Delhi 7(2): pp.64-71.

Panikkar, R. (1986). There is no outer without inner space. Paper presented at the International Seminar on Inner & Outer Space. New Delhi, November 20-26.

Peal, S.E. (1892). The communal barracks of primitive races. Journal of the Asiatic Society of Bengal, Calcutta.

Pillai, G. Shankara (1986). Spatial relationship from the outer to the inner - in ritual and performance. Paper presented at the International Seminar on Inner & Outer Space. New Delhi, November 20-26.

Radcliffe-Brown, A.R. (1964). *Structure and function in primitive society*. London: Cohen and West.

Ramanna, Raja (1986). Physical space in the context of all knowledge. Key-note paper presented at the International Seminar on Inner & Outer Space. New Delhi, November, 20-26.

Randhawa, M.S. and Prem Nath (1959). *Farmers of India*. I. New Delhi: Indian Council of Agricultural Research.

Randhawa, M. S. Sivaraman, M.S. and Naidu, I.J. (1961). Farmers of India. II. Delhi: Indian Council of Agricultural Research.

Rao, C. Hayavadana (1923-24). Rural habitations in South India. Quarterely Journal of the Mythic Society, Bangalore 14(4): pp.313-23.

Rao, V.K.R.V. and Desai, P.B. (1965). *Greater Delhi : A study in urbanization 1940-57*. Bombay: Asia.

Risley, Herbert (1915). *The people of India : Calcutta.*

Rivers, W.H.R. (1906). *The Todas*, London: Macmillan.

Rohitsingh, N. (1972). Manipur villages. Unpublished MS.

Roy, S.C. (1915). Orientation of grave-stones and houses in Chotanagpur. Journal of the Bihar and Orissa Research Society, Patna 1 : pp.277-80.

(1920). Distribution and nature of Asur sites in Chotanagpur. Journal of the Bihar and Orissa Research Society, Patna 6: pp.393-423.

Sachchidananda (1953). The tribal village as a social unit. Journal of the Bihar Research Society, Ranchi 39: pp.185-93.

1956 Social structure of a Chotanagpur village. Proceedings of the Indian Science Congress, Calcutta 43(3): p. 327.

Saraswati, Baidyanath (1984). The spectrum of the sacred : essays on the religious tradition of India. Ranchi : Anthropological Series (6).

Sarma, Jyotirmoyee (1952). The village organisation of the Kanikhars. *Man In India*, Ranchi 32(2): pp.64-81.

(1953). A Bengal village. *Economic Weekly*, Bombay 5(32-34): pp.901-910.

Shah, A.M. (1955). A dispersed hamlet in the Panchmahals. *Ecnomic Weekly*, Bombay 7(4-5): pp.109-16.

(1956). Caste, economy and territory in Central Panchamahals. Journal of Maharaja Saiyajirao University of Baroda, Baroda 4(1): pp.65-91.

(1973). *The household dimension of the family in India*. New Delhi: Orient Longmans Limited.

Sims, N.L. (1928). *Elements of rural sociology*. New York: Thomas, Y. Crowell.

Singh, K.B. and Ghandhoke, S.K. (1966). Village housing scheme in Lalgarh - an assessment. *Rural Housing Wing News Letter*, School of Planning and Architecture, New Delhi 6(3-4): pp.1-22.

(1967). Bhawanpura research-cum-demonstration project - an assessment. *Rural Housing Wing News Letter*, School of Planning and Architecture, New Delhi 7(1-2): pp.1-16.

Singh, R.D. (1956-57). The unity of an Indian village. *Journal of Asian Studies*, Harward 16(1): pp.10-19.

Singh, S. J. (1933). Habitations of the Maitais. *Man In India*, Ranchi 13(2-3): pp.165-88.

Sivertsen, Dogfinn (1963). *When caste barriers fall : A study of social and economic change in a South Indian village*. Norway: George Allen & Unvin Ltd.

Slocum, Walter L. (1962). *Agricultural sociology*. New York: Haper.

Smith, W. Marian (1952). The misal : a structural village group of India and Pakistan. *American Anthropologist*, Washington 54(1): pp.41-56.

Srinivas, M.N. (1951). The social structure of a Mysore village. *Economic Weekly*, Bombay 3(42-43): pp.1051-56.

(1954). Village studies. *Economic Weekly*, Bombay 6(22): pp.605-8.

(1955). *India's villages*. Bombay : Asia Publishing House.

(1956). The nature of the problem of Indian unity. *Economic Weekly*, Bombay 10(17): pp.571-77.

(1965). *Religion and society among the Coorgs of South India*. Oxford: Oxford University Press. Revised Edition.

Srinivas, M.N. and Shah, A.M. (1960). The myth of the self-sufficiency of the Indian village. *Economic Weekly*, Bombay 12(37): pp.1375-78.

Srivastava, L.R.N. (1962). *Gallongs.* Shillong: Advertisers Secretariat.

Staal Frits (1986). The centre of space : construction and discovery. Paper presented at the International Seminar on Inner & Outer Space. New Delhi, November 20-26.

Stephen, Fuchs (1960). *The Gonds and Bhumia of Eastern Mandla.* Bombay: Asia Publishing House.

Tambiah, S.J. (1969). Animals are good to think and good to prohibit. *Ethnology,* an International Journal of Cultural Anthropology. University of Pitsburg, Pitsburg 8(4): pp.423-59.

Tod, James (1957). *Annals and antiquities of Rajasthan.* London: Routledge and Kegan Paul. Originally Published in 1914.

Trivedi, H.R. (1961). *Mers of Saurashtra : an exposition of their social structure and organisation.* Baroda: Baroda University.

Unni, K.R. (1965). Rural house types. *Rural Housing Wing News Letter*, School of Planning and Architecture, New Delhi 5(2): pp.1-11.

Van Der Kroff, Justus M. (1954). Dualism and symbolic antithesis in Indonesian society. *American Anthropologist*, Washington 56(5): pp.847-862.

Vannucci, M. (1986). Sacred groves or holy forests. Paper presented at the International Seminar on Inner & Outer Space. New Delhi, November, 20-26.

Weiser, W.H. (1936). *The Hindu jajmani system.* Lucknow: Lucknow Publishing House.

Weiser, William H. and Weiser, Carlotte Viall (1951). *Behind mud walls.* New York: Agricultural Mission Inc.

B. GEOGRAPHY

Ackerman, E.A. (1941). Sequent occupance of a Boston, Suburban community. *Economic Geography*, Worcestor 17: pp.61-74.

Afsaruddin, M. (1964). *Rural life in Eastern Pakistan : A study of five selected villages.* Decca : Department of Social Studies, University of Decca.

Ahlmann, N. W. (1928). The geographical study of settlements. *Geographic Review*, New York 19(1): pp.93-128.

Ahmad, Enayat (1952). Rural settlement types in the Uttar Pradesh (United Provinces of Agra and Oudh). Annals of the Association of American Geographers, New York 42(3): pp.223-46.

Ahmad, Nafis (1956). The pattern of rural settlement in East Pakistan. *Geographical Review*, New York 46(3): pp.388-89. Rural Communities of East Bengal Series.

Ansari, Saiyad Hasan (1968). *Evolution and spatial organization of clan settlements: A case study of middle Ganga valley*. New Delhi: Concept Publishing Company.

Augelli, John P. (1952). Rural settlement types of interior Puerto Rico: sample studies from the Upper Loiza Basin. *Journal of Geography*, Miami 51: pp.1-13.

Aurousseau, M. (1920). The arrangements of rural population. *Geographical Review*, New York 10: pp.223-40.

Bhattacharya, A.N. (1956). Effect of tribal and caste factor on rural settlements in Uttar Pradesh, evolution and importance of the caste system. *The Indian Geographical Journal*, Madras 31 (3-4): pp.94-101.

Bhattacharya, A.N. and Verma, L.N. (1956-57).

Bhattacharya, A.N. and Vyas Ravindra Nath (1979). *Habitat, economy and society*. New Delhi : Concept Publishing Company.

Blache, P. Vidal De La. (1956). *Principles of human geography*. Emmanuel, De Mortonne. Ed. Translated from French by Millicent, Todd Bingham. London: Constable Publishers.

Bose, S.C. (1960). Nomadism in high valleys of Uttarkhand and Kumaon. *Geographical Reveiw of India*, Calcutta 22(3): pp.34-9.

(1962). Rural settlement and land-use: an essay in location. London: Hutchinsons.

Chisholm, Michael (1970). *Geography and Economics*. London, C. Bell and Sons. 2nd Edition.

Cozzens, A.B. (1938). The geographical background of some Mexican house types. *Annals of the Association of American Geographers*, New York 28: pp.43-4.

Cunningham, A. (1871). *Ancient geography of India*. London.

Davis, Kingsley (1951). *The population of India and Pakistan*. Princeton, New Jersey: Princeton University Press.

Demangeon, A. (1925-26). Agricultural system and schemes of distribution of population in Western Europe. *(The Geographical Teacher)*, 12: pp.199-205.

(1962). The origin and causes of settlements, in Wagner and Milkesell (ed.) *Readings in cultural geography*. Chicago: Chicago University Press. pp.506-17.

Desai, Anjana. P.A. (1985). *Spatial aspects of settlement patterns: A study of the Narmada Command Area of Mahesana District, Gujarat*. Foreword by A.B. Mukerji. New Delhi : Concept Publishing Company.

Dickinson, R.E. (1949). Rural settlements in German lands. *Annals of the Association of American Geographers*, New York 39(2): pp.239-63.

Durand, L. Jr. (1943). Dairy barns of Southeastern Wisconsin. *Economic Geography*, Worcestor 19(1): pp.37-44.

Edward, W. Soja (1980). The socio-spatial dilectic. Annals of the Association of American Geographers, New York 70: pp.207-25.

Finch, W.C. and Trewertha, G.T. (1946). *Elements of geography : physical and cultural*. New York: Lydolph & Laknewska.

Finlay, R. and Scott, E. M. (1940). A great lakes-to-gulf profile of dispersed dwelling types. *Geographical Review*, New York 30: pp.412-19.

Gates, D.S. (1933). The Sod houses. *Journal of Geography*, Miami 32: pp.353-59.

Hall, R.B. (1931). Some rural settlement patterns in Japan. *Geographical Review*, New York 21(1): pp.93-123.

Hudson, F.S. (1970). *Geography of settlements*. London: Macdonald and Evans.

Hudson, J.C. (1969). A location theory of rural settlements. *Annals of the Association of American Geography*, New York 54: pp.365-81.

Janki, V.A. (1953). *Geographical basis for the distribution and pattern of rural settlements in Kerala*. Journal of Maharaja Sayaji Rao University of Baroda, Baroda 2(2): pp.42-54.

(1957). *Historical geography of settlements in Kerala*. Journal of the Maharaja Sayaji Rao University of Baroda, Baroda 5(2): pp.57-76.

Jones, Emrys (1964). *Human geography*. New York: Chatto and Windus.

Kayastha, S.L. (1964). *The Himalayan Beas basin: a study in habitat, economy and society*. Varanasi: Banaras Hindu University.

Kaushic, S. D. (1959). Types of human settlements in Jaunsar Himalaya. *Geographical Review of India*, Calcutta 21 (2-4): pp.1-17.

Kohn, Chayde F. (1954). Settlement geography. in, Preston, E. James and Clarence, F. John. (ed.) *American Geography*. New York: Syracause University Press for Association of American Geographers.

Kniffe, F.B. (1936). Louisiana house types. *Annals of the Association of American Geographers*, New York 26: pp.179-93.

Lee, D.H.K. (1951). Thoughts on housing for the humid tropics. *Geographical Review*, New York 41: pp.124-27.

(1953). *Psychological objectives in hot weather housing*. Washington: United States Housing and Home Finance Agency.

Meston, B. (1935). The geography of an Indian village. *Geography*, New York.

Mobgunge, Akin L.

Money, D.C. (1967). *Introduction to human geography*. London: University Tutorial Press Limited.

Mukerji, A.B. (1957). Jat settlements and habitations. *Indian Geographical Journal*, Madras 32(1-2): pp.13-28.

Mukerji A. B. (1956-57). Nomenclature of Jat villages. *The Geographer*. 8-9: pp.19-26

Platt, Robert S. (1959). Field study in American geography: the development of theory and method examplified by selections. Department of Geography Research paper No. 1. Chicago, Illinois.

Scofield, E. (1938). The origin of settlement patterns in rural New England. *Geographical Review*, New York 28(4): pp.652-63.

Semple, E.C. (1947). *Influence of geographical environment*. New York: Henry Holt.

Sharma, R.C. (1972). *Settlement geography of Indian desert*. New Delhi: Kumar Brothers.

Singh, K.N. (1972). An approach to the study of the morphology of the Indian village, in Singh, R.L. (ed.) *Rural settlements in monsoon Asia*. Proceedings of the I G U Symposium at Varanasi and Tokyo. National Geographical Society of India, Varanasi.

Singh, R.B. (1975). *Rajput: clan settlements in Varanasi district*. Edited by. R.L. Singh. Varanasi, National Geographical Society of India, research publication. 12.

Singh, R.L. (1957). Typical rural dwellings in the Umland of Banaras. *National Geographical Journal of India*, Varanasi III Part II: pp.51-64.

Singh, R.L., Singh, K.N. and Singh, Rana P.B. (ed.) (1975). *Readings in rural settlement geography*. Varanasi: National Geographical Society of India Research Publication 14.

Singh, R.L., Singh, Rana P.B. (1980). *Rural habitat transformation in world frontiers*. Varanasi : National Geographical Society of India.

Singh, Sant Bahadur (1977). *Rural settlement geography: A case study of Sultanpur district*. Gorakhpur: Uttar Pradesh Bhoogol Parishad Gorakhpur.

Spate, O.H.K. (1952). The Indian village. *Geography*, New York 37(1): pp.142-52.

(1957). *India and Pakistan - A general and regional geography*. London: Methuen. 2nd edition.

Trewertha, T. Glenn (1946). Types of rural settlements in colonial America. *Geographical Review*, New York 36(4): pp.568-96.

Wagner, Philip L. (1962). *Readings in cultural geography*, Chicago: University of Chicago Press.

Whittlesey, D. (1929). Sequence occupance. *Annals of the Association of American Geographers*, New York 19(1): pp.162-65.

Yonekura, J. (1961). Comparative study of East Asian and Indian villages. Comparative geography in general with reference to social structure affecting the village pattern. *Geographical Review of India*, Madras 23(3): pp.6-15.

C. CLASSICAL SANSKRITIC LITERATURE

Acharya, P.K. (1927). *A dictionary of Hindu architecture*. Bombay: Oxford University Press.

(1934). *Architecture of Mansara*. Translated in English. Bombay: Oxford University Press.

(1946). *An encyclopaedia of Hindu architecture*. Bombay: Oxford University Press.

Agarvala, V.S. (1953). *India as known to Panini*. Lucknow: Lucknow University.

Apte, V.M. (1954). *Spatial and religious life in Griha Sutras*. Bombay: The Popular Parkashan Depot.

Baumer Bettina (1986). From guha to akasa : the mystical cave in the Vedic and Saiva traditions. Paper presented at the International Semiar on Inner & Outer Space. New Delhi, November 20-26.

Chakladar, Harnam. Chandar (1954). *Social life in ancient India*. Calcutta: Greater Indian Society. Originally published 1954.

Chaudhuri, S.B. (1955). Ethnic settlements in ancient India : a study of the Puranic lists of the peoples of Bharatvarsa. Part I. *North India*. Calcutta: General Printers and Publishers.

Jha, B. (1955). *Village in ancient India*. Journal of the Bihar Research Society, Ranchi 41(1):pp.68-86.

Jitatmananda Swami (1986). Chidakasha & Bhutakasha (The Indian view from the standpoint of modern physics). Paper presented at the International Seminar on Inner & Outer Space, New Delhi, November 20-26.

Kramrisch Stella (1986). Space in Indian cosmology and in architecture. Paper presented at the International Seminar on Inner & Outer Space, New Delhi, November 20-26.

Nilkanthasastri, K.A. (1963). Village in ancient India. *Illustrated Weekly of India*, Bombay 84(B113): pp.37-9.

Oldenberg, Hermann and Max Muller (S. B. E.) (1964). *Griha Sutras* Part I. Delhi: Motilal Banarasi Das. First published by Oxford University Press 1904.

Shamasastry, R. (1967). *Kautaliya Arthasastra* (transalated). Mysore: Mysore Printing and Publishing House. First published 1923.

Shastri, Manmatha Nath Dutt (1967). *Agni Purana* (A prose English translation), 2 vols. Varanasi: Chowkhamba Sanskritic Series Office. Chowkhamba Sanskritic Series 54. Originally published 1903-4.

Sukla, D.N. (1961). *Vastu-Sastra*, 1 (with special reference to Bhoja's Samrangana-Sutradhara). Lucknow: Vastu-Vanmaya-Parkasana-Sala.

Upadhyay, B.S. (1947). *India in Kalidasa*. Allahabad: S. Chand & Co.

D. HUMAN ECOLOGY AND EKISTICS

Athens Centre of Ekistics (1970). *EKISTICS*. Athens Centre of Ekistics, Athens:

Dastur, Aloo, J. (1954). *Man and his environment*. Bombay : The Popular Book Depot.

Doxiadis, C.A. (1963). *Architecture in transition*. London: Hutchinson.

(1968). *Ekistics, an introduction to the science of human settlements*. London: Hutchinson.

Mukerjee, Radhakamal (1928). The social ecology of a river valley. *Sociology and Social Research*, California 12(4): pp.341-47.

(1946). *Social ecology*. Calcutta: Orient Longmans.

(1968). *Man and his habitation*. Bombay: Popular Parkashan.

Nicholas, Ralph (1963). Ecology and village structure in deltaic West Bengal. *Economic Weekly*: Bombay 5(28-30): pp.1185-96.

Quinn, James A. (1950). *Human ecology*. New York: Prentice-Hall.

Waston, O.M. and Greaves, T.D. (1966). Quantitative research in proxemic behaviour. *American Anthropologist*, Washington 68(4): pp.971-85.

E. ARCHITECTURE AND PLANNING, INCLUDING REGIONAL SCIENCE

Clarke, L. David (ed.) (1977). *Spatial archaeology*. Cambridge : Peterhouse.

George Michell. (ed.) (1978). *Architecture of the Islamic world, its history and social meaning*. New York : William Morrow and Company, Inc..

Ghose, Benoy (1953). *Primitive Indian architecture*. Calcutta: K.L. Mukhopadhyay.

Ghosh, Bijit and Kulshrestha, S.K. (1973). A development plan for Chhatera village. *Urban and Rural Planning Thought*, School of Planning and Architecture, New Delhi 16(3): pp.121-47.

Havell, E.B. (1915). *The ancient and medieval architecture of India: A study of Indo-Aryan civilization*. London: John Murray.

(1927). *Indian architecture (its psychology, structure and history from the first Muhammadan invasion to the present day)*. London: John Murray.

Kennedy, R.W. (1953). *The house and the art of its design*. New York: Reinhold Publishing Corporation. Progresive Arhitecture Library.

Morris, R.N. and Mogey, John (1965). *The sociology of housing*. London: Routledge and Kegan Paul.

Rapoport, Amos (1969). *House form and culture*. With a foreword by Wagner, L.Phillip. New Jersey: Prentice-Hall.

(1970). The study of spatial quality. *Journal of Aesthetic Eduction* 4(4): pp.80-95.

(1975). The mutual interaction of man and his built environment: a cross-cultural perspective. The Hague: Mouton. World Anthropology Series.

Ray, Amita (1960). *Towns, villages and secular buildings in ancient India*. Calcutta: Mukhopadhyay.

Sasi Kumar (1963). Coastline of Kerala: evolving a settlement structure. Unpublsihed Master's thesis. School of Planning and Architecture, New Delhi.

Vanne, Troph (1965). Village settlements of Delhi and Punjab. Unpublished thesis for the degree of Master of Architecture, University of Melbourne, Parkville, Australia.

Volwahsen, Andres (1969). *Living architecture: Indian*. Foreword by Walter Henn. Calcutta: Oxford and IBH Publishing Company.

Wagner, L. Phillip. (1969). Refer to Rapoport, Amos (1969).

F. CENSUS OF INDIA, GAZETTEERS AND SETTLEMENT REPORTS.

Baden-Powell, B.H. (1972). The Indian village community: examined with reference to the physical, ethnographic and historical conditions of the provinces: chiefly on the basis of revenue settlement records and District Manuals. Delhi: Cosmo Publications. First published 1896 by Longmans Green, London.

Burman, B.K.Roy (1967). Chetlat - an island in the Arabian Sea. Socio-economic survey report on Cheltat Island, Union Territory of Lacadive, Minicoy and Amindivi. *Census of India 1961*, Vol. I, Monograph Series, Part IV. Delhi : Manager of Publications, Government of India.

(1986). Social processes in the industrialization of Rourkela (with reference to displacement and rehabilitation of tribal and other backward people). *Census of India 1961*, Vol. I, Monograph Series, Part VI. Foreword by Ashok Mitra. Delhi : Manager of Publications, Government of India.

Census of India Publications Part-IV Series. All India and State volumes for 1961 and 1971.

Census of India 1961 and 1971, Part VI, Village Survey Monography Series. Available from the State Census Superintendents.

Chhatera [Report of] (in Urdu)

(1880). Settlement report of Chhatera. Unpublished MS document. District Archives, Office of the Deputy Commissioner, Sonepat.

(1910). Settlement report of Chhatera. Unpublished MS document. Patwari of Chhatera and District Archives, Office of the Deputy Commissioner, Sonepat.

Chopra, Prabha (1976). Delhi Gazetteer. Delhi: Delhi Administration.

Gazetteer of Delhi District (1883-84) N.D. Compiled and published under the authority of the Punjab Government. Calcutta: Calcutta Central Press Company Limited.

Government of India (1966). *National Gazetteer of India*. I. Delhi: Publications Division.

Ibbetson, Denziel Charles Jelf (1883). Report of the revision of settlement of Panipat Tehsil & Karnal Parganas of the Karnal district. 1872-1880. Allahabad: Pioneer Press.

Innes and Evans (1907). *Gazetteer of Malabar*, Madras.

Kiran Prem (1970). *Haryana district gazetteer, Rohtak*. Chandigarh: Haryana Gazetteers Organization, Revenue Department.

Mitra, A. (1966). Report on house types and village settlement patterns in India. Vol. I. Part IV-A(iii). *Census of India, 1961*, Delhi: Manager of Publications, Government of India.

Mukerjee, V. Satya (1932). *Census of India, 1931*. Vol. XIX, Part-I. Report. Baroda. Bombay: Times of India Press.

Purser, W.E. and Fanshawe, H.C. (1880). Report on the revised land revenue settlement of the Rohtak district of the Hissar division in the Punjab. 1873-1879. London: W. Ball Printer.

G. DICTIONARIES AND OTHER REFERENCE BOOKS

Earnest, Weekly and Anne, Scott (1954). *Gem dictionary*. London: Collins.

Macdonald A.M. (ed.) (1972). *Chambers twentieth century new dictionary* (new edition). New Delhi: Allied Publishers Private Ltd.

Platts, John T. (1960). *A dictionary of Urdu, Classical Hindi and English*. London: Oxford University Press.

William, Geddie (ed.) (1964). *Chambrs twentieth century dictionary* (revised edition). New Delhi: Allied Publishers Private Ltd.

GLOSSARY*

ábádí	area reserved for residential use
achár aj	the priest who presides over post-death ceremonies; a caste group
ág	fire
ahlkár	a petty government functionary to discharge duties of an administrative nature, generally attached to the courts of land revenue department
álá	big-sized niche in the wall
álí	small-sized niche in the wall
almárí	almirah
amántí kawálá	trust mortgage
amáwas	the day with the darkest night occurring every two fortnights; *mawas*
án	defect; flaw
anáj	food grains
aobrá	rear closed dark room used mainly as a store
aobre	plural of *aobrá;* store rooms
aobrí	small *aobrá;* small-sized store room
aoṛhní	headgear of women. It is a sheet of long cloth
aragh	offering water to the Sun God or the Moon God, a symbol of welcome to a newcomer, a form of worship
arañṛì	workshop of the *Lohar*

---

* The system of transliteration followed in this book is that of Platts (1960). The diacritical marks have, however, been given in full in the glossary only.

ariyá samáj a modern reformist sect of the Hindus based mainly on the *Vedas*. Founded by Dayanand Saraswati about a century ago this sect discards idolatory and other later tendencies of Hinduism

ártá ceremony of worship or means of honouring someone by rotating before him/her a tray bearing lights and incense

asthal a substantial big-sized structure built with durable materials and used as a place of worship

astrá a weapon which the user keeps on holding while hitting the enemy

aṭárí covered space at the stair-case end at the roof terrace

aṭhgámá an eight-village group

bábá a respectful term generally used for elderly people and saints, etc.

bádsháhí saṛak the King's way, the royal road

bagaṛ open space in a *ghar, gher* or *baithak* when not located in its centre; open space enclosed or flanked by a group/cluster of houses; a closed-ended street occupied by households that are closely related or belong to the same caste

bahí ledger, account book

bahí-bháṭ the ledger of the *bhat* containing ancestral trees of and other information about villagers

bahú daughter-in-law. Every woman married into a village is called the *bahu* of that village

bail bullock

bail-gáḍí bullock-cart

baisákhí festival celebrated in the Punjab on thirteenth April every year, on the eve of harvesting

baiṭhak men's quarters, men's sitting room

bájrá millet; pearl millet

bákhal a closed-ended street belonging to households of the sme caste

bálmíkí new name given to the *Bhangis*, a civilized term for them

balorí flarish minor

Baniyá — trader caste

Banjárá — a caste group whose male members move from village to village to sharpen the grinding wheels and females selling general merchandise and other items of interest to women

Banjáran — woman of *Banjara* caste

banṛá — bridegroom, husband

banṛí — bride, wife

báǹṛì — ceremonial oil bathing and massage given to both, the bride and the groom before wedding

báǹsóǹ ke phúl — flowers of a particular variety grown locally in Chhatera and used on auspicious occasions

báṛá — land outside the *abadi* earmarked for religious purposes with a small structure built on it

báṛá — big-sized earthen pot for storing *ghee*

barámdá — *verandah*

barát — marriage procession of groom's party to bride's village

baṛhautrí — prosperity; increase of posterity; progeny

baríhá — twelve-village group

barmá — handpump for water

bárná — door; generally the term is used for the main door of a residential house, *ghar*

baṛolí — medium-sized earthen-pot in which butter milk is kept for consumption when meals are taken to the fields for those busy working there

barsáwan — winnowing

barsim — a sort of green fodder

básan — vessel/s or utensil/s, generally of brass

basauṛá — balls of cooked *daliya*

bastá — official papers tied in a red cloth; lab

baṭa'í — share-cropping

baṭná — paste made of gram flour, mustard oil, turmeric, etc., used for massaging the body of bride/groom at the *banrn* ceremony

baṭyaú — guest; traveller; son-in-law and his relatives

báwájí — *sadhu*, saint

bázár — market

beáh	marriage; a ceremony about two months before the actual day of marriage when the *purohit* of the bride's side brings some presents to the groom's *ghar* and performs certain ceremonies
be-biswedár	non-land owner
be-mátá	the Goddess who writes the fate of every person at the time of his/her birth
bețí	daughter, every woman is treated as a *beti* in her parents' village
bhábí	brother's wife
Bhádoṅ	the sixth month according to *Bikrami* Calendar. It falls during August-September of the Christian Calendar
bhagwán	god
bhágwán	lucky; fortunate; wealthy
bhá'í-bațwárá	distribution of *abadi* land of the village among the *biswedaran*; distribution among brothers; brotherly distribution
bhá'í-chárá	brotherhood: a type of land tenure
bhajan	devotional song
bhajník	a professional who recites *bhajans*
Bhaṅgan	sweepress, a caste group in the village
Bhaṅgí	sweeper; the lowest caste group in the village
bháṅṇṅjá	sister's son
bhát	gifts by a brother to his sister on the marriage of each of her children
bháț	bard; genealogist
bhátí	he who brings the *bhat*
bhaṭí	hearth
bhatíjá	brother's son
bhelí	lump, weighing about 4 kg
bhít	wall
bhojan	food; meals
bhujkat	three-cornered plot; literally, armless
bhúmíyá	mound of earth raised near the proposed *abadi* before a new village is founded. The first man who dies in the village is burnt or burried on this mound and a masonry shrine is built there. This man is deified as *bhumiya* or the earth-god

and is worshipped by all Hindu residents of the village being looked upon as its sole guardian deity

bhúṛ — waste uncultivable land
biloní — earthen pot for churning curds
biswá — measure of land equal to 5.42 sq.yds.
biswedár — land-lord, land-holder; plural *biswedaran*
biṭorá — a heap of dried cow-dung cakes
Bráhman — the highest caste group in the village community
bukhárí — an indigenous contrivance for storing grains
búṅgá — a heap of wheat and/or barley chaff for animal feed stored in a conically-shaped structure; *kup*
cháchá — father's younger brother
Chait — the first month of the *Bikrami* Calendar
chakí — grinding wheel
chaḷísá — forty-village group
Chamár — leather worker; a caste group; Cobbler
Chamáran — a woman *Chamar*
Chamarvá Paṅḍat — *Purohit* of the *Chamars*
charágáh — common grazing land of the village; *charan*
charán — common grazing land of the village; grazing; *charagah*
charkhá — spinning wheel
chaubárá — room on the first floor of a house with no *verandah* in front of it
chaubáre — plural of *chaubara*
chaubísá — twenty-four-village group
chaugámá — four-village group
chauk — central court
chauk-ká-jál — angle-iron frame fitted with iron bars fixed at the roof level, above the *chauk; jál gajáṅ wálá*
chauká — kitchen; cooking space
chaukbaṅd — a structure with a central court
chaukbaṅd ghar — central court house
chaukbaṅdí — the pattern of building *chaukband ghars*
chaukhaṭ — door/window frame

chaukídár — an important village functionary appointed by the *tehsildar*. His duties include; rounds of the village at night, assisting the village *lambardar* in collection of land revenue, to convey to the villagers any message from the *lambardar* or headman, etc., to run errands within and outside the village, to visit the concerned police station every week and lodge information there about the births and deaths in the village and to attend on the government functionaries visiting the village.

chauṅtrí — small stool-like stone platform on either side of the main entrance of the *ghar*; *saihmchi*

chaupál — community building used exclusively by males

Chawdhury — headman; leader; a prefix used generally for the *Jats*

cheháṅṛíṅ — funeral ground; *masanrn; marghat*

chháchh — sort of butter-milk; *lahsi; sit*

chhapṛí — roof-like straw cover over a cow-dung heap to protect it from rains

chhát — roof terrace

chhát-pitrál — rain water drain to remove water from the *chhat*

chhaṭí — sixth day; the ceremony performed on the sixth day after a childbirth

chháwá — covered space

Chhipí — tailor; a caste group

chhuchhak — presents given to a woman by her fatner or brothers at the time of each childbirth to her

chilam — top (earthen) portion of the *huka* which contains fire and tobacco

chitáh — pyre

chuchí — teat

chúlhá — fire place used for cooking

chúlhá tax — tax levied by the *gram panchayat* within the *ábádi* area on every household/*chúlhá*/hearth

chún — wheat flour

chúṅḍáwaṅḍ — system of inheritance of property where all the sons of a mother get equal share in the property of their father. *Chunda*, literally means, the hair tail of a woman, and *wand* means distribution.

chúṛ — laddle-shaped hearth on the platform in the *chaupal* used for boiling water for the *baratis*

Chúṛhá — sweeper

Chúṛhí — female sweeper

chúṛí — bangle worn by women

dádí — father's mother

dahej — dowry

daheṛ — threshold

dakshiná — after feeding their *Purohit* people make offering of cash to him, this is called *dakshina*; donation

dalán — covered space on either side of the *chauk* in a *ghar*

dalání — small-sized *dalan*

daliyá — bruised wheat, *jowar* or *makai* grain thrown into boiling water and boiled with pulses

dámád — son-in-law; *jamai*

ḍaṅḍá — stick

dar — main door; *barna*

darbár — court

darshan — holy view

darwájá — gate; *baithak* with a wide main gate which can take a tractor in

ḍáṭ — arch

dauhlí — while feeding his *Purohit,* the *jajman* has to make a present, in cash or kind, to the former. This present is called *dauhli*. Some of the well-to-do *jajmans* give a small piece of land to their *Purohit* as *dauhli* while feeding the latter on important occasions like *sharadh*, etc.

deh — sort of account

desí — of local variety

dewtá — god; angel

ḍhakná — earthen-plate for covering various types of jars

dharamshálá — a small road-side structure near the village *abadi* which serves as a resting place/house for travellers in the countryside

ḍholí — drummer

dhuniyá — carder

díwá — earthen-lamp; small lamp

Díwálí	the festival of lights
do-kaṛiyá	any covered space with its depth covered by two rafters
ḍolí	bridal coach
doḷrá	big jute cloth used for agricultural purposes
dúlhá	bridegroom
dulhan	bride
Durgá Bhawání	Goddess of Power, family deity of the *Baniyas*
Dussehrá	festival celebrated in the month of October every year to commemorate the victory of virtuosity over sin
faqír	saint; medicant, generally a Muslim
gáḍí	cart; bullock cart
gaihlaṛ	literally speaking, *gaihlar* is one who comes *gaihl*, i.e., along. When a woman marries a second, or subsequent husband, then the children (from her previous husband/s) who come along with her to the house of her new husband are called *gaihlar*; *khadehlar*
gair-biswedár	non-land-holder
gair-málkán	non-owners, i.e., those who do not own land
gál	street, *gali*
galí	street; *gál*
gaṅḍá	sugarcane
gaṅḍásá	chaff cutter
gá'oṅ	village, village community
gá'oṅ shámlát	property common to the entire village community
garaṛ	grinding wheel
gaudhaná	cow-like, narrow in front and wider at the rear
geṙú	red earth
ghar	house; residential house mainly for women and children
ghaṛiá	medium-sized earthen-pot for storing water
ghar jamá'í	a son-in-law who settles down permanently in his in-laws' place
gher	enclosure; place for cattle
ghee	clarified butter

ghee-ká'-diyá	small lamp burnt with clarified butter
ghoṛí	mare
ghoṛ-chaṛhí	the ceremonial mare ride by the bridegroom
ghuṅgaṭ	veil
gitwáṛ	open plot of land used for some small agricultural operations, for tying cattle, storing fuel and constructing *bitoras, kups*, etc.
gobar	cow-dung
gorá	cattle; place earmarked for cattle outside the village *abadi*
gorá deh	place marked for cattle outside the village *abadi*
Gordhan	believed to have been the *pali* once upon a time
Gordhan Púja	worship of *Gordhan,* believed to have been a *pali*. This *puja* is performed a day before the *Diwali* festival
gosá	cow-dung cake; plural, *gose*
gose	plural of *gosá*; cow-dung cakes
got	non-localized exogamous patrilineal clan; *gotrá*
gotrá	non-localized exogamous patrilineal clan; *got*
grám pancháyát	elected body of villagers to run village administration
grám sewak	village level worker of the development department
grihá	house
grihá parvesh	house-warming ceremony; literally, house entering
grihá-stambhá	in *sanskritic* literature, the term is used for the central post; literally, the pillar of the house; *Mul Stambha*
guṅgní	boiled gram
guṛ	molasses
guru	teacher
gurukul	the residence of the *guru;* a residential training institution
gwárá	an annual plant whose seeds are used as pulse

gyáras — the eleventh day of a *paksha* according to *Bikrami* Calendar

hadwáṛí — a place where dead cattle is taken and its skin is removed there; literally, a place for bones

hal — plough

haldí — turmeric

hálí — man behind the plough

halwá'í — sweet-meat maker

hárá — removable hearth that can be shifted according to requirements

Harijan — the children of *Hari,* i.e., God; people belonging to untouchable castes

Haryánvís — those belonging to the State of Haryana

háth — hand; arm length (18") used as a measure of length

hawan — purificatory fire lit on the occasion of life-cycle ceremonies and on festivals etc.

hawelí — spacious *pacca* double-storeyed residential structure

hissedár — partner, share-holder; literally, *hissa* means share

ho'í — festival celebrated for the welfare of children

Holí — festival of colours

Holiká — sister of King Harnakashyapa; bonfire burnt during *holi*

homá — purificatory fire; *hawan*

huká — hubble bubble

Jaith — a month in the Hindu Calendar, falling in May-June

jajmán — patron

jajmání — patronage; adjective decribing the system of economic exchange characteristic of rural India

jal — water

jál — net; steel rod cover over the *chauk* of the *ghar*

jal-dewtá — water god

jál-gajáṅ-wálá — angle-iron frame fitted with iron bars fixed at the roof level above the *chauk*; *chauk-ka-jal*

jalwá-pújan — five weeks after the birth of a male child, the woman who has delivered goes to the *kuwan* for *puja*

jamá'í — *dámád;* son-in-law

jáman common black plum; Java plum

Janam-ashṭamí birthday of god Krishna

jaṅgal wás an abode in the jungle; a place outside the village *abadi* near the *gora* where a marriage party coming from outside to marry a girl in the village first halts

janet marriage party of the groom that goes to the bride's village

jaṅglá window

Jáṭ a cultivating caste

jawár green small sprouts of barley

jháṛ-phúṅk white magical treatment

Jhímar basket maker; a caste group

jholí lap

jíjá sister's husband

Jogí a caste of traditionally singers of songs of patriotism and chivalry

johaṛ village tank

jot leather belts and ropes, etc., used for tying the plough to the bullocks, cotton wick dipped in clarified butter and burnt for *puja,* etc.

ju'í lice

júṭh left overs

Jún a *gotra* of the *Jats*

kabaḍí an Indian game in which two teams participate

káká father's younger brother

kamín the menial; a colloquial expression for service caste people working on *jajmani* system

kamrá room; room on first floor of a house with a *verandah* in front of it; plural, *kamre*

kamre rooms on the first floor of a *ghar* with a *verandah* in front of them; singular, *kamrá*

káṅdhiyá pall bearer, literally, the word *kandha* means shoulder

kanyá-dán the ritual gift of a girl

kaṛhávaní earthen-pot for boiling milk

kaṛí rafter

Kártik	eighth month of the *Bikrami* Calendar falling during to October-November of the Christian Calendar
karwá	small oil lamp-shaped earthen-pot used for *puja* on *karwa chauth* festival
karwá-chauth	festival celebrated by women whose husbands are alive for the welfare of the latter
kauliyá	pilaster
khadehlaṛ	literally, one who is chased; *gaihlar*
khalihán	threshing ground
kháp	group of villages; territorial unit belonging to families of the same *gotra* of a caste
khasrá No.	No. in the revenue records for the village lands
kharaṛ	a big-sized thick cloth made with home-spun cotton yarn
khát	organic manure
kháṭ	cot, bedstead
khatauṛ	workshop of the *Khati*
Khátí	carpenter
khaṭ-paṭ	troubles, quarrels, etc.
Khaṭík	weaver; a caste
khet	agricultural field
khichṛí	a very thick pudding made of *bajra* mixed with *mung ki dal* pounded in a mortar and cooked in boiling water in a coldrum
khíl	charred rice
khír	a pudding made of rice and milk. This sweet dish is treated as *pacca khana* and is considered to be a very good non-conductor of ritual pullution
kisán	agriculturist
khor	manger; trough for cattle
khuraihrá	*kharkhara*; groom; dandy brush
kiwáṛ	door leaf
kolhú	cane-crusher; expeller
koṛá	whip
koṭ	boundary wall around the *abadi*
koṭhá	closed dark rear room used for storage; *aobra; kothri*
koṭhí	an earthen container for storing grains, built locally

koṭhṛí — *aobra; kotha*

Krishí-darshan — a special television programme regarding agriculture. Literally, *krishi* means agriculture and *darshan* means a view

Krishna-pakshá — the darker *paksha* (fortnight) of a month according to the *Bikrami* Calendar

kuchá — a thing which is not quite durable

kul dewtá — family deity

Kumbhkaran — brother of demon king Rawan

Kumhár — potter; a caste

kunbá — extended family

kúp — heap of wheat/barley straw for storage; *bunga*

kuṛí — pit in which waste of the *ghar, baithak* as well as *gher* is dumped for making *khad*

kursí — chair

kuṭiyá — structure with trees around it used for religious purposes

kuwáṅ — well

lab — official papers tied in red cloth; *basta*

Lachhmí — goddess of wealth; *Lakshmí*

laḍú — sweetmeat ball

lahsí — butter milk; *sit; chhachh*

laihṅḍá — common land in the village earmarked for relaxation, stroll and grazing of the village cattle

Lakshmí — goddess of wealth: *lachhmi*

Lakshmí-pújá — *puja* of Goddess *Lakshmi*

lál ḍorá — red cord; an imaginary line (which does not exist on the ground) delineating the residential area from the rest of the village estate

lambardár — headman of a sector of the village responsible for collection of land revenue for the government

lambardárí — the post of *lambardar;* the institution of *lambardar*

lápsí — a glutinous delicacy made of toasted flour, brown sugar and water

lená'í — plastering

logaṛ — home spun cotton yarn

Lohár — blacksmith; it is a caste

loṭá	brass jug
lúh	extremely hot westerly winds that blow in the *Chhatera* region during the months of April, May and June
mahá-parlay	the day of complete destruction; the great doomsday
maihráb	arch
makán	house
makar sańkráńt	the first day of the month of *Makar* according to the *Bikrami* Calendar
malbá	the salvaged material; the receipts into the common fund of the village to be divided among members of the proprietary body
ṃálkán	owners: members of the village proprietary body
mámá	mother's brother
mán	respect
manautí	on certain shrines there is a practice that when some people come to pray they promise that when their desire is fulfilled they will come there again and make such and such presents
mańdar	a temple-like structure for religious purposes with a *pujari* living in it
mańḍí	whole-sale market, generally the grain market
Maniyár	a person of the *Maniyar* caste who sells glass bangles - a sign of *suhag,* i.e., of the marriedhood of a woman
máp	earthen jar for measuring wheat
marchá	chillies
marghaṭ	funeral ground; *masanrn; chehanrin*
masáńṛń	*marghat; chehanrin*; funeral ground
mashak	a big leather bag for carrying water; it is held under the arm like a bag-pipe
mátá	a deity near the *laihnda* worshipped by the villagers
mauj-mastí	to enjoy and have nice time
mauzá	territorial unit for land revenue collection which may not be inhabited even. It is the revenue village as against a social village
máwas	the day having the darkest night every two fortnights

má'yka parents' place for a woman

Meghnáth son of demon king Rawan

methí fenugreek

misal-e-hakiyat appendix to the revenue record book. The original record of rights prepared only during a land settlement. It contains the record of local customs and of the revenue assessments. It also contains a map of the village, a genealogical chart of all the land owners and old tillers, and other similar information.

Mishrá'yn wife of the *Purohit*

mithá'í sweetmeat

mohallá residential locality; small neighbourhood. The *Bhangis* have a system whereby individual families or persons sort of own different *mohallas*. If any other *Bhangi* wants to work in that *mohalla* as a sweeper, he has either to purchase that *mohalla* from the *Bhangi* household owning it or ask for his permission

mor a head gear made of papers of various colours pasted on a frame of bamboo chips, worn by the bridegroom

mukaṭ a head gear, generally made of silver, worn by a bridegroom on his forehead

múl-stambhá the basic pillar; this term is used in Sanskritic literature to denote the central post; *griha stambha*

muṅḍaihrá parapet

muṅḍan ceremonial removal of the hair of a child for the first time as a mark of ritual purification

muṅgholí small-sized earthen-pot for storing water. It is placed on the *paindha.*

murabí male member of a joint family chosen to look after the accounts and management of the joint family affairs

músal pounder

Musalmán follower of Islam; Muhammadan

nahán bár the day on which a woman takes bath for the first time after delivering a child

Ná'í	barber; it is a caste also
Naiṅṛi	barber's wife
námá	wealth
náná	mother's father
nauhrá	*katcha baithak* with an entrance not so wide where *rath* - chariot - may be parked
nawáb	Muslim ruler or lord
nawábí	royal; that belonging to a *nawab*
netá	leader
nikás	place of origin; literally, the outlet
ním	margosa
pachgaṅḍá	five sugarcane sticks brought on the *Dussehra* day
pachhiyá	westerly wind
pág	turban
pagwaṅḍ	a system of inheritance of property where all the sons of a person get an equal share of the property of their father. Literally, *pag* means turban, and *wand* means distribution.
paiṅḍhá	earthern jar for storing water
paiṅḍhí	place for keeping the *paindhas*
paiṛ	thrashing ground
pakshá	fortnight; according to the *Bikrami* Calendar every month consists of two *pakshas*
palá	door leaf
pálí	cowherd appointed by the villagers to take care of their cattle during the day time
palṭá	iron spoon
páná	sub-division of a village, revenue paying group
paṅch	village elder, member of the *panchayat*
panchá'yat	village council
panchá'yat ghar	building of the village council
panḍat	the colloquial expression for the *Brahmans*, especially the *Purohit*
paras	village rest house; *chaupal*
parchárak	preacher
pardáh	privacy; the avoidance of women from men
pardes	any place away from one's native place
paṛkálá	staircase
parlá-bagaṛ	the distant *bagar*

parlay	dooms day
parmeshwar	god
parshád	the consecrated things, generally eatables, distributed by some *saint* or after some *puja*, etc., or at some shrine
patal	tree leaf plate used for serving meals and snacks, generally to big gatherings
pátál	the universe below the one where we live
patáshe	sugar drops
paṭí	village sector
paṭídárí	a system of land tenure and land revenue collection
paṭṛá	short-legged wooden stool
paṭwárí	village accountant
paulí	the first covered space on entering a *ghar/baithak* through its main *barna* in the *ga'*
paunchi	ceremonial thread tied by a sister on the wrist of her brother on the occasion of *salono* festival
Phálgun	the last month of the *Bikrami* Calendar
phere	circumambulation
phúl	flower
pípal	a tree (ficus religiosa; the wisdom of *Buddha*)
píplí	string prepared like a garland with *pipal* leaves tied with cord. It is tied on the upper horizontal member, i.e., *sardar* of the *chaukhat* of the *barna* of the *ghar* on ceremonial occasions and is considered to be auspicious
piyá'ú	kiosk for free distibution of drinking water
pop-lílá	deep-rooted folk beliefs and orthodox views
prem	affection
paccá	a durable thing, a structure with long life expectancy
paccá bhojan	fried food
pújá	worship
pujárí	person in-charge of religious activities in a *maṇdar*
púlí	bundle of corn or of any other crop
Puṅjábí	literally one from the Punjab State; cloth vendor, all cloth vendors in this region are from the Punjab
punyá	virtuosity

púranmáshí	the day with the full moon night, occurring once every two *pakshas*
Purohit	a *Brahman* who professionally presides over all the religious and life-cycle ceremonies in the family of his *jajman*
purohitgirí	profession of the *Purohit*
purush	male human being
purwá	easterly wind
qabristán	burial ground
qabzá-bahál	reinstating the possession, a method of appropriating to each member of the proprietary body his due share in the *abadi*
qabzá-toṛ	breaking or eviction of possession, a method of appropriating to each member of the proprietary body his due share in the *abadi* involving some demolitions
rábṛí	thickened milk; a preparation of churned milk and flour
rahá'yshí ghar	residential house
rá'í	churner
ráhaṭ	wooden part of the Persian-wheel
raihyne ká/ wálá ghar	house for living
ráj	mason
rákh	ash
rakhwálá	he who looks after the stray cattle in the village or rather in the region so that these may not spoil crops
rakshá bandhan	festival on which every sister ties a hread on the wrist of her brother to symbolize that he owes the responsibility to come to her rescue whenever she is in distress
rákshas	demon
Rám	name of Lord Rama, a highly revered Hindu deity
Rám Lílá	enacting the epic *Ramayana* on the stage in October every year

Ráwan — the legendary ruler of *Lanka,* the present-day Ceylon (Sri Lanka), who had a war with Lord Rama and is viewed as a symbol of evil.

rok — a function organized in the village (as a safeguard against cattle diseases) in which the inhabited areas are sealed for forty-eight hours; literally meaning blockade; *rokna; tham*; literally, stoppage,

rokná — *rok; tham*, literally, to stop, to block

roshan dán — ventilator

roṭí — *chapati*, loaf

rúkh — tree

sabjí-wálá — vegetable vendor

sádhú — saint; medicant

safaid zamín — vacant land

ság — green

sagá'i — engagement; betrothal; a ceremony before marriage

saihan — courtyard, a term used generally by the *Baniyas*

saihmchí — *chauntri;* small stool-like stone platform on either side of the main entrance of the *ghar*

saká — Muslim water-carrier

sakúl — school

sál — multi-purpose *verandah* in the *ghar* where private life of the family members is lived

sálá — wife's brother

sálá — during a particular period (in Hindu era) of Indian history, buildings have been called *sálás*

salono — a festival celebrated in August every year when every woman ties a sacred thread, called *paunchi*, on the wrist of her brother and gets presents from the latter

samdhí — co-parents-in-law

samskár — life-cycle ceremony

saṅdúk — big-sized wooden box used for storing beddings, big clothes and other similar household things like home spun cotton yarn, etc.

sáṅjhí jagáh — common place

saṅkh — counch shell

sañkráñt	the first day of every month of the *Bikrami* Calendar
sáñp-mukhá	snake-mouthed; a plot of land whose front is broader than its rear
san	a kind of flax; hemp; *sanm*
sañṛñ	a kind of flax; hemp; *sanm*
sañt	saint; *sadhu*; medicant
sarádh	rituals performed for the benefit of deceased ancestors, the *Purohit* is fed and given *dakshna*
sárañgí	small voilin-type musical instrument
sardar	wide plank-like upper horizontal member of the *chaukhat* of the main *barna* of a *ghar*
sarpanch	headman; chairman of *gram panchayat*
sás	mother-in-law
sasur	father-in-law
sasurál	in-laws; in-laws's place
saṭá	speculation
sáteñ	a festival celebrated on the seventh day of a *paksha*
satún	pillar
sauṛ	quilt
sáwan	fifth month according to the *Bikrami* Calendar, falling during July-August of the Christian Calendar
semí	vermicelli
setiá	a woman's figure built (immediately before the *Dussehra* festival) with cow-dung on the outer wall of the *ghar* near the *barna* and decorated with clothes and jewellery, etc.
shaihtír	wooden log; wooden beam
shámlát	something common to a number of persons or households/group
shámlát-deh	common to the entire village community
shámlát- ṭholá	common to the members of a sector of the village, or to a group of households
shart-wájib -ul-arz	It is a village administration paper stating customs and conditions affecting the management of the village and includes a discussion of the following items: the *shamlat* land and its cultivation, management and use of derived income, graz-

	ing rights on *shamlat* land, customs about irrigation, canals and tanks. This paper forms a part of the *misal-e-hakiyat* of every village
shastrá	a weapon that is thrown at the enemy, manually or mechanically
shástrás	scripture
sherdahaná	lion-like; with a wider front and narrower rear
shramdán	voluntary labour
shudh	pure; ritually unpolluted
shukul-pakshá	the brighter of the two *pakshas*
síḍhá	food given to the *Purohit*
sím	boundary; boundary of the village estate; border
sím-joṛ-kí-biráḍrí	brotherhood of the common boundary
sít	*lahsi; chhachh;* butter milk
súdrás	the untouchables
suhág	husband; the symbol of a woman's marriedhood
súkhá sídhá	uncooked food given to the *Purohit*
Sunár	goldsmith; a caste in the village
Súrya Dewtá	Sun God
sútak	ritual pollution of the family members for thirteen days after the death of a person and for ten days after a childbirth
tadrá	pilaster
tál	universe
ṭáṅḍ	loft
ṭáṅḍí	small loft used generally for keeping utensils
ṭáṅgá	horse drawn carriage for passengers
tá'ú	father's elder brother
tausíh ábádí	the extended *abadi,* done generally at the time of settlement or of consolidation of holdings
tehsíl	group of villages (below the district level) for revenue collection
tehsíldár	government officer in-charge of land revenue collection in a *tehsil*
Telí	oil man
ṭewá	a ceremony performed a few days before the actual day of marriage; a paper containing date of marriage and some other details
thal	raised higher ground

thám	column; pillar
thám	*rok, rokna*
thanedár	Station House Officer of Police
thápá	hand print put generally on walls as a sign of happy occasion
ṭheká	very big-sized jute bag for storing grains
thok	village sector inhabited by the descendants of a common ancestor
ṭholá	village sector
tijorí	iron safe for keeping valuables
tilak	auspicious mark put on the forehead as a part of some function or religious ceremony
till	the sesamum plant and its seeds
ṭiṅḍá	a green summer vegetable commonly grown and relishingly consumed in North India
ṭoḍá	stone element supporting the roof of balcony projections
toraí	cucurbita
torí	cucurbita
totá	parrot
ṭúm	silver ornament
túṛá	wheat or barley straw used as fodder for cattle
úkhal	mortar for pounding grains, etc.
uláhná	complaint to a friend or relative; friendly complaint
updesh	religious discourse
uplá	*gosa;* cow-dung cake; plural *uple*
uple'	*gose*; plural of *upla*; cow-dung cakes
urlá-bagaṛ	the nearer *bagar*
vaisyás	traders
vardán	blessings in the shape of a word of honour given by some saint possessing spiritual/godly powers
vástú	architecture
veḍhá	obstruction
zamín	land
zamíndár	land lord; cultivator
zamíndárí	particular system of land revenue collection
zanáná	for women

APPENDIX - I

A JAT VILLAGE

Source: Purser and Fanshawe, 1880:28

THE PEN picture of a typical Jat village drawn by Sir George Campbell in his essay on the "Land Tenures in India" in the Golden Series and quoted in the Rohtak Settlement Report by Purser and Fanshawe is an excellent piece of work, which is as valid today as it was long ago when it was originally compiled. I think it would be only appropriate here to quote from this report.

The Jat community is of clansmen managed by a council of elders. There is no feature of communism in them: the bond is municipal rather than a community of property. The common interest in common property is hardly greater than that of the commonness of an English manor. The wasteland and grazing ground is held in common; certain common receipts are brought to a common fund, certain common charges are collected against the same fund and distributed in a cess on individuals according to their common holdings. There is a system of municipal management; and the community claims to exercise a certain limited claim over its members and to have a reversionary right to the land of members who cease to cultivate or fail to pay, but beyond this there is complete individual freedom. Such are the Rohtak communities. They are communities of clansmen linked sometimes by descent from a common ancestor, sometimes by marriage ties, sometimes by the fact of a joint foundation of the village. It must be noted, however, that not every proprietor has a share in the common interests of village. Gifts and sales are generally made without transferring this right and the donee or buyer is owner merely of so much land and perhaps of a house inside the village site, and of nothing more.

APPENDIX - II

THE PROCESS OF VILLAGE HABITATIONS

Source: Purser and Fanshawe, 1880:27-28

THE CORRECTNESS of this summary is well examplified in the history of Rohtak district. First of all the tribes of clans settled at one or more spots, holding a large tract in common. Presently as cultivation extended from each centre, boundaries were defined and separate estates formed inside which the land was still held in common. This was the case up to the regular settlement, till when no man held an invisible right of possession in the land which he cultivated, but was owner only of so many *biswas*, ploughs, *annas* or whatever the shares were called in the estate or a family grew stronger than the rest in numbers or desertions occurred, or new settlers were taken in. But still the shares did exist, and were the admitted standard of proprietary rights in a large number of villages. The local annals tell of half a dozen changes made at intervals in the shares on which each estate was held; and though there is no evidence or any periodical re-distribution of lands, these changes may possibly point to the existence of such a custom at an earlier date. But the existence of shares was not understood or recognized at the time of the formation of the record of rights, and each man was recorded as owner of the land which he cultivated. The people themselves acquiescend in this, and the immense breaking up of the jungle land, which took place shortly afterwards, consummated the change. But the old shares are still known, and in some few cases the common lands are still held according to them.

APPENDIX - III

THE PROCESS OF VILLAGE GROWTH : DELHI

Source: Mitra, 1966:223-224

QUITE A good percentage of villages of the Union Territory have a long history – in some cases extending to the pre-Muslim period. Detailed written records for many of these are, however, not available. The following account by Mitra (1966:223-224) gives a good idea of the situation.

The villages of the Union Territory are mostly multi-caste villages with one or two castes being predominant socially as well as economically. The predominant caste is usually the one which came and inhabited and owns most of the land of the village. Thus it is common to find people referring to a village as a Jat village or a Brahman village and so on. Thus when the original settlers came to inhabit a new village, they usually invited some households of other castes to come and settle in the new village with them. Take the case of Bhalswa Jahangirpur, a Jat village. The Jats who were the owners of land of the village first came to settle here some two hundred years back. As soon as they came here, they invited several households of other castes to come and settle down with them. The households who accepted their offer were all given a piece of land in one or the other sector of the village for construction of their houses. Thus when the village came up there were a number of small and isolated homesteads each quite distinct and separate from the other. But with the passage of time, the population increased and with break-up of many a family, more and more houses were constructed by the people of each caste around their own cluster, until a time came when the various clusters came to touch each other and in case where further expansion of the clusters was not possible, they constructed their houses a bit away but again only to form a separate cluster of their own. Thus we find that in some villages whereas some castes have one cluster each, others have two clusters each.

As for the forms, we found that in some cases a village instead of being one massive cluster contained two clusters. One the main cluster and the other a small satellite sort of cluster either just adjacent to the habitation site of the village or a little bit away from it, but for all practical purposes part and parcel of the village. Such cases are few. The satellite habitations usually crop up when some nomadic people come and want to settle down in a village either for good or for a considerably long period. They are usually not allowed to settle down in the village habitation but are given a piece of land outside the habitation for purposes of constructing their huts.

APPENDIX - IV

HOUSE, ITS DESIGN, PARTS AND THEIR USES

Source: Ibbetson, 1883:120-121

ENTERING THE street door of a private house you pass into the other room or *Dahliz*, beyond which you must not go without permission, and where your friend will come and talk. It is often partly occupied by some calves. Beyond this is the yard (*Chauk*) separated from the street by a wall, and in which the cattle are tied up in cattle sheds (*bara*), and the women sit and spin. Round this are the houses occupied by the various households of the family. In front of each is a room with the side towards the open yard (*dalan* or *tamsal*) which is the family living room. On either side of this will be a *sadri* or store room and a *chatra* or cook-room with its *chulha* or hearth: and there is often an inner room beyond called *Obri* or *Dobari* if with two doors, and *Kothra* or

Kothri if with one only. Upstairs is the *Chaubara* where the husband and wife sleep, while the girls and children sleep downstairs and the boys in the *Chowpal* or *Dahliz.*

APPENDIX - V

JAT HOUSES

Source: Purser and Fanshawe, 1880:60 and Gazetteer of Delhi District, 1883-84:42-43

THE DOORWAY opening in the streets are usually handsomely made of wood. Inside is the courtyard in which cattle are stabled, and beyond this the room where the household live. In many cases the door opens into this room itself. Through the gloom of the smoke, through the food which is cooking it may be seen that substantial wooden pillars support the roof, and that throughout the room, brass dishes, and *pongharas* and spinning wheels, baskets, receptacles of grain, etc., are scattered about in comfortable confusion. The subdued murmur of the grinding of the corn-mill is heard from the spinning recess. A ladder connects the roof with the ground through a trapdoor: on the top of the house, fodder is stored, cotton and grain are placed for drying while the family sleeps in the hot weather.

There is no great difference in the style of houses of Hindus and Muhammadans. The main thing that causes variations is the pecuniary conditions of the house-holders. The best way of noting the different parts of the Zamindar's dwelling will be to give a rough description of a sample house belonging to a well-to-do Jat. In the village main street, its front will be a blank wall some ten or twelve feet high, with door somewhere about the middle. Turn in here and you find yourself in the *dahlij* (or *dah lij*), which is a kind of porch; it is also called *deorhi*, as in parts of the Punjab. This is roofed with rough wooden rafters (*karis*) and opens on the inner side of the courtyard of the house, if it is deep, it will have supporting pillars, (*thamb* or *situn*), supporting the main cross beam (*shahtir*) which runs along its length. In the *dahlij*, horses and cows are fastened up, and the *takht*, a large seat, is often put there handy for a lounge or a mediative pull at the *hukah.* In our friend's house, if you look round to the left, i.e., north end of the *dahlij*, you will see a *khor* or *than* or manger put up in the corner. This is generally a box-like erection made of earth; the *than* for horse is, say, four feet high, the *khor* for cattle lower, either solid, or hollow underneath to admit of an arched recess (*tak*) a convenience which a thrifty zamindar is very fond of, and will always get into walls and spare places when he can. At the right hand end of the *khor* is the *kundi*, a hollow made in the top of the manger for the grain of the animal (when he gets any). The rest of the manger is kept for the fodder, and on the outside an edge is made either of wood or earth to prevent the food from falling when tossed about in eating. The inner door of the *dahlij* is not generally exactly opposite the street door, but on one side, so as to make a screen for *chauk*, where the women and children of the house pass much of their time, and, in the hot weather, sleep; the cattle too stand about in it. Going across the yard, we come to an ante-room or verandah, roofed like the *dahlij* and leading to inner rooms or *kothas* (also called *obras*). In the corner of the *dalan*, or in a corner of the inside room, will be *kothi* or house-grannary, made of hard earth well-mixed with chaff and cow-dung, and built up very carefully by the women folk a span height at a time. It looks white and clean, and stands four feet high or more. A good wife will generally adorn her *kothi* with fantastic representations of peacocks, parrots or other birds, done in chalk or with the red earth (*geru*), which is sold in the bazar: a big *kothi* will hold 50 maunds of grain; an average one about 30. Its lid is called *pahan*. The cooking of the family is done in the *dalan*, or, as is very often the case, the room at the east end of the north *dalan* will be open to it and the cook-room there (*rasoi*). The rooms which are here shown at the east end are the principal rooms of the house. Their chief furniture will be *charpais* or *khat*, one for each member of the family. One or two low stools for the women to sit on (*pidha*), the cotton spinning wheel (*charkhi*) and the women's clothes box, a wicker basket some two feet high (*pitar*); the men's clothes are kept in a locked box, together with ornaments or papers or other property of value. There is generally too a *chaj* or fan made of reeds, and its joints fastened with leather. For getting on to the roof, which is used for storing jawar stalks, and sleeping in hot weather, there is the *parkala* — rough set of steps built up into the inner side of the *dahlij*. The water for house-drinking is kept in an earthen vessel (*painda*) kept in the *rasoi*: it is brought twice daily, morning and evening, from the village well.

APPENDIX - VI

VILLAGE COMMUNITIES

Source: Purser and Fanshawe, 1880:26-27

NOTHING MORE true or apt can be written of these than was penned by the late Lord Lawrence, when Collector of Delhi, in 1844, on the estates of the district.

In no part of the North-Western Provinces are the tenures so complete and recognized as here; no districts in which the ancient Indian village communities are in such excellent preservation, or where the practice of our Civil Courts has done so little harm. They are admirably adapt to resist the evil effects of bad seasons, epidemics and other evils incidental to this country. Bound together by the ties of blood connection, and, above all, common interest, like the bundle of sticks .... they are difficult to break. Drought may wither their crops, famine and disease may de-populate their houses, their fields may be deserted for a time, but when the storm blows over, if any survive, they are certain to return. "The tie is of course less strong in some cases than in others. The most perfect types are found in the oldest and largest Jat and Rajput villages .... Sir George Campbell who was well acquainted with the Old Delhi territory speaks thus of the Jat community in his essay on the "Land Tenures of India" in the Golden Series. "They are tributary republics rather then subjects or tenants of- their conquerors. Those in possession of the village are were left in possession, and were allowed to manage their own affairs, subject only to the State right to receive its dues". Such is the case now, and how this came about can be easily traced. "In the grater part of the world, the right of cultivating particular portions of the earth is rather a privilege than a property; a privilege first of a whole tribe or a particular village community. In this last stage the land is partitioned off to these individuals as a matter of convenience, but not in the unconditional property, it long remains subject to certain conditions and to reversionary interests of the community, which prevent its uncontrolled alienation, and attach to it certain common rights and common burdens.

APPENDIX - VII

THE VILLAGE COUNCIL

Source: Purser and Fanshawe, 1880:28-29

EVERY VILLAGE has got a Village Council. Over each *Panah* or *thula* are headmen, a single *Panah*, if large, may have several headmen, or several *thulas*, if small, may be under a single headman. But at least as important as the headman and forming with them the village council or *panchayat* are the *thuladars*. These are a body of men recognized by the government, but exercising real power over the village. There is generally one representative for each family or group of families, among this body, the shrewdest man being usually chosen for the post. There is no formal election but the marked men of a village are but few and well known; and a sort of tacit assent of his fellow clansmen seems to constitute a man's right to join the village council. In this there is always sure to be some leader of the opposition, who perpetually demands that the account of the steward-ship of the more powerful faction be submitted to the voice of the whole village, and so keeps up a wholesome check on their proceedings. The council or *panchayat* settles everything of common interest for the village, ... the cultivation of any common lands, ... the rents to be paid for these, ... the realization of grazing and hearth fees, ... the exemption of certain persons from payment, ... the building and repair of village rest houses, ... the supervising of the system of special watchmen (*thikar*), ... the clearing of village tanks and such like. The accounts of the village funds should be submitted yearly for the sanction of the whole body of proprietors, but this is not done regularly. Certain other matters by general custom also need their special assent, such as the breaking up of jungle land, the grant of a revenue holding by the village, and the like. All the members of the whole body of proprietors are equal; all consider themselves immeasurably superior to the other inhabitants of the village. There are the trader, Brahmans, village servants and village menials; the distinctive sign of their inferiority is that they are all likely to pay the hearth (*kundi-kamini : kundi* = a home), to the proprietary body, unless exempted by consent or under special circumstances. The first are often well to do and more or less independent of the proprietary body. The latter are still almost at the mercy of the owners, though the old ... Such are the village communities, a body often of hetergeneous composition, but united by close ties, self-supporting, united, vigorous and strong.

APPENDIX - VIII

FOOD OF THE JATS

Source: Gazetteer of Delhi District,1883-84:44-45

THE MAIN food of the *Zamindar* is, of course, grain, wheat and channa; jowar, maki, bajra with milk and ghee; rice, if he is above the average in means. In the cold weather, beginning with *kartik* or *Mangsar*, he will eat jowar or makai mixing with it green food made of mustard leaf or cabbage. In *Chait* or even *Phalgun*, the jowar is changed for wheat or if the man is poor, he must eat barley bread. Bajra bread is good for the cold weather.

Meals are taken twice in the day – in the morning about ten, and in the evening somewhere about seven or eight. If a man, however, has hard work, he eats something, either bread or *khichri* made from bajra, or *dalya* of makai (*basi*)*[1] or dalya of jawar, or *lassi* (*sit* or *chhachh*) before starting for his work, or half an hour after he has begun it. If he is well off, he may treat himself to a sweetmeat ball (*ladu*) or gur, til and wheat meal. This is considered a morning comforter, and very strengthening. The *Zamindar*, he be well-to-do or poor, will have green food for part of his daily diet. When this is mixed with meal, he calls it *sag*, and when it is simple plant boiled in water its name is *Bhuji*. This last is made often from the tender plant of the *panwar* (cassia occidentalis), but this is only in the beginning of the rains; afterwards, when the fibres of the plant get strong and tough it becomes unfit for such use. Gur .... the raw juice will be mixed by the good wife with rice (*ras ki khir*), and served up as a savoury dish for the husband at his early morning meal, or mixed with milk it is a warming drink (*tasmai*). Again, when the boiling is going on, and the gur is nearly made, a favourite comestible is obtained by mixing it with milk, and boiling it to a thin consistency. Thus, which is called *shira*, is eaten with bread, much as we eat honey.

Men, women and children eat the same food

The general ways of cooking food are: (1) *roti*; (2) *dalya*; (3) *khichri*. The peculiarity of *dalya*, which is generally made from wheat, jowar, makai, is that grain is bruised rather than ground; it is then thrown into boiling water, in a couldron (*handi*) and boiled with salt and *dal* of *moong* or *moth*. *Khichri* is made from bajra mixed with *moong ki dal* and pounded in a mortar. When this is fine it is thrown into vessel in the same way as *dalya*, but is cooked longer and it should be cooked slowly; it should be thick enough to stick on a wall, when thrown there. *Dal* is made of *moong*, *moth* or *urd*; the grain used for the purpose is merely split up not ground. It is considered better to make the bread, one part of *channa* with two of wheat, salt being mixed also; this is called *misi* by *Zamindars*, *besni* in towns. The thick *roti*, made from

1. * Basi means stale, but in this sense it includes sad (which is strictly speaking fresh-cooked food).

wheat alone is called *pani ki roti*; the thin, like our (*chapatti*), made after rolling out, is called *phulka* or *manda*.

APPENDIX - IX

ADMINISTRATIVE HISTORY OF CHHATERA

Source: Field-work, 1972-73

"UNDER EMPEROR Akbar, Todar Mal divided all North India into administrative circles called *Pargunnahs*. Within the *Pargunnahs* again were *Thapas*. At that time Rohtak district fell under the *Subah* of Delhi" (Purser and Fanshawe, 1880:30).

Afterwards during the British period when the capital of the country was at Calcutta, Delhi consisted of three *tehsils*: Sonepat, Ballabgarh and Delhi (Chopra, 1976). Since 1861, Sonepat *tehsil* had remained attached with the Delhi district of the Punjab (Purser and Fanshawe, 1880). However, till 1911 Chhatera was a part of Alipore police station of Delhi *tehsil* of Delhi district of Punjab.

After the transfer of the capital from Calcutta to Delhi in 1911, the province of Delhi was re-constituted under a Commissioner. In September 1912 Delhi territory was separated from the Punjab. At that time, Chhatera was attached to Rai Police Station of *tehsil* Sonepat of Rohtak district of the Ambala division of Punjab.

In 1966, when Punjab was re-organized into Punjab and Haryana, Rohtak district was allotted to Haryana. In December, 1972 when a new district of Sonepat was created in Haryana, *tehsil* Sonepat was transferred to the new district.

APPENDIX - X

KOT

Source: Field-work, 1972-73

DUE TO the fear of enemy attacks, especially during the disturbed periods of history, every village has a tendency to make arrangements for guarding itself. In the Sanskritic literature, in history books, in books on architecture, planning and other subjects one comes across descriptions of the various methods in which this defence was achieved. The most commonly adopted method in this connection is that of making a wall around the *adadi* and restricting the entry to the village *abadi* only through one single gate.

When Chhatera was originally founded, there was a wall called *kot**,[2] around the *abadi*. In fact the *kot* was one of the first things to be built or the first development work to be undertaken in the village. This *kot* is reported to have been seven *hath* high, with equally (i.e., seven *hath*) deep foundations, and was thick like a *rail ki patri*, meaning a rail track (i.e., about five feet). The *kot* was made of mud. In fact logs of country wood were fixed in the central line of the *kot* and were gradually embedded in mud. These wooden logs gave strength to the wall, and especially resistance against *sendh*, i.e., against penetration with any sharp-edged instrument. The *kot* had a wooden gate with covered terraces on both sides of it where *lathi ke pakarniyan sote baithte the*, i.e., where those able-bodied young men who could wield the sticks well used to sit and sleep. Just outside the *kot* there was a seven hath deep ditch. All the *biswedaran* households of the village had their *ghars* inside the *kot*. All the *be-biswedaran* lived outside the

2. * Some people are of the opinion that it is the ditch in front of the village wall, and not the wall itself, which is called *kot*. But, without going into this controversy in any detail here, in this book the term *kot* has been used to mean the village wall.

kot. Originally there were only sixteen *ghars* inside the *kot* – eleven of Jats and five of Brahmans. The *ghars* of the *Khatis* were near the gate of the *kot* (behind the present *chaupal*), those of *Jogis* and *Lohars* were located in close proximity to each other al–most abutting the *kot*, while those of *Chamars* and *Bhangis* were some distance away from the *kot*.

The following description by Ibbetson (1883:120) fits the account of the *kot* given by some of the very elderly residents of Chhatera and of surrounding villages. "The village is generally surrounded by a mud wall and ditch as a protection against thieves, and is entered by gates, often of brick, and containing side rooms on village gated where the gossips sit .... when it grows hot under the huge bar tree or *peepal* which generally stands just outside". Ibbetson (1883:60) further observes "that outside the village walls and often in a separate colony beyond the village ditch, the houses of the menials will be seen".

As the population of the village started increasing, the *abadi* had to be extended and the *kot* was demolished, in stages, to accommodate new houses. By that time the law and order conditions in the region has also changed. Some remnants, or physical signs of the *kot* – though very fain – are still there.

INDEX